More Fighting for Canada

Five Battles, 1760–1944

Edited by

Donald E. Graves

with

Robert H. Caldwell

John R. Grodzinski

Ian M. McCulloch

Michael R. McNorgan

Brian A. Reid

and

Maps and illustrations by

Christopher Johnson

ROBIN BRASS STUDIO

Toronto

Copyright © Ensign Heritage 2004

The work of each contributor is copyright:

"From April battles and Murray generals, good Lord deliver me!" The Battle of
   Sillery, 28 April 1760 © Ian M. McCulloch 2004

"We're making history, eh?" An Inquiry into the Events that Occurred
   near Cut Knife Hill, North West Territories, 1-2 May 1885 © Robert H.
   Caldwell 2004

"A most dashing advance:" Paardeberg, 27 February 1900 © Brian A. Reid
   2004

"My God, look at them houses moving!" Combined Arms Action at Iwuy,
   10-11 October 1918 © Michael R. McNorgan 2004

"A perfect example of teamwork:" The Battle for the Melfa Crossing, 24-25
   May 1944 © John R. Grodzinski 2004

All rights reserved. No part of this publication may be stored in a retrieval
system, translated or reproduced in any form or by any means, photocopying,
electronic or mechanical, without written permission of the publisher.

Published 2004 by Robin Brass Studio Inc.
www.rbstudiobooks.com

Printed and bound in Canada by AGMV Marquis, Cap-Saint-Ignace, Quebec

National Library of Canada Cataloguing in Publication

More fighting for Canada : five battles, 1760-1944 / edited by Donald E.
Graves ; with Robert H. Caldwell ... [et al.] ; and maps and illustrations by
Christopher Johnson. – 1st ed.

Includes bibliographical references and index.
ISBN 1-896941-36-2 (bound). – ISBN 1-896941-37-0 (pbk.)

1. Battles–Canada–History. 2. Canada–History, Military. I. Graves, Donald E.
(Donald Edward). II. Caldwell, Robert H.

FC226.M66 2004   971   C2004-900117-5

Contents

LIST OF MAPS

Introduction:
The Tactical Level of War

"War is a simple art, but it is based on knowledge."

SIR ANDREW MCPHAIL, 1935

More *Fighting for Canada* is about the tactical level of war and that term requires some explanation. Professional soldiers generally regard warfare as having three distinct but interconnected levels: strategic, operational and tactical. The strategic level of war is the application of a nation's resources to achieve objectives critical to that nation and includes political and economic aspects, as well as military. The operational level of war (usually associated with the actions of individual armies) takes place within a theatre, or specific geographical area. At the operational level, commanders decide when, where and under what conditions to engage in battle and attempt to connect tactical actions to achieve operational, and possibly strategic, objectives.

The tactical level, the focus of *More Fighting for Canada*, is the level at which formations (corps, divisions and brigades) and units (regiments or battalions) plan and fight battles to achieve operational objectives. The tactical level is the sharp end of the business, and at the sharp end, leadership, training, weapons and experience become crucial. It is the level, echoing Sir Andrew McPhail's belief that "war is a simple art, but it is based on knowledge," where professional training meets an activity that imposes the most severe physical and psychological demands. This basic truth is clearly evident in the five battles that form the subject matter of *More Fighting for Canada* – Sillery, 1760; Cut Knife Hill, 1885; Paardeberg, 1900; Iwuy, 1918; and Melfa, 1944.

The tactical level of war is about combat and it is important that Canadians, soldiers and civilians alike, are aware of the realities of combat – perhaps more so today than when *Fighting for Canada: Seven Battles, 1758-1945*, the companion volume to this book, was published in 2000. I wrote in my introduction to *Fighting for Canada* that, despite the collapse of the former Soviet Union, "the threat of a war is still very much a part of global reality." The events of the last 30 months, which have witnessed Canadian troops sent overseas to serve in combat (although their government is determined not to admit it) and suffer casualties, have borne out the accuracy of that statement, which arose not from any particular prescience on my part but from a belief that warfare is an enduring part of the human condition. We may hate it, as well we should; we may try to do away with it, as well we ought; but we cannot simply ignore it, and we therefore must try to understand it.

To understand warfare, particularly combat, means that we must study it – and that is the purpose of the five authors, all them serving or former combat arms officers, whose investigations of five battles fought either by Canadians or on Canadian soil between 1760 and 1944 form the subject matter of *More Fighting for Canada*. If warfare is an art, as Sir Andrew McPhail believed, than it is a terrible art, and McPhail, a veteran of three years of fighting on the Western Front during the First World War, certainly knew of what he spoke. Since warfare, whether we wish it or not, is still very much with us, it is important that, following McPhail's advice, we acquire knowledge about it, and the five battles studied in this book each provide important lessons about the tactical level of war.

As the largest engagement to take place during the Seven Years' War on what would later be Canadian soil, the 1760 battle of Sillery was a bloodier and more bravely and skillfully fought action than the famous encounter on the Plains of Abraham that preceded it by eight months. Sillery presents a contrast in command styles – Lévis, the French commander, realized and anticipated the difficulties inherent in a spring campaign in Canada, while Murray, the British commander, disregarded those difficulties, to the peril of the men under his command. Sillery offers an object lesson in why personal ambition has no place at the tactical level, and it offers convincing evidence that when opposing forces are nearly equal in all respects, manoeuvre will often be the deciding factor.

The engagement at Cut Knife Hill fought in 1885 was not a battle in the accepted sense of the word – an engagement fought between two military organizations. It was really a conflict between two opposing societies. For this reason, the author has chosen to subtitle his study "an inquiry into the events that occurred" on or near Cut Knife Hill on 1-2 May 1885. Nonetheless, Cut Knife

Hill does yield some valuable lessons for the student of warfare. It shows that both ambition (although it has no place) and the will to survive can influence an engagement, positively or negatively, as much as tactics, training and weaponry. It emphasizes the paramount importance of ground and knowledge of ground, and underscores the universal axiom that when troops are fired upon, they will go to ground, and once they do, it is difficult to get them moving again. Experience gained at Cut Knife Hill demonstrates that commanders who do not plan for this will be less successful than those who do.

The battle of Paardeberg, fought in South Africa in 1900, was Canada's first major overseas battle and a celebrated action in this country's military history. Paardeberg offers compelling evidence that, despite a simple plan and good troops, Murphy's Law usually prevails at the tactical level of war and, thus, what can go wrong, will go wrong – and things went horribly wrong at Paardeberg. This battle also provides evidence that, despite changes in weaponry, the behaviour of soldiers under extreme stress and major tactical principles has remained remarkably consistent in the intervening century and more since Paardeberg was fought.

The action at Iwuy (pronounced "Eee-why"), fought on 10-11 October 1918, offers lessons in the conduct of a pursuit and the mounting of a quick attack on a withdrawing enemy, and also how to create a hasty defence when that enemy unexpectedly counterattacks. Iwuy was fought by elements of the Canadian Corps, the finest army that Canada has fielded in its history and an army whose outstanding qualities were due to the fact that it had thoroughly learned its trade in more than three years of uninterrupted operations. The Canadian Corps was also an army whose government gave it unqualified support – a rare occurrence in the political history of this nation that had never happened before and has never happened since. Iwuy also constitutes a historical footnote because it marked that last time that Canadian soldiers mounted a conventional cavalry charge.

And finally there is the battle of the Melfa River, fought in Italy in May 1944. This hard-fought, near desperate, action is a convincing demonstration that, despite grand strategic plans (which, in this instance, called for the destruction of an entire German army), victory often depends on much smaller forces; at Melfa, the outcome hinged on the actions of a handful of soldiers with three small armoured vehicles. Melfa also provides several important lessons for the student of tactical warfare: that there can never be enough planning; that, despite all planning, Murphy's Law will intrude and commanders must be prepared for it; that one battle rarely decides a war so a military unit, even if victorious, must be prepared to continue the fight; that in modern warfare getting to a battle is just as important as fighting it, so attention must be paid to often-overlooked administrative details; and, most important, that when the terrain does not permit the plan to be accomplished, commanders should have ready an alternate plan. Finally, Melfa is a fitting subject for study as it shows just what good junior leadership can accomplish, and since historical study is based on actual, not simulated, events, it yields useful information on how soldiers react under stress.

What follows, therefore, are five studies of five very different military engagements which offer five sets of lessons about the most terrible but most enduring of human arts.

Donald E. Graves
Wolf Grove, Upper Canada
St. Valentine's Day, 2004

MORE FIGHTING FOR CANADA:

FIVE BATTLES, 1760–1944

One Last Throw
of the Dice

In the morning of 13 September 1759, on fields once owned by a farmer named Abraham Martin a mile or more west of the walls of Quebec City, two armies, one British, the other French, met in battle. The issue was decided when Major General James Wolfe's redcoated British infantry fired a single, devastating volley – which one commentator has called "the most perfect volley ever fired on a battlefield" – into the ranks of *Général* Louis-Joseph Montcalm's opposing French and *Canadien* troops, inflicting such heavy casualties that they lost their will to fight and hastily retreated. A few days later, Quebec, the capital of New France, surrendered, and for all intents and purposes the rivalry between France and Britain for North America, a struggle that had been waged for nearly two centuries, came to an end, except for the details. At least, that is the popular wisdom – but as is so often the case, popular wisdom is wrong. There remained one last major military engagement to be fought and this was the battle of Sillery (often mistakenly called St. Foy), which took place in April 1760 on almost the same ground as the better known action of the Plains of Abraham.

As the author of the following study makes clear, the Chevalier de Lévis, the French commander who succeeded Montcalm after the disastrous outcome of 13 September 1759, did not accept that defeat as ending the war. He resolved on a last gamble, a last throw of the dice and, gathering all available forces, marched against Quebec City the following spring, determined to retake the capital city of New France and reverse the outcome of the British victory of 1759. The result was the bloodiest battle, in terms of casualties suffered, ever fought on what is now Canadian soil.

1

"From April battles and Murray generals, good Lord deliver me!"

The Battle of Sillery

28 April 1760

"The frozen Laplanders": The British army in winter, 1760

"Our inventions to guard us against the extreme rigour of this climate," Lieutenant John Knox of Murray's army wrote, "are beyond imagination: the uniformity, as well as nicety, of the clean methodical soldier, is buried in the rough fur-wrought garb of the frozen Laplander; and we rather resemble a masquerade than a body of regular troops." Knox added that "notwithstanding all our precautions, several men and officers have suffered by the intenseness of the cold, being frost-bitten in their faces, hands, feet and other parts least to be suspected." Here, a wood-cutting party with escort have ventured out of the garrison to get firewood to survive, all the while keeping a sharp eye out for Indians and *Canadien* militia waiting in ambush as they make their way back to town. This 20th-century painting is accurate in most details except for the anachronistic feather bonnets which the artist has placed on the men of Fraser's Highlanders (78th Foot). They would have actually worn flat blue bonnets with a tuft of bearskin on the left side. (Print after a painting by J.H. Macnaughton, author's collection)

"From April battles and Murray generals, good Lord deliver me!"[1]

❦ ❦ ❦

The Battle of Sillery[2]

28 April 1760

Ian M. McCulloch

O ghillean bithibh ullamh, le armaibh guineach,
Gu làidir, urranta, an onair an Rìgh;
Mun tig oirnne fada, bidh an Rìoghachd seo againn.
Is thèid sinn dhachaidh do Bhreatann a-rìs.

O Lads, make ready, with death-dealing weapons,
Strong, intrepid, in honour of the King;
This country will be ours before too long,
And we will return to Britain again.[3]

On the evening of 26 April 1760, a freezing rain stung the faces of the French infantry struggling in darkness across makeshift pontoon bridges spanning the Cap Rouge River, a tributary of the Saint Lawrence about ten miles above the fortified city of Quebec. Bolts of lightning flared occasionally, bathing the scene in a spectral light. It was now 6 P.M., a raw, miserable day's end, and their general, heavily cloaked, sat astride a black horse on the east bank of the small river, watching his army cross. The wind had built up to a relentless pitch but occasionally a cheer of *"Vive le Roi!"* would go up from the troops, roused from their mind-numbing march by the sight of their commander observing their progress and he would graciously acknowledge all cheering, lifting his *tri-corne* with its sodden ermine trim and bowing his head in salute.

The victor of Sillery, 1760: François-Gaston, Chevalier de Lévis (1719-1787)

Lévis replaced Montcalm after the latter was killed in 1759, taking command of all French troops in New France. He was a favourite of Pierre de Rigaud, Marquis de Vaudreuil, the na-tive-born Governor of the colony, and together they devised the daring strategy of retaking Quebec city in the spring of 1760 before British reinforcements could get up the St. Lawrence. Beloved by French regulars, colonial soldiers and *Canadiens* alike, Lévis quickly knitted together a highly motivated army of 7,000 men to attack the capital of New France. (Editor's collection)

François-Gaston, Chevalier de Lévis and major general (*maréchal de camp*) commanding His Most Christian Majesty's forces in New France, was a born soldier, a scion of an impoverished branch of one of the most ancient and noble families of France. He had entered the army as a cadet in his teens and in 1735 was commissioned *ensigne* in the *Régiment de la Marine*. By the age of 17, he was a *capitaine* serving in the Rhine campaign of the War of the Polish Succession (1733-38). He appears to have been an able combat as well as staff officer, serving with the Bavarian army during their invasion of Bohemia during the War of the Austrian Succession (1741-42), and then doing duty as assistant chief of staff to his cousin, the Duc de Lévis-Mirepoix, while attached to the army of Italy. Always short of money, François-Gaston could not expect to command a regiment of his own and therefore relinquished his company command in exchange for a brevet *colonel*'s position on his cousin's staff.[4]

When the Marquis de Montcalm was sent to North America in 1756, the then 36-year-old Lévis had been offered the post of second-in-command with the rank of brigadier. He accepted and soon proved to be the most popular of the French regulars with Vaudreuil and the *Canadien* seigneurs. Calm and totally professional, Lévis acted as the go-between for the irascible Montcalm and the Canadian-born governor, the Marquis de Vaudreuil, who detested each other. Lévis was the genius behind organizing and mounting the successful expedition against Fort William Henry in 1757, and in 1758 he fought at the battle of Ticonderoga, commanding the right wing of Montcalm's army.[5] He was also the mastermind behind the defensive positions prepared at Quebec that stymied Wolfe's army for three months in 1759. Unfortunately, a few weeks before the battle of the Plains of Abraham at Quebec, when it appeared the British would make a thrust at Montreal via Lake Champlain and Lake Ontario, Montcalm dispatched Lévis to that city with 800 reinforcements to counter the threat. He thus missed the final showdown between Wolfe and Montcalm that took place on 13 September 1759.[6]

On learning of Montcalm's death and defeat, Lévis immediately rode north to join the demoralized French army at Jacques-Cartier, some 30 miles upriver from Quebec, arriving 17 September. He was outraged at the disorganized rabble he found huddling at the river village and immediately set about restoring order and discipline as well as making plans to attack the besiegers and to succour Quebec immediately. The next day, however, the Chevalier de Ramezay surrendered the capital of New France and a grim Lévis was forced to leave a strong force at Jacques-Cartier for the winter and place the rest of the army in quarters up the Saint Lawrence River valley as far as Montreal. During the winter months he worked closely with Vaudreuil to develop a strategy for retaking Quebec. Their plan was to use the interior lines of the Saint Lawrence River to defeat the invading British armies one at a time – first retaking Quebec, then shifting the army to the south to counter any enemy thrusts from the Lake Champlain or Lake Ontario frontiers.[7]

The entire strategy depended on recapturing Quebec City as the first step and that prize could only be won if strong reinforcements, siege guns, gunpowder and food supplies were dispatched to North America before the Royal Navy could reinforce the British garrison of the city when the river ice broke up. It was a big "if," but Lévis and Vaudreuil believed it was possible and set about preparing the boats, guns, rations and manpower that would be necessary to execute the plan.

The French army numbered approximately 7,000 (for Order of Battle and Strength, see Appendix A). With Levis were all eight battalions of French regulars, his *troupes de terre*, led by veteran officers and NCOs with several years of campaigning experience in North America, particularly the elite of the army – the grenadier and *volontaire* (or light) companies – who had missed the main action at the Plains battle. Lévis also had a brigade of *troupes de la Marine* or colonial regulars organized in two battalions and led by the experienced Jean-Daniel Dumas, the Adjutant-General of the *troupes de la Marine*. As for the morale of the army, the Comte de Maurès de Malartic recorded that "the melting of the ice does not match the eagerness of our troops to start."[8]

Bushfighters: The *Canadien* militia

The Quebec militia in their distinctive red tuques possessed expert knowledge of the local terrain and formed an integral part of Lévis' vanguard leading the way, while the militia from the Montreal colony initially formed the reserve, then replaced the *brigade de La Reine* in the main battle line. Over the winter of 1759-60, three companies of militia were assigned to each brigade of *troupes de terre* and trained to act as skirmishers and sharpshooters. Others stationed near Quebec under the command of Major Jean-Daniel Dumas of the *Compagnies franches de la marine* raided outlying British posts. During the battle of Sillery they performed magnificently, taking post in the gaps between the brigades, and their accurate marksmanship resulted in a high casualty rate among British officers. (Painting by Francis Back, courtesy Parks Canada)

All the regular units were thus battle-experienced and, more significantly, reorganized. Lévis had taken measures over the winter to ensure that his commanding officers had instilled the necessary discipline and *esprit de corps* in his officers and men to fight the better trained and better equipped British. In addition, Lévis was a strong believer in the merits of using the militia, but not as heavy infantry as his late friend and former commander, the Marquis de Montcalm, had attempted the year before. He ordered that three companies of *Canadiens* be attached to every regular battalion and instructed that each be commanded by a hand-picked *capitaine* who could "manage the *habitants* with gentleness." The *Canadiens* were not to be assimilated into the ranks but used as independent companies of light infantry for screening marches and skirmishing. When their respective regiments were in line of battle, they were to take post in the gaps between the battalions.[9]

One of Lévis' last acts before setting out for Quebec in early April was to acknowledge the *Canadiens* who had cared for his regular soldiers all winter, giving them lodging, clothing and sharing their last morsels of food. "We should in this daring undertaking show our gratitude to the colony that has maintained us since our arrival," Lévis proclaimed as he marshalled his forces; the *Canadiens* had "received the soldiers as if they were their own children, and we cannot too highly praise their friendship and devotion."[10]

If Lévis was musing on these matters during the night of 26 April 1760, a loud thunderclap brought him back to the present as lightning illuminated the footbridges over the Cap Rouge River. They were alive with men clad in an assortment of rags, blanket coats, *justaucorps*, fur hats and capes to keep the freezing rain and cutting wind at bay. Their officers marched with them on foot, already soaked to the skin from the rainstorm that had started earlier that day when they had set out from Saint-Augustin at 3 P.M. (see map S-1).

Although it was only five miles to the crossing sites, the troops were exhausted from trudging through the thick cloying mud and slush of the spring thaw, their only meal a quarter pound of bread per man

Canada's first cavalry

A trooper of *Capitaine* de la Rochebeaucourt's *corps de cavalerie,* which was composed of some 180 *Canadien* volunteers, commanded by French regular officers and mounted on small, sturdy Canadian horses. Dressed in blue jackets, faced red coats and fur caps, and armed with carbines, these men were mounted infantry or dragoons raised in June 1759 as a mobile force to counter up-river movements during Wolfe's siege of Quebec. During the 1760 campaign they provided Lévis with a mobile scouting force that played a prominent part in the approach march to Quebec. This was the first cavalry unit organized in Canada. (Painting by Eugene Leliepvre, courtesy Directorate of History & Heritage, DND Canada).

that morning and nothing to drink but cold water. Before this they had spent nearly a week in open boats, trying to make their way down the ice-clogged Saint Lawrence. Those too sick to march had been left at Saint-Augustin to move down the river a few days later with the siege artillery when a safe anchorage closer to Quebec was secured.

The first troops to cross the Cap Rouge River, before the bridges were built, had been the Sieur de Rochebeaucourt's small cavalry corps at 2 P.M. that afternoon. Numbering some 180 men dressed in blue jackets faced with red, fur caps and armed with carbines well wrapped against the elements, these men were dragoons or mounted infantry, who had been raised the previous summer as a mobile unit to counter upriver movements and feints during the British siege of Quebec. Mounted on gaunt but sturdy horses, progenitors of the modern French-Canadian breed, their first task had been to guard the east bank of the Cap Rouge while the militiamen constructed the footbridges.[11]

Once these structures were completed, *Capitaine* de la Rochebeaucourt and his dragoons had pushed on to secure Ancienne Lorette, whose spire was visible, the village apparently free of British troops. By now, Lévis had forded the swollen river, its banks still lined in places with ice, and had taken up a post on the east bank. The Chevalier had been at the bridges since 2 P.M., when his advanced guard had crossed over, eager Quebec militia in their red tuques leading the way. They had been absent from their properties these last seven months and were now returning to their homes and fields to fight the British in this last-ditch effort. Many men of Quebec's outlying villages and hamlets who had remained on their lands for the winter now flocked to join the French army. Unfortunately most were weaponless, having been systematically disarmed by the British during the previous months. No mind, Lévis may have thought, they could at least serve as pioneers or labourers during the siege.

Next across the makeshift bridges were 280 aboriginal warriors led by *Capitaine* Corne Saint Luc of the *troupes de la Marine*. Many were Mission Indians returning to fight for their settlement at Lorette. A brave officer with a grasp of several native tongues, Saint Luc and his force had the job of locating the positions of British forces on the height of land to the south that resembled a long hump-backed whale. This promontory rose in the west at the point where the Cap Rouge River emptied into the Saint Lawrence , and its wooded and cultivated plateau stretched some 10 miles eastwards to the fortified city of Quebec which nestled against its easternmost cliffs.

Once over the river, Lévis discovered that the retreating British had neglected to tear up the corduroy road that traversed the sprawling Suëte marsh running north-south to the heights of Sainte-Foy. He immediately ordered Saint Luc and his Indians to move south and secure the head of the road, and then sent for his fiery second-in-command, *Brigadier* François-Charles de Bourlamaque. An experienced 44-year-old combat officer, Bourlamaque was of Italian extraction, an acknowledged expert throughout the French army on drill, and a self-taught engineer. A fellow officer, the Chevalier de Johnstone, described him as a man "of great knowledge in all the branches of his profession" who was very popular with the regular soldiers. Lévis ordered Bourlamaque "to advance as far as he possibly could without compromising himself until he heard the army was underway."[12]

Bourlamaque and Rochebeaucourt's dragoons, following closely on the heels of Corne Saint Luc's warriors, crossed the frozen Suëte marsh at last light on 26 April 1760 and approached a large wood sprawling across the road at the foot of the Sainte-Foy escarpment. There they joined Saint Luc and sheltered for the night in some nearby houses about one mile distant below the fortified village of Sainte-Foy. The French approach to Quebec was now secure but back at the northern Cap Rouge crossing sites, progress was slow. "It was a frightful night," recalled Lévis, "terribly cold and stormy, and the army, which only finished

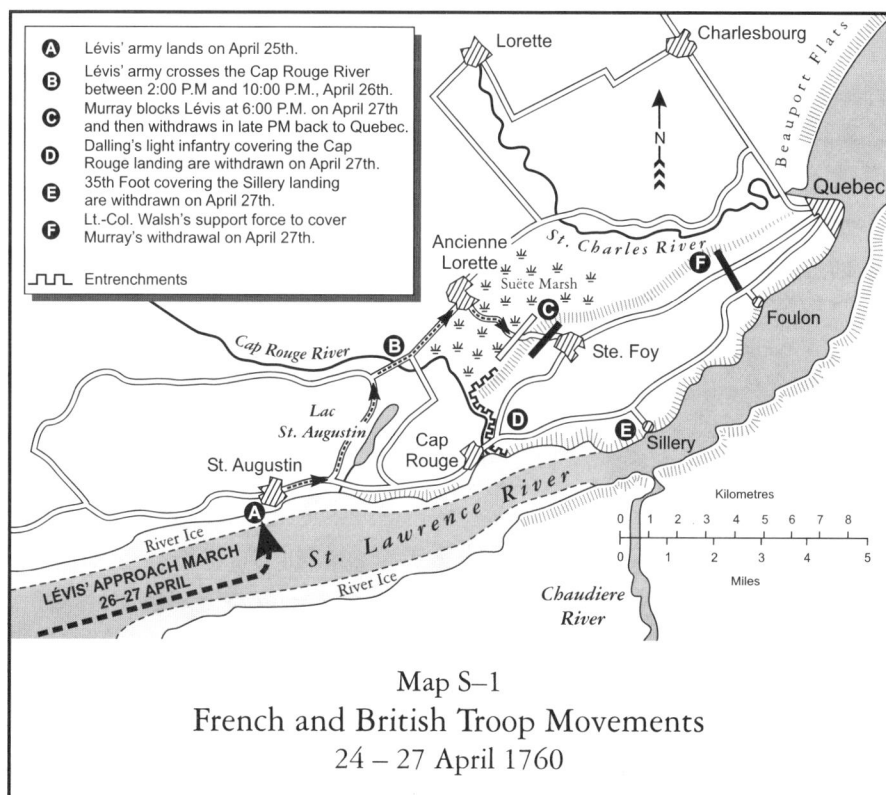

Map S–1
French and British Troop Movements
24 – 27 April 1760

crossing at a very late hour in the night, suffered enormously." When several bridges broke up, men waded waist deep in ice-cold water. "In the darkness," Lévis remembered, "the workmen could hardly repair them had it not been for the lightning!"[13]

Because of the storm, Lévis billeted his troops in the farmhouses of Ancienne Lorette for the night. French accounts claim the storm was one of the worst on record and that this unfortunate act of God was the main culprit in "retarding for some hours the march of the army" as well as rendering "it impossible for Chevalier de Lévis to defile on the church of Saint Foix [sic] at daylight as he had intended." This "mischance," as one of Levis' staff officers termed it, "gave the English time to come in force to mask the high road and save their detachments." The storm was indeed instrumental in delaying Lévis' approach march to the Quebec plateau but other events were also conspiring to ensure that the British arrived at Sainte-Foy in the nick of time.[14]

General James Murray was awoken, fully dressed in his uniform, at 3 A.M. on the morning of 27 April 1760, by Captain John Macartney commanding His Majesty's Sloop *Racehorse*. An hour before, Macartney's men had rescued a French artillery sergeant from an ice floe in the river and the unfortunate Frenchman was now slung in a hammock carried by four sailors waiting outside in the corridor. The prisoner, blue-lipped and shaking from his ordeal, was perfectly lucid in mind and speech according to Macartney and would the General care to converse with him? Murray had striven all winter to learn his opponent's exact whereabouts and intentions, and his rangers and light infantry forces had played a constant cat-and-mouse game of watch and wait, move and counter move, raid and counter-raid on the south shore and up the river towards Jacques-Cartier. Murray had also used the captured brandy stores of the city to good effect to reward *Canadien* informers and spies for any information on French troop movements or locations.[15]

Murray, the most junior of Wolfe's brigadiers during the 1759 siege, but the oldest at 39 years of age, had been left in command of Quebec over the winter, as no one else wanted the job, causing him to comment caustically to the Commander-in Chief in North America, Major General Jeffrey Amherst: "We have little cash, much labour, no prospects of fresh provisions, a great scarcity of fuel, and [are] ill-housed: but everyone is cheerful and happy in having Quebec. All those that did not like it are, thank God, gone to places they like better."

"Envy and ambition are the only springs that work him."
Brigadier General James Murray (1721-94) was appointed Governor of Quebec in September 1759. An experienced professional officer, he took stern disciplinary measures with the British garrison of the city during the very cold and inhospitable winter of 1759-60, as well as disarming the citizens and the inhabitants of the outlying districts. A fellow officer described the 39-year-old Murray as "hot in action" but "brave from ambition not zeal." After the war, Murray continued to serve as Governor of Quebec to 1766, but his pro-*Canadien* views and the measures he put in place to protect them from rapacious New England merchants led to his being recalled to Britain. (NAC, C-2834)

A short man with bright staring eyes, a hawk-like nose and a fiery disposition, Murray did not suffer fools gladly. He had been born at his family's seat of Ballencrieff in Lothian, Scotland, in 1721, the fifth son and fourteenth child of Alexander Murray, Lord Elibank, and his wife, Elizabeth "Bare Betty" Stirling. Two of his four brothers were avowed Jacobites and Murray's military career to date had been an uphill struggle to prove his loyalty and worth to the British Crown. A French official, François Bernier, who had remained in Quebec to assist Murray in civil administration and to represent the French king, gives us a good insight into the British commander's personality:

> The man is young, fiery, proud of his strength, decided in his ideas, and, having reached a position that he had no reason for previously expecting, is eager to distinguish himself. Of a naturally good character, he is nevertheless to be feared when opposed, and being easily inflamed is then ready to do almost anything. You know that too great an opinion of one's strength leaves one little opportunity for reflection and consideration, and frequently gives reason for subsequent regret.[16]

One of Murray's fellow officers during the 1759 campaign was less charitable. To this anonymous gentleman, Murray was the "poison Nightshade of the Camp," and whilst "hot in Action," he was "brave from Ambition not Zeal." In sum, Murray was "a Tolerable good Commander of a Brigade – Anything beyond that is too extensive for him!"[17] These candid assessments are borne out by Murray's own vow to his brother George in a letter written at the same time Bernier was reporting to Vaudreuil on the British commander. Murray wrote:

> I have now served two campaigns under three officers who were put over my head, and I don't find I have got a regiment yet, though I have had the strongest assurances from the ministers. I think I cannot miss it now, and I believe my enemies will agree that I have earned it....... I have 6000 as brave troops ever existed. Business may, and shall, be done with them, and those who have hitherto deprived me of my preferment may repine of it.[18]

James Murray's military career had started at the age of 15 when he was enrolled as a cadet in Colyear's 3rd Scots Regiment of the Dutch army in 1736. Murray considered the three years he spent with these hardened soldiers of fortune to be his true military education and claimed in later life, "I served in all ranks except that as drummer." But it was peacetime for the Netherlands and war was looming between England and Spain. In February 1740, anxious for advancement, Murray obtained a commission in Wynard's 4th Marine Regiment and participated in the 1740 British-American expedition against Cartagena in central America. The diseased-ravaged marching regiments that participated in that campaign lost officers and men in the hundreds, and on 20 November 1741 Murray transferred from the Marines to become a 20-year-old captain in the 15th Foot. For the next ten years he soldiered in the West Indies, Flanders and France, and participated in the 1746 Lorient expedition as the captain of the grenadier company. In 1749, Murray purchased a majority in the 15th and, a year later, the lieutenant colonelcy of the same regiment.[19]

At the outbreak of the Seven Years War, Murray met James Wolfe for the first time during the Rochefort expedition of September 1757. The following year he served under Wolfe at Louisbourg, earning the latter's respect for his "infinite spirit," and in 1759 commanded the left wing of the army on the Plains of Abraham. Murray's position as governor since the fall of Quebec had not been an easy one. Nearly a thousand British corpses, still fully clothed from a fear of contagious disease, were stacked like firewood inside the city walls, awaiting the spring thaw and a chance for burial. In the words of Grenadier James Miller of the 15th Foot, "we were totally unprepared for such a climate, neither fewel, forrage, or indeed anything to make life tolerable. The troops were crowded into the vacant houses as well as possible. Numbers fell sick and the scurvy made a

"A shapeless mass of ruins"

This was how the French Commissary of War, François Bernier, described Quebec shortly after its surrender in September 1759. Major Patrick Mackellar, Murray's chief engineer, assessing the damage and the city's potential to house the British garrison, was equally bleak in his journal: "The Buildings in general [are] in a most ruinous condition, and infinitely worse than we could have imagined; for besides those burnt, there was hardly a house in the Town that was not injured by either shot or shells nor are they habitable without repairs." This picture shows soldiers of the garrison, including kilted Highlanders of Fraser's 78th, climbing the road from the Lower Town to the Upper Town with the Bishop's Palace at the right. (Print after Richard Short, NAC, C-350)

dreadful havock among us. [I]n short, the fatigues of winter was so great that the living almost envied the dead."[20]

The British did not regard Quebec as much of a prize. It is "nothing but a shapeless mass of ruins," reported François Bernier, "confusion, disorder, pillage reign even among the inhabitants, each searching for his possessions and, not finding his own, seizes those of other people." Major Patrick Mackellar, Murray's chief engineer, examined the city with a critical eye after its fall and "found the Buildings in general in a most ruinous condition, and infinitely worse than we could have imagined; for besides those burnt, there was hardly a house in the Town that was not injured by either shot or shells nor were they habitable without repairs." The fortifications, in Lieutenant John Knox's opinion, were not much better, "our only defence and dependence six bastions, with their curtains of slight masonry forming a chain from Cape Diamond to Saint Rocque, no footbank to the curtains, no embrasures made, no covered way, nor out-work of any kind and cannon that were on the flanks so indifferent and worm-eaten that they were almost useless."[21]

One of Murray's first moves was to increase the security of the roofless and vulnerable city by establishing a series of outlying fortified posts at Ancienne Lorette, Sainte-Foy, Pointe Levy and Sillery. As Sergeant John Johnson of the 58th Foot explained, the detachments in these posts "were to watch the motions of the Enemy's Army, who for some time Lay hovering round bout the Garrison" and to serve as "a check upon their Skulking Parties of Indians and Canadians who during the Winter Season were a great disturbance to the Garrison." Many skirmishes were fought in and around these advanced posts during the winter of 1759-60, the British light infantry and rangers, ever-alert and equipped with snowshoes, usually gaining the upper hand.[22]

Murray was a professional soldier and the hard intelligence provided by the frozen French sergeant that the French were close at hand was news he had been waiting for these last two weeks. Each day more of his men fell sick and his garrison would be lucky if it could muster 3,000 men to counter the approaching force, reported to be at least 10,000 strong. Much print has been devoted to the story that Murray would have been completely surprised by Lévis if it hadn't been for the unfortunate French soldier who fell into the Saint Lawrence River during the 26 April windstorm. Several contemporary accounts, both French and English, mention this episode by way of suggesting it was the gunner's intelligence conveyed to Murray at 3 A.M. on 27 April that alerted him to his enemy's intentions.[23]

In fact, to give Murray some credit, he had known for some time that Lévis was coming in force and a few weeks earlier had taken almost every precaution he could think of to foil and delay his enemy on every likely approach. Murray had recorded in his journal in March 1760 that he was well aware his opponent "was determined to besiege us the moment the Saint Lawrence was open of which he was entirely Master by means of four [French] King's frigates, and other Craft proper for this Extraordinary River." On 17 April, he had noted that "The best intelligence was now procured that the French had armed six ships which had remained in the River last autumn with two galleys that they had built; [and] that they designed to bring down this squadron with a number of boats to transport the troops to Cap Rouge."[24]

To counter this threat, Murray posted his best troops, his light infantry under Major John Dalling of the 48th Foot, at the mouth of the Cap Rouge River, which was "the most convenient place for disembarking their Artillery and Stores, and for securing their retreat" (see map S-1). The Light Infantry corps were the "Chosen Men" of Murray's gaunt and sickly army, the best dressed for winter campaigning and the most adept in the use of snowshoes. Their first tasks were to destroy two bridges at the mouth of the Cap Rouge River and to fortify the houses on the east bank. Murray also posted covering detachments at Sillery and the Anse au Foulon farther down the Saint Lawrence River, thus denying Lévis all water access points onto the Quebec promontory and forcing his opponent into the only alternative – to land some distance upriver and try to flank the promontory from the land side. Murray had already ordered the 400-man detachment at Ancienne Lorette to fall back to Sainte-Foy in anticipation of this eventuality and had reinforced the redoubt surrounding the loop-holed village church on the heights with two 18-pdr. guns drawn there on 22 April "with infinite labour and trouble." The next day, when the ice in the river gave way everywhere, Murray had considered posting a 1,500-man force at Sainte-Foy "to

Lévis' intended landing place

A 1759 view of Cap Rouge by Hervey Smyth, showing the westernmost edge of the Quebec headland and plateau that runs down to Quebec city on the eastern end. It was the best place to land an army with artillery and siege stores; Murray correctly deduced his opponent's intentions to use it in April 1760 and entrenched his Light Infantry to cover the landing sites. Two bridges crossing at the mouth of the river at Cap Rouge were destroyed and the houses seen on the river shore at right were loopholed and fortified on 18 May 1760. Lévis was thus forced to land further up-river at St. Augustin and march inland via Ancienne Lorette. (NAC, C-783)

be at hand to strengthen any of my advanced posts and to prevent the enemy's landing but it froze so hard every night I could not venture on this measure yet, considering the sickly state of the men." As an extra precaution, however, he ordered every French civilian out of the city over the next three days, and most were allowed to take only what they could carry.[25]

Despite misgivings about its health, Murray felt his army was in good spirits for the task at hand and he professed "a strong confidence" in his infantry and artillery. His force included ten under-strength battalions of heavy infantry totaling 3,017 men (for the British Order of Battle and strength, see Appendix A), all veterans of the 1758 Louisbourg and 1759 Quebec campaigns; two companies of Royal Artillery commanded by Major John Godwin; a company of 110 "Chosen Men" or volunteers from the army under the command of Captain Donald Roy Macdonnell; a 78-man company of Rangers under Captain Moses Hazen; and the Light Infantry corps under Major Dalling numbering 337 men drawn from the ten battalions and organized into five companies.[26] "Our little Army which was in the habit of beating the Enemy and had a very fine train of Field Artillery" was a force this ambitious Scots general had no intention of "shutting up at once within the walls [of] a wretched fortification."[27]

Once the French sergeant had been given hot brandy and had told his tale, Murray called for his staff and issued orders. Ensign John Désbruyêres, 35th Foot, working as an intelligence officer, confirms that the Frenchman's information was certainly helpful. Dalling's Light Infantry at Cap Rouge "were hardly settled in this post when a man pickt upon a cake of ice during ye night of 26th & 27th brought certain intelligence that the French were in motion to come by ye way of Lorette & Saint Foy [sic] to cutt off our Cap rouge posts." Désbruyêres added that "this providential notice gave us just time to march out & it gave us the opportunity to bring in ye light Infantry."[28] "On this information I marched immediately with the grenadiers, picquets, Amherst's [15th Foot] and two field pieces to Saint Foix," Murray recorded, "ordering three other regiments, commanded by Colonel Walsh to march out and cover my retreat, and Major Morriss with Otway's [35th Foot] to Sillery." Before leaving Quebec, Murray gave the command in the city to Colonel Simon Fraser and ordered the remainder of his fit troops "instantly paraded and marched down to Saint John's gate, prepared to push out in case circumstances should require it."[29]

As they marched through "a thick and cold misting rain," the 35th Foot turned southwest towards Sillery while the main force pushed on west to Sainte-Foy, where Murray found the enemy "in possession of all the woods from Lorette to Sainte Foy." Lieutenant John Knox with the 43rd Foot picquet observed that the British commander "formed the line of battle on an advantageous piece of ground beyond Sainte-Foy and endeavoured to invite [the enemy] to action; in which they seemed as if inclined to indulge him, [but] afterwards retired to the woods behind them, hoping, by various stratagems, to decoy our troops to follow them, their cavalry and savages [making] frequent and ostentatious displays."[30]

The British artillery took good firing positions among the houses overlooking the Suëte Marsh, remembered Knox, and could easily reach the woods in which the French troops periodically emerged "in small divisions to appear more numerous, yet they would not advance." The British gunners fired round after round into the woods, which Knox thought "galled them immensely; for they were frequently thrown into confusion and seen to drag off many killed and disabled men." Dalling's Light Infantry, now recalled from their forward positions at Cap Rouge, joined in the skirmishing and tried once, unsuccessfully, to dislodge Huron, Abenaki and Mohawk warriors who had climbed the wooded slopes to the right of the British line to snipe.[31]

During the course of the morning, as Murray watched the French army building up, he was forced to consider whether his current position was the best spot to fight a pitched battle. By two o'clock, "perceiving they were only trifling and protracting time, the [general] gave the order for the demolition of our post at the church," wrote Knox. This decision was not hard. "Finding that their numbers were increasing and endeavouring to get round me by the woods [and] the weather being very bad … I thought it proper to retreat to the town," Murray recorded. He ordered the powder magazine and provisions in the stone church at Sainte-Foy blown up and had his gunners knock the trunnions off the two 18-pdrs. that he was forced to leave behind "on account of the badness of the roads."[32]

The retreat, Murray later recorded with some satisfaction, "was accomplished in a very regular manner. The enemy followed us with their irregulars but could make no impression on our rear." The chief reason, according to Knox, was Colonel Ralph Burton's reserve brigade posted on the Buttes à Neveu with ten well-served 6-pdr. field pieces "which obliged them to keep aloof."[33] The Saint John gate closed behind Murray's tired and bedraggled little army at last light, with the general, unsurprisingly, the last man to enter the city. For 12 hours nonstop, his force had been exposed to the elements, force-marched to Sainte-Foy and back, and had pulled field pieces by hand to and from the Buttes à Neveu. "Being extremely harassed and wet with a constant soaking rain," Knox remembered, "[we] were allowed an extraordinary jill of rum per man and some old houses at Saint Roques were pulled down to provide firewood in order to dry [our] clothes."[34]

As Murray dried himself out in his quarters he was probably thinking of the large number of French troops he had seen that morning and the relatively small number of fit soldiers he had to defend Quebec. He still possessed two manned blockhouses on the southern shore across from Quebec and consequently, he wrote, "I could not think of keeping post at Point Levi [sic] any longer. I ordered the officer commanding there to burn the blockhouses, spike the guns, destroy the provisions and come off with the first tide which was effected." Murray then passed the word for all battalion commanders to assemble that evening for a council of war to decide the next move.[35] If his own men were exhausted, wet and cold, he reasoned, then certainly the French, *Canadiens* and Indians he had seen that morning must be in as bad, if not worse, condition.

At dawn on 27 April 1760, as Murray had been making ready to march to Sainte-Foy, the French army was still strung out over a distance of five miles between Ancienne Lorette and Sainte-Foy on the Suëte Marsh road. "At daybreak," a staff officer remembered, "the Chevalier de Lévis having pushed the vanguard as far as the edge of the wood within sight of the enemy, set out to reconnoitering their position with the Sieur de Bourlamaque. He gave orders at the same time to the remainder of the troops who had marched the whole night, to cross the marsh and form in the rear of the woods."[36]

The French commander's reconnaissance quickly revealed that his way was securely blocked because "at six o'clock in the morning, the British appeared in order of battle to the number of [1,500] men on top of this hill facing the road on which we were marching." The British line was drawn up right to left between "the church of Saint Foix, several houses on their left and some in front of their lines. They had also lodged some troops in the latter and placed some field pieces there." Lévis realized that the woods that covered his army below Sainte-Foy were swampy and impassable and not conducive to forming a battle line "unmolested by artillery." If he decided to fight for the heights, he would be constricted by the main road and the unfavourable terrain between the woods and the British position "as 'twas not possible to march against them in front, without being exposed to a disadvantageous fight."[37] As his main objective was to put Quebec under siege, not give battle before it, Lévis resolved to wait until nightfall to advance using the woods on the British right as a covered approach to turn the enemy flank. Such a manoeuvre "would enable him to attack the British with advantage of daybreak [on the 28th]." Lévis decided that he would wait to see what night would bring.[38]

He rode back to Ancienne Lorette to halt movement of the army, telling each of his brigade commanders to keep their troops under shelter and to eat what meagre provisions they had. For many soldiers, breakfast consisted of a drink of cold water, a piece of salt meat and some bread. *Capitaine* Anne-Josephe-Hippolyte de Malartic recorded that his brigade in Lorette received the order to move at 6 A.M. but "two kilometers from his lodgings, the General stopped the advance telling the troops to wait for the clouds to dissipate." Two hours later, they were on the move again, "marching in single column, with the grenadiers taking the point." Between the tramping columns on the marsh road were "three [6-pdr.] field pieces which had accompanied the troops with great difficulty." As they marched, "the morning [below Sainte-Foy] passed in some firing and volleys discharged by the enemy at the vanguard."[39]

When Malartic's brigade, last in the order of march, arrived, it halted at the rear of the woods out of artillery range and waited for further orders. At 2 P.M., Malartic noted "that the church of Sainte-Foy was engulfed in flames, its roof blowing up. M. Bourlamaque sent someone to inform M. de Lévis that the English were retreating." The French commander ordered Bourlamaque "to pursue with the Grenadiers and the Cavalry. The grenadiers pressed the English rear guard and forced it to enter the city." Lévis now moved the main body of his army onto the heights in the freezing rain, a move that Malartic thought was "hard as it was painful."[40]

As Lévis stood beside the smoking ruins of what was once the Sainte-Foy church, he issued orders for his chilled and rain-soaked soldiers to get under cover as quickly as possible as he "judged it indispensable to give some repose to the troops after two day's very fatiguing march, the ground moreover being covered with snow." By 6 P.M., his entire army was up on the Quebec headland and needed no prompting to shelter in the numerous but scattered farmhouses and barns along the road from Sainte-Foy to the city. Eventually "our little army covered a space of a league and a half," recorded one of the French staff officers.[41]

Lévis posted his grenadiers, cavalry and Quebec militia within gunshot of the city walls, then made plans for the following day. His journal records that his intention was not to give battle. Instead, the Chevalier wished to use the next day, 28 April, "to land provisions which were needed, some field guns and in resting the troops." In his mind, the French commander was thinking ahead to his next task – to besiege the city. His opponent, however, had very different plans.[42]

Throughout the previous winter, Murray had hoped to cover the west side of Quebec and its dilapidated masonry walls with an entrenched fortification along the ridge of the Buttes à Neveu, and his chief engineer, Major Patrick Mackellar, had worked on plans all winter for such a contingency. As early as 3 March 1760, almost a full two months before the battle, Murray recorded that he was "determined to fortify the heights of Abraham" and "had detachments under proper officers to be selected in order to cut fascines and picquets for that purpose in order to be ready to fall to work as soon as the season would allow us to fortify." The fickle spring thaw, however, was not cooperating on land for the British as it had done on water for the French with the early breakup of river ice on the Saint Lawrence. From 23 April 1760, an impatient Murray had already tried, unsuccessfully, to commence entrenching at Wolfe's Redoubt, a fortification facing west on the site of the present day Musée du Québec. The work there was laborious and "advanced but slowly, the ground being so hard they could not drive their pickets above nine inches into it."[43] While Murray's plan to entrench the heights made tactical sense, it was just not feasible given the ground conditions.

On the evening of 27 April 1760, Murray convened "a meeting with the different Commandants of the Corps," recorded Lieutenant Malcolm Fraser of the 78th Foot, "[where] he declared his intention of fortifying himself on the heights and not to attack the Enemy, unless he should be forced to it." By occupying this height of land, Murray could, ideally, deny Lévis use of it for siege operations. But Murray did not tell his council everything. Secretly he believed that "the enemy, so near at hand, would never suffer us to fortify the heights of Abraham. [E]ven unmolested the chief engineer was of the opinion it would take ten days to execute the plan proposed [and with] the garrison so sickly it could hardly be supposed equal to the task of guarding both town and lines." Simply stated, Murray was going to leave the city and look for a fight.[44]

The first British troops to march out of Quebec on the morning of the 28 April 1760 were a screening force of some 525 men composed of Dalling's Light Infantry, Macdonell's Volunteers and Hazen's Rangers. French advanced posts were near the *Hôpital-Général* to the northwest of the city, recalled John Knox, so "our light troops pushed out and with little difficulty drove them to a greater distance." Malartic noted that "the English fired a few cannon shots on the Grenadiers and the *Canadiens* that the General had placed close to the city."[45] The sound of these guns no doubt alerted Lévis, who had been occupied with the Sieur de Bourlamaque since dawn in reconnoitering positions, that something was afoot.

The French commander rode forward to consult with *Capitaine* Charles d'Aiguebelle commanding the six companies of grenadiers that were now falling back to Dumont's Mill on the north side of the Sainte-Foy road (see map S-2). There he learned that the enemy garrison had been "seen issuing from Quebec" in force and "appeared disposed to march against us," and Lévis was soon able to confirm this information with his own eyes when two large columns appeared "on the heights with considerable artillery." At 8.30 A.M. he "gave orders to Chevalier de Montreuil, his adjutant-general, to make all the troops advance" while "the vanguard continued to occupy the redoubt on the right, the heights in the centre and Dumont's house on the slope of Cote d'Abraham." Lévis posted the Grenadiers at the mill to guard the Sainte-Foy road that was now key for the rapid deployment of his army.[46]

The French army was already awake as the "*Générale*" had been sounded at 7 A.M. and some units had "moved forward to gain a few more houses." As the British army appeared on the Buttes à Neveu, Lévis took up a good position to watch developments and to try to figure out his opponent's intentions.[47]

"A wretched fortification:" The western walls of Quebec

The western ramparts of Quebec were so described by General James Murray in his journal. This 1783 view by James Peachey, painted from the high ground to the west of the town known as the Buttes-à-Neveu, clearly shows the gun embrasures cut in the western walls by Murray's garrison in the winter of 1759-60 to permit them to fire on Lévis' batteries. It was here that Murray initially formed his battle line on the morning of the battle, with the intention to entrench and deny the French this important high ground which dominated the western wall and Upper Town. (NAC, C-1514)

After his men secured the Buttes à Neveu at 7.30 A.M. on 28 April 1760 and cleared the woods around it, Major John Dalling could relax for a few minutes until the main body arrived. Looking back down the slope towards the fortified town, he saw two large columns emerge from the Saint John and Saint Louis gates respectively and slowly make their way up to the heights, pulling small 22 field pieces by hand as no horses were available, other than for the general, his brigadiers and staff. Out of the Saint Louis Gate came Colonel Simon Fraser's brigade comprising the 28th Foot, the 47th Foot, the Second and Third Battalions of the Royal Americans or 60th Foot, and the 78th Highlanders. Farther to the north, Colonel Ralph Burton's brigade was marching out with Murray at their head: the 15th Foot, 35th Foot, 43rd Foot, 48th Foot and 58th Foot, each regiment helping the Royal Artillery gunners to pull their battalion guns with long drag ropes.

All these units were equipped with picks and spades, and all troops, if Sergeant Johnson of the 58th is to be believed, were eager to fight. "Any man," he recalled, "would have shuddered at the Sight to have seen a poor pitiful handful of half Starved, Scorbutic Skeletons, many of whom had laid by their crutches on the occasion and would not be prevailed to stay behind, although many of them were absolutely forbidden and would not be suffered to fall in the ranks with the Men." Johnson added that many of them "followed us out of the Gates in the Rear and fell in when we formed the line of Battel."[48]

Marching out that morning at 8 A.M. was a young lieutenant of Fraser's 78th Foot carrying a fusil, his broadsword slung at his waist. At least 200 of the Highlanders marching with Lieutenant Malcolm Fraser had "come out of the Hospital on their own accord." Once a proud regiment of some 1,500 men, its ranks had been winnowed by disease, death and battle down to 400 shivering, sickly men. Marching at the head of the 78th column were the grenadiers distinctive in their bearskin mitre caps, including Grenadier Sergeant James Thompson who remembered the day as being rainless, but "cold and raw."[49]

When the two columns were "about three quarters of a mile out of the Town," recalled Fraser, "the General ordered the whole to draw up in Line of Battle two deep, and to take up as much room as possible." This they did in the position that Wolfe had formed his battle line the year before, but facing in the opposite direction. The field pieces were positioned in the gaps between regiments and the sergeants acting as file-closers dressed the ranks (see map S-2).

Ironically, many British officers and men standing shoulder to shoulder on the Buttes à Neveu that morning had fought against each earlier almost 14 years to the day on a different continent. They had warily watched each other across a dreary rain-drenched moor near Culloden in April 1746, some in the British King's red coat under the command of William Augustus, Duke of Cumberland, others part of the clan levies that made up Bonnie Prince Charlie's army under the command of Lord George Murray. Many of these Scots had participated in the last wild charge of the Highland clans, including Lieutenant Fraser's father, killed on the bayonets of the British line.[50]

Stationed near two 12-pdr. field guns aimed at the French columns approaching from the west along the Sainte-Foy road was the British artillery commander, Major John Godwin. He too was a veteran of Culloden, where his small 3-pdrs., interspersed between Cumberland's battalions, had pounded the Scottish clans into a bloody ruin until, infuriated, they had come "running like troops of hungry wolves." For this April 1760 battle, Godwin's guns were deployed much as they had been on Drumossie Moor 14 years before, though the similarities ended there. Now he had twice the number of guns, mostly captured French ordnance, but each with twice the calibre and range.[51] He did not have as many trained gunners as he would have liked, so most of his pieces were manned by infantry with one of his gunners to lay them, and the gun detachments were commanded by infantry officers.

As the French came within range, Godwin ordered his guns to open fire. Just to the rear of the field pieces rolling back on their recoil in the mud were the men of the 78th. Their officers stood quietly in front, the cream of Jacobite gentry, broadswords resting lightly on their shoulders, waiting to go forward. Standing just to the north in the front line of the 58th Foot was Private William Lee, an ex-cordwainer from Nottingham, who had fought at Culloden on horseback as a volunteer trooper in the Duke of Kingston's Light Horse.[52] A few paces to the left of Godwin's gunners feverishly serving their pieces was a man Lee had missed in the bloody rout of Clan Macdonald that grim April day in 1745 – Captain Donald Roy Macdonell. He was receiving last minute instructions from his brigade commander and regimental colonel, Simon Fraser, the Master of Lovat, whose father had been beheaded in the Tower for treason after the rebellion. The 78th Foot was in some measure a regiment raised to restore the fortunes and reputation of Simon Fraser, his friends and their clansmen.[53] Macdonnell, described by a non-commissioned officer as "a good Soldier, a Brave Officer, and a Bold, Enterprizing man," was preparing to go forward with his volunteers and a company of rangers to cover the left flank of General Murray's small emaciated army.[54]

Many of the men in the 48th Foot, now anchoring the right flank of Murray's small army, had stood in the second British line at Culloden, bayoneting the few berserk Highlanders of Clan Macpherson who had pierced the first line. Former enemies, all were now wearing the red coat and standing together in this business against a common enemy, a Franco-*Canadien* army come to retake the capital. Even the British commander, James Murray, though not at Culloden, had something to prove. A victory today would unequivocally clear his name of the taint of Jacobitism. The alternative – defeat – was not a recognized word in the ambitious general's lexicon. As his army deployed into line, Murray reconnoitred the enemy from left to right, riding along the Buttes à Neveu with Major Patrick Mackellar and Lieutenant Thomas Mills, his aide de camp.[55]

He saw much to stir his blood. To the far left on the edge of the plains, barely a mile away, Murray observed that two unfinished redoubts guarding the heights and open ground around the top of the Anse au Foulon were already occupied by Indians and *Canadien* militia. Smoke still rose from morning campfires, gray-white against the dark green backdrop of the wet Sillery wood. This small forest framed the western edge of the plains, and stretched some two miles northward to the other side of the Quebec plateau. Two hundred yards north of where the Sillery road disappeared into the trees was a string of gentle hillocks. Murray's gaze was drawn to the largest of them, now held by elements of the French advanced guard, who appeared to be cleaning their weapons, and a party of enemy horsemen watching his army's movements. Mackellar thought that the enemy were there "early in the morning to seize advantage of the ground and to watch our motions."[56]

The situation on the far right of the field was the most interesting. There, the Sillery wood had been cleared for cultivation and ended in a series of copses bisected by two overflowing brooks swollen with spring melt. Murray could see behind these copses the Sainte-Foy road stretching back to the ruined church where he had been yesterday. It was now alive with columns of marching troops as the head of the French army wheeled into the fields and scrub behind the Sillery Wood and disappeared into the woodline. Murray firmly believed he had caught his opponent on the march and out of position and therefore decided "to give the enemy battle before they could establish themselves."[57]

He issued his orders quickly and a sense of his reasoning is gleaned from his later dispatch to Amherst. Murray claimed to be influenced by "the superiority [my] troops had acquired over the enemy ever since the last campaign, [which] together with the fine field train [of artillery] we were furnished with, might have tempted me with an action, supposing I had not been thoroughly convinced of the necessity of it."[58]

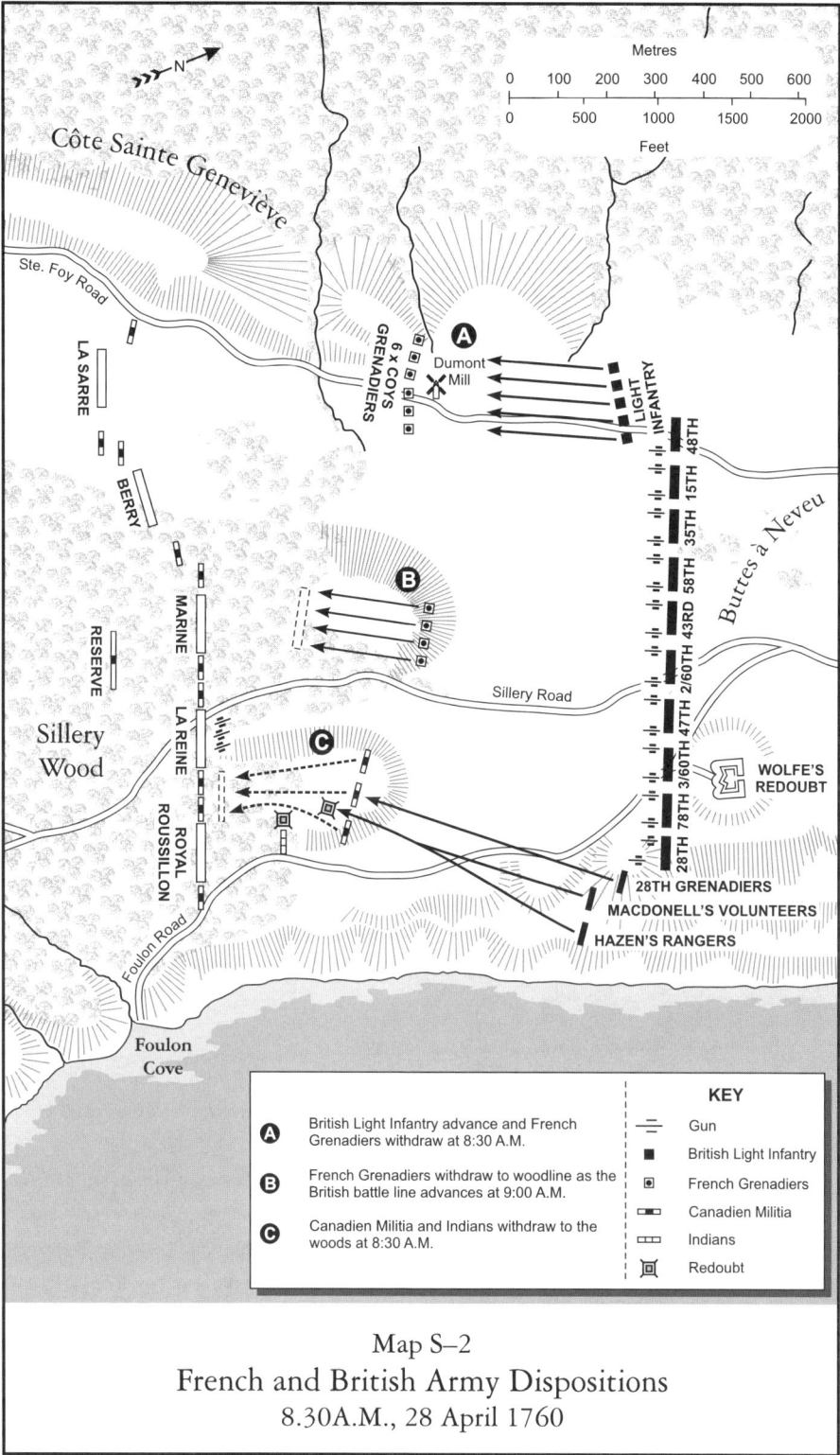

Metres

0   100   200   300   400   500   600

0   500   1000   1500   2000

Feet

Côte Sainte Geneviève

Ste. Foy Road

LA SARRE

BERRY

6 x COYS GRENADIERS

Ⓐ

Dumont Mill

LIGHT INFANTRY

48TH

15TH

35TH

58TH

43RD

2/60TH

47TH

3/60TH

78TH

28TH

Buttes à Neveu

Ⓑ

Sillery Road

MARINE

LA REINE

RESERVE

Sillery Wood

ROYAL ROUSSILLON

Ⓒ

WOLFE'S REDOUBT

28TH GRENADIERS

MACDONELL'S VOLUNTEERS

HAZEN'S RANGERS

Foulon Road

Foulon Cove

KEY

Ⓐ British Light Infantry advance and French Grenadiers withdraw at 8:30 A.M.

Ⓑ French Grenadiers withdraw to woodline as the British battle line advances at 9:00 A.M.

Ⓒ Canadien Militia and Indians withdraw to the woods at 8:30 A.M.

═ Gun

■ British Light Infantry

◉ French Grenadiers

▭▬▭ Canadien Militia

▯▯▯ Indians

▣ Redoubt

Map S–2

French and British Army Dispositions

8.30A.M., 28 April 1760

The enemy closest to Murray's line were six companies of French grenadiers who had been pushed back that morning from the Buttes à Neveu and were now posted at Dumont's farm and windmill on the extreme left. Murray deduced that this position was vital ground if he was to seize the initiative and fight a manoeuvre battle. The impetuous Scot, mounted on horseback, seemed oblivious, however, to the fact that the same soggy ground conditions that were preventing the rapid deployment of the French army to his front would apply equally to his own. Murray "thought this *the lucky minute* [author's emphasis] and moved the whole in great order to attack before [the French] could form." He therefore ordered his soldiers to drop their entrenching tools on the high ground and advance.[59]

But was the French army really off balance? Three of five brigades under the command of Lévis were already in battle formation deep within the Sillery Wood and only the advanced guard was in view from the British positions. Ensign John Désbruyêres, standing with the 35th Foot on the Buttes à Neveu, noted from his vantage point that the enemy's movements were deceiving, "the French appearing but small, their brigades being then sheltered in the woods."[60] Instead of being cautious, however, Murray saw what he wanted to see. Lieutenant Malcolm Fraser remembered that, when the order came, the thin, red, scorbutic line was told "to advance slowly, dressing by the right," and the army went forward, drummers beating out the cadence, leaving an excellent defensive position on high and reasonably dry ground with a small frontage of only 1,100 yards. Lieu-

Dumont's Mill

A detail of one of the plates on the base of the *Monument des Braves* by Charles Baillairgé recalls the mill that once stood on the northern escarpment of the Côte Ste Geneviève. Purchased from the Jesuits in 1741 by Jean-Baptiste Dumont, a Quebec trader, the mill complex included a house, a grange and a tannery and its fittings. Dumont put the property up for sale in 1779 and by the middle of the following century all that remained of the mill was its foundations. In 1855 a monument dedicated to Lévis and Murray was erected close to the windmill's original site. (Author's photo)

tenant John Knox recorded the unspoken thoughts that were on many of the British soldiers' minds as they marched about 800 yards forward. "We were insensibly drawn from our advantageous situation into low swampy ground where our troops [were] almost knee-deep in dissolving wreaths of snow and water."[61]

At least five of the battalion guns "bogged in deep pits of snow" on the move forward to the new position, so that of the twenty-two artillery pieces brought out of Quebec, only fifteen reached the new position. More than five hundred cursing men were employed in dragging and pushing the heavy pieces and their attendant ammunition tumbrels forward and the infantry line appears to have stopped two or three times during the advance to allow the artillery to catch up. Major Mackellar was of the opinion that this forward movement of the British actually gave their opponents ample time to form. "The snow and slipperyness of the ground … kept back our Cannon and saved [the French] being attacked sooner."[62]

In their haste to move forward and, dressing by the right, Murray's army reached their new position with all but two of their battalions north of the Sillery road (see map S-3). This left the 28th Foot and Fraser's Highlanders with the Ranger and volunteer companies on the extreme left flank now stretched very thin to cover a new frontage of some 400 yards in wooded and rough terrain compared to their former position with its 200 yards on open high ground. First contact with the enemy was made on the British left by Captain Donald Macdonell's volunteers of the army, 110 strong and supported by the 28th Foot grenadiers and Hazen's small ranger company. By 9 A.M. these troops had easily pushed the Indians and *Canadiens* out of the two unfinished redoubts that stood at the top of the Anse au Foulon, but, as Mackellar later pointed out, the enemy was fully formed and advancing in strength on this side of the battlefield, "favoured by the woods to conceal their movements."[63] Emboldened by his initial success, the intrepid Macdonell now went forward into these same woods with his small force, leaving the 28th Foot to consolidate around the two redoubts as the southern anchor of the British line.

It was a disastrous move. Most accounts of the battle state that the volunteers were overrun by the advancing French brigades, though one memoir specifically details their final fate. Sergeant Johnson of the 58th claimed "Savage Indians and Canadians who were advanced in the front of the Enemy's Right Flank and posted under some rocks and bushes, and entirely out of sight of Captain Macdonald and his Men ambushed them from the rear." Macdonell's force fell into disorder at "the very first fire," were unable "to recover themselves on a Sudden, after such

Un "sauvage"

An aboriginal warrior with a captured musket. During the winter of 1759-60, displaced Christianized Huron, Abenaki and Iroquois warriors of the Sillery and New Lorette missions joined *Canadien* militia and detachments of *troupes de la marine* in harassing British outposts around Quebec. At Sillery, some 280 warriors under *Capitaine* Corne St. Luc of the *Compagnies franches de la marine* formed part of Lévis' vanguard. They ambushed Captain Macdonell's volunteer company early in the battle and then spent the rest of the engagement in the rear looting the unattended packs of French soldiers. After the battle, they scalped British and French dead indiscriminately and killed British wounded. (NAC, C-3136)

an unsuspected surprize; and a regiment of french Regulars coming up instantly on them, Captain Macdonald and his whole Company, Officers and men were cut off. [E]xcept for Five or Six private men, they were all killed."[64]

The Rangers are, suspiciously, not mentioned at all and apparently did not fight very long on the left flank. A study of the casualty lists reveals that they appeared to have suffered very lightly in the heavy fighting, an indication that they never became decisively engaged, or worse, took to their heels as soon as the volunteers were overpowered and the full weight of the French army's right wing came against them. Having disposed of the British skirmishers, the French regulars kept advancing. The 28th Grenadiers in the two redoubts tried doggedly to hold what they had but were soon surrounded and had to fight their way out back to the main British line.

At the same time that Macdonnell and his men, flushed with victory at the redoubts on the left, were advancing boldly into the woods, the French commander's thoughts were concentrated on Murray's small army aggressively advancing at 9.00 A.M. As Lévis watched the British dressing to the right, "he concluded he would not have time to put his left in order to receive them" and "resolved on throwing the troops who were already in line a little to the rear so as to place them under the cover of the wood and to abandon Dumont's house." A position astride the Sainte-Foy road at La Fontaine's farm some 400 yards further to the rear seemed more prudent to Lévis as it would "allow the troops time to breathe, and to dispose them afterwards for marching against the enemy."[65]

At approximately 9.15 A.M., Bourlamaque galloped over to the Dumont farm complex, which consisted of several buildings, the most prominent being a loop-holed stone windmill. He found the 250 grenadiers there engaged in a firefight with advancing British light troops and ordered their senior surviving company commander, *Capitaine* Charles d'Aiguebelle of the *Languedoc* to retire by companies. A mounted officer in any 18th century battle was a prime target, and as he fell back with the grenadiers, Bourlamaque was hit by the British gunners. A round shot struck and killed his horse and also removed a large chunk of the brigadier's right thigh. As a party of grenadiers carried the stricken second-in-command to the rear, the last two French brigades moving up on the left were without orders. It was up to one of the oldest army officers in North America to make a command decision. [66]

This was 66-year-old *Lieutenant Colonel* Jean Dalquier de Servian, commanding the Brigade of *La Sarre*, which included his own battalion of the *Béarn*. Dalquier quickly took in the scene – his *Béarn* grenadier company with others was coming down the road towards him in full flight, no officers were to be seen anywhere and British light troops were nipping at their heels like terriers and whooping like savages. Dalquier, an experienced veteran and one of the best field commanders in New France, immediately ordered his brigade forward to support the retreating advanced guard. The Brigade of *Berry* commanded by Lieutenant Colonel Jean-Baptiste de Trivio on his right, numbering some 1,250 men in column, took their cue from Dalquier and also advanced. A staff officer with Lévis noted with a mixture of awe and disdain that the army's left wing "moved … *without being formed*" and "under the most murderous fire of artillery and musketry."[67]

A "Chosen Man"

This soldier represents one of many active and alert men handpicked from the marching regiments to be trained specifically for patrolling, skirmishing and bushfighting. Brigaded in a special corps known as the "Light Infantry," they were trained by the American Rangers in the use of snowshoes and armed with tomahawks, powderhorns and cut-down muskets. They proved their worth during the skirmish warfare that was waged around Quebec during the winter of 1759-60. At the Battle of Sillery they were initially successful on the right flank but over-extended themselves and were severely defeated by French regular columns supported by grenadiers and *Canadiens*. (Courtesy Parks Canada)

"In spite of our utmost efforts exerted on our part to prevent them, one of [the French] columns came without loss of time to sustain their flying grenadiers, now pursued by our light infantry," remembered Knox. The Brigade of *La Sarre*, numbering some 1,100 men and bolstered by d'Aiguebelle's grenadiers who now returned to the charge, completely routed the British light troops, who were "overpowered with great loss." This defeat was the direct outcome of the British light infantry's confidence born from a string of successes against French irregulars during the past winter. By 9.30 A.M. however, they had been thoroughly chastened and fell back to a gentle rise overlooking the right of the battlefield and occupied Dumont's Mill, grimly determined to hold there. Lévis now sent the remaining four grenadier companies of the advanced guard which had been posted in the centre over to the left with orders to retake the Dumont farm.[68]

It was vital ground for both armies as possession of this fortified mill and its stone manor house ensured stability for their respective flanks. Moreover, whoever possessed the windmill heights then had the ability to outflank the other in dead ground just to the north along the escarpment. The Dumont Mill would now become the scene of vicious fighting for the next two hours, much of it hand-to-hand with dirks, bayonets and tomahawks.[69]

M ajor Jean-Daniel Dumas, commanding the two battalions of *troupes de la Marine* in the centre, could hardly believe his eyes at 9 A.M. when he glimpsed the British army advancing from the Buttes à Neveu, two ranks deep, drums beating, colours flying. They marched slowly as if very weary, but they came on nonetheless, with battalion guns being dragged behind while others sent their round shots screaming into the forest canopy over his head. The recent commander of the forward base at Jacques Cartier, Dumas had been Murray's principal opponent all winter. His spy network in the city and countryside had kept close tabs on the British garrison and relayed information to him.

Only 16 days before, Dumas had reported to Lévis and Vaudreuil that Murray "has very few men left [and] I believe he finds it very hard to keep up a show. All the news received for the last three weeks tells the same story of sickness and mortality ... and if we allowed ourselves to trust common rumour we should conclude that there are not present in Quebec 2,000 men under arms." Dumas had concluded this report with a firm statement that Murray would not try to give open battle: "M. Murai, I think is too good a military man to do that." But now Murray was marching directly at him with a line that appeared to number

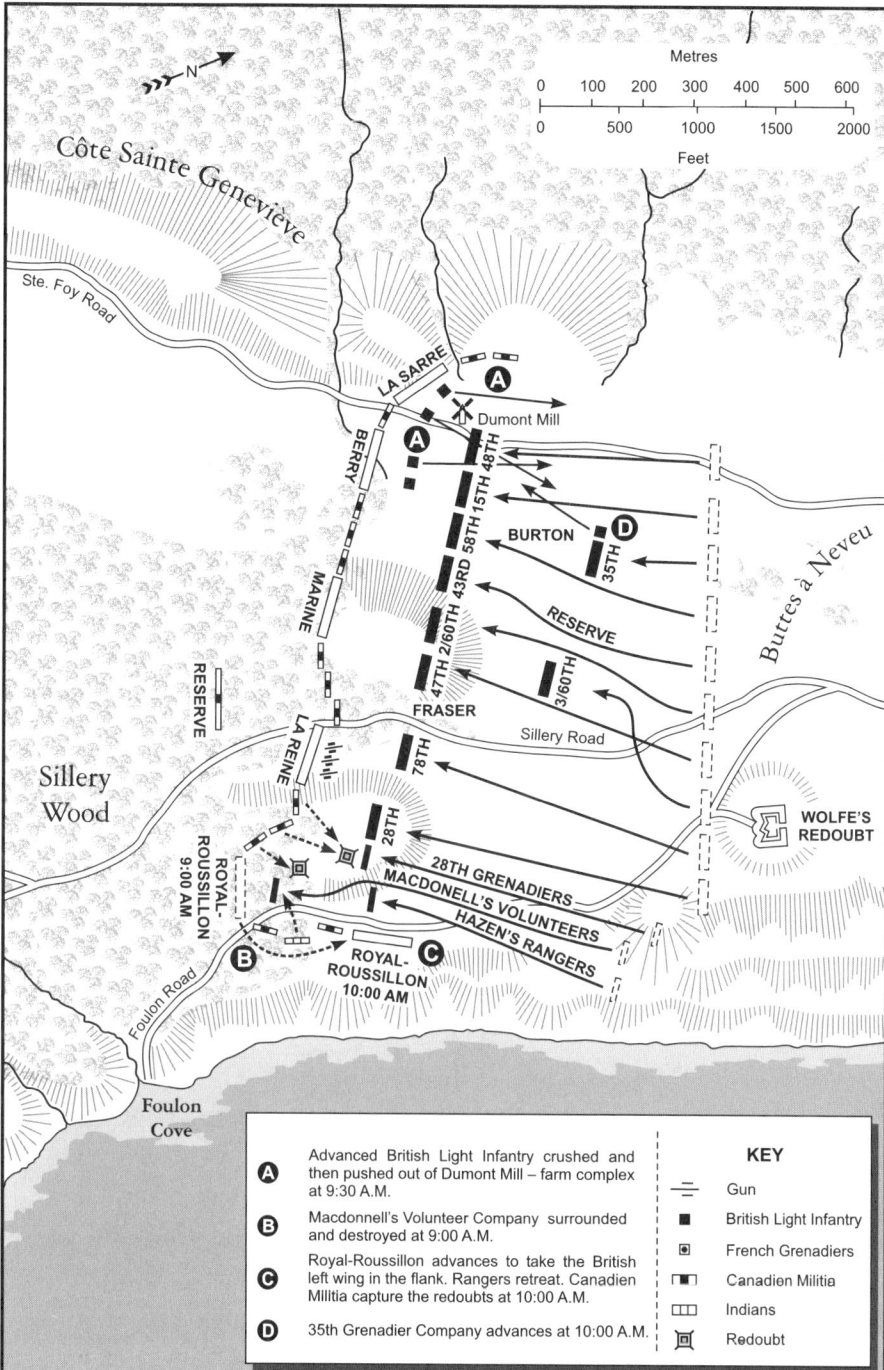

Map S–3
French and British Army Dispositions
9.00A.M. – 10.00 A.M., 28 April 1760

more than 2,000 men. Dumas obviously had been given wrong intelligence about the size of the British army. Perhaps he would now have to also revise his opinions of the general as "a military man"?[70]

Lévis' staff, positioned not far from where Dumas' brigade now held the centre, were equally confused. Their first thoughts were that the British intended to work "under cover of their lines and guns [to entrench] themselves on the heights before Quebec in order to keep us at a distance from the heart of the place," but they realized that when the British saw the French advanced guard "fall back some steps, they [the British] looked on the movement that was ordered as involuntary and believed they ought to advance so as to profit by the disorder in which they supposed we had fallen."[71]

It appeared to Sergeant John Johnson and the men of the 58th Foot facing *Canadien* marksmen and the colonial regulars in the centre that the French were no match for them. As they had reached their final position at 9.30 A.M., the 40 year-old ex-writing master was telling his men, "Look lads! They dare not face us in the open plain." The reason was obvious, for as Johnson later recorded, pieces of "Artillery were planted two on the Right flank of each battalion; and so as long as we had Ammunition to Support them we maintained our ground, and obliged their front line to press so hard upon their rear as to force them into the skirts of the Wood which was close behind them."[72] The British regulars had easily pushed Dumas' advanced guard skirmishers back into the Sillery Wood, but this rearward movement ended there. With the 58th stationary at a distance of only 50 paces from the tree line, Dumas' men and attached *Canadien* sharpshooters exacted retribution for their earlier rebuff.

The wisdom of not standing on the open plain soon became apparent to Private James Miller of the 15th Foot some 200 yards north of Sergeant Johnson. The 15th had advanced with the rest of their brigade, Colonel Ralph Burton at their head. Miller, on the right front of his battalion line, remembered his regiment was "drawn up in a hollow, with a height, in front, on which, the enemy balls struck, and flew over our heads." While Miller and his companions enjoyed the relative safety of dead ground, the centre and left companies of the 15th were counterattacked by two battalions of colonial regulars led by Dumas. Miller noted that "the fireing [sic] continued, in the center and left, where we repuls'd the enemy in our front." But then the drums rolled and "we unfortunately advanced. [Our regiment] drove them, but the French line, when hid by the bushes, kept up a fire, and with such effect, as threw us into confusion."

The French now "took an opportunity of cutting us up," Miller recalled, "they being drawn up under cover, and taking aim at leisure, while we could only see them through the intervals of the trees." The British guns guarding the battalion gaps, some from 200 to 400 feet apart in Murray's over-extended line, were ignored, the French directing their fire at the infantry battalions because they presented easier and wider targets. Over a period of 30 minutes, the British right took heavy casualties. "Ten Officers, from Twenty, were dropped," recorded Miller of the 15th Foot. "Twelve serjeants from twenty-four, and near two hundred Rank and file, from less than 400 in the field!" The 48th Foot to the north fared no better, nose to nose with the Brigade of *Berry* to their front and the Brigade of *La Sarre* with its host of *Canadien* sharpshooters and the remnants of the French grenadiers on their right.

On the extreme British right, Major John Dalling's Light Infantry had been damaged beyond repair and now recoiled in confusion from the windmill as they were pushed back. Their dashing commander had been wounded and 218 officers and men killed or wounded out of a total of 377 men. As the survivors broke and streamed back, they masked their own guns from opening up with canister on their pursuers. The disorder and rout, Murray later claimed, lost him his "lucky minute" as the Light Infantry "prevented Colonel Burton from taking advantage of the first impression made on that left [French] flank."[73]

At 10 A.M., Murray rode over to the right from the centre where he had been personally placing artillery pieces. He ordered the light infantry "to clear the front and regain the right; but in attempting this, they were charged, thrown into confusion, retired to the rear, and never again could be brought up during the action." Murray barked an order at his mounted aide, Lieutenant Thomas Mills, to ride to the 35th Foot in the reserve line to tell their commander "to march up

"The best trained battalion in all America"
This was how Wolfe described Anstruther's or the 58th Foot. This private is dressed in full marching order and is a member of one of the eight line or "hat" companies of his battalion. Trained by a young Lieutenant Colonel William Howe, who had commanded Wolfe's Light Infantry the year before, the soldiers of the 58th remained steady throughout the battle of Sillery and were one of the two battalions Murray used to cover his broken army's retreat to the gates of the city. (Courtesy Parks Canada)

immediately and cover the Right Wing of the army, the grenadier company to advance and take possession of a Mill to their front."[74]

Major Roger Morris and his Irishmen of the 35th watched as the mud-spattered and hatless Mills reined in at 10.15 A.M. and relayed Murray's order. The grenadier company on the right flank of the battalion shouldered arms and its commander, Captain Charles Ince, drew his sword and led his men north over the Sainte-Foy road. During the winter, Ince had been one of Murray's most reliable detachment commanders and had been responsible for the defence of two blockhouses at Point Lévis on the south shore, a difficult and dangerous assignment. Terminated just two days ago, it bore no resemblance to the almost suicidal mission his company was now ordered to undertake – recapture the windmill and the heights in the face of the massed fire of two French regiments, 800 *Canadien* sharpshooters and the remnants of the French grenadier companies.

"The situation our Company was in when we gave our first Fire," recalled one of Ince's officers, Lieutenant Eubule Ormsby, "was in a regular manner, the front rank kneeling, drawn up with a Ravine just in our front … about 50 or 60 yards from the Windmill, in which position we continued for a little time, when Captain Ince perceiving that our Fire had forced the enemy to withdraw from thence, … called out loud to follow him." The grenadiers of the 35th "immediately crossed the Ravine, by a little Gap upon the Right, only by one, or at most, two men abreast as the path was very narrow." The big Irishmen struggled to get across the obstacle "rendered still more difficult in many parts by a great quantity of snow which lay in drifts." As Ormsby brought up the rear of the company and finally scrambled up onto the open ground leading to the mill, now some 30 yards away, he saw the entire company running forward in no order. Grenadier John Maxwell remembered the "company was in great confusion and divided into several bodies." As he ran forward "with Lt Ormsby nigh the mill," he "set up a kind of Indian Hollow [holler], and [the Lieutenant] ordered me to hold my tongue." Around them the trampled snow was stained with blood, the dead and dying of both sides littering the ground. The mill doors were so choked with bodies that the only access was through the windows.[75]

"Soon after we got to the mill," Ormsby recalled, "Captain Ince was wounded [and] immediately called for me." As the young lieutenant reached his mortally wounded commander, Ince could only gasp, "My dear Ormsby, keep what we have got!" What the Irish had got was more than any man or grenadier could keep. "We were a good deal broke," stated another Grenadier Lieutenant, George Weld, a few months after the battle. Private John Stone noted that Ormsby, now in charge, "ordered [us] to fire where he saw the French stand very thick." but the returning fire was so heavy he ordered them to fall back.[76]

Lieutenant George Fraser, commanding one of the howitzers attached to the 48th Foot on the Sainte-Foy road, cursed as the 35th's grenadiers came back, because they masked his fire in much the same way as the Light Infantry had done nearly an hour before. As the surviving grenadiers returned to the dead ground of the ravine, Fraser's gun fired canister causing the *Canadien* militia in hot pursuit to dive for cover. As the French tried to move forward, the grenadiers turned and used the ravine as a trench while Fraser's gun swept the open ground to their front, mutually protecting one another. This caused Fraser to comment: "I know it was owing to the singular good behaviour of that company that the howitzer and ammunition cart I commanded were not taken before the Line Retreated and I told Lieutenant Ormsby, I should ever esteem them for it!"[77]

On the British right, it was now a waiting game for the French: as long as the guns kept up their withering fire, the French kept their distance. On the extreme left, around 11.00 A.M., the British line was being overwhelmed by sheer numbers and "the enemy possessed themselves of two redoubts upon our left," remembered Knox.[78] The rout of the rangers and volunteers on the left mirrored their Light Infantry comrades' embarrassment on the right. The bold and resourceful Captain Macdonell lay dead with most of his men forward of the southernmost redoubt, now occupied by *Canadien* militia under *Capitaine* Dominique-Nicolas de Laas. Captain Moses Hazen of the Rangers was seriously wounded and his men were falling back to the city with large numbers of the 28th Foot who, according to Lieutenant Malcolm Fraser of the neighbouring 78th, had been "exposed" and "obliged to give ground after an obstinate resistance."[79]

Murray, realizing that his left was in danger of complete collapse, ordered the 43rd Foot under Lieutenant Colonel Demetrius James to shift from the centre where there was little pressure and move as quickly as possible to his endangered flank. "I ordered Kennedy's from the center and the 3rd Battalion [Royal Americans, from the reserve line] to sustain [my left]." On the left, the 78th Foot was barely holding on, the only British battalion to face the fire of three French 6-pdrs commanded by *Capitaine* Jean de Louvricourt, a regular artillery officer situated on the French right wing (see map S-4). "The enemy played against the left of our army with two pieces of canon [sic]," Lieutenant Fraser recalled, "and killed and wounded us some men." As with the other battalions to the north, the 78th started to take heavy casualties. Sergeant James Thompson was kept busy as "it was my lot to act as covering sergeant to [Captain Alexander] Fraser," closing up files in his grenadier company as the Highlanders fell. Soon Thompson was obliged to replace his company commander, who "received a shot in the temple" which "killed him on the very spot on which he stood (and as not an inch of ground was to be lost), I had to move up into line which I could not do without resting one foot on his body."[80]

Lieutenant John Knox of the 43rd proudly recorded that his battalion passed to the rear of the 47th and 78th "by an excellent movement and made a vigorous effort to recover those works, and succeeded." Both the 43rd and Royal Americans "maintained them for some time with admirable firmness, but, at length being reduced to a handful, [we] were compelled to yield to superior numbers." Lieutenant Colonel John Young, commanding the Royal Americans, was struck down and captured by soldiers of the Brigade of *Royal-Roussillon* as, despite all efforts, the British left flank finally crumpled.[81]

This was the critical moment. It was now 11.30 A.M. and the Brigades of *La Sarre* and *Berry* had closed with the British right, now reinforced with the 35th Foot from the reserve line formed at a right angle to the enemy or *en potence*, a similar flank protection role they had executed at the Plains battle the year before. The Chevalier Johnstone, a former aide-de-camp to Lévis, later wrote that "the left of the French army which was in hollow ground about 40 paces from the British was crushed to pieces by the fire of their artillery loaded with grapeshot." Their commanding general began to doubt if his men could bear the barrage. "M. de Lévis perceiving their bad situation," recorded Johnstone, "sent M. de la Pause with orders for the army to retire some steps behind in order to occupy an eminence" behind the windmill and "parallel to the rising ground occupied by the English." There they could shelter behind its slope and wait out the artillery fire that was starting to slacken as British ammunition stocks rapidly dwindled.[82] An able staff officer, *Lieutenant Colonel* Plantavit de Margon de Lapause appears to have got a garbled version of his general's intentions or delivered the orders so precipitously that he nearly lost the battle "irremediably ... by his stupidity." Johnstone claims Lapause "ran along the line, ordering each regiment to the right about, and to retire, without any explanation of M de Lévis' orders." As the aide-de-camp points out, "some of the left of the French army [were] so near as twenty paces to the enemy," including *Lieutenant Colonel* Jean Dalquier's battered *Bearn* battalion and the Alsatians of *La Sarre*. Even "the best disciplined troops," opined

Metres

| 0 | 100 | 200 | 300 | 400 | 500 | 600 |

| 0 | 500 | 1000 | 1500 | 2000 |

Feet

Côte Sainte Geneviève

Ste. Foy Road

Dumont Mill

LA SARRE **(A)**

BERRY

35TH

35TH

MARINE

(B) 47TH 2/60TH 43RD 58TH 15TH 48TH

RESERVE

3/60TH

RESERVE

(C)

LA REINE

Sillery Road

Buttes à Neveu

78TH

Sillery Wood

43RD

28TH

(D)

3/60TH

WOLFE'S REDOUBT

ROYAL-ROUSSILLON
10:00 AM

Foulon Road

Foulon Cove

(A) 35th Foot ordered to right flank from reserve at 10:00 A.M. Grenadiers repulsed from the mill at 10:30 A.M. 48th and 35th retreat at 11:30 A.M.

(B) 43rd withdrawn from battle line and sent by Murray to shore up the left flank at 10:15 A.M. 3rd Royal Americans ordered from reserve to the left flank at 10:30 A.M.

(C) Lévis orders La Reine to attack the British left at 10:30 A.M. in concert with Royal-Roussillon but they mistakenly march to their own left. Montreal Militia in reserve ordered into main battle line to take La Reine brigade's place.

(D) 28th is broken at 11:00 A.M. 43rd and 3rd Royal Americans recapture redoubts briefly, but are flanked by the Royal-Roussillon brigade and retreat at 11:30 A.M.

KEY

Gun

British Light Infantry

French Grenadiers

Canadien Militia

Indians

Redoubt

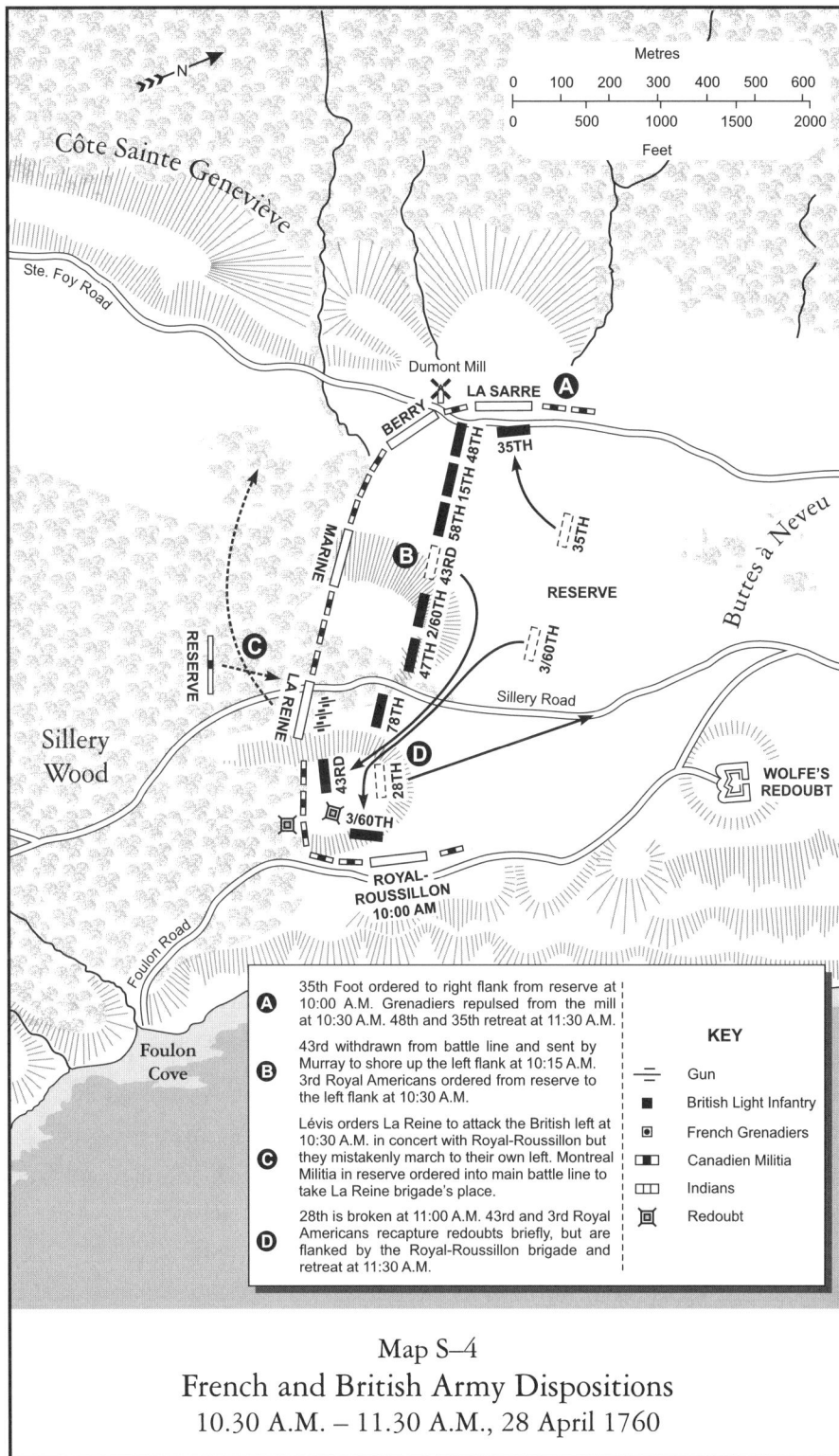

Map S–4
French and British Army Dispositions
10.30 A.M. – 11.30 A.M., 28 April 1760

Johnstone, "in that [circumstance] can scarce be expected to retire without the greatest disorder and confusion or exposing themselves."[83]

As Lapause reached the Brigade of *La Sarre*, he found *Capitaine* Maurès de Malartic, the brigade major, calmly telling his men to hold their ground and return fire. The brigade commander, Dalquier, had just gone down with a ball in his right chest, so Lapause shouted out his abbreviated orders to Malartic to turn right about and retire. The latter, a capable officer, immediately saw this would be disastrous and refused to comply with the orders. *Lieutenant colonel* Lapause tried to order Malartic's men back himself but the wounded Dalquier, "a bold, intrepid old officer" bleeding from his side, pushed forward into the din of the battle and shouted, "Now is not the time *mes gars* to retire when at twenty paces from the enemy!" He then ordered them to fix bayonets shouting, "Let us throw ourselves amongst them!"[84]

As the Brigade of *La Sarre* went forward with the cold steel, Malartic ten paces to their front, the Brigade of *Berry* turned about and joined the charge, screaming their support. The British right immediately broke, the 48th and 35th disintegrating into a running mass of broken men, and Lévis, watching from the centre, quickly issued orders for the Brigades of *Royal-Roussillon* and *La Reine* on the French left also to move forward at best speed. He then rode along the front of his centre, his hat upon his sword held over his head, the signal for a general advance. The orders for *La Reine,* however, were so badly communicated that instead of assisting the Brigade of *Royal-Roussillon* to finish off the left flank of the British army, it formed and marched to the right where the other two brigades were already in pursuit of the British.

Sergeant Johnson of the 58th (and many of his red-coated comrades) knew intuitively that it was only a matter of time before the battle was lost. "So long as [our guns] had ammunition to support us we maintained our ground," he later wrote, "but no sooner they perceived our Artillery had intirely ceased and that our Musquetry was so very light, they advanced boldly upon us, which in a little time forced us to give way." The 58th remained steady, however, as they went back,[85]

> keeping a good front towards them; but through the smallness of our number, and the quantity of the ground we had to cover, to secure the flanks of our line, the intervals between our battalions, so excessive large, they advanced

The general advance

The Chevalier de Lévis, commanding the Franco-*Canadien* army at the Battle of Sillery, rides in front of his cheering battle line, his tricorne held triumphantly aloft on his sword to signal the general advance against the broken British army. For a battlefield of trampled mud and April snow, the artist has made the grass overly long for the season. (Painting by Bompled, courtesy Directorate of History & Heritage, DND Canada)

and broke in hastily upon us like a hasty torrent from a lofty precipice and got into our front through those intervals which obliged us to retire in confusion, each one striving to shift for himself.

Many soldiers suffering from "Wounds, Scurvy, Sickness or real want of the common necessities," recalled Johnson, could not move as fast as their healthier comrades. "Faint and intirely unable for a precipitate flight," they fell victim to the tomahawk and scalping knife. Major Patrick Mackellar, despite being seriously wounded, was one of the lucky few to escape the battle's aftermath and bitterly remembered after the siege that the "dead, all the wounded men and several of the wounded officers who could not get off the field was, as usual, every one Scalped for the entertainment of the Conqueror." Knox devotes a page in his journal to the seeming inability of the French officers to prevent the killing of British wounded, claiming that "of the immense number of men who were unavoidably left on the field of battle, twenty-eight only were sent to the hospital, the rest being given up as victims to glut the rage of their savage allies!" [86]

The French witnesses deny complicity in such atrocities. In fact, Malartic claimed, "The *sauvages* were of no use to us during the fighting and stole things in the stores and knapsacks [to the rear]. They came back as soon as it was evident to them that we were masters of the battlefield to scalp the victims." Indeed, many British accounts mention that French officers attempted to save British wounded from the warriors after Murray's army had quit the field. Lieutenant Alexander Gregorson of Ardtonish, bayoneted twice by French regulars of the *Royal-Roussillon*, lay bleeding on the ground, helplessly watching "savages murdering the wounded and scalping them on all sides" and "expected every moment to share the same fate, but was saved by a French officer who luckily spoke a little English." Indignantly, Malartic added that their so-called allies "scalped many a Frenchman as well!" [87]

Thomas Mante, a former British officer who interviewed battle participants for his *History of the Late War in America* published twelve years after the battle, discovered that in the retreat "Amherst's [15th Foot] and Anstruther's [58th Foot] supported each other with great firmness; and retreated in some order. The return of the other regiments resembled a flight more than a retreat, till they got under the cannon of the wooden redoubts." [88] Murray must have been with these two battalions for he wrote to his brother that he personally commanded a retreat that was made "in tolerable order, by means of the corps the General himself had posted in the two unfinished redoubts [one being Wolfe's redoubt] and on an eminence." Murray later claimed that he was "the last man that enter'd the gates."[89]

During the retreat, the 15th Foot, Murray's old regiment, certainly remained steady under the leadership of another fiery little Scot, Major Paulus Aemilius Irving. Private James Miller of the 15th noted that his commanding officer "did all that a man could do to keep it in a body, in order to cover the retreat, ordering them to turn round frequently, and fire by platoons or Volleys." In "the hurry, he had like to have lost his *wig*," recalled Miller fondly, "however, [Major Irving] put it under his arm with great Sang froid, and said '[D]amn the old wig', a name by which he is known to this day by the old soldiers."[90]

On the left, the last regiment to fall back was the 47th Foot. It was "drawn up with a small rising ground in their front which till then covered them pretty much from the enemy's fire," recalled Lieutenant Fraser of the 78th. "Colonel Fraser who commanded the Left brigade … sent orders [to Colonel Walsh] it was absolutely necessary for the 47th to quit this ground, otherwise they must inevitably [be] surrounded in a few minutes." Corroborating Mante's assessment of a rout, Fraser's Highlanders were characterized by one of its own sergeants, James Thompson, as being "a raw undisciplined set" which "got into a great disorder" and became "more like a mob than regular soldiers." But "as soon as the Piper discovered that his men [were] scatter'd and … in disorder …he luckily bethought himself to give them a blast of his pipes," recalled Thompson. "This had the effect of stopping them short and they soon allow'd themselves to be form'd into some sort of order."[91]

Certain incidents occurred at this stage of the action that contributed to the French army's reluctance to pursue their retreating opponents too closely. During the retreat, Sergeant Thompson encountered the Ranger commander,

"Damn the old wig!"
Major Paulus Aemilius Irving, the feisty Lowland Scot who commanded Amherst's 15th Foot during the Quebec campaign of 1759-60, was known for cramming his trademark wig into his pocket during combat. His coolness under fire at Sillery became legendary in his regiment, one veteran remembering his battalion commander calmly ordering men to right about turn and fire disciplined volleys at pursuing Frenchman. In the heat of action, Irving risked losing his trusty wig: "he however put it under his arm, with great *Sang froid*, and said 'damn the old wig,' a name by which he is known, to this day, by the old soldiers." (Print after oil pastel, author's collection)

Captain Moses Hazen, who had been wounded in the thigh and was making his way off the battlefield with the help of his servant. The American saw a French officer exhorting his detachment onwards over an open field well to his rear.

"Do you see that rascal there, waving his sword to encourage those fellows to come forward?" Hazen asked his servant. "I do, Sir." Sitting down, the ranger captain quickly looked up and said, "Then just place your back against mine for one moment and I'll see if I can bring him down."

Sergeant Thompson watched incredulously as Hazen "accordingly stretch'd himself on the ground and resting the muzzle of his fuzee on his toes he let drive at the French officer … and 'afaith, down he was flat in an instant." Upon being congratulated for his extraordinary marksmanship, Moses Hazen shrugged and said, "A chance shot may kill the devil."[92]

For his part, Malartic, leading the Brigade of *La Sarre* forward, was wounded "in the chest as I was advancing. The hit made me fall backwards and left me in a state of shock." As the French officer came to, he found himself

in the arms of a Sergeant and Private who wanted to bring me back to my feet. I begged them to let me die right there. As they were lifting me against my will, I felt something cold slither to my stomach. I opened my vest, found it had been pierced and saw that the bottom part of my breast was quite black and swollen. I found the bloody bullet under my belly [and] was placed in the tender cares of a surgeon [at the *Hôpital-Général*].[93]

By 6 P.M. Malartic had joined his wounded brigade commander, Dalquier, in the hospital, which, being outside the walls of Quebec, now came under French control. The scenes that unfolded there had never been seen before in New France, the casualties on both sides outnumbering the entire total for the previous year's campaign. One of the sisters who nursed the wounded spoke for all:

It would require a more eloquent pen than mine to depict the horrors we were called upon to witness and to listen to during the arrival of the wounded who came in for 24 consecutive hours. The cries of the dying and the grief of their friends were indeed heart-rending and one needed almost a super-human strength to sustain the ordeal. Although we prepared 500 cots … as many more were needed. Our stables and barns were crowded with the unfortunates.… The misery was heightened by a scarcity of linen, and we were obliged to sacrifice even our own clothing.[94]

Murray's "*lucky minute*" had turned into three hours of almost non-stop fighting. From the moment the British Light Infantry and French grenadiers had been engaged at Dumont's Mill to the full-scale retreat back to the safety of the city, both armies had fought and grappled like two wounded bears: slowly, painfully and viciously. Some men were still loathe to leave the battlefield, their bloodlust up. When ordered to "Fall back" the 43rd Foot had cried out angrily, "Damn it, what is falling back but retreating!"[95] Lieutenant John Knox went back with these men and confessed afterwards that the battle had been "immensely warm for near two hours" with heavy casualties on both sides, particularly among the officer corps. The British army that had marched out that morning had been 3,111 strong. One hundred and thirty officers were killed or wounded, as well as 979 rank and file. The combined casualty rate of 1,109 all ranks represented a full third of Murray's effective strength and twice the number of casualties Wolfe's army had suffered the year before on almost the same ground.[96]

On the French side, Lévis submitted a return of 993 killed and wounded, 95 of whom were officer casualties. In a letter to Louis-Antoine de Bougainville commanding at Île aux Noix, the wounded Bourlamaque wrote, "We have lost the elite of the officers of *La Sarre, Berry, Béarn* and *La Marine*, all wiped out, so too our Grenadiers, 1000 men are killed or wounded I believe." He added as a caution, "Don't mention the contents of this letter to anyone and always diminish our loss."[97]

All French accounts reflect the fact that their men were too exhausted to give chase to the fleeing British regiments. *Capitaine* Pierre Pouchot of the *Béarn* Regiment, though not present at the battle, later recorded that the French soldiers and militia

pursued them to beneath Quebec but not very rigorously. Our soldiers were exhausted by their discomforts & weakened by poor food. We have seen that they had left their quarters on the 20th & since that time they had continuously been without tents and exposed to the snow and rain. It is certain that, if they had been able to run, very few English would have returned to Quebec & we would have remained masters of the place.[98]

A fellow *Béarn* officer, *Capitaine* Malartic, was quick to add that the French regular battalions had been "reduced to a very few people by the end of the battle," a reference to the high officer casualty rate and the resulting lack of command and control which hampered Lévis from "following the enemy as energetically as he

Artillery embrasures

The Royal Artillery, assisted by 300 "additional" gunners supplied from the infantry regiments, had to make open-
ings in the western curtain walls of the city similar to the battery pictured in this print in order to provide counter-
battery fire against the French siege lines on the Buttes à Neveu. (Courtesy Museum Restoration Service)

would have desired and possibly entering the city." While the British "abandoned
their artillery, which consisted of 22 field pieces, [including two howitzers], all
made of cast iron, as well as a vast amount of ammunition and a large number of
tools," noted Malartic, the footworn and hungry French soldiers and militia were
more interested in scavenging British haversacks and canteens for food, drink
and valuables.[99] To the defeated, all was despondency and despair and, for a day
or two, the bonds of discipline inside the walls of Quebec broke and "immense
irregularities were hourly committed," claims Knox. Prompt and stern measures
were necessary and a grim Murray moved quickly and ruthlessly. On 30 April
1760, a man was hanged without trial as an example to the rest and all liquor
"not belonging to the King" was spilled to prevent the men from getting it. Murray was also quick to issue a public order about his defeat:

> The 28th of April has been unfortunate to the British arms but affairs are not
> so desperate as to be irretrievable. The general often experienced the bravery
> of the troops he now commands and is very sensible they will endeavour to
> regain what they have lost. The fleet may be hourly expected, reinforcements

are at hand, and shall we lose in one moment the fruits of so much blood and treasure? Both officers and men are exhorted patiently to undergo the fatigues they must suffer, and to expose themselves cheerfully to some dangers – a duty they owe to their KING, their COUNTRY, and THEMSELVES.[100]

In private, Murray recorded that his next course of action would be an aggressive defence. "As we had the advantage of a numerous artillery," he wrote in his diary, "the enemy by the best accounts ill-furnished in that respect, and our wall bad, the best we could do was to endeavour to knock their works to pieces before they could mount their cannon." By keeping his men and officers busy around the clock, morale soon improved to the point where Lieutenant Knox could record in his journal:

> We are roused from our lethargy; we have recovered our good humour, our sentiments for glory; and we seem, one and all, determined to defend our dearly purchased garrison to the last extremity. [T]he general and Lieutenant-Governor visit the guards and working parties frequently to encourage the men and influence them to diligence and alertness.[101]

On the evening after the battle, 28 April 1760, the French started entrenching on the Buttes à Neveu using, ironically, the British tools that had been conveniently left there earlier in the morning. From the outset, Murray's attempts to outgun the besiegers had a telling effect, forcing Lévis to record in his journal that

> the enemy soon had 60 cannon unmasked on the attacked fronts. This artillery, served with the greatest activity not only retarded the construction of the batteries, but prevented the workmen transporting material; the balls plunging behind the heights, left no spot unprotected. The troops were obliged several times to decamp.[102]

In effect, Lévis was going through the motions of a formal siege without the men, guns and equipment he truly needed. As Ensign John Désbruyêres of the 35th Foot related to his patron, Colonel George Townshend, in a letter: "We had some reasons to think that Mr. De Levy ye French General considering the slowness of his approaches had meant nothing else by his coming so near us but to take post and hold himself in readiness to make the most of what succours might

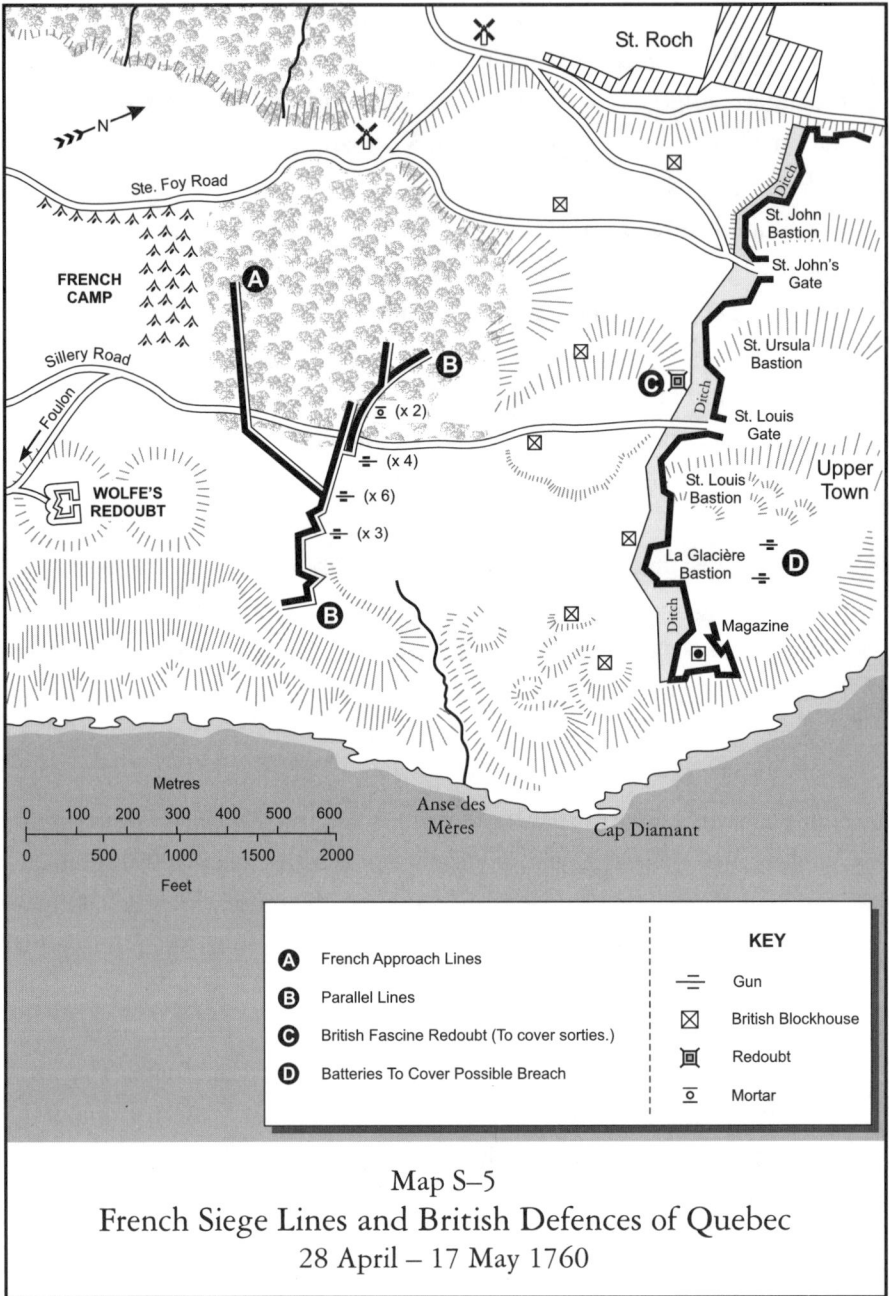

St. Roch

N

Ste. Foy Road

Ditch

St. John
Bastion

St. John's
Gate

FRENCH
CAMP

Sillery Road

Foulon

St. Ursula
Bastion

Ⓐ

Ⓑ

Ⓒ

Ditch

St. Louis
Gate

ō (x 2)

(x 4)

WOLFE'S
REDOUBT

(x 6)

St. Louis
Bastion

Upper
Town

(x 3)

La Glacière
Bastion

Ⓓ

Ⓑ

Ditch

Magazine

Metres

| 0 | 100 | 200 | 300 | 400 | 500 | 600 |

Anse des
Mères

Cap Diamant

| 0 | 500 | 1000 | 1500 | 2000 |

Feet

KEY

Ⓐ French Approach Lines

Ⓑ Parallel Lines

Ⓒ British Fascine Redoubt (To cover sorties.)

Ⓓ Batteries To Cover Possible Breach

Gun

British Blockhouse

Redoubt

Mortar

Map S–5
French Siege Lines and British Defences of Quebec
28 April – 17 May 1760

be sent from Europe." Both armies anxiously watched the river for reinforcements.[103]

They did not have long to wait. On the eleventh day of the siege, at 9 A.M. on 9 May 1760, the British garrison "had the inconceivable satisfaction to behold the *Leostoffe* frigate sail up into the bason and come to anchor," Lieutenant Knox recalling that

> the gladness of the troops is not to be expressed: both officers and soldiers mounted the parapets in the face of the enemy and huzzaed, with their hats in the air, for almost an hour the bay and circumjacent country for several miles resounded with our shouts and the thunder of our artillery; for the gunners were so elated that they did nothing but fire and load for a considerable time.[104]

It was the beginning of the end for New France, though Lévis stubbornly clung to the slender hope that the next ships to arrive would be French. Unbeknownst to him, his and Vaudreuil's plea for reinforcements had not fallen on deaf ears. A store ship laden with artillery munitions which would have been of great use to his siege train had arrived in the Saint Lawrence in November 1759, but had taken refuge in the Saguenay River and become ice-bound there.[105]

Early on the morning of 11 May 1760, four officers of the 43rd Foot who had spent a sleepless night on the ramparts with their men under arms were relaxing in their mess tent on camp stools sharing a pot of pease porridge. They had taken off their coats to enjoy the warmth of the early morning spring sunshine when "a shell pitched within a yard of the tent" sent them scrambling for cover. "They had barely time to stretch themselves at their length," wrote Lieutenant Knox, "when the shell burst! But, by being extended flat on the ground they happily received no other damage than losing their mess which was overset in the bustle." The puny French siege batteries had finally opened fire and Lévis recorded despondently that the barrage "would have been successful had our little artillery been of a better quality. 'Twas composed of [six] iron 12–pdrs. and [six] iron 18-pdrs, only one 24, and although the best in the Colony had been selected, most of the guns on the second day were unfit for service, and the remainder soon threatened to be in the same state."[106]

Four days later, three more British warships arrived in the evening twilight:

Les canoniers-bombardiers

Elite troops of the *troupes de la marine*, these gunners received higher pay than their infantry counterparts and served as grenadiers when away from their ordnance. Here a gun detachment trains on an iron gun, giving a good idea of the crew and equipment needed for siege operations. It was dangerous duty as the iron guns in New France were often old and worn cast-offs from warships and exploded during the siege, with dire results for the gunners. (Courtesy Parks Canada)

HMS *Vanguard* of 70 guns, HMS *Diana*, 32 guns, and the sloop *Lawrence* that Murray had dispatched several days earlier to get help. The disappointed Lévis now realized that his last throw of the dice had failed and an immediate retreat to Montreal was now necessary. He ordered his siege artillery removed from its batteries and dragged down to the Anse au Foulon to be reloaded on his supply boats under cover of darkness and the protection of his two frigates. "He did not hesitate in ordering a retreat," wrote one of his staff officers, "being well assured that *L'Attalant* [sic] and *La Pomone* ill-equipped, without guns and men, were not in a condition to resist the enemy's vessels and protect our transports having our provisions on board. He immediately sent orders to these vessels to re-ascend the River to a place of safety," after the guns were loaded.[107] Unfortunately for the French, bad weather prevented the message to retire up the river from reaching *Capitaine* Jean Vauquelin, the flotilla commander. This competent officer had commanded the frigate *Aréthuse* at Louisbourg in 1758 with great gallantry, where it had been the only ship to escape the harbour and elude the British fleet during the siege.

On the first flood tide at 4.30 P.M. the next morning, 16 May, 1760, the Royal Navy moved quickly, cutting their cables and running before the wind up to where Lévis' supply ships were still at anchor. They caught the French by surprise and the *Pomone* was "run ashore by the Frenche camp under there batterys," according to Andrew Knox, Master of HMS *Vanguard*. Once "the *Pomona* [had] struck, the *Dianna* and *Lowstaff* [sic] followed the rest up the River."[108]

The *Atlante,* commanded by Vauquelin, fought back fiercely, shielding a large fleet of batteaux as far as Cap Rouge, where they could be safe from an immediate attack. Then he engaged in a running rearguard battle with the *Diana* and *Lowestoft* frigates for almost three hours, buying much-needed time for the French army to get their batteaux at Saint Augustin safely upriver to Jacques Cartier. All the lesser transports anchored at the Anse au Foulon, however, were destroyed by the *Vanguard* except the small sloop of war, *La Marie,* which by throwing her guns overboard was the only ship of the fleet able to escape upriver. After destroying the sole means Lévis had of taking off his siege artillery, the Royal Navy turned its attention to the French army and "laid [its] broadside to the right flank of the enemy's trenches, and enfiladed them for several hours so warmly, that, between this fire, and that of the garrison, they were intirely driven from their works."[109]

Vauquelin succeeded in giving his opponents as good as he got and his gunners, aiming high, did great damage to the rigging of the pursuing British ships. A cheer went up from his sailors when a lucky shot sheared off the foretopmast steering sail of the HMS *Diana*. Other damage was extensive, the *Diana*'s master recording in her log that the frigate "was very much shattered in masts, rigging, and sails, and likewise received damage in the hull." Vauquelin's crippled frigate *Atlante* could get no further than Pointe-aux-Trembles so he ran his vessel aground, nailed his colours to the mast and fought until his powder ran out. At 11 A.M., sword in hand, Vauquelin ordered the mizzen mast chopped down so his surviving crew could use it as a raft to get to shore. Then he and his officers waited on board, their colours flying defiantly. By 11.30 A.M., boarding parties from the *Diana* had "brought the first and second Captn, officers, and sume of

Rearguard action

The French frigate *Atlante*, commanded by *Capitaine de frégate* Jean Vauquelin, trades broadsides with the frigates HMS *Diana* and HMS *Lowestoft* on 16 May 1760. This hard-fought but long-forgotten naval action in Canadian history signalled the end of the Franco-*Canadien* siege of Quebec and caused the withdrawal of Lévis' army to Montreal. Vauquelin fought a rearguard action for three hours until his crippled vessel could get no further upstream than Pointe-aux-Trembles. There he ran her aground, nailed his colours to the mast and fought until his powder ran out. (Print of painting by Thomas Weber, courtesy Directorate of History & Heritage, DND Canada)

the people on board us" the master noted, but "our cutter was bilg'd and lost upon a rock in boarding the enemy."[110]

The British naval officers were highly impressed with Vauquelin's fighting spirit and seamanship, so much so that the British naval commander, Commodore Robert Swanton, asked how he could serve the French captain. Vauquelin requested to be sent back to France at the first opportunity, to which the Commodore immediately complied. "This noble and generous behaviour of the English," noted the Chevalier de Johnstone, "did honour to their nation, far beyond what De Vauquelin met with from De Berryer, Secretary of the Navy, on his arrival in France." The returning Vauquelin was thrown into prison and court-martialled for losing his fleet.[111]

Early on the morning of the 17 May 1760, the wounded Patrick Mackellar was jubilant: "Finding our garrison vigilant and active, our Superiority of Fire increase, and three of our ships of war arrived which had driven away their Shipping or run them aground, they at night quitted the Siege and went off with the loss of all of their Artillery, ammunition, provision baggage, Shipping and about 3000 of their best troops." Mackellar added with some satisfaction that "they disappeared like a beaten army."[112]

With the siege lifted, however, Murray's officers and men began to openly question his generalship and his decision to give battle on 28 April. Lieutenant Charles Stewart, 78th Foot, who had fought under Lord George Murray at Culloden, was heard to exclaim from his hospital bed, "From April battles and Murray generals, good Lord deliver me!" Another 78th Foot officer noted that General Murray's "conduct on this occasion is universally condemned by all those who are not immediately dependent on him" and that it would give him "great pleasure to relate something more to the advantage of this gentleman who is, in many respects, possessed of several virtues, and particularly all the military ones, except prudence." In his assessment of his general's performance on 28 April, Lieutenant Malcolm Fraser identified the marching French army on the morning of battle as a "bait too tempting and that [Murray's] passion for glory [got] the better of his reason." Voices from the ranks were just as blunt, Sergeant John Johnson of the 58th commenting that "it was General Murray's duty to use all possible means to preserve [Quebec] and to defend it to the last extremity, and not throw away such brave men on a vain delusion of gaining to himself great honour."[113]

Censure at home was also to be expected. Murray's initial dispatches on his defeat came as a shock to a British public. Horace Walpole spoke for most when he wrote: "Who the deuce was thinking of Quebec? America was like a book one has read and done with: but here we are on a sudden reading our book backwards." To Sir Horace Mann, Walpole wrote, "General Murray got into a mistake and a morass and was enclosed, embogged and defeated."[114] Another critic commenting on Murray's explanation to attack rather than defend observed in the *Annual Register,* "It is hard to understand how the chance of holding out in a fortress should not be lessened after a defeat of the troops which compose the garrison," but added sympathetically that "these are matters not so easily comprehended by those who are at distance from the scene of action.[115]

The French success at the Battle of Sillery on 28 April 1760 was at best a Pyrrhic victory. Lévis won the contest decisively, but his exhausted and hungry army, exposed to the elements and the loss of so many active and dynamic officers as well as elite soldiers, was not up to the task of besieging Quebec. To do so would have required significant reinforcements, guns and ammunition. Both sides had lost approximately a thousand all ranks by the end of the siege – for Murray, a third of his effective strength. In the overall strategic scheme of things, Lévis had been defeated, for his daring campaign had truly been "all or nothing." His attempt "instead of recovering the Capital of their Country," noted Mackellar, "facilitated the loss of the whole."[116]

The fall of Montreal and the capitulation of New France later that year were now a foregone conclusion. On 8 September 1760, Montreal surrendered as the combined armies of Murray, Amherst and Haviland converged on it from the north, south and west. Murray remained unapologetic for the Sillery battle, a defeat rendered insignificant by the successful lifting of the siege by the Royal Navy and subsequently overshadowed by the ultimate conquest of New France later that summer. He wrote defiantly to his brother, George: "I fought a battle; I lost it. What then? Is every day of battle a victory?" He would also later claim, with some justification, that his attack had seriously damaged Lévis' army, emphasizing General Amherst's post-battle comments on the Montreal campaign that Murray's action had "left him nothing to do."[117]

As a military action during the Seven Years' War, the battle of Sillery ranks as a bloodier, more bravely and skillfully-fought action than that of 13 September 1759. The Plains of Abraham, however, has continued to hold the public's imagination for time immemorial, rooted in an unshakeable mythology that has grown up around the daring surprise landing and climbing of the cliffs at the Anse au Foulon and the noble and tragic deaths of Wolfe and Montcalm. At Sillery, the French army possessed the initiative throughout and the only complete surprise achieved that fateful day was that inflicted by Murray on his own men, who were not psychologically prepared for the action foisted on them by their ambitious commander. "When we marched out, we thought the General did not intend to give battle," confessed Lieutenant Malcolm Fraser. "We thought he meant to throw up works on the rising ground before the town." How true then were the prescient words of François Bernier, the French commissary, written several months before the battle of Sillery – that James Murray was a commander who had "too great an opinion of [his] strength" leaving him "little opportunity for reflection and consideration" and much for "subsequent regret."[118]

The Battlefield Today

In Quebec City today, the ground over which the two armies fought almost 250 years ago is covered completely with streets, houses and thriving neighbourhoods, although parts of the battlefield where Murray started his advance forward to close with Lévis' army are preserved as open ground between the Musée du Québec and the head of the Anse au Foulon. The Merici convent stands on the spot where two unfinished redoubts

Bellona of Sillery

On the site where Dumont's farm and stone windmill once stood on the British right and French left, stands a monument to Murray and Lévis designed by the famous architect-engineer Charles Baillairgé. A large column or pillar surmounted by the Roman goddess of war, Bellona, this monument can be found in a small park at the north end of the Avenue des Braves, a downtown city boulevard running north-south on the approximate line of the furthest advance made by the British. The monument was initially erected on the site in 1855 and inaugurated 19 October 1863 by Lord Monck, Governor-General of Canada. (Author's photo)

anchored the left wing of the British army. Dumont's farm and stone windmill on the British right are also gone, although a monument to Murray and Lévis designed by the famous architect-engineer Charles Baillairgé was erected on the site in 1855. It was inaugurated 19 October 1863 by Lord Monck, Governor-General of Canada, and consists of a large column surmounted by the Roman goddess of war, Bellona. It stands in a small park at the north end of the avenue des Braves, *a downtown boulevard running north-south on the approximate line of the furthest advance made by the British.*

A Battle That Should

Never Have Been Fought

British seapower overturned the results of the French victory at Sillery, and in the century or so that followed, it also preserved Canada from her more powerful and aggressive neighbour to the south. During the American Revolutionary War of 1776-1783, the War of 1812-1814 and during the American Civil War, the Royal Navy's control of the sealanes enabled military reinforcements to be sent to her threatened North American colonies as required and also created a countervailing threat against the extended coastline of the United States. Seapower, however, proved less useful after the separate colonies of British North America confederated into the Dominion of Canada in 1867 and the infant nation expanded into the hinterland of the continent west of the Great Lakes. For nearly two centuries, much of this vast area had been controlled by the Hudson's Bay Company (whose initials gave rise to the joke that it had been "Here Before Christ"), but in 1869 the HBC transferred much of its western territorial holdings to the infant nation of Canada.

At this time, there were two distinctly different groups living on the western plains: the indigenous aboriginal population and the Métis, a predominantly French-speaking people who were the result of the relations between French fur traders and hunters, and Indian women. While both groups hunted the countless herds of buffalo that roamed the area, the Métis lived in fixed settlements and also engaged in farming. Their system of land tenure differed from that in use in the rest of Canada, outside Quebec, and they feared that the annexation of the former HBC territory by the Canadian government would result in the loss of their farms. In the autumn of 1869, before Canadian authorities had taken actual control of the western territories, the Métis rose in a putative revolt under Louis Riel, their charismatic, if unstable, leader. Riel managed to negotiate a settlement of his people's grievances with the Dominion government although he was forced to flee to the United States after his revolt had ended peacefully. Fourteen years later, at the request of the Métis, he returned to Canada to lead another rebellion against the established authorities in an effort to alleviate his peoples' grievances.

Riel expected to find ready allies among the other major group that shared the plains with the Métis – the Indian peoples. By 1884 their way of life had been destroyed by the demise of the buffalo herds and they had been reduced to an abject state of near-starvation. The Canadian government, in an attempt both to control and succour them, negotiated a series of treaties with the Indian nations that saw them give up their rights to their traditional hunting grounds in return for assignment and movement to limited reserves where they were promised assistance to become farmers, education and medical treatment. Reasoning that the Indians, as had the Métis, had suffered a loss of livelihood from end of the buffalo, Riel was confident that they would join his plans for rebellion.

He overlooked, however, the fact that the situation in the west had changed since 1870. There were now numerous white settlements, a paramilitary force, the North West Mounted Police, and, most important of all, the area was connected to eastern Canada by telegraph and nearly connected by the Canadian Pacific Railway. His belief that he would find ready allies among the Indian nations was wrong – many Indian leaders proved loyal or at least neutral in the forthcoming conflict, although some who wished to stay out of the fighting were unwillingly dragged into it by the pressure of events.

One such was the Plains Cree chief, Poundmaker, a born leader who, at Cut Knife Hill near Battleford in May 1885, inflicted a stinging defeat on the Canadian militia and North West Mounted Police in a battle that should never have been fought.

2

"We're making history, eh?" An Inquiry into the Events that Occurred near Cut Knife Hill, North West Territories

1-2 May 1885

Poundmaker, probably early 1880s

Ever the traditionalist, Poundmaker holds a flintlock trade musket with the barrel not yet shortened for handiness on horseback. His hair, in a single swatch, reaches almost to his knees. This was a difficult time for Poundmaker because he knew that Plains life was ending and he and all the Plains peoples faced an uncertain future. (Saskatchewan Archives Board, S–B97)

"We're making history, eh?"

∞ ∞ ∞

An Inquiry into the Events that Occurred near Cut Knife Hill, North West Territories 1-2 May 1885

Robert H. Caldwell

"haw, nkusis, pustayowinisah; aka napawisi; aka wiya nantaw totasoh. mayatan awako. Usam nama wihkats kisihkimitin nantaw kit-atuhtayin: usam kisakihtin. a-kitimakisitik ayisiyiiniwak kantupayitsik. a-wih-kakwa-kimutitsik misatimwah; maka kiya miyusiw kitam: mihkawikiw. kistah kimiyusin: namuya kikitimakisin," itaw ukusisah.

Translation from Cree:
"Here, my son, dress yourself; do not be ashamed; do nothing foolish to yourself. This is no way to be. I never bid you go to the scenes I need not blame: I love you too much. Poor men are they who go on the warpath, for they hope to steal horses; but you, your horse is handsome; he is fleet of foot. And you yourself are handsome; you are not poor," he told his son.

SAKAWAW (ADAM SAKEWEW), "THE STORY OF THE CHERRY TREE", IN LEONARD BLOOMFIELD, *PLAINS CREE TEXTS*, VOL XVI, PUBLICATIONS OF THE AMERICAN ETHNOLOGICAL SOCIETY, ED. FRANZ BOAS, (NEW YORK, 1934), P.62-63.

It was but noon of yesterday
He bade farewell, he marched away!
The rifle bright and bayonet seen
Above the Queen's Own garb of green....

They bore the foodless, dreary march,
The nights that chill, the days that parch,
Through drifted wilds their way they take,
Their pathway is the frozen lake,
Yet buoyant, bright and bold are they,
Our boys in the North-West away.

They could not fail, they knew not fear
When Otter led the charging cheer.
They charged the open, they laid low
With Gatling fire the Red-skin foe....

C.P. MULVANEY, "OUR BOYS IN THE NORTH-WEST AWAY", *THE GLOBE*, 24 MAY 1885.

CITED IN C.P. MULVANEY, *THE HISTORY OF THE NORTH-WEST REBELLION OF 1885*,

(TORONTO, 1885), P. 73-74.

It is not known when Poundmaker was born, but in the 1870s he was probably in his thirties. Poundmaker was not a hereditary chief. His mother was a Métis, a sister of the famous Cree hunter Mistawasis, one of the signatories to Treaty No 6. in 1876. His father, Skunk Skin, an Assiniboine, who was also a well-known hunter – a buffalo-pound maker – from the Battleford area of the North West Territories, passed his name to his son. Poundmaker, while not known for his hunting or warrior skills, was respected for his abilities as an orator and as a leader who could gain the respect of "white fur traders, missionaries, Mounted Policemen, Indian Department officials, and politicians."[1]

To white people seeking a romantic, classical image of a Plains Indian, Poundmaker certainly met the requirements. He looked like an Indian should look. A writer for the *Toronto Mail* described him as "noble looking," reminding him "more of Fenimore Cooper's heroes than do the majority of North-West Indians." The reporter went on to say

His eyes are black and piercing. One moment they twinkle merrily at some humorous remark, and the next they flash with fire as something is said that is not agreeable to him. His nose is long and aquiline, while his lips are thin and his mouth devoid of that sensual character so peculiar to so many Indians. His hair hung in one long plait for more than a yard down his back, and was tied round with a red bandanna. The scalp lock was decorated with a mink skin, while from each temple there hung one long lock of hair twisted round and round with brass wire. He wore no coat, but his vest was richly decorated with brass-headed nails in true barbaric fashion.[2]

In 1876 Poundmaker was a councillor in the Red Pheasant band of Plains Cree and Mixed Blood Indians from the Battleford area. He attended the Treaty No. 6 negotiations, spoke during the proceedings and signed the treaty as a head man for Red Pheasant. Poundmaker had proved to be a tough negotiator. Peter Erasmus, the translator for Alexander Morris, the Lieutenant-Governor of the Territories who conducted the proceedings, remembered him speaking these words: "The governor mentions how much land is to be given to us. He says 640 acres, one square mile for each family, he will give us – This is our land! It isn't a piece of pemmican to be cut off and given in little pieces back to us. It is ours and we will take what we want."[3] It is noteworthy that this incident was not included in Governor Morris's own account of the treaty signing.[4]

Assiniboine camp, 1874

George M. Dawson, the celebrated surveyor, took several pictures of an Assiniboine camp during his survey of the North West. We see Plains life as it was before settlement pressure in the early 1880s. In his *American History Book of the Indian*, William Brandon asserted: "Something happens to a man when he gets on a horse, in a country where he can ride at a run forever, it is quite easy to ascend to an impression of living in a myth." (NAC, C–81793)

Poundmaker did not follow the band to their reserve, but instead kept to the plains, hunting the rapidly disappearing buffalo herds. A number of Cree families accompanied him and they lived for several years as, in anthropological terms, hunter-gatherers, hunting buffalo in the summer and wintering either in the traditional area along the Battle River or in the Cypress Hills far to the south. By about 1879 Poundmaker had formed his own band in the new, post-Treaty era.[5]

In 1880 Poundmaker was declared a chief by the Canadian government, and it surveyed a reserve for his band west of other Cree and Assiniboine reserves along the Battle River. In the summer of 1881 the survey was completed for the band, at a strength of 171 people, but immediately after the reserve was authorized, the band returned to the plains one last time, for the late summer hunt. It was a failure. Starving and in rags, they moved north to the new reserve.[6]

The buffalo herds were almost gone, however, and reports "of hardship and of death by starvation were legion during the 1880s."[7] The expansive plans of the Canadian Pacific Railway (CPR) and white settlement in the region gained momentum as part of Canadian Prime Minister John A. Macdonald's "National Policy" while, concurrently, the government persisted in its attempts to place all Indians on reserves.[8] Nevertheless, during this period the Plains Cree "were both flexible and active in promoting their own interests" and were "willing to accommodate themselves to a new way of life."[9] Moreover, through the treaty process they were committed deeply to a policy of peace with the whites, while at the same time they demanded that treaty agreements be fulfilled, and that they be allowed a high degree of autonomy. During the 1870s and early 1880s survival, and therefore treaty-making, was a natural extension of traditional Plains Indian life, which had always demanded negotiation and conciliation in order to improve their existence.

Between 1872 and 1882, the three most powerful Cree Chiefs, Big Bear, Little Pine and Piapot, had concentrated "more than fifty per cent of the total Indian population of the Treaty 4 and 6 areas" in the Cypress Hills, and they sought government approval for a large Cree reserve in that area. They failed, and

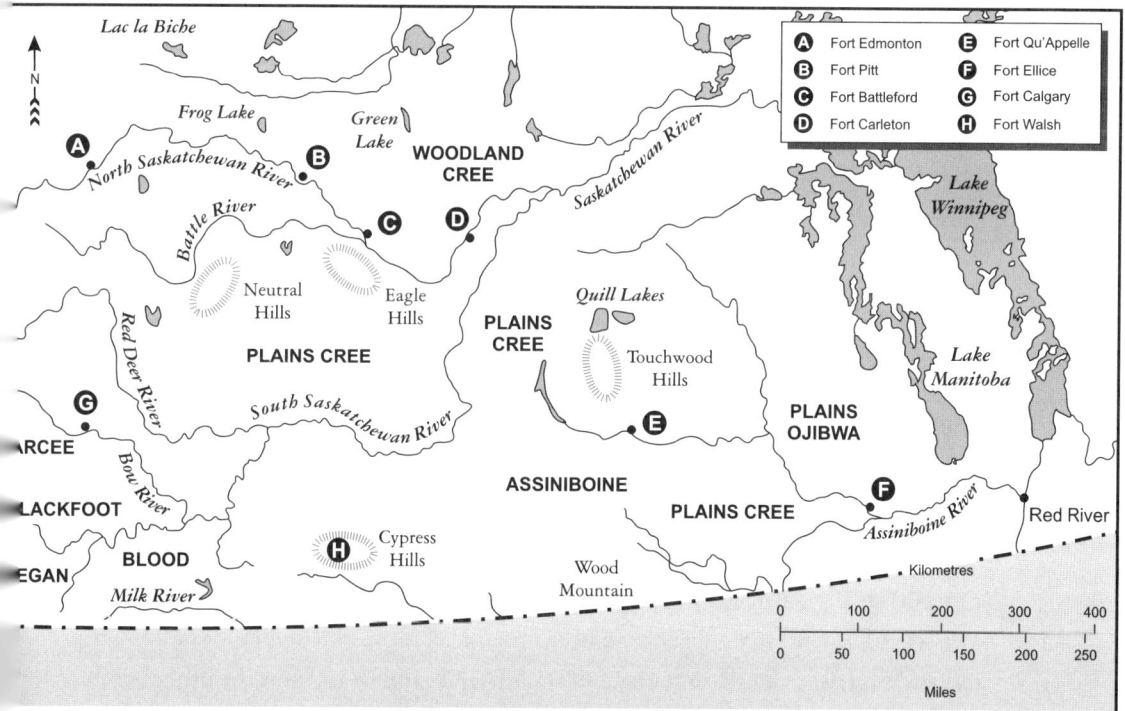

A	Fort Edmonton	E	Fort Qu'Appelle
B	Fort Pitt	F	Fort Ellice
C	Fort Battleford	G	Fort Calgary
D	Fort Carleton	H	Fort Walsh

C–1

The North West Indian World Prior to 1873

in 1882, no further food was issued to them. The Indian Department farm "that had been located near the NWMP [North West Mounted Police] Fort Walsh was closed," and in 1883 Ottawa ordered Fort Walsh to be closed, in an attempt to force the remaining followers of the three chiefs to take reserves in the "Qu'Appelle, Battleford and Fort Pitt" areas. Nevertheless the three chiefs, older and more experienced than Poundmaker, continued to seek autonomy for their peoples through their demands for contiguous reserves. Their strategy was to concentrate their peoples during the summer in increasingly larger councils, in order to demonstrate their solidarity to the government. Thus, in the early 1880s, a cycle began, whereby the government tried to discourage the summer concentrations, while the chiefs continued to urge their people to meet in larger numbers.[10]

At this time Louis Riel was living in western Montana, teaching at a Catholic Seminary. Whether or not Riel inspired revolt in the Canadian Indians he might have encountered is uncertain. William Bleasdell Cameron, a Hudson Bay Company employee at Frog Lake, and in 1885 a hostage of Big Bear, remembered that the chief had told him Riel believed that "much blood will flow."[11] Moreover historian Douglas Light has observed that the *Saskatchewan Herald* of 5 August 1883 claimed that Riel, still in Montana, "was attempting to get Canadian Indians to commit acts that would embarrass the Canadian government."[12]

Poundmaker was considered a "good indian." In 1882 and 1883 he and his band tried to adapt to farm life on their reserve, cutting hay, raising cattle, providing wood "and all the attributes of becoming 'civilized,' even abandoning Indian clothing for European dress."[13] Throughout 1883, however, conditions deteriorated for the northern Plains Indians on and off reserves. In the spring a number of Assiniboines died of consumption on their reserve, and an Indian agent, Thomas T. Quinn, travelled to Maple Creek in the south, to find Big Bear and the other bands and persuade them to return to reserves in the north. On 20 July Big Bear, Lucky Man and Piapot, with an escort of North West Mounted Police and wagons full of food, were escorted to their new reserves. Piapot chose land near Qu'Appelle while the other two chiefs selected an area near Battleford.[14] Perhaps to punish Big Bear, who was never in the government's favour, the authorities directed his band to take a reserve near Frog Lake, more in Woodland than Plains Cree country, about 75 miles west of their friends and relatives in the other bands of the River Peoples of the Plains Cree. These developments forestalled an Indian concentration that summer, but the government "was convinced" that a grand council was planned for 1884.[15]

Plains Cree warrior

In a picture probably taken in the 1870s or early 1880s, a Plains Cree sits on his pony surveying a world that is fast collapsing about him. He wears a typical Plains blanket coat and cap and carries a long-barrelled rifle, which indicates that hunting methods have changed, and he perhaps has taken to shooting the few remaining buffalo he can find at long range. This warrior has probably known hunger but remains proud and even defiant. (NAC, C-33473)

During the summer of 1883 Poundmaker grew disillusioned with farming life. Always a traveller, he returned to the southern plains to visit with the great Blackfoot Chief, Crowfoot, who had adopted him as his son,[16] and when he returned, the *Saskatchewan Herald* claimed that: "Poundmaker is back from his tour in the south. He is so set up by the attentions paid to him that he is not quite sure whether he is the Commissioner or a common Indian. He has discarded paint and donned a blanket."[17]

The year 1883 ended badly for everyone – settlers and Indians alike. In the autumn a severe frost hit the area and crops were ruined. Winter set in early, the snow fell deep followed by severe cold, and starvation "was rife amongst the Indians and Métis."[18] This situation demanded government aid, but instead the Deputy Superintendent General of Indian Affairs, Lawrence Vankaughnet, in Ottawa, *reduced* the amount of food available for distribution and also cut departmental staff. Ironically, in the midst of these stressful times, the government opened the Indian Industrial School in Battleford in December 1883.[19]

The winter of 1883-84 caused a further polarization of Indian attitudes. Leaders like Poundmaker and Big Bear, who were inclined towards conciliation based on oratory and reason, urged restraint but younger male Indians saw armed rebellion as a possible solution to their problems and moved increasingly towards that option. Among this group were Poundmaker's brothers, Yellow Mud Blanket and Seepeekwaskun (Blue Horn), and Basil and Tom Favel, Shooting Eagle and Little Pine.[20] The latter chief, another traditional Plains Cree leader, returned in April 1884 and settled with his band on the Lucky Man reserve, adjacent to Poundmaker. P.G. Laurie, editor of the *Saskatchewan Herald,* began 1884 by continuing his earlier sarcastic remarks about Poundmaker: "Ever since Poundmaker came back from the south last spring, he has been at cross purposes with the [Indian Department] Agent, to everything dictated to him Poundmaker objected, saying that the Commissioner said it was not to be so …… Lately the man of the blanket took possession of a lot of fish belonging to the [Indian Department] and sold them, converting the proceeds to his own use."[21]

By the spring of 1884 the North West had been lashed by hard times for over a year and an economic depression had set in. Settlers and businessmen had invested heavily in the Saskatchewan District of the Territories, anticipating the railway route, but these whites saw their money vanish when the railway bypassed them to the south. The region was undergoing extreme stress, and unhappiness was recorded not only among the Indians but also by settlers, the Indian Department, the NWMP, white businessmen and many Métis. It was not surprising that those with the least money or influence to get capital or to recover it – Indians and many working-class Métis without connections in Winnipeg – grew agitated and began to think in terms of political action to redress their grievances.[22]

During the summer conciliatory Indian leaders were sorely tested. In April Big Bear waited for a meeting with the Indian Commissioner and Lieutenant Governor of the North West Territories, Edgar Dewdney, but the *Saskatchewan Herald* wrote of Big Bear's frustration: "He has seen a great many head men in the Department, but there was always one above him. This trip, however, he will see the one who has no one else to refer to, if it takes him all summer."[23] Dewdney, however, never met with Big Bear, and Indian efforts to improve their circumstances with the government were further frustrated by its next action – when Lucky Man, as chief of his reserve, wished to redress Indian grievances, the government representatives silenced him by removing him as chief.[24]

On Saturday, 14 June 1884, many Indians gathered under Big Bear and Poundmaker at Battleford in order to have a "Thirst Dance" but, following a

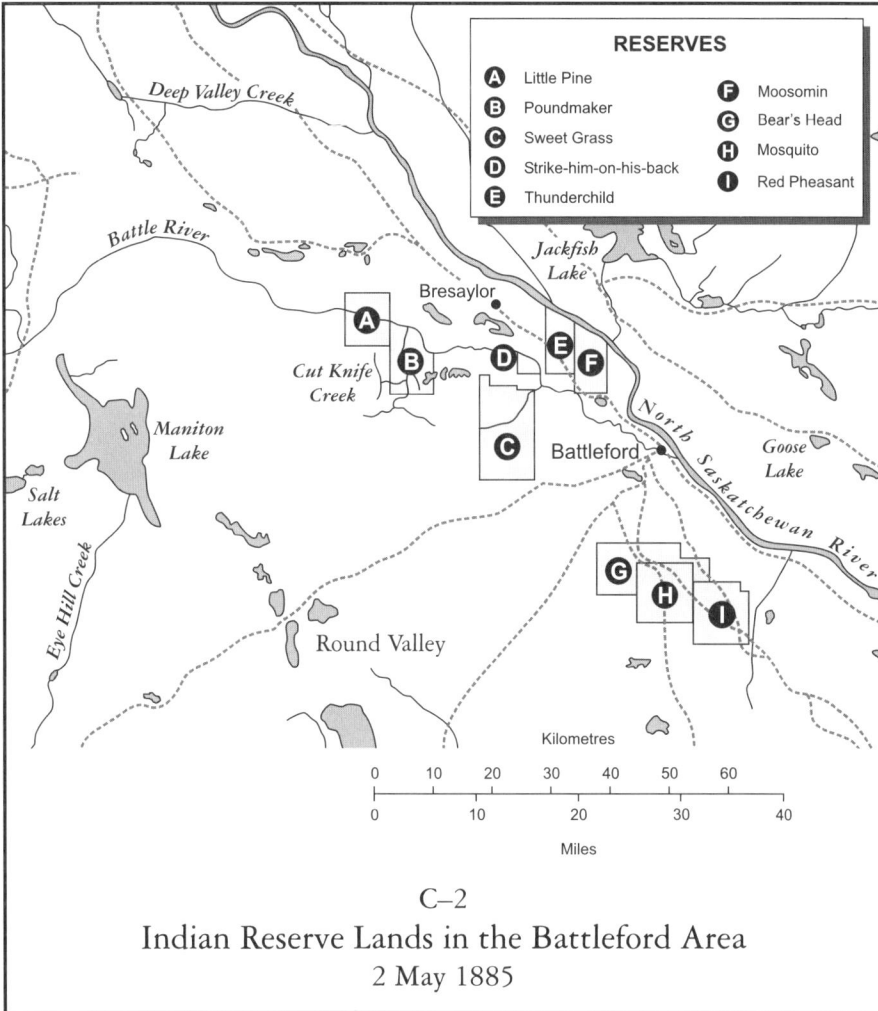

C–2
Indian Reserve Lands in the Battleford Area
2 May 1885

confrontation with the NWMP and Indian Agent J.M. Rae, they moved west to the camp on the Lucky Man and Little Pine reserve. The camp was possibly the largest-ever old-style Plains Indian camp. Nevertheless the Thirst Dance galvanized the Indians in the area, and many moved to the camp. Big Bear's aim apparently was to unite the Indians in a concentrated voice to renegotiate Treaty No. 6. Rae visited the reserve with a small Mounted Police escort and ordered those gathered to disperse. When they did not, Rae withdrew.[25]

A further incident followed, caused by a troublesome farm instructor. Rae and a larger escort this time, under command of Superintendent Lief Crozier, a veteran and respected NWMP officer, confronted the large and volatile camp. Crozier wisely calmed the Indian's defiant mood with four ox-teams of food which he delivered to the camp, now located in the Poundmaker reserve.[26]

Matters began to come to a head. In the spring of 1884 the Métis community on the South Saskatchewan, known as the South Branch Métis, arranged for Louis Riel to return to the North West Territories from Montana. He was supposed to lead the campaign for government action to secure the position of the inhabitants of the area within the new and expanding Dominion of Canada.[27] It was Riel's initial intention to form an alliance of protest so strong that the Canadian government and its agents could not ignore it, with a power base in the multi-racial cohesion of Canadian town and country settlers, as well as English and French Métis, and the Indians. At first, Riel did not think in terms of a protest founded on a threat of violence, and he was, after all, neither a Plains Métis nor a Plains Indian, both of which had threatened violence prior to his arrival. By 1884, however, the Indians had again concentrated and demanded that treaties "be revised" and an "Indian Territory" be provided to them. The Canadian settlers had threatened violence, inasmuch as they "warned" Ottawa about the possibility of rebellion.[28]

Nonetheless Riel did not advocate rebellion.[29] It was his intention to compel the government to resolve the grievances of Western Canadians in a way that

North West Mounted Policeman

This carefully posed photograph could almost have served as a recruiting poster for the NWMP in 1885, showing as it does a handsome and well-groomed constable wearing the 1882 uniform with pill-box hat, scarlet jacket and white gauntlets. This order of dress was never worn on patrol. (Saskatchewan Archives Board, S-B79)

had been successful at Red River in 1869-70: by taking hostages and bargaining from a position of power to achieve a negotiated settlement.[30] This plan rapidly fell apart, because in the 15 years since, circumstances and attitudes in Canada and the North West had changed dramatically – a change the Métis and Riel had not grasped.

Fighting broke out on Cree Chief Beardy's reserve at Duck Lake on 26 March 1885; a large mixed band of Métis and Indians of unknown strength – perhaps several hundred – decisively defeated an advancing force of about a hundred mounted and sleigh-borne NWMP and Prince Albert civilian volunteers commanded by Superintendent Crozier. The civilian volunteers had exerted much pressure on Crozier to deploy his policemen, volunteers and their 7-pdr gun to face down the Métis-Indian force, but Crozier's losses were 12 killed and several wounded.[31]

The battle at Duck Lake lasted approximately 30 minutes but it was decisive. The Métis proved they had the ability to take advantage of the government's military weakness in the west, and Riel, perhaps hoping that the unfinished Canadian Pacific Railway would prevent any military solution on the part of the Canadian government, expected it to dispatch an envoy to negotiate with his people, as in 1870.

In the North West the period between the Duck Lake battle on 26 March and the relief of Battleford on 24 April was fraught with rumour, racism and hyperbole which brought out extreme responses by all peoples in the region. The situation was reinforced by the cowardice and subterfuge of government officials, the dishonesty of leading Métis figures, a crisis in Indian leadership, and by Riel's hard-core and insidious representatives, who interfered with Indian-white relations in the Battleford area.[32] The government now could disregard the Cree movement for "an Indian Territory" since, as the Cree did engage in some acts of violence, Lieutenant Governor Dewdney chose to label these "acts of rebellion."[33]

Recent research by historians Douglas Light,[34] Bill Waiser and Blair Stonechild has shed new light on these events. Waiser and Stonechild used sources hitherto not consulted in government Sessional Papers – for example, testimony provided at the "Rebellion Trials" published in 1886 – in order to provide the Indians' perspective.[35] In the process they have revised the reasons for white panic and over-reaction to the Indian threat which created the "siege" of Battleford and widespread fright through the region.

To understand Poundmaker and the Cree and Assiniboine who congregated

in the temporary camp on his reserve in the spring of 1885, we need to understand the swift sequence of events that followed Duck Lake. Panic set in among
the settlers and townspeople of the Battleford area, and within three days more
than 500 people were housed within the walls of the local mounted police fort.
Concurrently a large group of Cree families travelled to Battleford to declare
their loyalty and to receive food since many were starving. En route agents of
Riel attempted to sway them to support his cause and move *beyond* Battleford to
reinforce the Métis in the Batoche area.[36]

These Cree, led by their principal Chief, Little Pine, who was ill from mal-
nutrition, rejected the overtures. Riel's men were more successful at firing up
the Assiniboine on their Reserves south of Battleford, whom they persuaded to
return to the old Plains ways of warfare. As Waiser and Stonechild have put it:
"For years, they had heard stories of the now defunct Assiniboine warrior societies; here was their chance to recapture some of the tribe's former glory." Yet, they
remained in the Battleford area.[37]

On Little Pine's arrival at Battleford on 30 March 1885, the situation quickly
went out of control. Government Indian Agent John Rae refused to meet with
Little Pine, Poundmaker and other Indian leaders because he was afraid of Riel's
agents who were nearby. Several Cree Indians briefly looted some white homes
and stores, but all of the Indians quietly departed from Battleford, although the
Métis – both Riel's followers and others in the area – continued the looting for
several days afterwards. Then Assiniboine warriors killed some white people on
and near their Reserves, but these deaths were personal grudges and not part of
a general uprising. Nevertheless the situation in the early days of April 1885 had
deteriorated, principally due to the work of Riel's men. Waiser and Stonechild
concluded that although "this campaign of terror was actually the work of Métis
and a few Stoney [Assiniboine] and that the Cree were just as upset about how
things had turned out at Battleford," these factors were inconsequential to the
hundreds of people shut up in the stockade.[38]

Little Pine died shortly afterwards. As his death followed the recent death
of the Cree Chief Red Pheasant, Poundmaker, young, unproven and unknown
to many Cree and Assiniboine, was now handed responsibility for an increasingly frightened camp, who had banded together for protection, fearing that
the government would retaliate. Nevertheless, it was doubtful that Poundmaker
had much control over this camp. As alarm increased, the regenerated warrior
societies of the Assiniboine and Cree would have increased their influence.[39] Also
influential were two senior Métis who remained in the Indian camp, Norbert

Delorme and Andre Nault.[40] The situation in the Battleford area was very tense. All that was needed now to sharpen opinions and provoke decisions on both sides was the horrifying news of the Frog Lake massacre of 2 April.

On that day several unruly warriors from Big Bear's band, frustrated with the delays resulting from negotiation, killed nine white men at the small settlement of Frog Lake in the Moose Hills, on the North Saskatchewan River near the present town of Lloydminster. With these deaths, any hope of future Indian diplomacy with the government also died.[41]

Almost concurrently, Prime Minister John A. Macdonald of Canada ordered the new nation's first large military mobilization. Minister of Militia and Defence Adolphe Caron and the Major General Commanding the Militia, Frederick D. Middleton, divided the mobilization responsibility between them. Caron negotiated the call-out of troops, ordered supplies and arranged rail transport with CPR officials while Middleton travelled quickly through the American railway system to arrive in Winnipeg well ahead of his eastern troops, ensuring that he would command them.[42]

Macdonald took a first-hand interest in the government's military response to the events in the west. He was concerned about protecting the southern border

Railway transport circa 1885
A Canadian Pacific Railway train at an unnamed station in the North West. Note the telegraph poles as well as the militia tents pitched on the right. This was a typical station along the Canadian transport system that could move a militia soldier, mail and stores to support him from Toronto or Montreal to the North West in five or six days. More importantly, because of the telegraph, the government could manage the campaign directly and an account of an event could be published in an Ontario or Quebec newspaper within two days of its happening. (NAC, C-5824)

and routes from the United States, as well as providing useful cavalry for Middleton's newly formed North West Field Force. In a letter to the general, he advised that

> The first thing to be done is to localize the insurrection. The C.P.R. must of course be guarded … parties should be sent to watch the people and stores coming in at Emerson by rail. The different trails across the border should also be watched… A force should be placed at Battleford, and, if possible, a line of communication from [there] to the railway … to prevent the flame from spreading westwards [where] … there are Mounted police stationed, as at Regina, Maple Creek and Edmonton, but where there is no military organization, the [NWMP] officers … have been authorized to swear in the inhabitants as Police Constables. This will give them a right to act with the Police force and bring them into some sort of training … the roads will be almost impassable for infantry and the services of a mounted force will be nearly, if not quite indispensable. You will have Lord Melgund on hand for that purpose at Winnipeg. Captain John Stewart, formerly commanding the Militia Cavalry at Ottawa, and a dashing young fellow, is now a ranchman south of Calgary. He is here just now and will raise a corps of Western prairie men – cow boys and others who can ride and shoot … I asked [Caron] to telegraph you if you would want cavalry from Ontario and Quebec… If you can get men enough from the prairies, they would, of course, be much more serviceable than town bred men who compose our cavalry … there is a good cavalry corps in the Eastern Townships of farmer's sons.… I hear that artillery batteries are volunteering all over Canada. Some you might want, but I fear their nine pounders would be too heavy for prairie work.[43]

None of the dissident groups in the west realized the speed with which large military forces could be concentrated at this time of year. Moreover they would soon see the products of modern technology – railways, telegraphs, high-explosive artillery, machine guns, preserved rations and ammunition, and an unlimited resupply capability — as well as different responses to the tactical dilemma caused by the recent introduction of the breech-loading rifle.

Thus, due to the aggressiveness and intransigence of the Métis on one side, and Macdonald and his officials on the other, by 17 April 1885 an odd collection of about 600 NWMP and Ontario militia found themselves on the forlorn north side of the South Saskatchewan River at a place called Saskatchewan Landing.

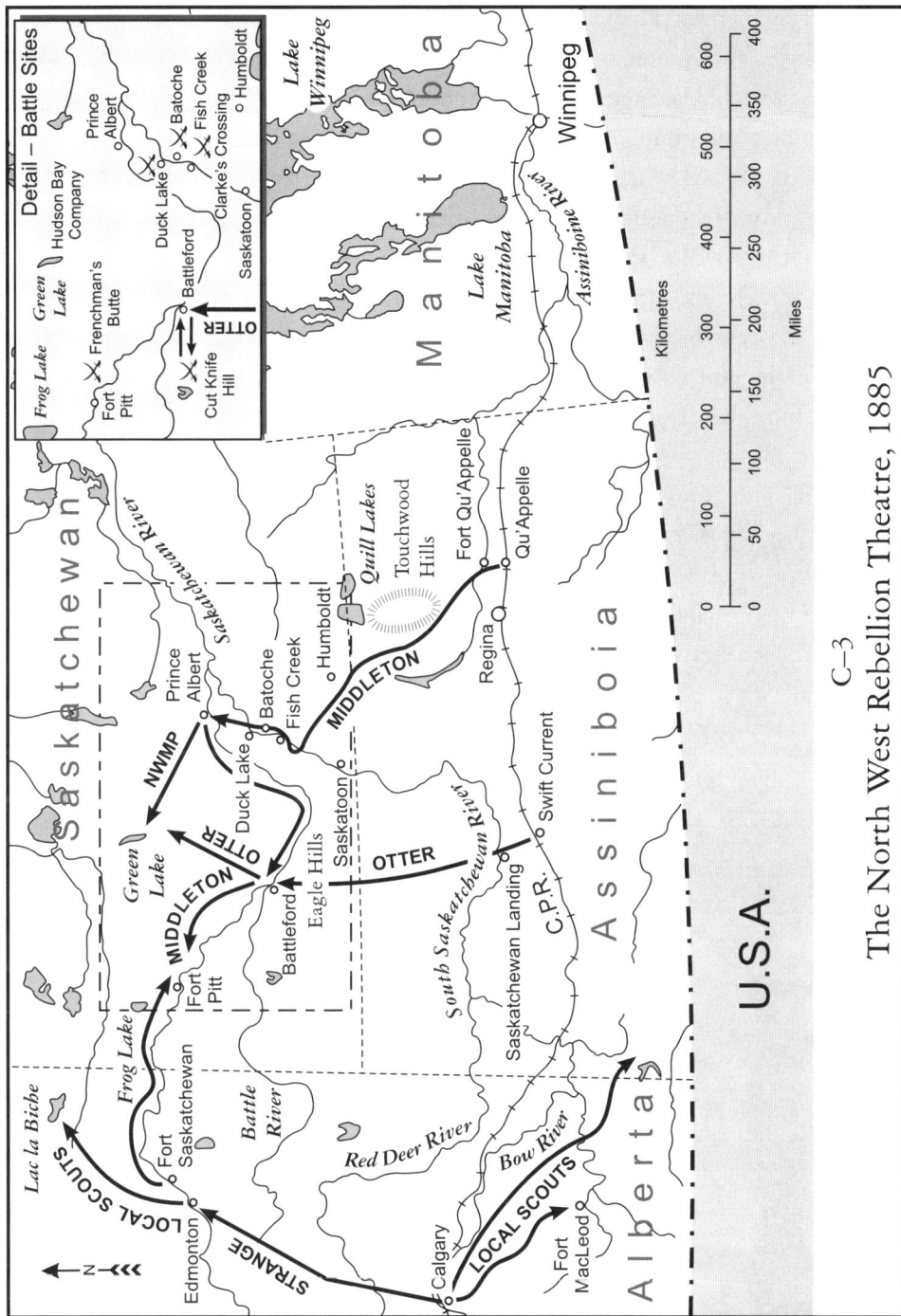

C–3

The North West Rebellion Theatre, 1885

They sited their tents in perfectly straight lines, by unit and no doubt regimental seniority, as they waited several days for the river to open for navigation so that steamboats could take them north to rendezvous with Middleton's column, moving fast overland from Qu'Appelle towards Batoche. The boats, coming from the west, were delayed by ice and low water levels, and the troops were ferried across the great river by the steamer *Northcote* between 15 and 17 April. In a sense the Militia had moved to the west *too* fast, ahead of favourable river navigation.

Now there was a new plan. This force was to break camp and prepare to move, tactically but as quickly as possible, to relieve Fort Battleford, about 150 miles to the north. Lieutenant Colonel William Dillon Otter was in command of this force, which came to be known as the Battleford Column or, simply, Otter's column.

William D. Otter was born in Toronto in 1843 and educated at Upper Canada College in that city. He joined a Toronto militia unit in 1861 and by 1866 was adjutant of the Queen's Own Rifles (QOR). He fought with his regiment against the Fenians at the battle of Ridgeway in 1866, a debacle which demonstrated that a lack of discipline among hastily enrolled volunteers could lead to a breakdown in cohesion, followed by a rout. Otter never forgot the lessons of Ridgeway, foremost being the requirement for discipline in all aspects of militia training. By 1874 he was commmanding the Queen's Own while maintaining his civilian occupation as an accounting clerk. Although a stickler for discipline – he was, after all, an ex-sergeant major – Otter apparently followed the militia custom of maintaining popularity with his subordinates, as commanding officers who made plans without consulting their officers were soon voted out of their appointments.

In 1880 Otter published *The Guide*, a handbook for the Canadian soldier. While unwritten rules

Militia infantryman, 1880s

His tunic was scarlet, trousers dark blue and accoutrements white, but the white coating was scraped off during the Rebellion to improve concealment. In Otter's column, C Company of the Infantry School Corps and the Sharpshooters Company of the Foot Guards were dressed this way. (Painting by Ronald B. Volstad, courtesy Department of National Defence)

Lieutenant Colonel William Dillon Otter

This picture of Otter in winter uniform is undated, but it was probably taken when he commanded C Company of the Infantry Corps School in Toronto in the mid-1880s. Otter was a civilian bookkeeper without significant family money who had to struggle for advancement and social standing in Toronto. He took militia soldiering seriously and this appealed to the various British army senior officers responsible to the Canadian government for the post-Confederation militia. (NAC, C-5366)

governed the militia culture and command arrangements, *The Guide* detailed the technical realities of military life. It was not a critical work; it did not attempt to solve the current dilemma created by the breech-loading rifle which had a major effect on land warfare, nor did it provide instruction in command and leadership. Basically, *The Guide* was an administrative text concerned with the *minutiae* of military service and it was a clear example of the professional immaturity of the Canadian militia in the late 19th century.[44]

In 1883 Otter was appointed the commanding officer of C Company of the Infantry School Corps at Toronto, part of the regular infantry force. This was a full-time appointment and Otter was to spend the remainder of his adult life in the regular force. As C Company was an important part of the Toronto military garrison, he was the natural choice to command the elements of that garrison – C Company and those in the Queen's Own who volunteered for service in the North West.

All of Otter's men had heard about the Duck Lake battle at the end of March, and more recently, of the Frog Lake Massacre. There was a thrill of impending action in the tent lines, and reactions differed about this possibility.

The average Canadian militiaman, or Mounted Policeman, was disciplined, but not fully trained and ready for war. Most joined for the adventure of active service in an age that glorified battles, heroism and colourful commanders. Otter's volunteer officers more often than not also lacked training, but both groups made up for this technical deficiency with their offensive spirit. The other ranks, many of whom were university students, were led by non-commissioned and commissioned officers who derived their military ardour from the late-Vic-

Superintendent William M. Herchmer, NWMP

Herchmer served as Otter's chief of staff and was probably asked by Middleton to keep an eye on Otter, his column commander, who was an inexperienced easterner. Middleton did not want a battle with high casualties, and his greatest fear was that an eastern militia officer seeking fame and reputation in an age that revered military exploits, would make a rash and costly decision. Herchmer's role in Otter's decision to attack Poundmaker – against Middleton's orders – remains unknown, as does the experience of most of the NWMP senior officers during the rebellion. (NAC, PA-42142)

torian phenomena of men's clubs, secret societies and hierarchial new professions. It produced a cohesive spirit that bonded young men together with older men, and created strong small groups that stuck together.[45] Many officers joined the Active Militia and volunteered for service in the North West Field Force for self-serving, *noblesse oblige* reasons to sustain or elevate their status in the community. Their standard of discipline would become critical when these citizen-soldiers came under fire.

The night before the column was to depart, Superintendent William M. Herchmer, NWMP, Otter's newly appointed chief of staff, attempted to remind the junior officers of the seriousness of the forthcoming operation. Lieutenant Richard S. Cassels, serving in Canada's premier city militia regiment, the Queen's Own, took exception to an outsider advising him how to behave. In his diary, Cassels wrote

> We are all amazed at Colonel Herchmer's conduct tonight. He, probably with the best intentions in the world, undertakes to read us a lecture on the proper exercise of discipline in a volunteer regiment, hinting very plainly that our men are allowed too much liberty. We do not appreciate his entirely uncalled for and, to say the least of, not over-polite criticism of his hosts. Our men are a fine willing lot of fellows, and friends that one knows intimately are not to be ordered about like a parcel of slaves.[46]

Cassels's words speak volumes about the autonomy and self-confidence within a Canadian militia unit at the time. He also, implicitly, revealed the gap that existed between experienced mounted policemen who had spent many years in the North West, and the newly arrived eastern militia, who had been told little or nothing about conditions and traditions in the region.

This was particularly true of Superintendent Herchmer, who had formerly commanded in the area. In the spring of 1885 Herchmer had been commanding the large NWMP detachment at Calgary. He was considered both an effective soldier and policeman and, during the third week of March, as the situation deteriorated, he had been ordered east with as many of his men as he could spare, to build up a reconnaissance screen in the Regina-Qu'Appelle area. He took along men he knew from neighbouring detachments, including the recently enrolled and already-famous Australian, Constable Charles J. Ross,[47] and arrived at Regina with about 40 police, 24 horses and 4 wagons. Leaving his force there, Herchmer went on to Qu'Appelle, eventually conferring with the two principal architects of the campaign, Lieutenant Governor Edgar Dewdney and Major General Middleton. There is no record of that meeting, but Middleton was probably impressed with the police officer's knowledge and judgement, and likely recognized him as a man who knew the country and could be trusted not to blunder into trouble.[48]

Briefly, between the end of March and mid-April 1885, Herchmer's modest NWMP force, now with two small 7-pdr mountain guns in tow, was used as a flying column to create a show of force and keep the peace in the Medicine Hat–Swift Current area.[49] During these troublesome times they were the first line of defence north of the American border, and operated as Prime Minister Macdonald had directed, guarding the CPR and the border. The NWMP, however, was no longer in charge of the operational situation. Herchmer and all mounted police officers were now working directly for the Department of Militia and Defence, specifi-

NWMP No. 1064, Constable Charles Joseph Ross

Born in New South Wales, Australia, in 1857, Charles Ross emigrated to the United States, where he scouted for the US Army on the western frontier in the 1870s and early 1880s. He joined the NWMP in 1884 at age 27. By the spring of 1885 Ross was trusted as a man who knew the west and was given important tasks such as delivering dispatches, which required travelling by day and night over great distances. He was with Herchmer's NWMP detachment screening the border when they joined Otter's force and was appointed chief of the five-man scout section for both Otter's columns. He probably fired the first shot at the battle of Cut Knife Hill. (Saskatchewan Archives Board, S–B10433)

cally General Middleton, and "in accordance with the General's instructions," Herchmer secured the area between Swift Current station on the railway and Saskatchewan Landing, a ferry and possible embarkation site on the South Saskatchewan River.[50] About 175 miles east, events were moving rapidly. Middleton had begun his march from Fort Qu'Appelle on 6 April with the troops from the CPR at Qu'Appelle station.

Meanwhile, Indians in the districts between the railway line and Batoche – which included the File Hills reserves just west of Fort Qu'Appelle – had pledged their allegiance to the government, as had the Indians in the great Blackfoot reserves to the west.[51] Nevertheless the Indians in the area covered by Treaty No. 6 were still unfairly considered a threat. As we have seen, the news of the Frog Lake Massacre of 2 April swept through the North West and mass hysteria quickly followed. Middleton wrote Major General Thomas B. "Jingo" Strange, his most westerly column commander, on 6 April and advised him, rather pompously, that "everybody is scared and is losing their senses. I do not believe I shall fire a shot, though I intend being cautious. There has been an awful lot of mismanagement somewhere. They are sending me 2000 more men and two Gatlings besides the 1000 I shall soon have (at present I have only 350 and no Cavalry)."[52]

Middleton was describing the siege mentality across the region. The two largest white settlements on the Saskatchewan River system, Prince Albert and Battleford, were filled with refugees; inside the stockade at Fort Battleford were over 500 men, women and children from the surrounding communities.[53] This caused Middleton reluctantly to change his plans: he ordered Otter's forces building up in the Swift Current–Saskatchewan Landing area to relieve Battleford. Thus he separated these troops from his main mission, which was to advance upon the Duck Lake and Batoche area, Riel's strongholds. To relieve Battleford, Otter's force would have to operate independently, out of telegraph contact and over a hundred miles from Middleton's column.

Herchmer remembered that at Swift Current,

Otter arrived, and I was informed that the police were to join the column under his command, and that it was the General's wish that he should consult me on all points. Colonel Otter appointed me his Chief of Staff. I therefore handed over the police to Superintendent Neale, who moved out to the Saskatchewan River, with orders to camp there until the arrival of the troops, and patrol both sides of the river.[54]

Herchmer, an experienced police officer who had been in the North West since the 1870s, was now the chief adviser to a militia officer who, until a year earlier, had been a bookkeeper in a Toronto office.[55]

Herchmer headed up Otter's staff, which included Lieutenant – often referred to as Captain – James W. Sears, from Otter's C Company, Infantry School Corps, who was the brigade major (in modern military parlance, the operations officer or G3). Sears had served in a line infantry regiment of the British army. Captain William G. Mutton, Queen's Own Rifles, was the brigade quartermaster and the surgeon was Dr. Fredrick W. Strange, MP.[56]

On Saturday, 18 April 1885, Otter's column departed from Saskatchewan Landing. They had been allocated a large number of teams and wagons, driven by civilian teamsters who had left their quarter-section homesteads and sought the pay of government contract work with the Field Force, to carry the troops – the first Canadian use of "carrier-borne" infantry. Lieutenant Cassels of the Queen's Own remembered that there were "enough teams to carry all our provisions and a great portion of our men; half at least will be able to drive at a time and we ought to make good progress. We see no vegetation and the country seems very wretched."[57] Rifleman J.A. Forin, a law student at the University of Toronto who had enrolled in Company H of the Queen's Own, described the country north of the Saskatchewan River as "very monotonous and one only has distant hills to

Typical farm wagon as used in the Canadian North West

This was the type of wagon used by Otter's columns, and up to ten troops could be seated inside its narrow box. All farm wagons were similar in design and construction, and most used a two-horse team. A wagon box was approximately 10 feet long and 4½ feet wide. The wagon stood only about 5 feet high and the wheels were generally standard – 44-inch in the rear and 36-inch in the front. (Catalogue illustration, courtesy Canada Science and Technology Museum)

look to for hope of change. Buffalo tracks and bones and little slews [sic] of water are the only thing visible besides the prairie grass."[58]

The Otter-Herchmer column was not a balanced force and largely consisted of marching infantry. While strong in artillery with B Battery's two 9-pdr rifled muzzle loader (RML) field pieces, the two NWMP 7-pdr. guns and a Gatling gun, it was woefully short of mounted troops who could conduct screen operations. Mounted Police Constable Charlie Ross, the Australian-born veteran of US Army frontier life in the American west, was in charge of five scouts hired by Herchmer. They were mixed-blood North-Westers: Josie Alexander, Peter Ballendine, Adam Ballendine, John Todd and John Pambrun.[59] All were men born of the country, who knew the trails and Indian habits. At least two of these five scouts were permanent employees of the NWMP. Yet, they were not enough. A force of more than 400 troops moving on the open plains required a screen and flank security force of at least 40 mounted men.

The first night out, Cassels recorded that now "we are in an enemy's country," and

> for the first time, form a "laager." The wagons are placed in an open square, each face about two hundred paces long. The horses are tethered in the inside and the tents are pitched on the outside, doors opening toward the wagons. The men are ordered to sleep with their arms beside them, and at the first alarm to make for the wagons. [60]

As the number of wagons allowed the dismounted men to ride, the Otter-Herchmer column made excellent progress. Lieutenant Colonel J. Elton Prower, an ex-British infantry officer and at the time a lieutenant in the militia, was attached to the gunners of B Battery in the column. He remembered that, because the wagons carried "about ten men in each," they were able to move "thirty-five miles a day instead of fifteen."[61] The new Swift Current–Battleford Trail, which was a good one, linked the Battleford area with the railway. It was not an original plains trail, but had been developed after the railway was constructed across the southern plains in 1882. In the spring of 1883, a group of enterprising Métis freighters marked this new route and a passenger stage coach service was begun, as well as regular freighting service. John Todd, one of the scouts for the column, was a member of that survey party.[62]

As the column moved north into the traditional wintering areas of the Plains Cree and Assiniboine, now their Reserve areas, the possibility of contact with the

Indians increased, and the column paid greater attention to security. When he felt that the ground was suitable for ambush, Otter screened the column with infantry skirmishers. Lieutenant Oscar Pelletier of the 65th Mont Royal Fusiliers was the second officer attached to B Battery and remembered that,

> Undulations in the ground became progressively more frequent … the prairie was gradually replaced by a series of elevations, which were covered with bushes and the occasional tree … we followed a coulee … which placed the road between two high hills [and] made us all fear an ambush. From the top of the hills, we could have been shot like ducks … we moved slowly. Mounted Police examined the trail ahead of us, while a group of men on foot detached themselves from the group to cover the flanks of the trail. As the brush was thick and difficult, it was impossible for men on horse-back to navigate beside the trail. Luckily, the enemy was not as ambitious as he could have been … he could easily have stalled our march and caused inevitable loss of life. Our scouts, it seems, had been in daily contact with enemy runners, spying on our march since we had passed the south branch of the Saskatchewan River. This contact had allowed the leading men to choose our route with extreme care. In choosing campsites, they looked for places where it would have been difficult for us to be dislodged without significant casualties for the attackers.[63]

Pelletier's description of men covering "the flanks" of the trail raised the question of the balance between security and speed.

The main weakness of the Otter column was the absence of a mounted screen that knew tactics, as well as plains lore. It needed a scouting force who knew the doctrine for an advancing battalion-sized column and *also* the lay of the land, Indians and their ways. The NWMP were not capable of fulfilling this requirement. While Middleton used Boulton's Mounted Infantry Corps, consisting of mostly ex-British army settlers from Birtle and Russell in Manitoba, to accomplish this task, Otter and Herchmer had no equivalent.

This is not surprising as Otter's column was never organized as a balanced force to operate independently; it was merely an *ad hoc* artillery, infantry and police force that had been given an independent task en route to join Middleton's larger, balanced, all-arms force. There is no evidence that either Otter or Herchmer requested additional mounted troops to ensure the security of their column and provide a highly maneuverable addition to their force. The "scouts" that were available to range ahead and on the flanks of the column were a mere handful – Constable Charlie Ross and his five Métis – and these men only knew one side of the equation: the nature of the ground and the habits and inclinations of plains peoples. They cannot be blamed for not knowing British tactical theory, because they had never been taught it.

On 22 April 1885, as the column approached Battleford from Swift Current, the scout force encountered a mounted Indian party somewhere south of the Mosquito and Red Pheasant Reserves. The former was Assiniboine, the latter Cree. This was ideal ambush country, being "very hilly and broken and ... we came to a belt of thick scrub." Otter and Herchmer reacted to the change in the ground by deploying two infantry companies as skirmishers. Lieutenant Cassels, Queen's Own, was with one of these companies, and remembered that following the deployment the "all clear" was sounded and they moved back into the column. Suddenly "five shots" were heard "toward the head of the column and all is excitement. Our skirmishers are ordered to the front and after a tremendous double [march] we reach a piece of rising ground and see in the distance a number of Indians making north ...... Our scouts have had quite a little skirmish, wounded one Indian ......"[64] Otter and Herchmer, who were trying to make the best possible speed, had not kept their two companies out in skirmishing order as the column passed through more dangerous terrain. Moreover, there seemed to be poor control between the scouts, the forward troops and the column commanders.

On 23 April the column halted two or three miles south of the Battleford area, two hours before sunset. They would not relieve the fort until they had full daylight. Lieutenants Pelletier and Prower – with their diverse backgrounds, one a French-Canadian militiaman and one an ex-British infantry officer – held different opinions about this cautious plan. Both agreed, however, that the caution came from Herchmer and not Otter. Pelletier stated that

> we could see the sliver of terrain which separated the Battle River from the north branch of the Saskatchewan River ... Fort Battleford ... we saw a reddish glow, of a fairly large size, rising from the site of the Hudson's Bay ... store. This aroused much excitement within our camp ... Colonel Otter ... consulted his unit commanding officers ... to decide ... [if we should] ... cross over to Battleford. Had we gone, we could have prevented a possible attack by the savages. Colonel [sic] Herchmer, however, as commander of the Mounted Police, a man very knowledgeable about the ground that we would have had to cross to get there, argued against it. As was made all the clearer by

7-pdr. RML gun

The small 7-pdr. RML (Rifled Muzzle Loading) guns used by the NWMP after 1876 were originally 3-pound smooth-bore pieces made in Britain in 1808-09. They were designed as mountain guns, to be disassembled and carried in pack saddles. With the development of artillery technology in the 19th century, the barrels were bored out to 3 inches and rifled. The two 7-pdr guns used in the battle fired both case-shot and high-explosive ammunition in the affair. Although NWMP guns, they were manned by B Battery, the Battery Commander, Major Charles Short, commanding one gun, and Captain R.W. Rutherford commanding the other. B Battery accounts, especially Rutherford's, claimed accurate shooting, but their fire was not decisive and both guns ceased firing after their wooden carriages broke down. The failure of his artillery gave Otter an excuse to withdraw from an engagement that he could not win. (NAC, PA-118756)

the next morning, the terrain which separated us from Battleford would only have allowed our men to walk in two lines. Had these lines been cut by the enemy, in the middle of the night, it would have exposed us to a disaster.[65]

Prower claimed that Herchmer "advised a halt, thinking the brush would be too favourable to Indian tactics." An experienced infantryman, Prower had more faith in disciplined firepower than Herchmer apparently did, and he disagreed with the decision to wait. Available to the column were the single-shot Snider breech-loader rifles of the infantry, as well as the rapid-fire Winchesters of the NWMP, not to mention the high-explosive and case-shot effect of the two 9-pdrs and two 7-pdrs and the potential effect of the Gatling gun. In Prower's opinion, if the Indians did attack at last light in the willow scrub, the result would "not have been doubtful and had we advanced we should have had them in a net with the deep river and fort at their back. As it was we lost them."[66]

It was at this point Cassels reported another incident involving the scouts, Indians and reinforcing supports of Mounted Police. While the column camped, everyone could see "smoke arising from the settlement ... [and while] ... we should like to press on and render help ... [I]t is not considered advisable to advance when night is approaching."[67] The scouts deployed towards the town, came into contact with Indians and fired upon them. Prower remembered that the scouts "crept out from our lines and relieved Battleford ... [and] in returning had stumbled upon some Indians asleep in the brush. Both sides, alarmed, commenced to fire, and one Indian, we afterwards heard, was hit."[68] Reinforcements of 25 mounted police from Fort Battleford now made contact with the scouts and all returned safely.

This was the second time that Otter's handful of scouts had contacted Indians or Métis and had fired quickly and been reinforced, only to see their enemy melt away. Perhaps the scouts and the officers in the column were learning a false lesson about Plains people and their ability to fight from other than ambush positions.

The column finally arrived at Fort Battleford on the morning of 24 April. Otter reported this by telegram – which has not survived – sent to General Middleton, Caron or Dewdney, or all three. That same day, however, a dramatic and decisive event was taking place when Middleton's column, about 100 miles to the west, received a stiff set-back by an entrenched Métis and Indian ambush at Fish Creek. Following this rebuff, the general's view of the campaign in the North West took on a note of caution. Otter and Herchmer would soon become aware of his declining confidence and his changed attitude about fighting Indians and Métis.

Throughout military history there are periods where critical questions about a seminal decision are raised, but the answers are not forthcoming. The seven days from 24 April to 1 May 1885 in Battleford was one of those periods. Otter's forces were in the Battleford area for exactly a week before a select part of it – the Flying Column – moved out towards the Poundmaker Reserve. Yet this period was as confusing for the participants as it is for historians. The questions are obvious. Why would Otter, who had been promoted from the ranks of his Toronto militia regiment for his high sense of duty, responsibility and devotion to rules and orders, decide upon an audacious and Custer-like stroke against Plains Indians? The decision was highly uncharacteristic of the man, an ex-sergeant major, careful Toronto bookkeeper and author of a military manual, *The Guide*, which laid great stress on doing things correctly.

Central to this is the role, if any, Herchmer played in the decision to attack

Poundmaker's camp. Surprisingly, we know little about the information received by, and the influences upon, Otter and Herchmer during this fateful week, and, equally, we know little about the pressures placed upon the senior officers by the militia officers in the column, as well as the leading citizens of the lately "besieged" Battleford. Did the irate citizens or settlers, many of whom were under arms in the locally-raised Battleford Home Guard or Battleford Rifles, demand that the militia and mounted police take punitive action? Did the column's officers urge Otter to take offensive action?

That they did so was the belief of Lieutenant Colonel George T. Denison, commanding officer of the Governor General's Body Guard and a rear area base far to the east of Battleford, in Humboldt. Being the senior Toronto militia officer in the theatre, he heard first-hand that Otter "was, I believe, much urged by some of his officers to march out and attack Poundmaker ... Middleton refused permission ... but after further pressing, said that ... Otter was on the spot, and must take the responsibility of acting as circumstances would direct. This is as near as I could gather as to what passed."[69] Other than Denison's statement that Otter was influenced by his own officers, there is no direct evidence to support the pressure that might have been exerted by leading citizens such as P.G. Laurie of the *Saskatchewan Herald*.

Otter and Herchmer probably faced similar circumstances to Superintendent Crozier at Fort Carlton a month earlier. There, the local citizens, under arms, had pressed him to venture out with a mixed force consisting of themselves and the NWMP, and the result was the debacle at Duck Lake. Although no evidence exists for it, there was another possible source of pressure, and that was from the NWMP itself. Was Herchmer one of the officers who "much urged" Otter to take offensive action? Had Herchmer received private communication from senior members of the force, who wanted their reputation restored after the initial set-backs?

Later, after the 1885 Rebellion was concluded, it was rumoured by a journalist in eastern Canada that, at an unspecified date "near the end of April," a "half breed" had arrived in Battleford with a remarkable story. He was a recently escaped prisoner from Poundmaker's camp and had told Otter and Herchmer that the "half breeds would fight the Indians ... if the Indians were attacked by the troops, and if attacked at once before Big Bear and his braves, who had been sent for by Poundmaker, arrived, he had no doubt Poundmaker would be easily defeated."[70] The informant warned that "If joined by Big Bear, Poundmaker would either attack the town of Battleford or join Riel in an attack upon it in case Riel withdrew westward, as was at that time considered probable." Did this information reinforce Otter's and Herchmer's natural instincts, as well as their officers' urgings, to undertake a punitive operation against Poundmaker's camp? We will never know. What is certain is that shortly after Otter's relief of Battleford, rumours began about a move against Poundmaker's band.[71]

In the meantime, Otter's force camped in front of Old Government House at Battleford, across the Battle River about a mile from the fort. He remained there until 29 April. Herchmer took command of all the NWMP forces in Fort Battleford, giving him a strength of 75 police and about 50 horses. He began a program of aggressive patrolling in every direction, and detachments of police made several trips to the troubled Assiniboine Reserves to the south.[72] Lieutenant Pelletier remembered that "The information obtained by our scouts varied considerably in estimating the number of warriors serving the great chief."[73]

Meanwhile, Middleton, off-balance because of the Fish Creek defeat, sent a garbled telegram only partly deciphered: "If you can spare Queens Own send to Prince Albert … forming depot at Clarks Crossing."[74] Middleton knew that the Queen's Own was Otter's best unit and it was clear that he now had to pause and develop a rear area base for his wounded from Fish Creek and supplies, at Clarke's Crossing. His "Flying Column" scheme was finished; he would now have to be more deliberate and operate from "base areas." By 25 April, Middleton had formulated a new operational plan and signalled Minister Caron: "Would not be safe to risk defeat so shall relieve Prince Albert then join with Otter in attacking rebels."[75]

A day later, 26 April, less than two days after Otter had arrived in Battleford, Middleton's change of mind became apparent to the staff at Battleford. He replied to Otter's news of his relief of the fort: "Glad to hear that you have arrived. Act for defence of Battleford on your own judgement. You have sole command. [two words indecipherable] … with me at Prince Albert. Tell Herchmer I am well satisfied with his promptness." Otter drafted in the margin: "Glad to hear of your narrow escape, hope wounded are doing well. Herchmer has been of great assistance." Middleton also telegraphed Otter about his urgent need for medical support: "If you have field hospital with you send it to Clarkes Crossing for my wounded, with a force to guard it." Otter's reply was garbled and almost indistinguishable: "… ? arrived. Will send it forward."[76]

What had Otter said when he reported relieving the "siege" of Battleford? He apparently demonstrated timidity or lack of confidence, which prompted Middleton to advise him that "you are in sole command." Had Otter seemed doubtful of his responsibilities or at least given that impression? Was Middleton telling

Otter that he suspected that it was Herchmer who had carried him through the operations thus far? If so, how did Middleton know this? Did he get a telegram from NWMP officials? Did Otter resent the inference that the column's success was due to Herchmer?

At this point, Otter made a decision. He sent a startling proposal to Middleton, suggesting that he conduct a punitive foray against the Indians concentrated on the Poundmaker Reserve to his west. The original copy of this signal cannot be found, and the definitive work on the telegrams of the Rebellion avoids any comment on the message traffic between Middleton, Otter and Dewdney on 26 April. We have, nevertheless, Middleton's immediate reply: "You had better remain at Battleford until you ascertain more about Poundmaker's fort and the kind of country he is in."[77]

But Otter duplicitously had not mentioned that he had also sent a similar telegram to Lieutenant Governor Dewdney, seeking *his* support for an offensive operation. To Dewdney, Otter wrote: "I would propose taking part of my force at once to punish Poundmaker … leaving 100 men to garrison Battleford … great depradations committed. Immediate decisive action necessary…."[78] Dewdney, perhaps not aware that Middleton had urged caution upon Otter, replied: "Think you cannot act too energetically or Indians will collect in large numbers. Herchmer knows country to Pound Maker's reserve … Must depend … [on] Him to get through be sure to secure good reliable scouts."[79] With that, Otter, Herchmer and Sears began to prepare a Flying Column with selected troops from their garrison at Battleford.

Four days later, there was a final flurry of telegrams between Otter and Middleton. Otter and Herchmer would have known that telegraph communications could not keep pace with events, and that at least a day was required for Middleton to send or receive a message. This was due to his isolated position at Fish Creek, which meant that his outgoing messages were relayed through Humboldt, Qu'Appelle and Swift Current. Incoming telegrams followed the route in reverse.[80]

Thus, on 29 April, Otter telegraphed Middleton with the direct question, "Am I to attack? Please give me definite instructions." Middleton replied clearly two days later: "Fighting these men entails heavy responsibility. Six men judiciously placed would shoot down half your force. Had better for the present content yourself with holding Battleford and patrolling about the country." Upon receipt, and having decided that his Flying Column would depart that night, Otter and his staff signalled: "Poundmaker hesitating between peace and war

– am going to-day to try and settle matters with him." Middleton's reply, dated 1 May 1885, never reached them. In it, he *again* advised Otter not to attack: "Don't understand your telegram about Poundmaker. Hope you have not gone with small force, he must be punished, not treated with. You had better confine yourself to reconnoitring for the present."[81]

But Otter had already made his decision – he was going to march against Poundmaker. Neither Lieutenant Cassels nor any other officer in the column has left any evidence that there was a detailed plan of action for the punitive operation against Poundmaker's camp. For example, what action would the column take if the Indians were contacted en route, or, at the Indian camp? No one seemed to know what do in any situation. On the morning of 1 May Cassels spent his time "getting things in shape." He had been assigned to C Company, Infantry School Corps, because the Queen's Own were only providing one company for the forthcoming operation. For Cassels and his fellow subalterns in the column, the aim was *not* clear. As he recalled:

> The object of the expedition is, we hear, to make a reconnaissance. It is not thought that there will be any fighting to do and if there is, Poundmaker has, we hear, only two hundred men and ought not to be able to do very much. The brigadier and staff evidently think that Poundmaker will surrender if we get near him at all.[82]

A number of other essential aspects of the Flying Column advance are also unclear but this is due to lack of evidence and not Otter's planning. First, it is not certain where the command element – Otter, Herchmer and Sears – were to position themselves, but they were probably to be behind B Battery in the order of march. Second, it was not clear if the NWMP mounted element used their own scouts to complement Constable Ross's five-man party. Finally, it appeared undefined where the combined brigade surgeon's group was positioned in the column, but presumably they were with the wagons carrying ammunition, rations and other stores, behind the dismounted NWMP detachment. This small medical and logistical element unfortunately carried no water. The three war correspondents from Toronto and Montreal newspapers apparently rode in wagons with the militia infantry, but their accounts are not informative about such details. (For the detailed Order of Battle of the Flying Column, see Appendix B). Outlined in the table below is the Order of March Otter and Herchmer used for the move from Fort Battleford to the Poundmaker Reserve on the night of 1 May 1885, and which was retained for the second advance across Cut Knife Creek on the following morning. Otter, Herchmer and the staff apparently used regimental seniority when they allocated the infantry units their places in the column. Prower remarked on this, claiming that his garrison battery gunners, artillery, "took the precedence over the other dismounted men in the order of march" but this was probably only to keep the battery together as a unit.[83]

Order of March 1–2 May 1885

Advanced Guard

Note that all combatants were either mounted or riding in the 48 wagons used by the column. (Strengths are added in brackets.)

Scouts – Constable Charles Ross NWMP and five mixed-blood men of the North West (6)

NWMP Mounted detachment (50)

B Battery. Two 7-pdr. guns and the Gatling followed by the Garrison Battery in two sections in wagons (88). Each section commanded by an attached infantry officer. B Battery took two NWMP 7-pdrs, which they manned. The Battery did not take their two 9-pdr Rifled Muzzle Loaders (RMLs) due to reports that the ground was too soft for the weight of these heavier guns. As it turned out, the reports were wrong.

Main Body

C Company, Infantry School Corps (ISC) (46)

Governor General's Foot Guards (GGFG) (21)

Queen's Own Rifles (QOR) (62)

NWMP Dismounted Detachment (23)

Wagon teams not committed to carrying personnel. The Brigade Surgeon's group probably travelled here (minimum 5).

Rear Guard

Battleford Rifles (43)

The total strength of the column, counting 48 teamsters and five in the medical group was 392 men.[84] The teamsters were counted because they were armed and later sustained one fatal casualty. This was a considerably higher figure than

Lieutenant Colonel W. D. Otter's Flying Column
1–2 May 1885

LIEUTENANT COLONEL W.D. OTTER
AND STAFF

SCOUTS
MEDICAL
LOGISTICS
WAR CORRESPONDENTS
TEAMSTERS

ARTILLERY

B BATTERY RCA (88)

CAVALRY

7-PDR GUN   7-PDR GUN   GATLING GUN

NWMP
MOUNTED
DETACHMENT
(50)

GARRISON
BATTERY
[COY (–)]

INFANTRY

| GGFG COY (–) (21) | C COY ISC (–) (46) | QOR NO.1 (COY) (62) | BATTLEFORD RIFLES COY (43) | NWMP COY (–) (23) |

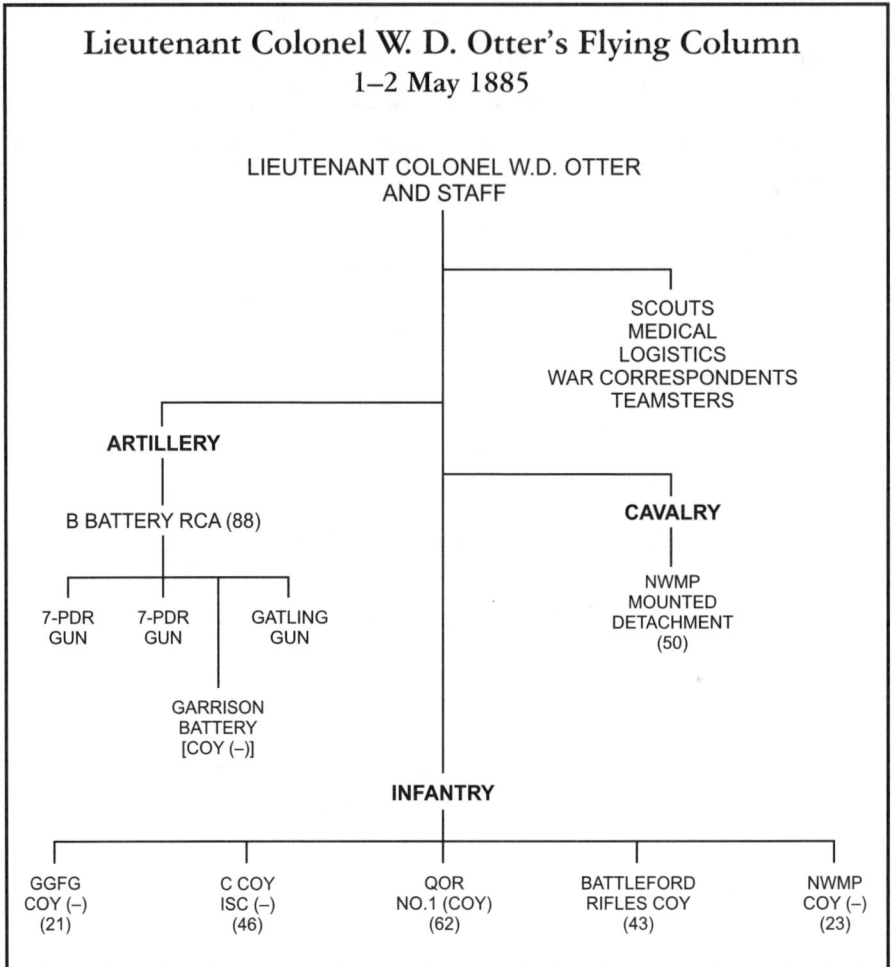

325, which Otter used in his official dispatch and which became the accepted figure for the column strength.[85]

Otter's Flying Column had formidable firepower. There were about 300 Snider-Enfields and 75 Winchesters in the force. The Snider riflemen could easily load and fire five aimed shots a minute. If the Winchesters were also firing at that rate, then the combined effort of the rifles was 375 x 5 or about 1800 rounds a minute. This was an impressive rate of fire and very high combat power. Added to that were the multiplying effects of the artillery's guns and the Gatling.

Otter and Herchmer also based their Flying Column on the success of their lightning, five and-a-half-day dash from Swift Current. The 48 teamsters' wagons allowed the dismounted men to ride and thereby arrive on any battlefield relatively fresh.

Small arms in use during the 1885 Rebellion

The following illustrations are from the collection of S.J. Gooding, editor of *The Canadian Journal of Arms Collecting*, and are reproduced with his permission.

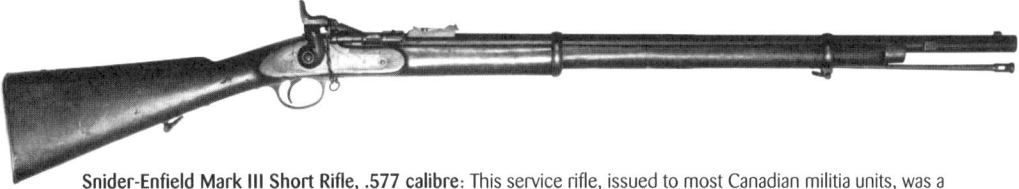

Snider-Enfield Mark III Short Rifle, .577 calibre: This service rifle, issued to most Canadian militia units, was a single-shot breech-loader chambered for the .577 Snider cartridge. Its overall length was 48½ inches and the barrel length was 30½ inches. The recoil was comfortable enough that volunteers could shoot it accurately to about 100 yards and it could be loaded, fired, unloaded and reloaded quickly, in about ten seconds.

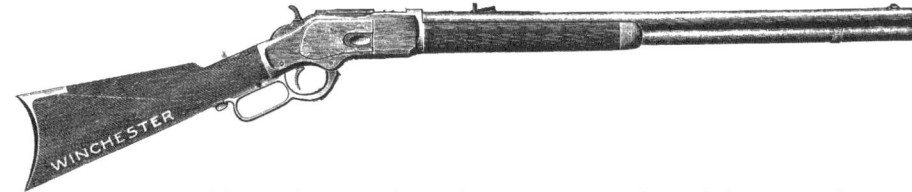

Winchester Model 1873 rifle: In 1873 the Winchester arms company designed a lever-action rifle strong enough to handle the pressure of a centre-fire cartridge. This rifle was extemely popular throughout North America, and the common chambering was for the .44-40 Winchester cartridge, an accurate short-range round which could be reloaded with simple hand tools. The Model 1873 was offered in musket, rifle and carbine versions, and the latter had a 20-inch barrel. The Model 1873 carbine was the fast-firing weapon of choice for western horsemen, but as inter-tribal warfare in the Canadian North West ended in 1870, this weapon arrived too late to influence that conflict. The Model 1873 remained in production until 1923.

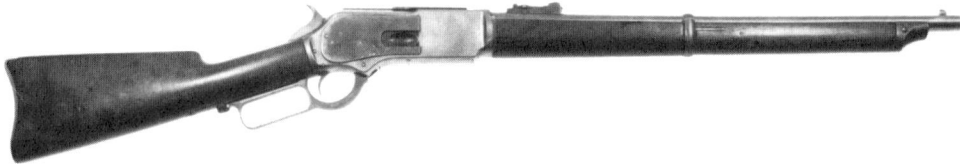

NWMP Winchester Model 1876 carbine .45-75: Between 1878 and 1885 the NWMP changed its standard small arm from the Enfield Snider cavalry carbine to the Winchester Model 1876 carbine in .45-75 calibre. This weapon was designed to fire a heavier cartridge than the short-action Model 1873. The Model 1876 carbine was a lever-action, magazine-fed rifle with a barrel length of 22 inches. The magazine held nine rounds, and the carbine could fire a round about every two seconds. These weapons were modern, impressive and intimidating.

Commercial shotgun: As Plains Indians grew accustomed to reserve life, the double-barrelled smooth-bore shotgun, usually breech, but sometimes muzzle loading, became popular. These shotguns were cheap and offered the ability to fire birdshot, large-calibre buckshot, or ball projectiles. They were a very close-range weapon and only effective to about 60-70 yards. Many Indians in the battle were armed with these weapons.

On Sunday, 1 May 1885, when the Flying Column departed from Fort Battleford at 11 P.M., Lieutenant Prower remembered that spirits were very high: "we hardly realised [sic] we were on anything but a picnic, until the quartermaster distributed lint [cloth for bandages] and gave us parting advice as to how to behave when hit."[86] Disturbingly, shortly after leaving, Prower noticed a "high column of smoke ascending from the prairie on our left front" which was "the Indian signal of our advance."[87]. *Toronto Daily Mail* correspondent W.W. "Billy" Fox also noticed "a dense column of smoke ... several miles in front" and this was "answered by another column of smoke further on."[88] Although it was dark, Cassels saw the smoke as well, but he again expressed the overwhelming confidence that the militia had in themselves: "There is, of course, no chance of surprising him [the enemy]. His scouts have probably long ere this noticed our advance, for signal fires have been burning all afternoon on the distant hills, but we want to reach him before he has time to move off."[89]

All accounts of the first phase of the column's move towards the Poundmaker Reserve emphasize its initial speed. Prower, still concerned about the excessive caution outside Battleford, noted that if "we had been timid in delaying our entrance into Battleford, we were making up for it now."[90] Cassels recorded that they pushed on "rapidly til nightfall," when they made a "laager" and waited "til the moon rises." They ate and rested "quietly and discuss[ed] the prospects for tomorrow."[91] For eight of the men in that laager, it would be their last meal.

The column probably halted just west of Drumming Creek, now known as Drummond Creek, which Prower described as "a very deep ravine ... and it took us some time to get the guns and wagon-train across."[92] Following several hours of rest, the men moved at about 3.30 A.M., when the moon had risen, but the final march to the reserve was through much more difficult country. Prower described the trail as a "long, bush road, rough and stony, with thick jungle on either side, deep ravines at intervals of a mile or so ... a few dozen ambushed Indians could have stampeded the whole train."[93] Cassels recorded that "the road ran through wild and rolling country, so that we did not move quickly." He remembered his thoughts as the night wore on:

I was too excited to feel sleepy and had lots of time to indulge in meditation; sometimes I would wonder whether anything was likely to happen and whether some of us would not come back again, but as a rule I, and I think, most of the other fellows, had very little thought of danger. We certainly felt serious, but why no one could tell.[94]

First light on 2 May 1885 was probably at about 4 A.M. By that time the column had moved onto Poundmaker Reserve land, passing "a few houses but no one was visible."[95] They now approached the large site of the original Indian camp, east of Cut Knife Creek, which Otter's scouts had discovered five days earlier. It was abandoned. By the time that Cassels, with C Company of the Infantry School, had come up behind the NWMP and B Battery, he could see that the former camp had been very large.

> The marks of numerous teepees and fires could be plainly seen and it was evident that the camp had been but lately vacated. We halted at this camp for some time while the scouts searched some clumps of bush that were near by. In front of the camp was a large creek and rising from this on the far side were high hills intersected with numerous ravines … we could see far away on the distant hills a herd of cattle grazing and one or two mounted men riding about. Here, evidently, were our friends.[96]

Colour Sergeant C.F. Winter, Governor General's Foot Guards, confirmed this assessment. He remembered seeing

> a solitary enemy horseman appeared over the brow of the high ground where the road up from the creek crossed the summit – rode towards us a short distance, then putting his horse to the gallop rode around in a circle three or four times, waving a blanket at the side of his mount and trailing it behind him — then disappeared over the top … Our scouts interpreted the maneuver as of distinct hostile intent and said it was meant not only as a challenge for us to come on, but was also a signal … to concentrate for some preconcerted movement.[97]

The Indians had been alerted by a scout probably posted on Cut Knife Hill to the south or one of the nearby elevations. Indian legend holds that this scout was an elderly man, Old Jacob.[98] One cannot be sure which troops of the column he saw from his position.

It is not clear why the Indians had moved their first camp, or who had planned the second camp, but it appeared to be sited for defensive purposes. Any enemy advancing from the east would have to pass through a defile – a crossing on Cut Knife Creek – and if they followed the Indians' tracks they would be forced to ascend a hill and gather themselves upon a large plateau in sight of the new camp, which was hidden from the creek. These two manoeuvres would test the training

Topographic Overview of the Cut Knife Hill Battlefield

N
↑

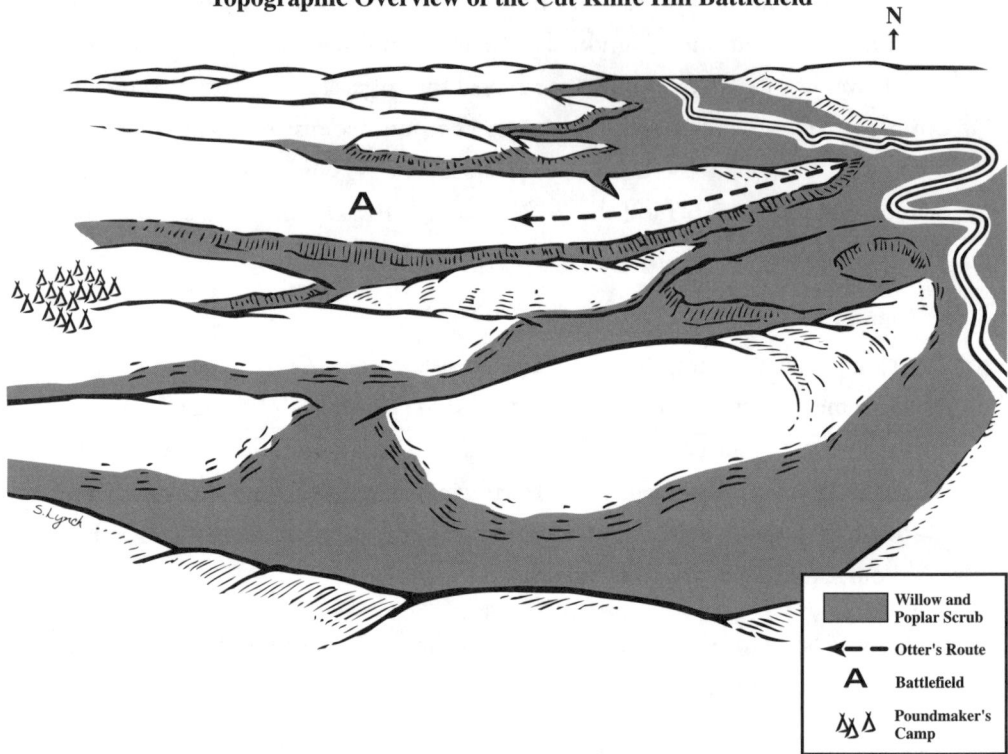

	Willow and Poplar Scrub
	Otter's Route
A	Battlefield
	Poundmaker's Camp

A perspective of the battlefield

This modern artist's simplified perspective of the battlefield is from Poundmaker's position, but elevated about 30 feet to improve the view for the reader. *To show the nature of the ground, the trees and shrubs have been removed from the illustration but their location has been indicated with shading.* Probably every Indian knew the ground from this perspective, and they also knew that a government force with troops in wagons and horse-drawn artillery following a fresh trail would advance up the ravine-lined open slope to the high level ground that created the plateau. They were correct. From Otter's perspective the open rising ground allowed easy access for his force, and, if the column kept together, he and his staff would retain control until first contact. Otter avoided the cautious approach, which would have meant securing at least one ravine *first*, with infantry in skirmishing order, until the open ground permitted his force to concentrate and move in tactical bounds.

and discipline of any force, and the Indians would also be given time to take the attack away from the women and children.

Except on the northwest side of the battlefield, ravines surrounded the plateau. These ravines were not open, but they were thick with low, thin-branched willow scrub up to six feet high.[99] This scrub surrounded the plateau, although there was less of it on the northwest side which had no ravine. Also interspersed around the site were clumps of tall poplar trees. Although there are no photographs of the Cut Knife battle, sketches of the battle and photographs of Batoche and Fish Creek do not show the willow scrub as leafy. The grass "had not yet begun to grow"[100] and leaves were not out on trees. Prower noted that the "flowers were just out and all traces of snow had disappeared, except in the ravines....The buds had just begun to show, but there enough of them to 'ware brush' when near Indians."[101] The willow scrub was so thick that it provided cover from view. It was through gaps in the scrub, especially lower down in branches nearest the ground, that the Indians would fire their close-range shotguns, smooth-bore muskets and in several cases arrows at militiamen and policemen on the slightly higher ground along the fringes of the plateau.

This scrub allowed the Indians and Métis to fight their sort of war, shooting and moving, with close-range weapons. More often than not, shots at fleeting or imagined targets through the scrub were missed, which explained why casualties were so low on each side. Due to the closeness of the fighting, when a target appeared clearly defined, the shot was usually on target with a fatal bullet in the head and indeed there were several head wounds on the Indian side.[102]

Captain Ernest J. Chambers, the popular historian of the Canadian militia in the late 19th and early 20th centuries, visited the battle site in July 1885 with Herchmer and Major Charles Short, Acting Commanding Officer of B Battery. Chambers had been present with Middleton's column at Fish Creek and Batoche, and he understood plains fighting. His description of the ground is one of the best we have:

The battlefield was a glacis-like hill side. With the exception of a very shallow depression or coulee a little to the rear of the centre of the position held by Colonel Otter's men, and which coulee, the day of the fight was occupied by the corral and hospital, there was no cover from the surrounding elevations except a few buffalo "wallows." The position held ... and as clearly indicated by the rows of empty cartridge shells and the holes cut by the gun trails in the sod on recoil, was in the shape of a horseshoe, the toe up-hill, the heel on the creek at the bottom of the hill. The rim of the horseshoe was defined by ravines or coulees, all connected in such a way that it would be possible for the Indians, who occupied these natural trenches to move under cover completely round both flanks and across the front of the position of the troops without being observed by any but those who exposed themselves uncovered against the skyline. The coulees were not as deep, as precipitous, as heavily wooded, or individually as formidable as natural defences as the coulee ... at Fish Creek, but in combination they made a much more deadly man-trap. The centre of the glacis within the horsehoe, the depression already mentioned alone excepted, was swept from the ravines in front and on both flanks. Had the troops not succeeded in keeping the troops out of the shrub-lined banks of the creek – it was quite a considerable torrent – the position would have been shot-swept from the rear as well. And it was not only the immediately surrounding coulees that held hidden foes that trying day … Major Short … felt convinced that his guns were drawing a vicious fire from the crest of a commanding hill so far to the left that the scouts declared the Indians had no weapons that would carry so far … [upon visiting] … there were several shallow rifle pits on the top of the hill looking down over the battlefield … with numerous very long, solid, brass cartridge shells scattered about.[103]

The hill that concerned Charles Short was Cut Knife Hill, south of the B Battery position, and because their guns were initially facing north and west, that hill was on his left. Later the battery front would change to the left or south, and the major was able to fire onto it.

We left Otter, Herchmer, the staff, the senior officers – and possibly Ross and the scouts – in daylight, looking up at the hills from the site of the deserted Indian camp. They could not see the new camp and in front of them was Cut Knife Creek, with dense willow scrub on either side of the creek bed. To the west were gently rising hills and to the south was the dominant feature, which the Indians called Cut Knife Hill. No one reported that they had seen the trail left by the Indians withdrawing from the first camp. There was no record of any decision or plan being made, or any alteration to the Order of March after the Indian scout was observed. On Otter's part, apparently, there was no hint of hesitation, or withdrawal, or inspiration to parley with any Indians that his force might meet. Did the disappointment at finding the first camp empty fuel the al-ready aggressive attitude of his militia officers? Because he had no plan when they intended to surprise Poundmaker's Indians in the first camp, we can assume that he had no plan of action when his force followed the trail to the second. What was clear, though, was that surprise had been lost. The length of the column, perhaps 700 yards from nose to tail, could be seen easily, and the noise made by the teams and wagons would soon give them away. Lieutenant Robinson L. Wadmore wrote on his sketch map, later published, that the column approached the creek crossing at 4.45 A.M.[104]

Lieutenant Prower did not mention any delay getting over Cut Knife Creek, other than "in finding a ford." During the jockeying for crossing places across the creek, Prower managed to get forward behind the guns. Lieutenant Cassels, with C Company of the Infantry School, remembered receiving new orders. He was now "to cross the creek, climb the hill, and have breakfast and rest the horses before pushing on." This made sense to the young subaltern, because the herd of cattle and mounted Indians could be seen "at least two miles away."[105] He was right. These Indians and the cattle were on the slopes of the actual Cut Knife Hill, over a mile south from the column, and in a different direction than the one he was facing to his west.

From his later discussions with militiamen who were present, Chambers described the creek as being "quite a considerable torrent," and in their opinion it was a formidable obstacle. It created a textbook defile because on the west side of it there was about four hundred yards of "scrubby marshy lands" – the willow scrub at the foot of the plateau.[106]

Once across the creek, a strange sense of calm seemed to descend upon the column. As the scouts, the mounted element and "B" Battery – the advanced guard – gathered itself beyond the willow scrub lands west of the creek, and began to ascend, Cassels was far enough forward to observe the head of column. What he saw was alarming. He carefully noted that as the column "began to climb the hill … [t]he scouts were riding quietly near the guns, the men had dismounted, and were walking by twos and threes along the trail."[107] It appeared that the column had let its guard down. Perhaps lulled into a state of somnolence, they were almost sleepwalking, a phenomenon that most soldiers experience following a night move.

It has never been clear what Constable Charlie Ross's tasks were once beyond the creek crossing. We do not know where Ross deployed his men as they came up out of the scrub, or which of the scouts were "riding … near the guns" rather than deploying forward to cover the wide plateau. How did Otter expect him to communicate with the senior officer in the advanced guard? Or the officer commanding the lead element of the column, the NWMP mounted group? Because they were mounted, they could act as *arme blanche* cavalry and charge. Was that an option? Was Ross to determine the axis of advance for the column on, or near, the well-marked trail left by the Indians en route to their new camp? Was Ross to look for *alternate* routes that could become an axis for a flanking attack? If so, what sort of attack? With the mounted NWMP group? With the infantry in firing lines? Certainly, the camp could have been more effectively threatened from directions other than the main Indian trail leading to it from the east. There are no answers to these questions. All of Ross's actions to date — to fire first at any Indian that he saw — indicate that Otter, who had lost surprise, did not have a well thought-out tactical plan that was integrated with the action that each arm would take upon contact.

As a result, when Ross encountered a small group of Indians at the west end of the plateau, he acted as he had several weeks earlier on the trail to Battleford: he fired at them. Prower was behind the guns, with the garrison battery gunners who were prepared to act as infantry to protect them, and he remembered that the men in the column "heard the report of a rifle followed by a regular volley from the mounted police ... about a hundred yards in our front."[108] That rifle shot was probably fired by Ross.

The Indians, or the Métis, for no one is sure who this advanced group were, returned fire. Now was the time for a command decision by Otter, yet there was none. Without even a subaltern's order, and with the column spread out nose-to-tail on a slope, the battle of Cut Knife Hill had begun. The time was about 5.30 A.M.

The NWMP mounted element, nearest the scouts who fired, dismounted as they had been trained to do. One policeman was killed instantly. Known thereafter as "the first man to fall," No. 565 Corporal R.B. Sleigh was shot in the mouth, and "shortly after ... No. 907 Corporal WHT Lowry ... [NWMP was] ... mortally wounded."[109] The leading element of the NWMP mounted contingent apparently consisted of Sleigh and Lowry. While Sleigh knew Indians, he, like the rest of the column, had most likely never been on this remote slope on the Poundmaker Reserve. Horse handlers, probably one for four horses, now took their mounts into a depression back down the slope, where they were protected from observation and fire. All the horses in the column would eventually be held there.[110] The B Battery gunners under Lieutenants Pelletier and Prower deployed as they were trained. The gun detachments brought the two 7-pdrs and the Gatling into action across the front of the plateau, facing west. The troops in the rear, if they had not heard the small arms fire from the vanguard, now heard the fire from B Battery's heavy weapons.

Cassels, who was just behind B Battery, described the opening of the fight:

as the scouts reached the top of the first steep ascent, I heard a rattle of rifles ahead and then in a minute or two saw the police and some artillery lying down firing briskly over the crest of the hill and the guns and Gatling also working for all they were worth. At the same time bullets began to fly round us and puffs of smoke floated from the bushes [on the right and left], showing us where they came from. Evidently we were in a trap.[111]

For his part, after the first burst of firing Prower looked to the rear and saw that

> The infantry sprang from their seats, those who were already across the stream, the guns and Gatling were rapidly fronted and unlimbered, and the wagons commenced to form a sort of lager [sic]. The garrison battery were formed up, wheeled to the right, extended, and commenced to advance, closely supported by the foot soldiers and others as they crossed the ford. Then a mistaken order was given to retire, followed by a counter order to advance, and we advanced until we came within about two hundred yards of a deep ravine, when the fire getting hot the men laid down and began to fire into it.[112]

None of Ross's scouts was hit – wherever they were – and presumably they dismounted and went to ground along with the police and the garrison troops of B Battery. Colour Sergeant Winter remembered that the infantry on the slope behind them

> hastily scrambled out of the wagons – the units were quickly formed up in some kind of order – Colonel Otter galloped off to the front, while the officers of his staff followed with such parties of the little force as were more immediately available, extending them [to the right and left] as they "doubled" up to the top of the hill some 400-500 yards from the side of the creek … the advance guard … had retired with several killed or wounded …were responding briskly to the enemy's fire which came from ravines about 300 yards away, full of small trees and brush, with the fire spreading fast to right and left of their position.[113]

In the Indian camp, meanwhile, panic reigned. Women and children bolted from their tipis and ran for cover in the nearby ravines. Cree and Assiniboine men, plus the 40 or so Métis under Delorme and Nault,[114] grabbed weapons and ammunition and ran, or rode if a horse was handy, towards the sound of the firing. No one was sure, then or later, who had influence over the Cree and Assiniboine warrior societies in the camp. Later, a well known warrior, Fine Day, claimed that he was in charge, but the present Cree tradition is that he was *not* in command. Few orders were necessary since everyone in camp knew their duty: to keep the fighting away from the women and children.[115]

Coming Day, a Cree from the Sweetgrass Reserve, remembered that he and other Indians were already up, ready and waiting in a ravine. They only needed orders for deployment.

At the opening of the fight I was down in this valley to the south of us, at this side of the ravine, on this slope of the hill. When the warning came at the tent that the troops were on the their way, I rode down with our other men right down into the position which was just spoken about, down on the slope of the hill on this side of the ravine. Evidently we had arrived pretty early on the scene. I was riding on this slope of the hill and I could see the police and other troops strung out from the creek clear up the side of the hill with their infantry, etc. The first new view I had of them was … [indicated on ground] … I saw a Mounted man and evidently it was the officer in command of the police and behind them were men on foot. That was the first view I got of these with the exception of those who were coming up the valley in wagons. I got a very close view of this Mounted man. At that time quite a large body of Indians were coming up. I got so clear a view of the man that I could tell the colour of his garb and of his horse. Speaking of this mounted man, just as he came above the horizon here on this hill I had my gun lifted to shoot at him. Little Crow, an Indian beside me, put up his gun and said, "Don't shoot; let them shoot first." On the front part of the policeman's saddle was something red – evidently part of his equipment he was carrying. It was a bay horse with white face and legs … at the same instant that my gun was thrown up, this mounted policeman wheeled his horse and went down the hill and gave the troops a command. A bugle shortly afterwards sounded. The troops then came up and fired at the other Indians but not at the Indians lying on the edge of the slope to the south … when the first guns were fired … the sun was just above the horizon. Immediately after they opened fire, then the Indians did themselves (we four men lying there). Just about that time when I was busy pulling my shells out of his pocket and firing, the wagons started coming up and unhooking their horses and putting their wagons into circles in the bush there … [indicated on ground] … They were very active in getting these things in there. They evidently had their coats on because we could see them all swinging their coats off in this bluff. By this time … the troops were quite visible all over here and the Indians then started taking to the ravines to get under cover … [at] that time … I saw this team wheeling into line. I did not know what it was, but it was evidently the artillery horses bringing in the guns, as just after that a big gun roared.[116]

During the opening few moments there was considerable confusion – more on the Indian-Métis side than the militia-police side. Basil Favel (Junior) of the Poundmaker Reserve recalled that, aroused by the alarm, he

vaulted on a horse, and came tearing down [from the camp]. I was a little late in arriving and it was this old Jacob … who heard the troops arriving. I rode down this ravine. They fired on me but they did not hit me. Shortly after I arrived down over the hill … [indicated the ground] … here I was with another Indian who was killed immediately afterward. I went along to … another Indian … [he] asked me for a smoke and I was in the act of bending over to light his pipe as a bullet passed over me, just cutting him through the ear. About that time there were five Stony Indians that came over this rise … I wheeled and turned back … I ran to where Fine Day was and passed them and ran on over the hill. Right after I ran down … to a deep buffalo path … I threw myself down … another Indian came down and lay down beside me. He had no gun. "I haven't a gun, but I'm going to sneak up on a policeman, grab him and get his gun" … I got up onto a rise and in a certain position the police were lying so thick … I could get a shot into the whole bunch. I would jump up and … fire five or six shots without picking any particular target.[117]

Lieutenant Oscar Pelletier, forward near the guns, was seriously wounded by an enemy bullet "in the very beginning of the battle," while his section of gunners was "first advancing to secure an advantageous position on the ground." Pelletier's account sheds light on the nature of gunshot wounds in the battle, as well as on the effectiveness of the Brigade Surgeon's staff – from the Queen's Own and B Battery – and the attached regimental stretcher-bearers, who had set up a rough field dressing station.[118] He recalled that his garrison gunners

set up a skirmish line behind the guns and opened fire. This provided the enemy with less leeway in attempting to shoot towards the field guns. It is at this moment that I was hit by a bullet, which pierced my left thigh through-and-through, thankfully without breaking the bone. I will permit myself to mention here that the bullets used in this battle against us were mostly of

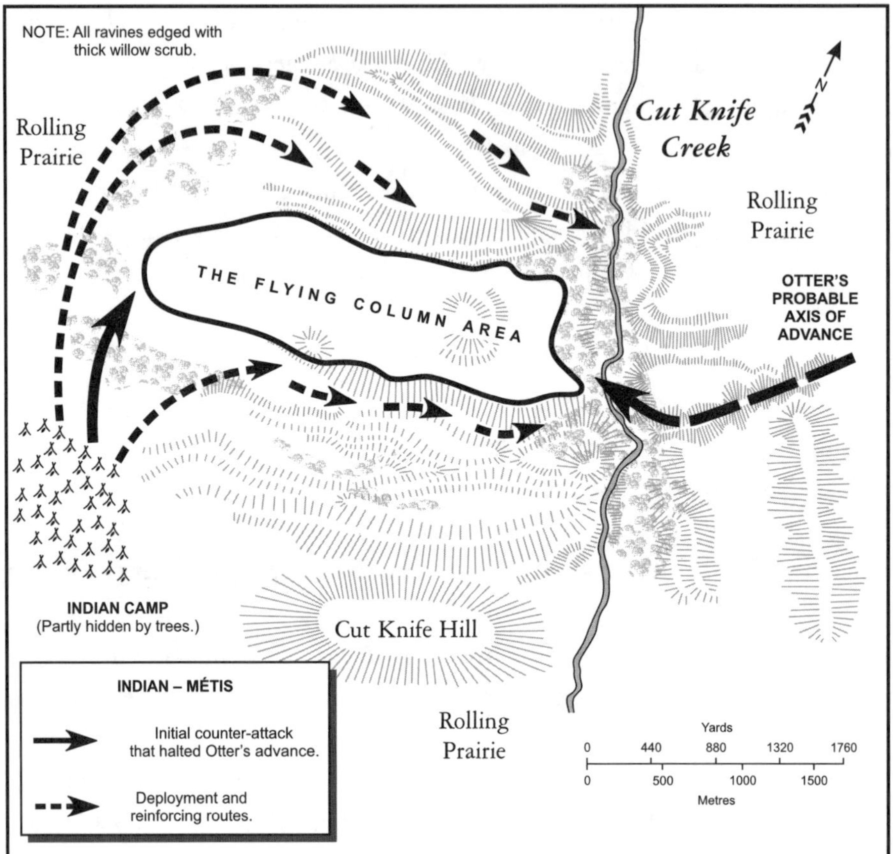

NOTE: All ravines edged with
thick willow scrub.

Rolling
Prairie

*Cut Knife
Creek*

Rolling
Prairie

THE FLYING COLUMN AREA

OTTER'S
PROBABLE
AXIS OF
ADVANCE

INDIAN CAMP
(Partly hidden by trees.)

Cut Knife Hill

INDIAN – MÉTIS

→ Initial counter-attack
that halted Otter's advance.

--→ Deployment and
reinforcing routes.

Rolling
Prairie

	Yards		
0	440	880	1320	1760

0	500	1000	1500

Metres

Map C–4
Sketch of Indian – Métis Counter-attack
and Deployment Routes
2 May, 1885

hunting type, whether fired from hunting or military-type rifles. Hunting
bullets cause excessively painful and difficult wounds, and cause greater loss
of blood than modern weapons, since the calibre of these bullets is infinitely
larger than those of modern weapons… I remained almost paralysed on the
ground, until some stretcher bearers from the Queen's Own Rifles came to
my rescue. They carried me inside a laager which was placed behind the line
of fire, in a depression in the ground. It would be unfair and ungrateful of
me not to mention the admirable dedication that the stretcher bearers played
during this brief but heated event. They had to expose themselves to enemy
fire, to retrieve the wounded and even the dead. Since the enemy would certainly have performed brutalities on the bodies of our dead, had they gotten
their hands on them, we retrieved all but one, Private Osgoode, from the

Governor General's Foot Guards, who rolled down a ravine after being mortally wounded. The slope was too steep to attempt any recovery… The interior of the laager, where the wounded were taken, had none of the facilities or surgical devices which can be found in a modern-day dressing station.[119]

Surgeon-Major Frederick Strange, whose responsibility it was to ensure surgical care, had only two Field Paniers[120] normally found in a regimental field medical kit. Assisting Major Strange was Surgeon-Captain Leslie, from the Queen's Own, and the hospital sergeant, Gaston Labat, a "precious man in these circumstances." He was from France and had joined B Battery as a medical sergeant several years earlier.[121] Pelletier remembered that

> The wounded received all the care and attention … permitted by circumstances. But, as war always brings the unexpected, a *lack of water* was … [soon noticed]. Enemy riflemen had positioned themselves behind our lines, on hills which overlooked Cut Knife creek, which was our only source of water. For a while, we were completely deprived. The well-directed fire of the enemy prevented our men from approaching the creek, whose bank was fully exposed.[122]

Captain R.W. Rutherford, RCA, the officer in charge of one of the 7-pdr. guns, and later a major general in the Canadian army, provided the best account of the opening action from a gunner's perspective:

> No sooner had we got well up on the hill than we saw the Indians on our front and right flank swarming around us and who instantly opened a heavy fire upon us. …… We brought the two guns and the Gatling to the top of the hill and got them into action at once. The Indians were so close upon us that we fired case shot. They came on with war whoops and jumping up and tossing their blankets up above them and to the right and left of them as to misdirect our aim, then fell on the ground and fired at us. So sudden was the charge … to captur[e] our guns and the Gatling that the men were surprised and began to fall back when Major Short sprang forward and called out the men to him, they did and also some Police and 'C' Co. who were with us and drove them back. They at once got undercover knowing every inch of the ground and poured in a deadly fire upon us.[123]

Sketch of the battlefield by Captain R.W. Rutherford, B Battery RCA
This is the best period sketch of the battlefield. Rutherford stressed aspects of the battle that he was familiar with, particularly the opening phases. He suggested that the Indians and Métis were in position when the column arrived on the plateau. The gun is in the withdrawal position. (Copied from the *Toronto Globe*, 23 May 1885)

Cassels saw some of the B Battery men bolt, and, as a Toronto Protestant, he could not resist the opportunity to criticize French Canadians. What he saw may have been the partial execution of the mistaken order to retire that Prower mentioned earlier, or what Rutherford described as the men falling back. Prower did not remember the Indian assault, but he clearly saw Major Short's first charge at a small group of warriors firing from the scrub surrounding a small pond. He recalled that they "were using their firearms against our flank. They were quite isolated, and when a dozen battery men under Major Short charges into them all but one bolted and were shot in the open."[124]

Otter or Herchmer did not exploit or reinforce these local initiatives by Short and the troops in the advanced guard, although this in fact was the *turning point* of the action. There was no ravine or natural obstacle between the advanced guard, then commanded by the spirited Short, and the Indian camp. Not surprisingly, the Indians fought the hardest here – in the open – to defend their camp.

While the mounted police and B Battery demonstrated effective, tactical re-action, their response had forced a situation that was rapidly spiralling out of control. Otter, Herchmer, Sears, and the officers commanding their respective contingents to the rear, were losing any initiative that their training and discipline might have given them, particularly as the Indian fire increased not only from the front but from the north, or the right flank of the column.

This fire was largely ineffective because too few Indians had breech-loading rifles,[125] but the sound and smoke must have alarmed Otter and Herchmer, as well as their inexperienced troops. Little direction seemed to come from Otter. The dismounted policemen, and now C School, as they deployed to the right rear behind these forward troops, began to fight their own little battles. By occupying all the available ground, Otter lost the ability to decisively influence the course of the action in a disciplined and concentrated manner, as his men, in extended skirmishing order, were now fighting like Indians in small groups, firing at fleeting targets, but unable to manoeuvre on their own. Only Ross seemed to have the authority to rove around the ravines on the fringes of the battlefield.

At the front of the position, Rutherford, with his gun detachment, remembered that after their charge forward to carry the crest of the hill,

> We soon settled down to hard work and every man made the most of the ground for cover. Not a[n Indian] shot was fired but was at a man and their fire was terribly good. They were now swarming around on our right and left flanks and tried to completely surround us … The enemy gradually crept up and got possession of a hill on our right which commanded our position but Major Short called for more volunteers and made a dash for it and drove them back. The Guards and 'C' Co. were the principals in this case and they held the hill for the rest of the day.[126]

These troops had begun fighting in and around the edges of willow scrub and ravines, and this was to last for over six hours.

Cassels recalled securing the right flank to the rear of B Battery and that the NWMP and C Company of the Infantry School were in a serious situation. As he described it,

> half an hour we had quite hot enough work and the bullets came flying about us … we were exposed to fire from three sides and had to grin and bear it. After half an hour or so we had quite silenced any fire on the right … [and to] our immediate front and could easily keep the ravine clear as the Indians could not reach it without exposing themselves and this they never dared to do.[127]

Thus, within the first 30 minutes of the battle, the leading troops in the column had fanned out across the front and to the immediate right flank. It is

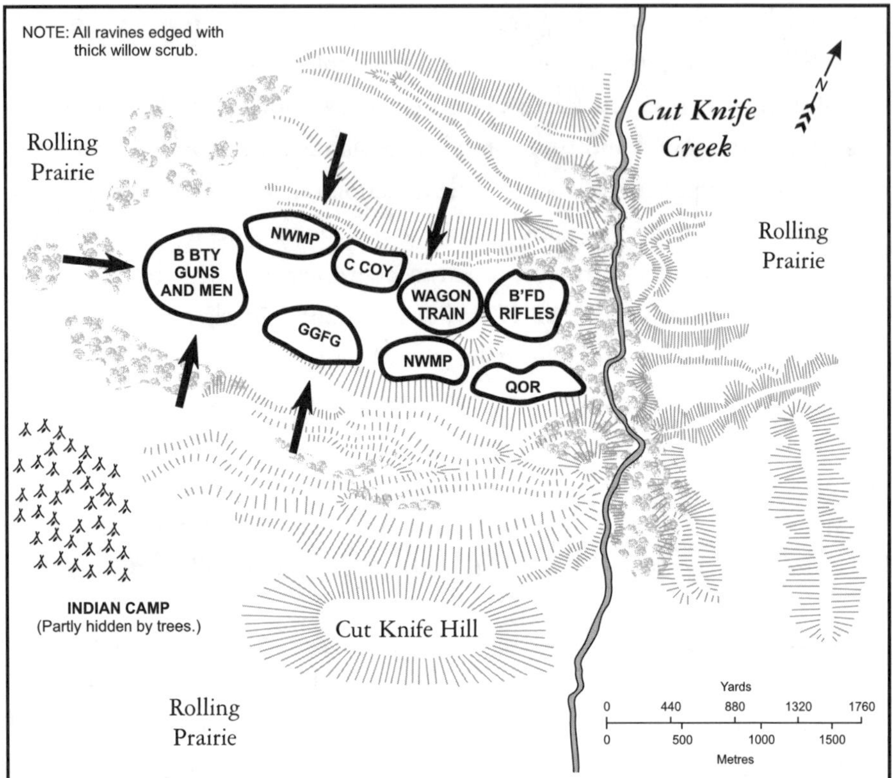

NOTE: All ravines edged with thick willow scrub.

Cut Knife Creek

Rolling Prairie

NWMP

B BTY GUNS AND MEN

C COY

WAGON TRAIN

B'FD RIFLES

GGFG

NWMP

QOR

Rolling Prairie

INDIAN CAMP (Partly hidden by trees.)

Cut Knife Hill

Rolling Prairie

Yards				
0	440	880	1320	1760
0	500	1000	1500	
		Metres		

Map C–5
Flying Column Deployment Following the Initial Check,
Threatened From Both Sides
2 May, 1885

uncertain whether or not C Company had sent some troops to the left early on, until the Queen's Own arrived. While the 56 or so men of the Queen's Own and the 20 of the Foot Guards might have been used to manoeuvre around the firm base of the NWMP, B Battery and C School, towards the Indian camp, Otter and his staff were now required to commit them to holding the left side of the plateau. Moreover they briefly lost control of the 55 men of the Battleford Rifles, probably the least disciplined and trained in the column, who spread themselves out on the left near the Queen's Own. Otter's staff were required to move them to secure the rear, probably in response to war whoops and firing of two or three Indians or Métis. With this final deployment of the Battleford volunteers, Otter's only reserve was Charlie Ross and his five scouts.

Lieutenant Cassels described the situation:

Roughly speaking we occupied a triangular inclined plane – the apex resting on the creek and the base running along the crest of the hill. In front of the hill and parallel to the crest a ravine, about two hundred yards distant and running down from this ravine on the right there was open ground, but on the left for a long distance the whole country was rolling and bushy, and it was from this side that the heaviest firing seemed to come. "C" School was ordered to protect the right flank and clear the ravine on that side, while the Queens Own and Guards were assigned a similar duty on the left. The Battleford men were to look after the rear. The police and artillery were busily engaged in front.[128]

Hereafter Cassels admitted that "except in my own vicinity, I know nothing but hearsay. I saw no more of the Guards, Battleford Rifles, and our fellows [the Queen's Own] till we were on our way home." [129]

For the next five and a half hours the NWMP and B Battery would remain holding the ground of tactical importance, the open western flank facing the Indian camp. The remainder of the column was extended behind this anchor on the sides of the plateau. Otter, Herchmer and Sears managed these reinforcing deployments well, and slowly but surely the militiamen improved their ability to react to incursions around their perimeter. The area, however, was far too large for them to secure permanently. It would have been impossible, moreover, to control at night, and Otter probably began to think about this factor early on in the battle.

Prower recalled that after the

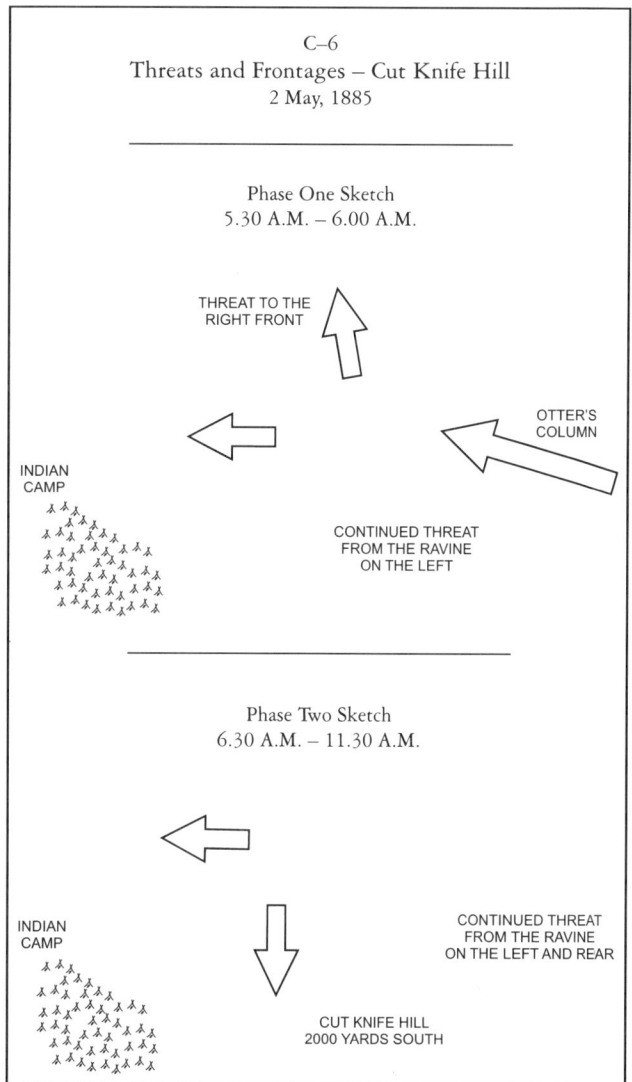

C–6
Threats and Frontages – Cut Knife Hill
2 May, 1885

Phase One Sketch
5.30 A.M. – 6.00 A.M.

THREAT TO THE
RIGHT FRONT

OTTER'S
COLUMN

INDIAN
CAMP

CONTINUED THREAT
FROM THE RAVINE
ON THE LEFT

Phase Two Sketch
6.30 A.M. – 11.30 A.M.

INDIAN
CAMP

CONTINUED THREAT
FROM THE RAVINE
ON THE LEFT AND REAR

CUT KNIFE HILL
2000 YARDS SOUTH

initial burst of activity, possibly less than 30 minutes long, which he described as "warm work … half a dozen of our men had been knocked over." Then, he recalled, "the fire slackened and we had time to look about us … The Indians … knew that tactical value of the ground well … They had carefully prepared the ravines for our reception by digging rifle pits."[130] He described the initial position as being

> in the shape of a horsehoe, with the ford at the opening of the heel; the guns … at the toe of the horsehoe and on the highest ground, and from them we had a good view of the whole field. Round the guns were the garrison battery men and most of the [NWMP who] … seem to have attached themselves to Major Short. At a short distance on our right front was a small body of sharp-shooters … on our left in very extended order were the Queen's Own …

Prower, however, was the only witness to note a change in the direction of the column's deployment after the original contact. Once the scouts, he claimed, "with their Winchester repeaters, succeeded eventually in clearing the *right* ravine … *then our left became our front.*"[131]

Cassels remembered that after they had secured their right flank, Otter visited Lieutenant Robinson L. Wadmore, commanding the C Company contingent, and "ordered Mr. Wadmore to take the men up to the Front and reinforce the line there and at the same time he asked me to take a couple of men and carry some ammunition to the fighting line."[132] Cassels and his ammunition party reached the "guns and the front of the line," where he recorded that "the fighting is still hot and several men are hit." Cassels "stayed near the guns" for a considerable time, in fact until the withdrawal order was given. He remarked that gradually the fire slackened, and "bullets come in any quantity only from the left."[133]

B Battery, with their right secure, now faced south and began firing across the complete western side, from north to south. They had a clear mission – to deny the Indians the open ground to the west – and there were plenty of targets, particularly to the south. Rutherford recalled that

> we shelled the [tipis in the Indian Camp] on our right front, the ravines where the enemy sharpshooters were and all points where they appeared. On a hill about 2000 yards to our front where we had seen the cattle grazing stood a large number of people which were first [thought] to be prisoners and friend-lies witnessing the fight, but from the constant communication that seemed

to be going on between them and the field we became convinced they were the enemies headquarters staff who were directing the fight and so we shelled them out. We afterwards learned that Poundmaker was there conducting the operations.[134]

Then disaster struck. Rutherford was not sure of the exact time, but after settling into a routine of shelling targets across their wide panorama,

the 7 pr gun carriages began to crack and break up. Major Short's first, then mine. So we were in a bad way. The bullets were coming at us hot and thick but there was only one thing to do and that was to stick to our guns and work them and we did though after we had to pick them up after every discharge and tie them to the trails.[135]

Nearby, Prower, remembered that

At the third or fourth round the trail of the gun-carriage broke, and by the time the other one had fired a dozen shots the cap-squares came off the woodwork, the gun turning a somersault after each discharge. Of course No. 1 gun was useless, and it was most fatiguing for No. 2 gun detachment to have to lift the gun on to the carriage after each discharge, while the ground was strewn with friction tubes, fuses, etc. which had been jerked out of the axle-tree boxes.[136]

Perhaps out of frustration, Short led a second charge, this time "a dash for the Indian camp with a dozen or so of men behind him, but the fire was too hot and they had to retire."[137]

Otter's situation was deteriorating. His column was now deployed thinly over an area that was secured, but hardly under his complete control. His artillery capability was reduced, and he had no reserve other than Ross's five men, who had thus far survived. Otter could react to incursions or threats only by withdrawing troops from one area and shifting them across the several hundred yards of the plateau to another threatened site. At least twice he used Ross's scouts to assist in reinforcing threatened spots. Now it was the Queen's Own's turn to demonstrate how discipline and cohesion count in small wars.

The Queen's Own, following the Foot Guards, had been the last eastern militia unit to deploy into the line. For some reason, first-hand accounts from this unit are scarce. Rifleman J.A. Forin simply stated that the "QOR formed skirmishing line and I went to extreme left. Had hot fire thru [sic] my overcoat. Fighting continued for 7 hours. Enemy punished severely. Number of QOR wounded."[138] The only detailed account of the Queen's Own manoeuvring into the network of willow scrub ravines to the south was kept by Colour Sergeant Samuel C. McKell, whose diary was found in Otter's papers. McKell was at the forefront of this distinguished unit's actions on the left, and recalled that the Queen's Own

> formed the left front with the Battleford Rifles protecting the left flank and rear. We occupied a hill without cover on the left but owing to a heavy cross fire we had to retreat off it afterwards and we charged & took it again & held it for the remainder of the day ... it was here poor George Cooper was wounded also [?] Wounded in shoulder and myself hit on the temple & knocked down ... Afterwards we were told to send 20 men to help the Battleford Rifles to clean out the brush ... this we did I being senior non com [NCO] of those sent ... having no officer we went into the brush about 60 yds but the artillery then started to shell the brush or seemed to do so but afterwards I found out that it was a bush on the opposite side of us ... we retired out of bush & it was here that Lloyd was hurt. I ran up to carry him in but owing to have 3 rifles to bring in I made slow progress with him but Acheseon came up & took him by the arm & shoulders & dragged him along ... I helping with one hand & dragging with the other 3 rifles we carried him back about 20 yds when ambulance corps took hold of him we remained firing.[139]

Amazingly the Queen's Own had no one killed, but did have five men wounded. They were Colour Sergeant George E. Cooper, and Privates George W. Watts, J.S.C. Fraser, Charles A. Varney, and George E. Lloyd. All survived.

A possible Indian account fits with the Queen's Own actions on the left, nearest the web of deep ravines. Sapostokun, referring to the militia as "police," described the confusion of the fighting on this difficult ground:

> The report got around that the police were leaving so I came over the hill, but it was only a rumour. We were met by a volley of shots from the hill. When we were met by this volley, the police came charging up that hill, on the *south* side and we were on this side of the hill. We would come up and shoot at them and they at us and we had it out. Shortly after I went down to

a lower position when you can see the opening in the muzzle of the other fellow's gun. I did not have any one pushing me to get into the hear of the fight – I had good heart that would carry me through. Their shooting was so close that the dirt would be kicked up by the bullets ... into our faces as we ducked from the shots ... I came around and was caught on this side of the hill. I lay down. The rest of the Indians went over the hill ... it was after I came over [the] brow of this hill ... [the account then included details of the ground where he moved for the rest of the battle].[140]

Most accounts by militiamen of the action mention a lull in the firing sometime in the morning. Cassels wrote that the fire "of the enemy seemed to be almost completely silenced ... and before we left ... had nearly died," while, for his part, Winter noted that "for some time after early morning our men had all noticed the gradual dying away of the enemy's fire; the camp in the distance was seen to be breaking up, the cattle herd being driven off, and all signs pointed to an Indian withdrawal." Prower, with B Battery, observed more indecision on the part of Otter, as well as planning based on concensus. Prower was close enough to observe that at

Private, Queen's Own Rifles, on active service in 1885

Modern-day artist R.J. Marrion produced this image of a rather shaggy Queen's Own private serving in Otter's column in the NWFF in 1885. His tunic is entirely dark green and his accoutrements have been dyed black. He is armed with the standard .57 calibre Snider-Enfield "two-band" rifle. (Courtesy Canadian War Museum)

the time of the lull … the commanding officer with Colonel Herchmer came up to the guns and discussed the situation with Major Short … Herchmer seemed to be for getting back across the stream as quickly as possible. The major was for rushing the camp, but the commanding officer took the middle course and we remained where we were for nearly six hours.[141]

The Queen's Own action on the left blurred into the final Indian incursion, which was an attempt to infiltrate into the left rear of the militia-NWMP position. If successful, the Indians and Métis would have denied the column a route out across the Creek for the wagons and guns. Otter himself remembered that *both* the left and right rear flanks were threatened. He later wrote that

The right rear, which took in the ford, was menaced, and a part of the Battleford Rifles, under Captain Nash, assisted by individual men of "C" Company, Governor's Guards and Q.O.R., with Constable Ross (Chief Scout) of the Police, undertook to clear the coulee at that point; this they did most effectually, capturing four ponies whose riders were shot by them. A similar duty had now to be performed on our left rear which was entrusted to parties of the Queen's Own and Battleford Rifles, and proved one of the sharpest brushes of the day. The enemy's fire here was, however, only partially subdued, as there remained a few men whom neither bullets nor shells seemed to reach, and who were only dislodged at the end of the day by sending Ross with his scouts by a long detour to the rear and flanking them.[142]

Colour Sergeant Winter summed up the latter part of the morning in a matter-of-fact way, and expressed his disappointment about not seeking a battlefield decision:

about 10 a.m., firing from the enemy practically ceased, and for a couple of hours thereafter men lay on the grass in the bright sunlight of a beautiful May day, resting, discussing the morning's doings, and wondering what the next move would be … much wonder was expressed that we did not push on to the enemy's camp, but evidently our Commander felt that the object of the reconnaissance had been achieved in locating the Indians and preventing them – at any rate for a time – from joining … Riel at Batoche.[143]

During this period, Otter, Herchmer and Sears planned to withdraw. This was the only operation that they developed which used their firepower in a disciplined way, to exploit their technological advantage over the Indians. By concentrating their firepower they could move wherever they wished. All accounts agree that the conduct of the withdrawal from the hill, across the creek, up the heights on the east side and the subsequent 30-mile retreat back to Battleford, was accomplished with high skill and discipline. Here Otter's theoretical knowledge matched the discipline of his troops, and the two were an unbeatable combination.

Unlike at Ridgeway almost 20 years earlier, the Queen's Own did not bolt, nor did any soldier in B Battery, C School, the Governor General's Foot Guards, the Battleford Rifles or the North West Mounted Police contingent. Even the civilian teamsters did not panic. The steadiness of B Battery and the NWMP in

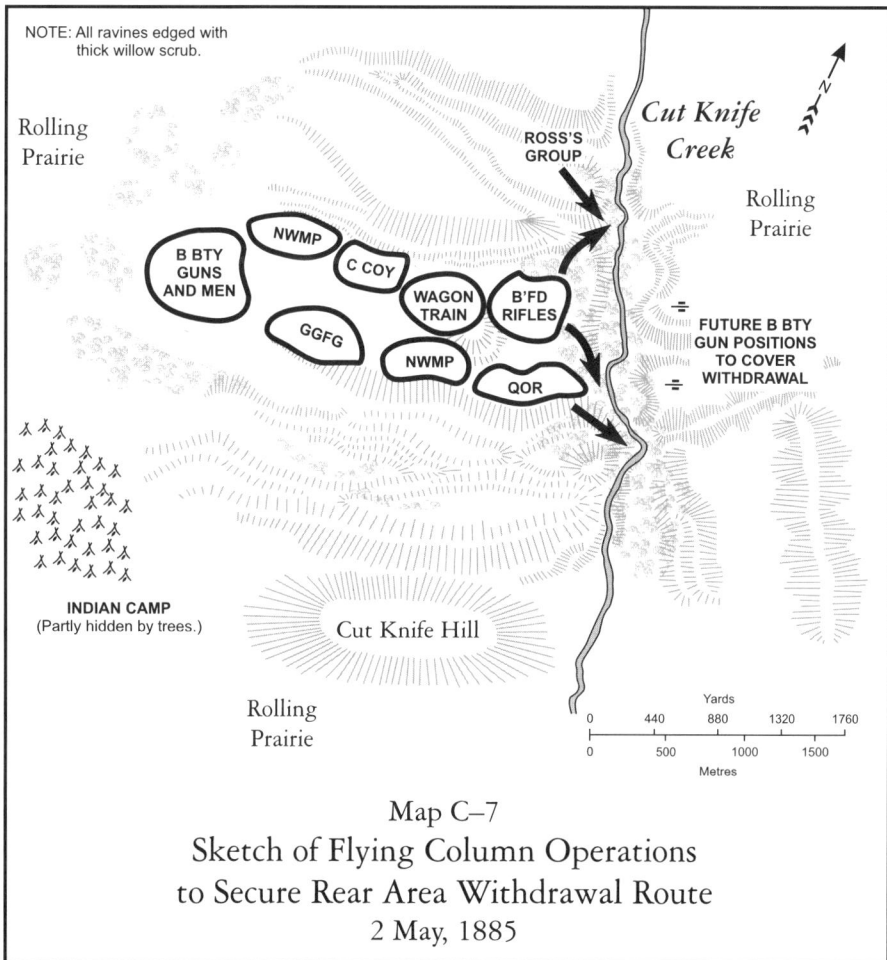

Map C–7
Sketch of Flying Column Operations
to Secure Rear Area Withdrawal Route
2 May, 1885

the withdrawal may have contributed to the solid composure of all other troops. The operation was conducted with crashing volley firing, and orderly movement was directed to the rear using controlled leap-frog fire and movement. There were no casualties sustained during this concentrated, disciplined phase of the Cut Knife operation, other than the death of a foolish English teamster who remained exposed in the willow scrub for one last shot. Prower remembered with pride that the retirement

> was as orderly and sedate as the advance on the field had been disorderly and confused. The men had got accustomed to the whistling of balls and the more nasty singing of the richochets [sic], and if they were retiring there was no doubling allowed: but alternate lines, composed where I was of garrison battery men and the Mounted police, retired at the quick, one line passing through the other, which knelt down and delivered fire. It was a pretty sight and very well done.[144]

The weight of contemporary evidence and later interpretations have suggested that, had Poundmaker pursued, the withdrawing column would have been destroyed. This was probably incorrect. Only one officer in the column, Prower, seemed to be aware of the inherent potency of Otter's column. Such lethality was not in the individual, aggressive power of Scout Charlie Ross's repeating Winchester rifle; it was, in fact, in the concentrated fire of the militia Sniders and NWMP Winchesters, *if they were controlled.* Prower was convinced that the column on the prairie, in the open, was so powerful that no Indian force could defeat it. When Prower saw that the "waggons [sic] were 'bunched' on the prairie about half a mile from the ford," he was certain "we were going to camp there, as our force on the prairie, near no brush or uneven ground, was a match for all the Indians in the North-West."[145] Prower was suggesting a "zareba" type of defence, which Middleton would use outside Batoche in a few days time, and which was standard British army practice when camping on open plains.

The staff work for the withdrawal was, by all accounts, excellent. Cassels remembered that when he recrossed the creek, "we found everything prepared for a start and we got in our wagons without delay and made off."[146] W.A. Harkin of the *Montreal Star* dramatized the withdrawal but nevertheless captured the essence of the operation:

Colonel Otter had already given orders to withdraw from a position of such disadvantage … Our troops fought their way out inch by inch, our front always to the enemy. No praise is sufficient to describe the bravery of officers and men. Everyone showed himself a hero. Colonel Otter with his staff was in every part of the field, and his orders were as cool and decided as if in a sham battle. Our men were badly used up before the withdrawal began.[147]

Toronto Mail journalist "Billy" Fox, who was present, later reported that the NWMP and Battleford Rifles "were ordered to fire the prairie and scrub to prevent the enemy from following us. This was done."[148]

Not even the most severe critics of Otter criticized his handling of this part of the operation. Needler, for example, declared that "the handling of that movement puts Otter foremost among the commanders of the whole campaign."[149] The irascible young journalist H.A. Kennedy claimed that the "victorious Indians, coming boldly out into the open, swarmed down after us over the battlefield we were leaving in their possession. They were checked by the steady rearguard fire."[150]

Otter's own account described the plan and the discipline of the troops as they executed it.

At eleven o'clock, that is, six hours after the beginning of the engagement, our flank and rear were clear, but the position we occupied was not tenable over night, while both guns were practically useless through broken trails, and the wounded required proper attention. Further, the object of the reconnaissance had been accomplished, inasmuch as he had declared his intentions, but Big Bear, or at least his men, had effected a junction before my arrival as the number of the enemy was fully five hundred fighting men, including some fifty half-breeds. I therefore concluded to withdraw and return at once to Battleford in case a counter-attack might be made on that place – placing the Battleford Rifles on the opposite side with one of the maimed guns, the wagons, dead, save Pte Osgoode, G.G.F. Guard, whose body had rolled into a deep ravine and could not be recovered, and wounded were taken safely over the creek, followed in turn, by the various corps …… A few of the enemy, on perceiving our withdrawal, followed to the edge of the ravine, but were quickly driven back by the Gatling, under Major Short, which brought up the rear and two rounds from the 7-pounders … under Captain Rutherford, with the gun bound up with rope and splints to keep it together. The crossing was effected without the slightest loss, and the enemy failed to follow, although, had they done so, much delay and loss of life might have been entailed upon us, as the country was favourable to them.[151]

Here Otter, perhaps underestimating his own power, was expressing his debt to Poundmaker for not allowing a pursuit. On the other hand, he discounted his other options. For example, if he was serious about seeking a decision against the concentrated Indian-Métis force, he could have sent for the remainder of his force, while he remained undefeatable in a zareba.

The Flying Column arrived back at Battleford at 11 P.M. that night. Cassels remembered that they drove

for about an hour and then stop and water the horses and have something to eat and not before we need it. We have had nothing since last night and are almost exhausted now that the excitement is over ...... The journey is very trying to the poor fellows who have been hit; they are made as comfortable as possible with blankets, but the jolting over the rough roads causes them agony.[152]

In addition to the initial casualties in the NWMP mentioned earlier, the following men were killed during the battle: Private W.B. Osgoode, 43rd Battalion, and Private John Rodgers, Sharpshooters Company, Governor General's Foot Guards; Brigade Bugler Foulkes, C Company, Infantry School Corps; Private Arthur Dobbs, Battleford Rifles; and Teamster Charles Winder. The total killed was eight, with 14 wounded.[153]

According to Douglas Light there were five Indians killed in the battle: Hole in the Nose, Medicine, Nahpatay Kesick and two unidentified, one Cree and one Assiniboine.[154]

The battle of Cut Knife Hill had ended but the controversy over this action had just begun and would continue for more than half a century. Foremost among the causes of this controversy was the the question of whether the plateau on which Poundmaker's camp was situated formed a trap for the Flying Column. An assumption that this was so pervades the evidence from the Militia and police but observers in the Indian camp both deny and confirm this assertion. There were several people in that camp who could read and write English and French,

Unnamed Cree woman and Miserable Man's wife with horse

Women played a pivotal role in Indian society in both peace and war, but there are few photographs taken of Plains Cree women at the time of the 1885 Rebellion. These two photographs portray typical young women who were present in Poundmaker's camp on 2 May 1885. (NAC, C-20854 and C-18963)

including two prisoners, Robert Jefferson, a 27-year-old Englishman farm instructor and school teacher,[155] and Father Louis Cochin, OMI, from France. Both were young and bright and provided a glimpse into Indian organization, decision-making, tactics and the effectiveness of the Flying Column.

Jefferson claimed that "since the outbreak" of the rebellion the Indian "tenting place had been moved" and up to the day before the fight the Indians were "in the valley of Cut Knife Creek" three miles from Cut Knife Hill. Further, he confirmed that the Indian Camp was moved deliberately the same day as the column left Battleford "over the creek on to the plateau that extends and is commanded by the [H]ill … scouts from the barracks – Halfbreeds – had espied the camp while it rested in the valley."[156]

Jefferson implied that the Indians knew that the column would follow the trail of the Indians up the plateau, because that trail "left no doubt as to the direction that had been taken and the scouts, following it, rode up to the top of the plateau and found themselves almost in the centre of the camp, which was arranged in a semicircle facing the east, flanked by ravines on each side, and sheltered by massed poplars and willows behind."[157]

From Jefferson's account we can determine that the warriors of the Assiniboine warrior society in the camp were nearest the vulnerable and open east side of the plateau. He also observed that the overall estimate of Indian combatants was much lower than the militia and police claimed. He described the Indian actions thus:

> The Stonies [Assiniboines], or rather some of them – had met the first onslaught, but were quickly recruited by Crees. Mostly young men … without any previous experience of fighting. Not more than fifty altogether, had taken part in the battle. This was excusable since few were decently armed, and the weapons and numbers and tactics of their enemy were new to them. As soon as the guns reached the top of the ridge, a rush had been made on them; it had nearly succeeded and caused the loss of two men.[158]

The militia illusion that the Indians were waiting in ambush for the column was also corrected by Jefferson. He reminded us that an "Indian camp can never be said to be asleep," and he confirmed that there had been an old man who was acting as a look-out. Jefferson's memoir fitted with the accounts of the column:

> [the look-out's] alarms and demonstrations quickly roused the sleepers and, when the first soldiers came to the summit of the rise, they saw the Indians – like ants disturbed in their hill – streaming in all directions from the tents, the whistle of shells and the rattle of the Gatling apparently cleared the front of everything moving before any opposition was encountered. The empty tents bore the brunt of the fusillade, an attempt was made by a few Indians in the first stage of the fight to rush the guns, which, had the attacking body been stronger might very well have succeeded. One old Cree and the Nez Percee were killed in this diversion.[159]

From the Indian perspective, Jefferson was very critical of the militia-police action on first contact and noted that the

> soldiers were so slow in taking advantage of their surprise attack that their opponents succeeded in establishing in a ravine that flanked the *east* side of the road up the hill. There, though only a few – not more than fifty – they kept up so continuous a sniping that the advance was stopped and the result was practically determined.[160]

This was Otter's enemy force on his right.

In Jefferson's opinion the Indians were now able to exploit their newly won initiative, since the fire from the two B Battery guns and the Gatling were largely ineffective. Jefferson described how the Indians used the ravines to their advantage, and also how exposed – and useless – B Battery was on the commanding position at the western end of the plateau, proving that ground of tactical importance in the defence is not always useful to support counter-attacks or battlefield movement. Finally, he asserted that the Indian warriors worked

> down the ravine, improved their position till they were potting the soldiers from behind as well as from the front and the side. The guns, along with part of the force, kept the mound that commands the camp but they had no enemy in front of them, and so long as they remained there, inactive, they were worse than useless for the enemy was gaining courage … from their elevation the [gunners] had a fine view all around and took pot shots at the odd Indians that they caught glimpses of, but they were themselves exposed to enemy snipers.[161]

Jefferson had a very negative opinion of Otter's handling of the operation:

> Had Otter followed up his advantage of surprise and come right on when he reached the top of the hill and instead of being awed by a few casualties, pursued closely the flying enemy, there is little doubt that he would have attained his object, as, in order to protect the women and children, the Indians would have surrendered.[162]

Jefferson also provided an important insight into the political circumstances in the Indian camp. He suggested that the Indians "might even have given in if a flag of truce had been sent forward instead of a Gatling gun." In Jefferson's view, knowing the Indians as he did, if the flag of truce and parleys had not worked and if "the Indians had elected to fight … [Otter] could have dispersed them with charges of horse." This was so because the "weak point of the Indian's case was their anxiety to keep the fighting as far as possible from their women and children." Instead, Jefferson mused, Otter failed because he "allowed them to fight on their chosen ground" - the plateau fringed with willow scrub-covered ravines.[163]

Finally, Jefferson summed up the dangerous nature of the operation by concluding that

Otter had been forbidden to make any offensive movement, so he called this a reconnaissance in force. Had it proved a success, it would likely have received another name. But for the grace of God and the complaisance of Otter's Indian opponent, it would have been left to strangers to name it, for there would have been no survivors.[164]

Father Louis Cochin, also a prisoner in the camp along with a number of local mixed-bloods from the Bresaylor settlement, was clear on the dates of events leading up to the battle. He remembered that the Indians "took us from camp to camp, till April 30. At this date, we camped on the shore of ... Cut Knife Creek."[165] Cochin confirmed that Poundmaker personally protected him and his Catholic parishioners among the warriors, "the greatest number" of whom were Assiniboines, but ironically so did the "several partisans of Riel" who were in the camp.[166]

On the morning of 2 May 1885 Cochin was aroused by the alarms of the Indians, and he remembered that they were "running in confusion towards the slope which descended the brook. Five among them had arrived at the summit of a hill and were already disappearing from the other side, when a shot from a gun was heard in that direction, followed immediately by a volley, intermingled with cannon shots."[167] Cochin was the second witness at the battle who suggested that the Indians, or the Métis, had prepared rifle pits:

> The soldiers, numbering two or three hundred, were on an elevated ground, flanked at a good distance by a number of small excavations, as in trenches, and from there they [Indians or Métis] could shoot without exposing themselves to any danger. Little by little they surrounded the soldiers. The shells, and grape-shot which fell on them made them feel anxious. Nevertheless at each cannon shot they replied by joyful cries, joined with ironical exclamations. Many seemed to be so little aware of the danger that they loaded their guns with their pipes in their mouths.[168]

At around noon, Cochin observed Poundmaker's action taken to stop an Indian pursuit.

> After a hard battle, the soldiers ... [left] on the battlefield one of their dead and a large quantity of ammunition, which the Indians gathered with ardent zeal. The Assiniboines and the Cree wished to pursue the soldiers, but

Chief Poundmaker, 1885-86

The best known picture of Poundmaker, it was taken when he was in captivity after the Rebellion. Although carefully posed, the photographer has nevertheless caught the powerful, almost magnetic, personality of the young chief. (NAC, C-1875)

Poundmaker prevented them. It was his intention not to leave his reserve, but only to keep himself on the defensive; and I believe that at that time the poor chief sincerely deplored this battle which came unawares, and which he would have preferred avoiding. In going over the battlefield I saw only five Indians killed and a few wounded.[169]

The evidence from the Indian camp, although clear on other matters, is not so certain concerning the assertion that the plateau formed a trap for Otter's Flying Column.

Otter, of course, submitted an official report which could stand as model of how such a document should be written, but a certain smell of duplicity lingers about it. Clearly his ambition had clouded his professional judgement. In his report, Otter totally avoided answering the big questions raised by the battle: Why had he gone in the first place? Why had he gone behind Middleton's back? What was the purpose of the operation? Was that aim translated into a plan, and subsequently into orders that were passed on to the scouts or the advanced guard? What was his response to the loss of surprise? Why did he maintain his priority of speed over security after he crossed Cut Knife Creek? We certainly know that a plan was not passed on to the officers in column. Otter's version of the battle differed from other accounts:

Crossing the creek our advanced guard, the Scouts and Police, were almost at the top of the lower hill before our presence was discovered, and the general alarm sounded hardly had our scouts gained the crest of the hill when the advanced part of the enemy was met, who opened fire upon our men with vigor – the Police immediately extended on the brow, and the guns, supported by

"B" Battery, were pushed forward into the same line, opening fire with shrapnel on the camp. The Indians who had evidently been taken by surprise, very quickly gathered themselves together, and attempted to surround; so large was their force that it required the whole of ours to be placed in the fighting line to meet the attack.[170]

This account seemed to answer the question why he had not exploited his mid-morning advantage.

For his part, Superintendent Herchmer's report of the action took only a few sentences and it concentrated on the initial action:

Our scouts, on ascending the slope, signalled "Enemy in Sight," and closed in. Fire was almost immediately opened on us, and a number of armed men were seen coming over the hill and descending from the camp. Before returning the fire our men were ordered to dismount and extend. Our dismounted party also came up on the double and extended, driving the Indians over the hill. The guns, manned by "B" Battery, R.C.A., got into action about the same time … [following the death of Sleigh and the mortal wounding of Lowry] … No. 36, Sergeant J.H. Ward, seriously [wounded], and … No. 402 Trumpeter P. Burke, mortally wounded … Both Lowry and Burke died the next day; Ward has recovered … The poor fellows deserved a better fate.[171]

From Herchmer's perspective as chief of staff, as well as a senior Mounted Police officer, a great deal more had happened than he chose to state.

As for the three "war correspondents" from Montreal newspapers who accompanied the Flying Column, W.W. Fox of the *Toronto Daily Mail* reported that

we saw a lot of cattle and some Indians on the low hills at Cut Knife Creek, and started for them. The police, under Herchmer, led, followed by the guns. All at once, on getting to the top of the hills, we came upon Poundmaker's teepees, about 120 in number. The Indians had laid a trap for us, lying in a huge semi-circle in the ravines and bluffs.[172]

W.A. Harkin of the *Montreal Star* contributed several vivid and detailed accounts using the same wording as Fox. Harkin perpetuated the theory that the column was caught in a trap.[173]

Howard Angus Kennedy, a young English journalist who was at the battle as a self-styled "war correspondent" for the *Montreal Daily Witness*, summed up many opinions when he wrote that Otter had wanted to "finish Poundmaker" but "got caught instead."[174] He wrote much, but few copies of the *Witness* have survived. Kennedy continued to comment on the battle for many years afterwards, downplaying the claim that the column was ambushed in a trap, and instead asserting a more serious claim; that Otter was defeated. He moved to the North West, and in 1924 led the criticism against Otter's version of the Historic Sites plaque which commemorated the battle.[175]

For the rest of his life Kennedy was soured by the notion that the battle had been a victory. In the 1920s he wrote a small textbook for the *Ryerson Canadian History Readers* series, titled "The North-West Rebellion," and in it portrayed Otter as a bungler, who was saved by the brains, bravery and cool discipline skill of the militia and NWMP:

Otter decided to take half his force and "finish Poundmaker," who was supposed to be in command of the Indians thereabouts … we started for the Indian camp … hoping to catch the "enemy" before they awoke in the morning. We got caught instead … the Indians rushed from their tents, and met us at the top of a long open turfy slope which we had climbed after crossing the … Creek … We were completely surrounded … Our men opened out in skirmishing order, lying down along the crest of the slopes and firing down into the gullies. They were as brave and cool as veterans … though few had ever been under fire before.[176]

Thousands of Canadian school children have probably read this version of the battle. In a later article published in 1935, Kennedy dramatized the battle, emphasizing that the operation had fundamentally failed:

"We're making history, eh?" The young Mounted policeman who spoke had been riding beside me in silence for an hour. Few of us were in any mood for conversation, and most of us could hardly keep our eyes open. The day before, we had set out from Battleford three hundred strong. We had ridden all night to catch the Indians at dawn, asleep in their tents on Cutknife Hill. We had failed. After the most disastrous fight of the campaign we were now in full retreat, carrying wagon-loads of dead and wounded.[177]

University of Toronto Professor G.H. Needler, who was at the battle as a rifle-man in the Queen's Own, also believed that Otter had fallen into a carefully laid trap and his criticisms of Otter and Herchmer were scathing:

> it is hard to believe that … [Otter and Herchmer] and their Battleford inform-ants could be such simpletons in the estimate of Poundmaker. Far from being any surprise, while … [we] were making … [our] night journey in wagons Poundmaker had silently placed a cordon of men at the edge of the ravines all along the three sides of the triangle … Otter's scouting as they walked into the trap was certainly lax, and the discipline of the Indians was perfect as they kept in hiding until the whole force was in it. It seems incredible that they could think there was not an enemy nearer to them than Poundmaker's camp, about two miles farther on, till all of a sudden bullets began to fly … just a matter of yards away. Otter got the shock of his life.[178]

Some militia officers in the North West Field Force were also critical of Otter. On 7 June 1885 Lieutenant Colonel H.J. Grasett, Commanding Officer of the 10th Royal Grenadiers battalion in Middleton's Column, wrote to a relative back in Ontario summing up the events in the rebellion. Grasett had not been with Otter, but as a Toronto militiamen he could not resist providing a brief glimpse of Otter's experience as well as that of a rival Toronto militia unit, the Queen's Own:

> Otter and his column are down in their boots at the comparative failure of their operations and they greatly regret that the success which followed us was not shared by them. From what I have heard of the "Cut Knife" engagement with Poundmaker it cannot be claimed as a victory for our side and it is now generally admitted that Otter made a mistake in attacking the Indians with a force insufficient to beat them. The march of the Q.O.R. on Battleford which had been lauded to the skies turns out to have been done in wagons, so much for "war correspondents."[179]

In contrast, however, when General Frederick Middleton retold his version of all the events in the North West Rebellion in 1893, including Cut Knife Hill, he had a good deal of praise for Otter's withdrawal. Middleton was also clear that Otter had been well served by both his militiamen as well as his staff. He made no mention of Herchmer, the NWMP, or Poundmaker and the Indians.

[Otter's] movement which led to the engagement was made without my orders, though … Otter had the approval of Lieutenant-Governor Dewdney, to whom however he should not have applied on such a purely military matter. Otter's force numbered about 325 men with two seven-pounders and one gatling, the enemy being estimated at about 200. After six hours' engagement, the trails of both guns having been broken, finding his position not tenable at night, and considering the object of his reconnaissance accomplished, he concluded to return at once to Battleford in case a counter attack might be made on that place. His casualties amounted to eight killed and fourteen wounded, including one officer … Pelletier, 9th Battalion, doing duty with artillery. Though this affair could not be considered a success, it reflected great credit on the untried officers and men engaged in it. The retirement – a difficult operation, especially with raw troops – appeared to have been remarkably well carried out by … Otter, who in his dispatch wrote very highly of the conduct of both men and officers, naming some especially, in addition to his personal staff, namely: Lieutenant Sears, 38th Staffordshire regiment, doing duty with C Company School Corps, and Captain Mutton, 2nd Queen's Own Regiment, Brigade Quartermaster.[180]

And what of Otter's perspective? His action on the Poundmaker Indian Reserve has been surrounded with confusion and controversy. To Otter, the militia, many Toronto cronies and newspapermen who were *not* present, the fight was considered a battle won. In the 1920s, Otter, then a general in the Canadian army, personally drafted the first version of the Historic Sites plaque.[181] He did this for good reason. Immediately after the battle, and for years afterwards, he had faced criticism about his unprovoked attack on Poundmaker's camp. At the least, many considered the battle an unnecessary action that resulted in a setback for the militia, who had attacked a camp with over 1,000 Indian and Métis men, women and children asleep in it, and failed to obtain a decision.[182]

In fact, Otter's attack had a *reverse* effect on the Indians, because Poundmaker – hitherto uncommitted in his support to the Métis rebels in Batoche – was afterwards forced to seek their assistance because Otter had removed the option of negotiation. As contemporary historians Blair Stonechild and Bill Waiser have observed:

By attacking Cut Knife, Otter had made a peaceful resolution of the situation extremely doubtful, if not impossible, and did more in a few short hours to push the Indians into the arms of the Metis than Riel and his followers had been able to accomplish over several months.[183]

These two historians buttress this assertion by pointing out that three days after the battle Hayter Reed, the controversial Deputy Indian Commissioner in Battleford, had advised Lieutenant Governor Edgar Dewdney of the North West Territories that: "This engagement ends hope of an amicable settlement of the difficulties that have risen ... It is probable that an Indian war is on our hands."[184]

But no Indian war took place. After surrendering, Poundmaker, Big Bear and two other chiefs were charged and tried for treason-felony, were found guilty and sentenced to three years in penitentiary. Poundmaker, "whose classical features and humble pride captivated the imagination of the press and public," became a subject of eastern Canadian sympathy. Petitions were sent to Ottawa, and he was released in the spring of 1886, having become ill, after having served only six months of his sentence.[185]

The controversy over the Battle of Cut Knife Hill has not yet been resolved and it is possible that it never will be. This study, which raises more questions than it answers, demonstrates that, by grappling with lack of evidence concerning the decisions and motives of the leaders, we can acquire only a superficial understanding of the battle. For example, absence of evidence has clouded the confused question of the government's policy towards the Indians in March-April 1885, and therefore the reasons for the battle in the first place. Neither Middleton, nor Dewdney, nor Indian Department officials in Battleford, nor the NWMP, seemed to share a clear idea of what was expected of them, and this allowed Otter to seize upon the self-promoting opportunity for an independent operation. Moreover we are still unsure of the pressures brought to bear on him. Otter's plans and decisions, along with Poundmaker's, and the influential elements in his camp, remain unclear, because they tended to be reactive and not proactive.

On the other hand, by concentrating on the evidence of the individual junior leaders and riflemen on both sides, we are provided with a clear understanding of the confused and frightening phases of the battle. We can attempt to understand the action through the experience of these men, and we can see images, as well as faces, emerging through the smoke and the Indian war whoops. These images and faces were missing in the official reports, along with any meaningful evidence.

Finally, there is another benefit to studying the lower levels of this battle: recognition is provided to those on both sides who fought bravely, with sincerity in their hearts, and whose names are long forgotten, on that grassy hill, 118 years ago.

The Cut Knife Hill Battlefield Today

Today, the battlefield is still part of the Poundmaker Reserve in east-central Saskatchewan, between North Battleford and Lloydminster, and it is easily accessible by car. The band has taken on the responsibility for the preservation and interpretation of the site, which is about 30 miles (about 50 kilometres) west of North Battleford, Saskatchewan.

There are two principal highways that bracket the Indian Reserve: Highway 16 (the "Yellowhead" Route) in the north, which is the main road through to Edmonton and the Pacific coast; and Highway 40, which is the main road west to Wainwright, Alberta, where it becomes Highway 14 and also proceeds to Edmonton.

Connecting these two highways is a partly paved and partly gravel road designated 674, which runs north and south beside the Poundmaker Reserve. The town of Paynton, Saskatchewan, on Highway 16 connects with 674 in the north, and the town of Cut Knife is at the southerly intersection on Highway 40. Both of these towns are off reserve land. Most modern road maps show, as a designated "point of interest" on 674, the "Chief Poundmaker Historical Centre," which is at the west end of the plateau where the battle was fought.

We do not know Otter's route from Fort Battleford on the night of 1-2 May 1885, but he was possibly on or near the first 20 kilometres of Highway 40. Travelling along this highway provides some insight into the country that he passed through, including crossing Drummond Creek, which his troops called Drum or Drumming Creek. Turning off Highway 40 onto 674, and then turning onto the reserve, visitors pass beside the actual Cut Knife Hill, just over a mile south of the battlefield. This is not marked but is easy to identify. For these reasons the best route to the area is the southerly route, although it may be about six miles greater to travel.

Once on 674 – from either the north or south end – there are signs showing the way to the Historical Centre. There is ample parking at the Centre, and a short walk away is the Historic Sites and Monuments Board of Canada plaque (the fourth version), which is set into a cairn. It briefly describes the events in Cree, English and French. In an arc surrounding the cairn are interpretive panels that explain various aspects of the battle. These panels, unfortunately, do not indicate the site of Poundmaker's first camp

*in the Cut Knife Creek valley, the route Otter used to cross Cut Knife Creek, or his route
to the battlefield.*

*There is a small museum in the village of Cut Knife, which is famous for Tomahawk
park. An enormous eight-ton stone is suspended as a tomahawk and serves as a symbol
of unity and friendship between the white and native communities in the area.*

*In Battleford itself – now a small town overshadowed by the larger North Battleford
– is the original Fort Battleford, operated as a National Historic Site by Parks Canada.
They are highly knowledgeable about the "siege" of Battleford and Otter's column when
it was camped in the area. On the Internet, the "Chief Poundmaker Historical Centre"
can be reached by entering the title in any major search engine.*

A Victory for
Citizen Soldiers

As the 19th century drew to a close, Canada's internal problems, as evidenced by the 1885 Rebellion, lessened and the new nation looked with confidence to a bright and shining future. An expression of this confidence was the nation's interest in foreign policy, an interest that ultimately saw expression in the government's decision (hastily made as ever) to contribute troops to the war in South Africa. Canada had sent contingents overseas before – the Papal Zouaves were raised in Quebec to defend the Vatican in 1868 and Canadian voyageurs participated in the Nile expedition of 1884 – but these were private, not government undertakings.

In the summer and autumn of 1899, as tensions heightened between Britain and the Boer republics in South Africa, English Canada began to agitate for Canadian military assistance to the Imperial forces. This agitation became a positive clamour after Boer forces invaded British territory in October, and in response the Canadian government approved the dispatch of a regiment of a thousand infantry to fight alongside Imperial troops in South Africa. Faced with opposition from Quebec, the government did not send units of the tiny regular army or the militia but decided instead to raise an entirely new force, designated the 2nd (Special Service) Battalion, Royal Canadian Regiment, from volunteers drawn from across the country. The 2nd (Special Service) Battalion may not have been popular with the politicians but it was widely supported by English Canadians and it was raised, organized and dispatched in record time. The first calls for recruits went out on 14 October 1899; less than 16 days later, the new unit was boarding a ship bound for the war.

It was fortunate that, despite the enthusiasm with which it was created, this new regiment had more than two months of training before it was committed to action. This was because the Boers, amateur soldiers only in name, proved to be skilled opponents who inflicted a series of embarrassing reverses on the British army. The Boers' qualities as soldiers became apparent in February 1900 when the Canadians encountered them in a major action fought along the banks of the Modder River near a little rocky hill the locals called Paardeberg.

3

"A most dashing advance:" Paardeberg

27 February 1900

Farewell to Manitoba

The Transvaal contingent leaves Winnipeg. This patriotic scene was repeated across Canada as the hastily recruited first contingent rushed to concentrate in Quebec City before sailing to South Africa. By the size of the crowd,
a high proportion of the population of Winnipeg must have turned out to bid the troops farewell.
(NAC, C-12272)

"A most dashing advance"

∞ ∞ ∞

Paardeberg

27 February 1900

Brian A. Reid

Good-bye Dolly I must leave you,
Though it breaks my heart to go,
Something tells me I am needed,
At the front to fight the foe,
See, the soldier boys are marching,
And I can no longer stay –
Hark! I hear the bugle calling,
Good-bye Dolly Gray [1]

Major General Sir George Colley[2] died badly. Bravely perhaps, for by all accounts he was a brave man, but he died stupidly and needlessly, and therefore badly. Things had not gone well for him from the very start on 10 January 1881, when he had marched from Pietermaritzburg at the head of an army he called "as queer a mixture as was ever brought together." It was hardly as bad as all that, but it still was a hastily thrown together hodge-podge, made up of 12 companies drawn from four different infantry battalions along with 120 mounted infantry-men (most of whom could not ride), a small naval detachment and six artillery pieces.[3] Colley, who was appointed Governor of Natal in April 1880 and had replaced General Sir Garnet Wolseley as the High Commissioner for South-East Africa, had mounted this expedition to put down the Transvaal Boers, who had risen in armed rebellion against the Crown on 16 December 1880. Within four days of their declaration of independence the Boers had surrounded and

---

* The orders of battle of the British and Boer forces on the western front are contained in Appendices 1 and 2 to this study.

"annihilated" a small column of British redcoats near the little town of Bronker's Spruit (now known as Bronkhorst Spruit), killing or wounding 155 officers and men out of a total strength of 259. The Boers acknowledged losses of two killed and five wounded. The Boers may have been regarded as rustic and untutored by the Imperial authorities, but they were nobody's fools; to block the expected British counter-move into the Transvaal, they crossed the border into the Crown colony of Natal and posted 2,000 men about Laing's Nek, the only pass in the Drakensberg Range through which the British could mount an invasion.

By 28 January 1881 Colley was camped at Mount Prospect, just three miles from Laing's Nek. It seems Sir George believed an unflattering assessment of the Boers written less than a week before they rose in armed defiance of British rule, that they were "incapable of any united action, and they are mortal cowards, so anything they do will be a flash in the pan," while ignoring a contrary report from the British military command in the Transvaal that there were "from 6,000 to 7,000 rebels in the field, who, under good leadership, would exhibit courage, discipline and organization,"[4] for in the next two weeks he fought and lost two battles and a third of his men. That Colley was a determined man is evident, as he wrote to his sister, "reinforcements are now arriving, and I hope it will not be long before I have force enough to terminate this hateful war." He decided upon a plan to seize the apparently unoccupied Majuba Hill, an extinct volcano that towered 2,500 feet above the camp, as he had appreciated that if the British held the peak, this would force the Boers to abandon their positions and allow him to march into the Transvaal. Given its importance, it seems odd that the Boers had failed to post a picquet on the peak, but this sort of thing happens even in the best of armies.

Be that as it may, at 10 P.M. on Saturday, 26 February, Colley led 490 soldiers and 64 sailors on a night advance, rather a climb, to the top of Majuba Hill. Just before four o'clock in the morning the first British scouts reached the peak and found it, as the general had suspected, unoccupied. Within an hour the main body was on the peak and deploying by companies around the perimeter, with some in reserve in the slight depression of the saucer-shaped peak. It is axiomatic that after a position is captured, the attackers must be able to defend it, and the preparations usually include digging in. Inexplicably Colley, who believed from the activity he had seen in the Boer camp below the mountain that the enemy were abandoning their position, refused to permit any digging and lay down to take a nap. If the general was prepared to be caught napping, the Boers were not. They may have been alarmed, they may have been surprised, but once the initial

Majuba Hill

The humiliating defeat of British regulars on this hill by a smaller Boer force on 27 February 1881 led to the hasty capitulation by the British government and a burning desire for revenge on the part of the British army. Nineteen years later the opportunity would arise. (From William Harding, *War in South Africa,* 1899)

shock had worn off, they were far from frightened. Instead they were furious that the British were fighting on a Sunday and a small force of 180 selected marksmen led by General Nikolas Smit soon began to make its way up the slope covered by a thousand Boer rifles firing from the camp. Colley seems to have had no other plan in mind than to hold his position, meet the Boers with a volley when they charged, and then counterattack with fixed bayonets and drive them back down the slope, just the sort of tactic that usually worked against natives armed with spears.

The actual battle went much differently; instead of charging, the Boers crept up on the British and mowed them down with rifle fire. By 1.30 P.M. Colley was dead, shot in the head while shouting orders to his troops, and the British had fled down the mountain in uncharacteristic panic, although isolated pockets held out until overwhelmed. In one of these little fights Lieutenant Hector Macdonald, an ex-colour sergeant who had made the great leap to commissioned rank, and 20 men of the Gordon Highlanders held their ground until reduced to a single soldier, and then Macdonald, with his ammunition expended, fought with his fists and feet while shouting great Highland oaths until he was literally wrestled to the ground by the Boers. (In recognition of his courage the Boers allowed him to retain his sword after the battle.) That may have been the only positive thing that happened to the British on 27 February 1881 because Majuba was one of the most humiliating defeats in British history – 180 Boers, mostly farm boys had assaulted and routed 554 British regular soldiers and sailors, in the process killing 93, wounding 133 and capturing 58 against Boer losses of one killed and five wounded.[5] The British army, however, had been humiliated before in the opening battles of wars and had a habit of rebounding to win the final victory. It was not to be this time. Prime Minister Gladstone's government capitulated with indecent haste and granted the Boers their independence; Queen Victoria was definitely not amused, neither was her army, which believed with good reason that it could have crushed the Boer uprising if the craven politicians had not intervened.

To the Boers, Majuba signalled the end of British oppression and the freedom to live their own lives without the ceaseless meddling and haughty condescension that had so endeared the English ruling class to their subjects from Dublin to Botany Bay. No one who was on the summit of that sugarloaf hill could have possibly foreseen that the Boer independence was destined to survive less than two decades, or that nineteen years later to the day the hated *rooineks** would erase the disgrace of Majuba near a squat *kopje* (hill) called Horse Hill, or in Afrikaans, Paardeberg, on the north bank of the Modder River.

E ven though the humiliation of their defeat rankled, Britain might have been content to tolerate the existence of the two impoverished Dutch-speaking republics of the Transvaal and the Orange Free State alongside the Crown colonies of Cape Colony and Natal had not gold been discovered in the Transvaal in 1886. Suddenly this nearly bankrupt republic found itself awash in riches. The Boers, however, lacked the expertise and population to exploit the find and were forced to accept numbers of largely-English speaking workers, the *Uitlanders* (foreigners) , to run the mines. Eventually there were so many foreign workers in the Transvaal that the Boers feared they might conceivably seize power at the ballot box and petition London to be re-absorbed into the Empire; thus the Boers saw nothing wrong in forestalling this possibility by denying the *Uitlanders* the

---

* *Rooineks* (red necks): a derogatory term for the British from their sunburnt necks.

franchise while imposing heavy taxes on them in a flagrant violation of the basic democratic principle of "no taxation without representation." It may have been, from the point of view of the Transvaal Boers, a necessary measure to ensure their national survival, but at the same time it was unbelievably ham-handed and one that managed to enrage liberals and conservatives alike.

While the British pursued the cause of justice for the *Uitlanders* loudly and determinedly, it seems that some of them had other, more covert objectives in mind. These included both obtaining the revenues from the gold mines and securing their hold over the southern tip of the African continent. Finally (and this was never very far from the surface, even if usually left unsaid) there was the little matter of settling the score for the defeats of 1880-1881. As for the Boers, they were stubborn, arrogant and largely ignorant of the outside world, always a dangerous combination. Contemptuous of British resolve and fighting ability, they convinced themselves they could defeat the British Empire in battle and that they enjoyed wide support among several European powers and the United States, who would often support any people fighting against Britain.

If there was a point beyond which war became inevitable, it was the Jameson raid into the Transvaal in December 1896, an attempt to overthrow the Transvaal government by a combination of a *coup d'état* and an armed invasion from British territory. The coup did not happen and the raiders were surrounded and forced to surrender at Doornkop on the outskirts of Johannesburg on 2 January 1896. The Transvaal government treated the captured raiders, who after all had no claim to being treated as other than brigands, with remarkably leniency, freeing most and imposing token jail terms on the leaders, who included a number of serving British officers. (Their treatment of the prisoners stands in marked contrast to that accorded by the Upper Canadian government to the members of the Hunters' Lodges captured after the battle of the Windmill in 1838.[6]) This blatant violation of the Transvaal's sovereignty not only hardened attitudes on both sides but alienated many Boer citizens of the Cape Colony and Natal.

To say that Canadians were generally ignorant of the issues involved would be a monumental understatement. Few Canadians knew or cared much about South Africa, except for the plight of the *Uitlanders,* a matter that had been largely created by a barrage of propaganda that painted the Boers in the darkest of colours. For example, Canon Knox Little declared in a polemic disguised as an essay that "it is probable that even the most corrupt of the South American republics cannot surpass the Government of the Transvaal in wholesale corruption." Knox Little must have been on a roll, for he then fulminated that the Boers

> detest progress of any kind, are frequently regardless of truth and unfaithful to promises when falsehood or betrayal of engagement will suit their purpose. They are subject to alternations of lethargic idleness and fierceness of courage which characterize many wild animals. Some of them are, of course, not bad fellows to get on with, if there is no reason for crossing them. They delight in isolation, detest work, dislike paying taxes, hate all progressive ways, cling to the most wretched stage of semi-civilization with unparalleled tenacity, and love what is called "independence" – that is, selfish self-seeking up to the verge and over the verge of license. They are utterly uncultured – indeed, have no conception of what culture means; their very language is incapable of expressing high philosophical ideas; and the pastoral home life so much insisted upon by their panegyrists thinly veils in many cases – such is the testimony of the many credible witnesses who have lived among them – the most odious vices.[7]

While the good canon may have been an extreme case, he was by no means alone in his efforts to create an atmosphere of animosity towards the Boers that found a receptive audience in Canada. This was true even in Quebec, where the image of the Britain bullying two small, non-English speaking republics did not pass unnoticed. In the summer of 1899 the Canadian parliament passed a resolution supporting the *Uitlanders*, although that was as far as Prime Minister Sir Wilfrid Laurier, who was faced with widespread opposition to war in the Quebec wing of his governing Liberal party, was prepared to go. Meanwhile many, but not all, of the Australasian colonies had offered troops to the British government and the Canadian Department of Militia and Defence had received a number of offers of volunteers from militia commanding officers. Moreover the opposition defence critic, Colonel Sam Hughes, had characteristically ignored the chain of command and, as a citizen of the Empire, submitted an offer directly to the British government to raise and command a battalion or even a brigade for service in South Africa.

As war clouds gathered and Britain began to reinforce its South African garrison, the British government sent telegrams to the Dominions thanking them for their offers of volunteers and providing details regarding the size and composition of the various contingents. Canada's quota was four independent infantry companies, each of four officers and 121 men.* While officially the Canadian government had made no such offer, the British were very well aware of the feeling in the country and hoped to goad the Canadian government into action. If so, the ploy failed miserably. Prime Minister Laurier restated his opposition to participation in an Imperial adventure in South Africa and then left on an official visit to Chicago.

In the meantime, on 9 October 1899, the Transvaal government issued an ultimatum to the British, ending with the note that if a satisfactory reply was not received within 48 hours, a state of war would exist. With no such answer forthcoming, on the evening of 11 October parties of Boers invaded British territory from both the Transvaal and the Orange Free State. This brought Laurier scurrying back to Ottawa to chair a hastily assembled cabinet meeting. Whatever the feeling in Quebec, English Canada was aflame with imperial enthusiasm and demanded a place in the war. On the 14th, the government announced that it was prepared to provide a contingent of eight companies, 1,000 men in all.

All at once the government had reversed its position and offered to provide twice the suggested quota. A few days later Canada upped the ante again by offering to send a complete infantry battalion instead of independent companies. This offer was accepted by Britain within days, but in the meantime orders had gone to the Military Districts across the country to begin recruiting men for the eight companies (see Table 1 below). Instead of mobilizing contingents from selected militia units, which would have unleashed an orgy of intrigue and infighting between militia regiments vying to be selected, and causing an adverse political reaction in the large number of units that would have necessarily been excluded, the government decided to create a new permanent force unit and man it with a regular cadre and volunteers enlisted for a fixed period of full-time service. In this way, as widespread militia representation as possible could be assured, while the regular Royal Canadian Regiment of Infantry provided a source of unit tradition and pride as well as a means of perpetuating any honours accruing from service in South Africa.** It was a typically Canadian compromise, a triumph of pragmatism and improvisation over principle and policy.

---

* Each company was to consist of a captain, three lieutenants, a colour sergeant, four sergeants, five corporals, two buglers and 109 privates.

** The award of the battle honour "South Africa" to a number of militia regiments came about three decades after the war, partly as an afterthought to the transferring of First Word War battle honours won by units of the Canadian Expeditionary Force to militia regiments.

What was the state of Canada's army in 1899? Traditionally the Dominion's defence had rested on two discordant pillars – the militia and the might of the British Empire. Those who believed in the former held that Canadian settlers rallying to the colours *en masse* had defeated both the Americans in 1812-14 and Papineau's and Mackenzie's rebels in 1837-38.[8] No matter how many times Canadians may have chanted the mantra, however, the truth was that British and Canadian regulars had done the bulk of the fighting and bleeding in both crises. Still, this myth had a practical benefit; it fostered the idea that every male citizen had a responsibility to come to Canada's defence in time of need.[9] Furthermore, for a government that refused to accept any meaningful fiscal responsibility for its own defence, the policy it fostered was, in a word, cheap.

Slowly and reluctantly, for Canadian governments avoided anything that smacked of military innovation and expense, the militia evolved from an organization based on compulsory universal service, the sedentary militia, into one that relied on formed bodies of volunteers, the active militia. The British noted with some frustration that the enthusiasm of successive Canadian governments for greater political independence did not extend to making any meaningful fiscal contribution to their own defence. Instead, Canadians placidly accepted reductions in the British military and naval establishment in North America as long as any additional Canadian spending on defence could be avoided.[10] In short, Canadians conditioned themselves to do nothing and hope for the best. Even the threat of Fenian invasion and the Red River rebellion of 1870 did not spur the Canadian government into forming permanent bodies of troops, that is, regulars. It was not until the British withdrew their garrisons in 1871, that the Canadian government grudgingly created two small artillery batteries to act as schools of instruction for the militia and to maintain armament and stores left behind by the departing Imperial troops. In the aftermath of the Red River Rebellion the Canadian government also maintained a rifle battalion manned by militia called out* for full-time service at Fort Garry in Manitoba until 1877. In 1883 additional permanent units of infantry and cavalry, known respectively as the Infantry School Corps and the Cavalry School Corps, were formed to take over the role of schools of instruction for their branches of the service. In 1885, when the Métis rebelled in Saskatchewan, the government rushed a hastily assembled force to the west over the partly completed Canadian Pacific Railway and crushed the uprising.

---

* The term "call out" is used in the Canadian army to describe a militia soldier "called out" or employed for a fixed period of full-time service.

Table 1 – Recruiting the First Contingent

Company	Recruiting Area
A	Manitoba, British Columbia
B	South Western Ontario
C	Central Ontario
D	Eastern Ontario
E	Western Quebec
F	Eastern Quebec
G	New Brunswick, Prince Edward Island
H	Nova Scotia

By the end of the 19th century the self-perpetuating militia myth had mutated into a dogmatically held belief that part-time Canadian volunteers possessed military virtues far superior to those of the finest of regulars. The militia had established roots in virtually every community in the seven provinces and many members of parliament were or had been senior militia officers, including both Surgeon-Lieutenant Colonel Frederick Borden, the Liberal Minister of Militia and Defence, and Colonel Sam Hughes, the Conservative defence critic. Furthermore, a succession of governments from both political parties had used the defence budget as a tool for dispensing patronage and pork rather than as a means of improving the country's security. Three decades after the Fenians had first revealed major flaws in Canadian defences, the militia was still little more than a cross between a service club and a volunteer fire department rather than an effective military organization, and was capable of little more than parading and strike-breaking.

The change in Canada's offered contribution from eight independent companies to a battalion, the Second (Special Service) Battalion, Royal Canadian Regiment of Infantry, created extra requirements beyond the initial 1,000 men. First, of course, there was the commanding officer (CO), a lieutenant colonel, who would be responsible for the success or failure of the unit. If it did well, the CO could expect to reap the rewards in praise, promotion and awards; if it did poorly, he could expect censure. While there was some latitude in shifting blame – the "shit flows downhill" principle – the consequences of failure in battle and the responsibility of command bore heavily. Fifty-eight-year-old Colonel William Dillon Otter was named to command the Special Service battalion as a lieutenant colonel; indeed he was the obvious and perhaps the only choice for the post given his stature and seniority. Otter had enlisted in the Queen's Own Rifles

Hurry up and wait, Canadian-style
This picture shows the First Contingent's troopship, the converted Allan Line cattle boat SS *Sardinian*, with the 2nd Battalion, Royal Canadian Regiment formed up, waiting for the order to embark. The cramped and primitive conditions resulted in the troops renaming the vessel the "Sardine." (NAC, C-12276)

in Toronto in the early 1860s, and his approach to training and discipline was coloured by his experience at the debacle at Ridgeway in 1866 when the militia had fled from a Fenian force of less than half their number. A member of the permanent force since 1883, when he had transferred to the Infantry School Corps, Otter had commanded the Battleford Column in the North West Rebellion. His penchant for strict discipline and "no frills" soldiering, at least for his subordinates, would bring him in direct conflict with the free and easy militia approach to military life. Once in South Africa, however, he gained the confidence of his British superiors and proved no more prone to stupid decisions than his Imperial contemporaries. William Otter rose against obstacles of poverty and intrigue to end his life as Canada's first general.[11]

Infantry battalions consisted of eight companies, organized into right and left "half battalions" of four companies each. To command the two half battalions, there were two majors, one of whom also understudied the CO as the second-in-command of the battalion and filled in for him in his absence or if he became a casualty. These appointments went to two regulars, both veterans of the North West Rebellion; Lawrence Buchan, an infantry officer and professional rival of Otter (to say they heartily disliked each other is not to overstate the case) was named second-in-command, while a gunner, Oscar Pelletier, received the second majority. There were other officer appointments to fill: adjutant, quartermaster, machine gun officer, transport officer and two medical officers, for example, as well as the staff non-commissioned officer positions such as regimental sergeant major, regimental quartermaster sergeant, chief clerk and armourer.[12]

In what can only be termed a near-miracle in organization and improvisation, the Special Service Battalion was assembled in Quebec City, issued with weapons, uniforms and equipment, loaded aboard a converted cattle-boat, the SS *Sardinian* and steaming toward South Africa before sunset on 30 October 1899. The unit, however, was hardly more than a collection of individuals; Otter considered most of the men were no better than raw recruits and fully half were without any military experience whatsoever, while the officers, who probably were a cut above the average of the Canadian militia, were the weak point of the battalion. In light of that unflattering assessment, Otter's emphasis on strict discipline and comprehensive training was not far out of place.* The battalion was fortunate that it spent two months training on the lines of communications after its arrival, with its only taste of action the inclusion of C Company and the machine gun section on a raid on the Boer enclave at Sunnyside on the last day of 1899.

In the meantime, the war in South Africa had not gone well for the British. The Boers, who enjoyed a numerical superiority at the outset, had advanced into British territory, trapping and laying siege to the garrisons in Mafeking and Kimberley in the northen Cape Colony and Ladysmith in Natal (see map P-1). Not only that but they had inflicted a series of humiliating defeats on the British army, destroying its reputation and ruining the career of its commander-in-chief in South Africa, General Sir Redvers Buller. It is not too much to say that the Boers had victory in their grasp by the end of 1899, but lacked the strategic

---

* To use the example of the creation and despatch overseas of the battalion in1899 compared with the time taken to despatch a modern Canadian Forces battle group overseas is mendacious; the differences in both the scope and complexity of the equipment and training are staggering. The only pieces of equipment in 2 RCR with any degree of technical sophistication were two Maxim machine guns and two heliographs in the signals section, while the only transport was seven riding horses.

vision, and the ruthlessness, to exploit the opportunity. It was a fleeting opportunity, and one that was lost forever; the British government undertook a massive reinforcement of its forces in South Africa and appointed Field Marshal Lord Roberts to replace the unfortunate Buller.

The successes of the Boer forces came as a nasty surprise to the professional British military establishment, which was, in a word, "regimental" in the extreme. In contrast to the tightly structured and highly disciplined British army, with its men recruited from the meanest social classes and its officers drawn from the aristocracy and the upper middle class, the Boer forces were very much a "peoples' militia," with every male of military age liable for service in local units called commandos, based on the peacetime administrative structure of the two republics. Unlike the British army, which had a ratio of infantry to cavalry of about six to one, the commandos were made up of mounted men, along with small professional state artilleries equipped for the most part with modern guns that outranged their British counterparts, and some specialist units and small foreign contingents. Furthermore, the Boers elected their own officers, and could and would change leaders if dissatisfied with their performance. Individual Boers, burghers, also had the option of joining another commando, and even withdrawing their services, if the mood struck them, or if the requirements of hearth and home dictated. Despite what must have appeared to have been massive structural flaws to the British, the commando system was one of those things that worked well in practice, if not in theory.

Boer tactics were rudimentary with little sophistication or subtlety of grand design: in the defence they would occupy a carefully selected piece of ground and defend it from small one- or two-man trenches; when attacking they would ride up and dismount under cover and then advance towards the objective, making the best possible use of the ground. It is interesting that the Boers would measure the range to various visible points from their trenches as an aid to controlling small arms fire, a technique that was not practised by the British army at this time. While their artillery outranged the British, it was plagued by poor ammunition and guns were usually deployed singly, with little effort to concentrate fire. In this regard the Boers suffered versus the British, who understood and practised the employment of massed artillery. The Boers also employed a few pom-poms, automatic cannon that fired a 37 mm high-explosive shell, but made no great use of rifle-calibre machine guns, while the British did the opposite but quickly adopted the pom-pom after encountering it in battle. In fact, the very existence of this weapon seems to have come as an unpleasant surprise, which seems a little

Lieutenant Colonel William D. Otter, Commanding 2nd Battalion, Royal Canadian Regiment

A tough, no-nonsense soldier with the soul of a bureaucrat and the charisma of a long-dead mackerel, Otter, however, possessed sound tactical sense and was no more prone to stupid decisions than his British contemporaries. (From William Harding, *War in South Africa*, 1899)

(Above) Major Lawrence Buchan, 2nd Battalion, Royal Canadian Regiment

Otter's second in command and Right Half Commander of the 2nd Battalion, Buchan was gregarious and outgoing, and his obvious concern for their welfare earned him the affection of the men of the unit. However, his personal antipathy towards Otter led to overt disloyalty which has sullied his reputation ever since. (From William Harding, *War in South Africa*, 1899)

Major Oscar Pelletier, 2nd Battalion, Royal Canadian Regiment

The Left Half Commander of the battalion, Pelletier was wounded in the night engagement of 27 February 1900. This was the second time he had been wounded while serving under Otter's command; the first being at Cut Knife Hill in 1885. (From Gaston Labat, *Le Livre D'or*, 1900)

odd as it was designed and manufactured in England. One last point: the Boers were armed with modern Mauser magazine rifles of German design that were superior to the British Lee-Metford and Lee-Enfield rifles.*

The British army experienced considerable difficulties in coming to grips with the unique demands of war in South Africa. The stereotyped tactics and rigid control that had proven so successful in the post-Waterloo era failed against the Burghers; the story of the private who complained that the Boers were not playing fair because they shot the officers first may have been apocryphal, but it certainly indicates a rigidity of mind set. To his credit, Roberts recognized the nub of the problem and set about correcting it. Tight formations and massed ranks were abandoned in favour of dispersion and fluidity of movement; however, it was harder to break the habits of careers spent in an atmosphere of tactical sclerosis, and it would take a post-war reorganization to set things right. Not everything needed to be discarded; in many cases adaptations were sufficient. In the attack, the forward troops still deployed as skirmishers in the firing line, while the remainder of the force formed in support and reserve "lines,"** although the men were spread out in depth and breadth. As the supports built up, the firing line was reinforced until sufficient firepower was massed to overpower the defenders. Then, a last volley and a charge by excited, cheering men with fixed bayonets would usually suffice to win the day. At least, that was the theory; unfortunately no one had bothered to run it past the Boers for their agreement.

As January 1900 ended, the Boers were deployed blocking the possible routes they appreciated the British must use if they attempted to take the offensive, that is, along the major railway lines. On the western front, the majority of the Boers were disposed in a large arc north of the Modder River based on the Magersfontein position under the commander of General Piet Cronje, who had taken the surrender of the Jameson raiders in 1896. Others were investing Kimberley and Mafeking, while smaller parties roved the countryside to deny access to British scouting parties. In all, the Boer forces numbered perhaps 7,000

---

* The Mauser was superior to most other rifles at the time. The United States army adopted a .30 calibre version as the Springfield Model 1903 after encountering it in Spanish service in the Spanish-American War, while, but for the outbreak of the First World War, the British army likely would have discarded the Lee-Enfield in favour of a Mauser-action rifle.

** The lines were actually made up of bodies of troops in loose or open formation; thus a support line might consist of several companies or battalions arrayed in depth.

to 8,000 men from the two republics, rebels from the Cape Colony and small contingents from places such as France, Scandinavia and the United States.

By early February 1900 Roberts was ready to move against them. The most obvious course was to advance along the central railway line, the very option that had formed the basis of the prewar planning; the field marshal, however, decided to base his advance on the western railway. The commander-in-chief, with 37,000 men and 36,000 horse, mules and oxen, would march 80 miles across country to the central railway below Bloemfontein, with a detour to relieve the siege of Kimberley. Roberts's striking force was made up of a cavalry division, 6th and 7th Divisions from the United Kingdom, and the newly organized 9th Division, composed of 3 (Highland) Brigade and 19 Brigade, formed from the second battalions of the King's Shropshire Light Infantry (KSLI or Shropshires) and the Duke of Cornwall's Light Infantry (DCLI or Cornwalls) and the First Battalion, the Gordon Highlanders (the Gordons) as well as the 2nd Battalion, Royal Canadian Regiment (2 RCR), all taken from garrisons on the lines of communications.[13]

To remove the army from the logistical pipeline provided by the railway required special arrangements for its supply and maintenance in the field. A large supply park of ox-drawn wagons continually replenished from depots established along the railway would trail the army, while horse- and mule-drawn wagons would accompany the divisions.* To mobilize this large transport network required not only pooling unit transport but also the collection of 2,000 wagons and 20,000 draught animals. Units were restricted to ammunition mules, a water cart, an ambulance or two, and a few light baggage wagons to carry no more than the barest of shelter and two days food and forage. While the massive logistical reorganization has been criticized, reliance on unit transport would have resulted in chaos, as well as the carrying of a plethora of non-essential items such as officers' mess furniture and personal kit, despite strict orders to the contrary. There is, after all, a certain irreducible minimum that must stay with the soldier: boots, clothing, load-carrying equipment and helmet; a field dressing; a weapon and as much ammunition as possible; and some food and water. (In 9th Division only 2 RCR retained their greatcoats, which were carried rolled and slung across the body.) As any infantryman worth his salt will tell you, everything else can be dispensed with, at least for short periods. The unit transport could carry a

---

* Oxen required a halt of several hours during the day to chew their cuds; thus, as their progress was usually slower than horses and mules, the practice was not to mix the means of transport.

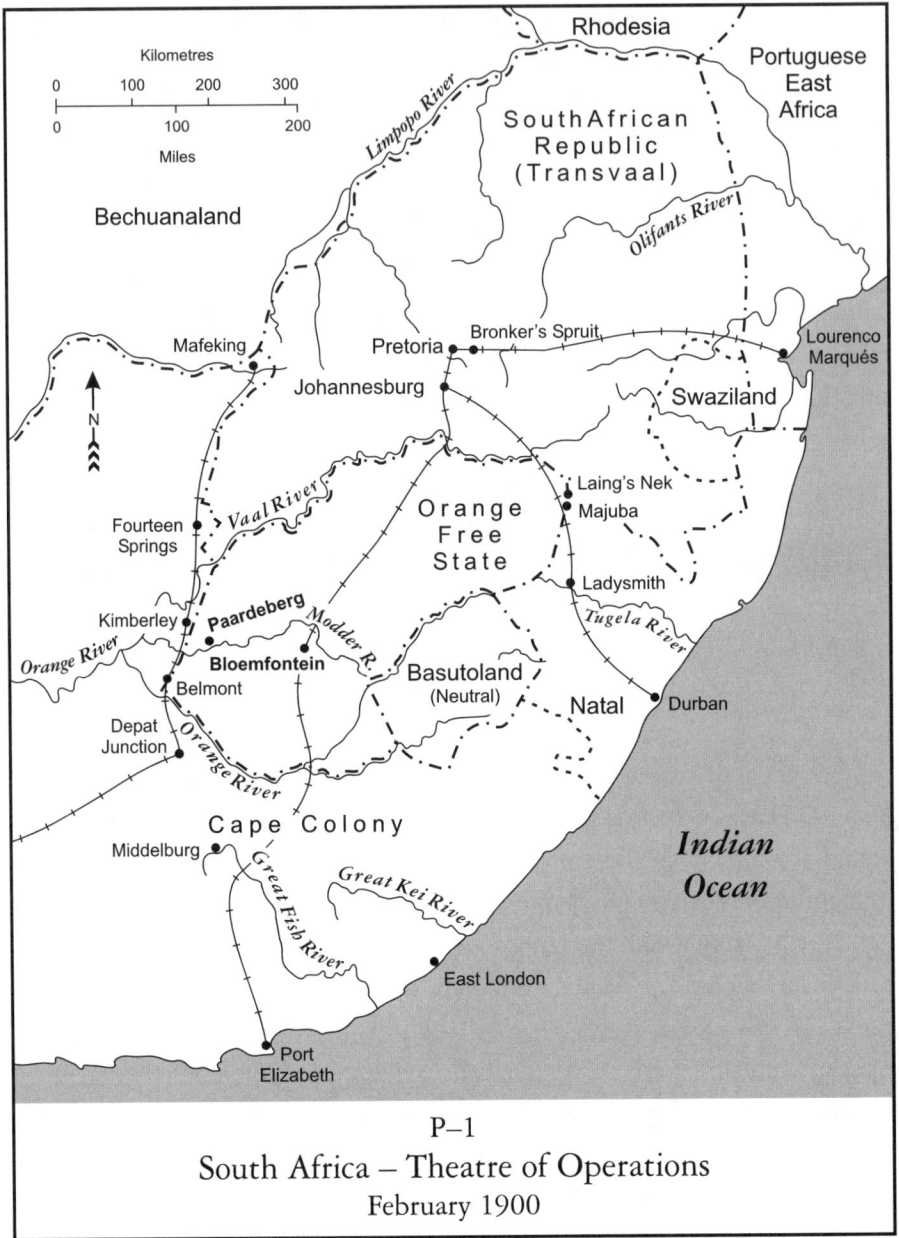

P–1
South Africa – Theatre of Operations
February 1900

blanket per man and a rubber groundsheet for every two.[14] Spare uniforms, tents and other such frills would come along later, if at all. Like the men, the animals would have to rely on forage carried with the army.

Late on the afternoon of 12 February 1900 the Canadians clambered on a train and steamed up the track to Graspan, the next station along the line, to join the rest of 19 Brigade (see map P-2).[15] Graspan was the jumping-off point for the British offensive, and the cavalry division and two infantry divisions were already marching into the Orange Free State. Nineteen Brigade would trail the army on the morrow. The brigade bivouacked under the stars and before dawn began to march east towards Waterval Drift* on the Riet River, which flows northwest to join the Modder near Modder River Station. The 13th was a desperately hot, dry day and progress was slow; upwards of 50 men dropped out, and although most straggled in later on their own, 14 men were unable to continue the march. The first day's objective, the hamlet of Ram Dam, a desolate farm squatting at the foot of a ridge, was reached in the early afternoon. Columns of dead-tired troops in sweat-stained khaki and burning boots wheeled into position and halted. Where was the water? All that was available was a slimy pool, alive with unnameable wriggly things and churned into mud soup by hundreds of animals jostling for space with men filling their canteens and cooling their bodies. After a hot march thirsty soldiers are not discriminating and the men gulped down canteen after canteen of the foul brew, one proclaiming that he had drunk five canteens and was still thirsty.[16]

The preliminary moves on 13 February 1900, especially by the Cavalry Division, had alerted the Boers that the British were up to something, but Cronje took little action other than to despatch *Commandants* Froneman and De Beer, with some 800 men, to attack the British forces in the area of Klip Drift. However, instead of launching an attack which could well have disrupted Roberts's plans, the Boers took up positions along a line of low *kopjes* and ridges, blocking the approach to Kimberley and Cronje's *laager* itself. The Boer commander had completely misread Roberts's intentions and assumed that the British could not move far from the railway and therefore were feinting to draw him out of the Magersfontein trenches to divert his attention from the main thrust, which must come either from Modder River Camp or Jacobsdal. His deployment reflected this faulty appreciation of the situation: several hundred men were sent to the west under Liebenberg and Breytenbach; De Wet and Andries Cronje (a younger

---

* *Drift:* a ford or river crossing.

Canadians on the road to Paardeberg

This picture of the 2nd Battalion, Royal Canadian Regiment, was taken on a rest halt during the pursuit of Cronje. The four officers in the foreground are (left to right) Lieutenant M.G. Blanchard, Lieutenant A.E. Hodgins, Lieutenant J.M. Ross and Captain H.M. Arnold. Note that the officers are wearing issue uniforms and kit and are carrying rifles. (NAC, PA-173037)

brother of General Cronje) were roving more than 30 miles away with some of his best mounted burghers; another 800 men were now facing Klip Drift, leaving him with hardly more than 5,000 men to hold the Magersfontein trenches facing the main approach up the railway.[17]

The 9th Division was to cross Waterval Drift, turn north and occupy Jacobsdal. After a march of 12 miles as hot and trying as the day before, the Canadians reached the *drift* in the early afternoon of St. Valentine's Day, 1900. If the troops were ready for a rest, they were in for a rude shock. Two naval guns were stranded at the *drift*; the combination of a mud-bottomed river, a few tons of heavy gun and soft, sandy banks being too much for the 32 oxen hitched to each gun. Detailed to assist in the passage of the guns, teams of 200 Canadians grasped long ropes hitched to the wheels and hauled the obstinate dead-weights through the *drift* and up the bank to the flat, open *veldt*.[18] Private Chester McLaren of B Company wrote of the afternoon's work at Waterval:

We reached here at noon and we did all this heavy work till 6 o'clock with only a hard-tack biscuit, but at 6 o'clock we had a good dinner served to us of fresh beef and soup, and we didn't do a thing to it. Oh, no! I was mess orderly for the day, and in addition to my share of the hard work had to get water from the river, a quarter of a mile distant, and get all pots and kettles ready for breakfast, and by 8 o'clock I was rolled up in my great coat and sound asleep. Shortly after the orderly corporal came around and ordered us to draw four day's ration of biscuits. We had to go from wagon to wagon before finding them, and before we had them distributed it was 12 o'clock. We only touched the ground before we were sound asleep. We were again called at 3 o'clock, and started at 5.[19]

This time it was the Canadians' turn to lead 19 Brigade, detailed to protect the rear of the army. Leaving a further seven men unable to proceed, the battalion moved off at first light on 15 February. The sky was hazy and a gentle breeze was blowing, which made the journey seem more like a pleasant stroll than a forced march. Before 9.00 A.M. the battalion had covered nine miles to the day's objective at Wedgraal Drift and thrown out a screen to cover the arrival of the brigade. It was a relatively easy day and from their position on the screen McLaren and his comrades were even able to watch the storming of Jacobsdal.[20] The same day Lieutenant General John French's Cavalry Division relieved Kimberley in a wild charge that swept through the Boer defences. Meanwhile, back at Waterval Drift, an ox-drawn supply train of 200 wagons was waiting to cross the Riet, guarded by a small body of mounted infantry. Christiaan De Wet with a thousand riders swept up the Cape Colony side of the Riet, brushed aside the escort and fell upon the wagons loaded with several days' supplies. Roberts, after some vacillation, decided that he must abandon the convoy as lost, as he was not yet aware that Cronje was offering himself up for destruction. He had to balance the possibility of jeopardizing his grand design against the shortage of supplies. Roberts persevered with his plan, the convoy was lost and the army went on short rations.[21] Despite Otter's initial belief that the seven Canadians left behind, unable to continue, had been captured, they were safe* and actually, in the words of the historian of the Gordon Highlanders, had foiled a "nasty-looking" attempt to seize control of Waterval Drift itself.[22]

---

* One of the Canadians, Private Gordon Corbould of A Company, then joined with some mounted infantry and was waiting to rejoin his comrades when they arrived at Paardeberg.

Meanwhile, Lieutenant General Charles Tucker's 7th Division had already captured Jacobsdal five miles from Wedgraal after a sharp skirmish with its Boer defenders. Cronje belatedly realized, after the siege of Kimberley was raised and his flank turned, that a noose was being tightened about Magersfontein. Before nightfall he decided to abandon his strong position north of the Modder and take up a new position to cover the route to Bloemfontein; he therefore ordered his burghers to congregate at his *laager* ready to march. At the same time he ordered Du Toit, *commandant* of the Transvaalers around Kimberley, to fall back to Fourteen Springs, and suggested to Ferreira, the Orange Free State head *commandant*, to retire eastwards and meet him farther up the Modder. Approximately 5,000 Boers accompanied Cronje on his march; of these, nearly 1,000 were on foot while the remainder rode indifferent horses.[23] Meanwhile French, out of contact with the main army, was pursuing Kimberley's besiegers to the north. On the morning of 16 February Lieutenant General Thomas Kelly-Kenny's 6th Division on the Modder spotted the dust from Cronje's convoy and began to race him for the series of *drifts* over the Modder. Boers hindered with wagons and families, and with many of the burghers dismounted after the loss of their horses, could still easily outstrip marching British infantry. The British had to stay close enough to catch Cronje before his entire party could cross over a *drift* and escape behind a mounted rearguard. A hastily mounted force was able to prevent a crossing at Klip Drift; the next crossing place was near the little hill called Paardeberg. Contact was regained with French just after dark and after that he dashed, if that is the correct term for weary men on exhausted horses, for the Kimberley-Bloemfontein *drift*.

Brigadier General Horace Smith-Dorrien's 19 Brigade marched through Jacobsdal; although the town had been captured on the previous day, and the brigade advance guard had already passed through, the troops were canny enough to search the buildings for lurking enemy, and food. Chester McLaren and his comrades "commandeered a good-sized calf," and McLaren was "lucky enough to get his hands on a pair of ancient hens," which proved too tough to eat, so they "drank the broth and ate the calf, and were full and contented for once."[24] In one of the homes Private Russell Hubly of G Company found an old gray-headed woman grieving over her husband, who lay dying of a head wound,[25] while Private Bill Warren of C Company had a more unusual experience; while checking a house, he found a dead Boer in a bedroom, and a frightened woman and her newborn baby in another room;* hastily murmuring an apology, he made his

---

* In 1918 Warren was in England, recuperating from a wound suffered at Passchendaele, when he was introduced to a young South African, who mentioned that he was from Jacobsdal. Furthermore,

way out, after helping himself to some food from the pantry.[26] At this time, which was no later than mid-morning, Roberts, who had established his head-quarters at Jacobsdal, still had not realized that the Magersfontein position had been abandoned. He first directed the 9th Division to guard against an enemy advance from the south, but later ordered Colvile to march towards Kimberley that evening. Shortly after 6.00 P.M. the orders were changed again, this time to march to Klip Drift.

Nineteen Brigade left Jacobsdal on a gruelling night march that did not end until dawn on 17 February when it reached Klip Drift. The brigade rested un-til late afternoon and, after a hasty meal, set out on another overnight march, trudging all through the night in the dust of the Highland Brigade. Marching by night was more comfortable, as the temperature cooled to the merely warm; against this, there was the poor footing and the danger of injury as men cursed and stumbled over the rocky, uneven plain.

Cronje, meanwhile, had reached Vendutie Drift just upstream from Paarde-berg, where he halted for rest and a meal in the late morning of 17 February. Oxen were outspanned, horses unsaddled and some of the burghers stretched out for a quick nap. Suddenly there was a boom, a swish and the explosion of a British shell. Smoke drifted lazily over a hill a mile and a half to the north; General French, with 1,200 cavalry and two horse artillery batteries, had ar-rived in the nick of time. The sensible thing to do would have been to salvage as much of the Boer army as possible, but Cronje refused to abandon the families and the supplies and resolved to make a fight of it from a hasty *laager* on the north bank of the Modder midway between Koodesberg and Paardeberg Drift. Once his wagon and animals pulled into the *laager*, the Boers began to extend outposts upstream and downstream along both banks of the Modder. This not only prevented any approach by the British, but kept open an avenue of escape, at least for riders, and, if they could extend far enough west, for the wagons at Paardeberg Drift. Cronje had no great opinion of British fighting abilities and expected to be relieved before the British could pound him into submission. Few of his subordinate commandants shared his opinion, and several, includ-ing *Commandants* Tollie De Beer, Grobbleaar and Douthwaite, urged him to take immediate action to escape, while *Commandant* Ferreira, who was now

---

the young man added, on the day he was born, the British had attacked the town and killed his father in the fight. Later, a soldier had searched the house, badly frightening his mother. After drawing a sketch of the house to establish his *bona fides*, Warren told him to tell his mother that she had had no need to fear his presence.

riding to his aid, sent in a messenger suggesting that he break out to the north. Although Cronje was determined to hold his ground, he was unable to prevent several hundred burghers slipping away from the *laager* in small parties, some to join the fighting outside the British ring, but most to return to their homes.[27]

The old fox had been run to ground but the trap was still not closed as the road to the south lay open. Soon a cloud of dust approaching along the Modder from the south heralded the approach of the mounted infantry. For the time being, Cronje would be in a trap of his own making, as the British began to build up a cordon around him, but the issue was still in doubt as commandos under De Wet and Ferreira had been summoned.* It would depend on who got there "firstest, with the mostest."

Cronje's *laager* lay on the north bank between two *drifts* across the Modder, which snakes in a deep, wide gorge across the *veldt*. The usually shallow river was in flood, with the current running at nine miles per hour. A series of *kopjes* ringed the *veldt*, close to the river in the west at Paardeberg, swinging out a few miles in the north, approaching the river again at Koodesberg, and running rather closer along the south bank. The dominant feature was a high peak, soon to be dubbed Kitchener's Kopje, near the southwest extremity (see map P-3). The position resembled a shallow, oval platter, with a gouge down the long axis. The *laager* formed a semicircle on the north bank with Boers entrenched on both sides of the river. Cronje's men began to extend their positions downstream to within a mile or two of Paardeberg Drift; they dug narrow, deep slit trenches, scattering the soil so that they were invisible from ground level. By the end of the battle many trenches would include a dugout in the walls to provide protection from the searching lead balls of British shrapnel shells.

Before dawn on 18 February 1900, 19 Brigade began to arrive south and west of Paardeberg Drift. All around were the sights of the battle to come. The Highland Brigade had deployed to the east of the *drift* and would later attack northwards at about the same time as the RCR forded the Modder. This attack would prove futile, although a number of Scots were able to cross the river between Paardeberg and the Boer outposts at the bend. Beyond them were the men of the 6th Division and some mounted infantry holding the ground they had taken up to block Cronje's escape. During the day, in response to Kitchener's orders, they would mount unsuccessful frontal assaults north and south of the

---

* Ferreira was killed by accident on 19 February, when he prodded a sleeping sentry with the butt of his rifle. The startled sentry clutched at his trigger and shot him. He was replaced by De Wet.

Boer tactics

A not too subtle example of British propaganda. Here we see some fiendishly featured Boers enticing pure-hearted British troops into an ambush by waving a while flag. (From Hopkins and Halstead, *South Africa and the Boer-British War,* 1901)

river. Batteries were steadily pumping shells into the wagon *laager*, just visible in the distance. Away to the east French's men were blocking Koodesberg Drift and warily probing the Boer trenches. In the early morning light of 18 February, Smith-Dorrien halted his three battalions, with the fourth, 2nd Duke of Cornwall's Light Infantry, still on the road escorting the division's transport (a duty taken by each battalion in turn on a daily rotation) and awaited orders. Lieutenant General Sir Henry Colvile, the division commander, was with Lord Kitchener, who had assumed command because of the sudden illness of Roberts. (His assumption of command was disputed at first by Lieutenant General Kelly-Kenny, the commander of the 6th Division, who was senior to him, until he was shown a paper signed by Roberts appointing Kitchener to succeed him.) The first order was to take up a position near some field guns to the south. There was no time for breakfast; instead a cup of coffee, a biscuit and a hurried rum ration were gulped down by tired men on empty stomachs.

Soon a staff officer galloped up to Smith-Dorrien with orders to cross the river and secure a feature, Gun Hill, three or four miles distant across the *veldt* to the northeast to prevent any escape in that direction. When he asked where

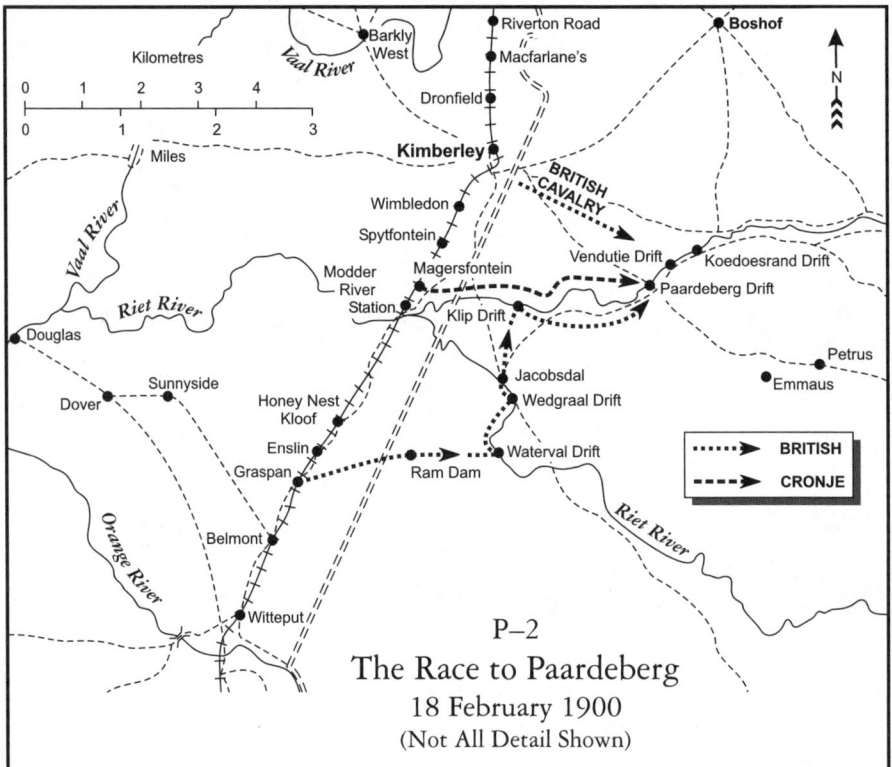

P–2
The Race to Paardeberg
18 February 1900
(Not All Detail Shown)

his brigade was to cross, the staff officer replied, "The river is in flood, and as far as I have heard, Paardeberg Drift, the only one available is unfordable; but Lord Kitchener, knowing your resourcefulness, feels sure you will get across somehow." With these helpful words, the staff officer turned and galloped off, leaving Smith-Dorrien to his own devices. The brigade commander, who, as a 20-year-old lieutenant, had survived the hell of the Zulu massacre at Isandlwana by a combination of guts and good luck, was not one to waste time. Ordering his brigade to follow, he galloped to the river; he must have still been fuming, for he unhesitantly plunged his horse into the rushing stream upstream of the *drift.* After regaining the bank with some difficulty and somewhat chastened by his brush with death, he moved to the *drift,* where he found that his horse could just get across without swimming, but the current was very strong and the river at least 50 yards wide. It was too dangerous for tired infantry encumbered with weapons and packs to cross unassisted. The engineers got a rope across which they securely anchored on both banks. Some men crossed by the rope, while others linked their arms for support. The brigade, as well as its supporting battery, struggled across through rushing mud-brown water that reached up to the men's armpits and completely submerged the field guns. Besides the guns, ammunition wagons and limbers, the only other vehicle able to cross was one of the Canadian Maxim machine guns mounted on large, two-wheeled carts pulled by a horse or mule, the other being temporarily out of action with a damaged wheel.

By 10.15 A.M. the crossing was complete, except for the DCLI guarding the transport and two companies of the King's Shropshire Light Infantry. As they crossed, the first battalions swung to the west to avoid Boer fire and the Shropshires secured Gun Hill by 11.00 A.M., after which the Gordons extended the line to the northeast. As the RCR crossed, they were directed to work up the bank and prolong the line from the Shropshires to the river. In the meantime, the field guns and the Canadian Maxim had come into action at Gun Hill and began to engage the Boers in the *donga* (gully) and along the river bank. In effect, the 19 Brigade deployment threatened the Boers and made their withdrawal east back along to the river bank to the *laager* inevitable; this makes what happened later during the day all the more tragic.[28]

Smith-Dorrien seems to have been seized with an uncharacteristic bout of inertia and allowed the Canadians to proceed in accordance with his ambiguous orders to cross the river and take up position despite his perspective from Gun Hill. It may be that he intended for Otter to picquet the crest and extend north-

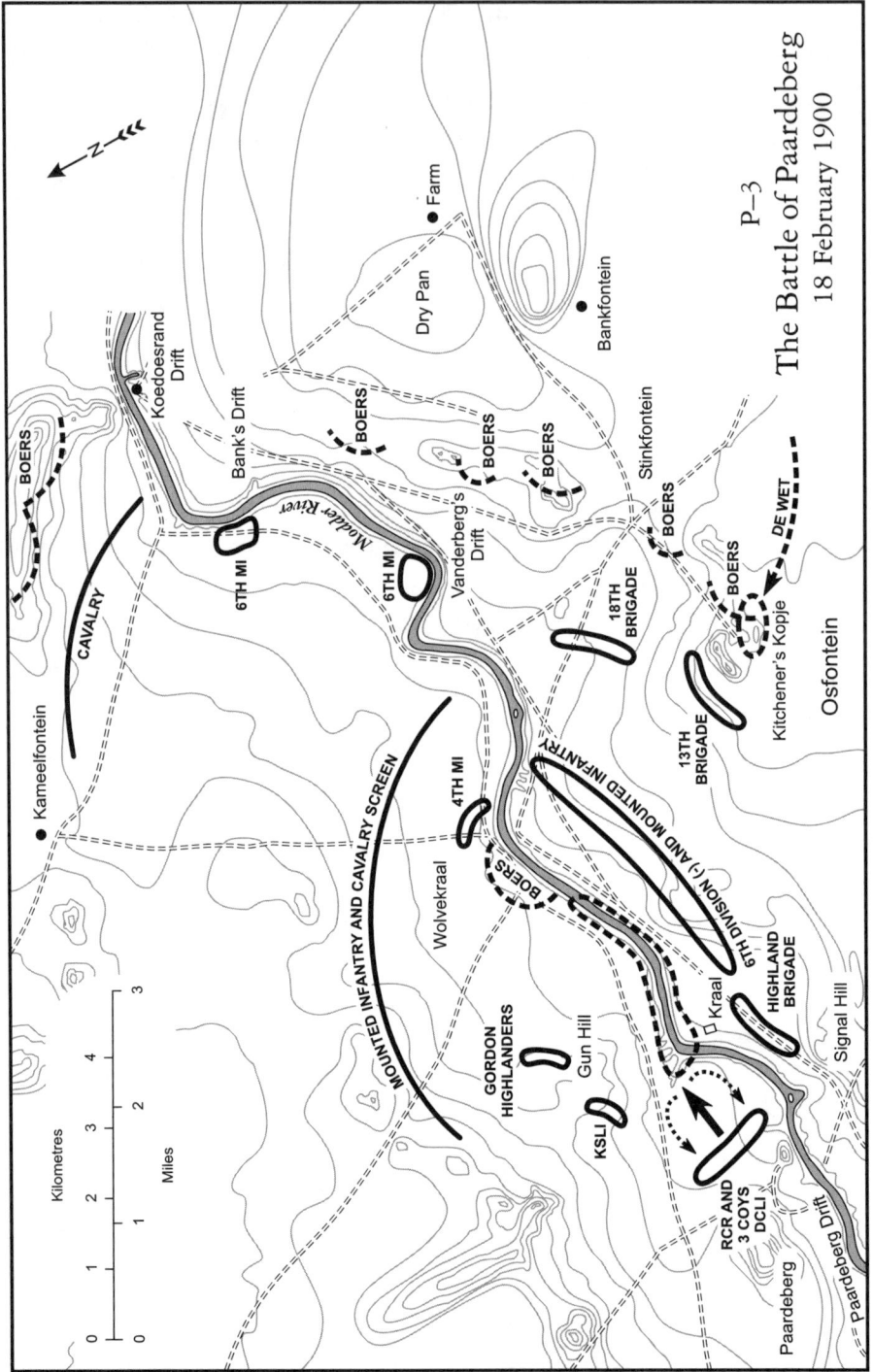

The Battle of Paardeberg
18 February 1900

P–3

wards from the Paardeberg feature, as he felt his task was to prevent an escape to the northeast, while Otter believed that the 9th Division had been ordered to attack with 19 Brigade left (north of the Modder) and the Highland Brigade right on the south bank. Otter was not one to question orders, and the Canadians had yet to experience how handily an unseen enemy could mow down exposed soldiers. The brigade was newly formed and had not trained together; it was incumbent on Smith-Dorrien to make his intentions perfectly clear to Otter, which he did not.

As companies emerged from the river they swung right behind a hill and ridge extending from the bank where a track ran from the *drift* to Gun Hill. The plan and formation were simple: A Company would lead, followed by C Company close behind, with D and E as their supports, while the remaining companies would be in reserve. Major Lawrence Buchan would advance with the firing line, with Otter and Major Oscar Pelletier doing the same with the supports. The spacing between the men increased to five paces (12-13 feet) as the companies moved steadily forward, crested the knoll, and headed down along the long, open forward slope. Private James Halkett Findlay, a 27-year-old from central Ontario, was struck by a bullet in the heart and became the first member of the battalion to die in battle. The open ranks of hunched men in wet, leaden khaki advanced steadily in long, thin lines until they were within about 300 yards of the Highlanders and within accurate rifle range of the greenery lining the banks, where the order to lie down was given, and the men dropped into the meagre cover provided by the little folds and the rock-hard anthills that dotted the *veldt*. On orders, sections then rose and doubled forward 30 yards or so, to drop and crawl into concealed fire positions again. Concealed sections should cover moving ones by fire but the presence of friendly troops to the front effectively prevented this. Still, the advance progressed slowly down the hot, barren slope as bullets snarled and screamed about the troops. Here and there, dark stains on still khaki forms dotted the field as Boer fire began to take its toll. Sergeant William Scott (a celebrated oarsman from British Columbia) died leading his A Company section in one of these short rushes. Finally, the Canadian line reached a point 500 to 800 yards from the Boer trenches; an A Company non-commissioned officer estimated that this had required no more than three or four rushes per section. Here the advance halted and the firing line opened fire, in a position Smith-Dorrien felt was "rather closer … than necessary" and well within effective range of the Boers. The firing line was reinforced with C Company, then with D and E and part of B. The rest of B as well as F and G Companies were a few hundred yards to the rear in support, while H Company was in reserve, but all were under Boer fire. As the firing line was built up, fresh troops were superimposed on men already in place; officers found themselves commanding men from a number of companies. While the advance by a series of short rushes, the reinforcement of the firing line, and the retention of supports and reserves were all in accordance with British doctrine, not all the problems of adapting tactical drills to South African conditions had been solved.

The troops huddled in the available cover and scanned the banks for a glimpse of the enemy. The day was very hot, the men had not eaten since the previous afternoon and the sun beat down unmercifully; even those who had been prudent enough to save a biscuit or two in their pockets found that the river water had reduced the hardtack to a pulp. To shift position in an effort to gain better cover or to escape the sun's relentless rays was only to invite a burst of well-aimed Mauser fire. In the early afternoon a violent thunderstorm soaked the Canadians without relieving their thirst or improving their firing positions. Among the men with rifles, who at least had the satisfaction of being able to shoot back, moved other brave men – stretcher bearers, ammunition carriers and chaplains – who courageously exposed themselves as they moved from front to rear and made the return trip. Captain Henry Arnold, the A Company commander, was shot through the head as he raised himself to scan the banks with his binoculars. Two stretcher bearers were shot down while trying to carry Arnold to safety on a stretcher; two more followed and one fell; finally Surgeon-Captain Eugene Fiset was able to reach Arnold and, after bandaging his wounds, bear him from the field with the aid of the remaining stretcher bearer. Several, including the battalion's Roman Catholic chaplain, Father Peter O'Leary, and Privates Curphy and Page, had narrow escapes as they selflessly laboured in aid of their fellow men.

Smith-Dorrien, in an effort to lessen the Boer pressure on the Canadians, ordered the KSLI to move forward and sent his supporting field battery to a position where it was able to fire directly down the *donga* and along the river bank. These moves had some effect, but the Boer fire persisted; and was taken by some for "overs" from the area of Gun Hill, which led to calls to "hold fire," which in turn only resulted in the Boer fire intensifying again. The Canadian advance on the right may actually have outflanked the enemy along the river bank, but no attempt was made to explore this approach. Whether this was because the fire from Gun Hill prevented the troops from moving forward, whether the tactic had been discarded as impractical given the relative strengths, or whether no one had thought of it, is one of the unanswered questions of Paardeberg.

Father Peter O'Leary, Roman Catholic chaplain, 2nd Battalion, Royal Canadian Regiment
Rather old for active service, O'Leary earned the respect and deep affection of the men of the Royal Canadian Regiment by his demonstrated bravery in caring for the wounded under fire at Paardeberg. In an era not renowned for religious tolerance, a Protestant soldier called him "the finest man I know." (NAC, C-006337)

Otter felt that while he was faced by 1,200 Boers, the situation was not difficult. (His assessment probably included those extending along the Modder holding the Highland Brigade and 6th Division at bay.) He was pleased by his men's steadiness and fire discipline in their first action, while he termed the Boer fire as "slow" as the enemy husbanded their ammunition until a Canadian exposed himself. Unfortunately fate, or British generalship, intervened in the form of Major General Horatio Herbert Kitchener.

Cronje could not escape without outside assistance. If the British cordon could be maintained, it could only result in his capitulation and a victory without heavy casualties; Kitchener, however, would have nothing to do with a waiting game. All day he ordered attack after attack on the Boers. Finally he turned to the 9th Division baggage guard, provided by 2/DCLI. Colvile was directed to order Lieutenant Colonel William Aldworth of the Cornwalls to cross the river and carry the Boer position, without passing the order through Smith-Dorrien, Aldworth's brigade commander. Taking three and a half companies, Aldworth forded the river and moved forward into the Canadian lines. Some writers have claimed Aldworth was overwrought or even deranged and had hastily launched an unauthorized attack on his own; in fact he had obtained permission to feed his men before crossing the river, not usually an indication of an overwrought officer, and Otter's report confirmed that the attack was a planned operation. At about 4.00 P.M. Aldworth arrived in Otter's position and imperiously told the

Canadian officer that he had been sent to resolve the situation at the point of the bayonet. One of his companies moved into the firing line, followed in about 30 minutes by the others. In the meantime Aldworth and Otter were discussing the enemy situation and the form the attack would take. Lieutenant James Cooper Mason of B Company of the Royal Canadian Regiment overheard part of their rather heated discussion (in their defence, both were under considerable stress at the time) and organized covering fire for the Cornwalls as they moved into a position to attack.

Finally, at 5.00 P.M. Aldworth decreed that a general advance would take place. At 5.15 P.M. bugles sounded the charge. Canadians, frustrated by a long, hot day under fire, leaped to their feet and, as a number of their officers shouted for them to fix bayonets and join the charge, surged forward as the Cornwalls passed through their lines. Private Douglas Williams, C Company's baby-faced bugler, stood to attention on an anthill and sounded the charge, while A.J. Cawdron, his counterpart in D Company and the ex-bugle major of Ottawa's Governor General's Foot Guards, found his bugle cords had become tangled with his rifle and, horror of horrors for a guardsman, was forced to adopt a non-regulation posture. The attack was a frenzy of cheering men running towards "the hateful line of foliage which had been spitting out death and destruction at us all day." At least 1,000 men must have joined the charge: 600-700 Canadians,

Bugler Douglas Williams, C Company, 2nd Battalion, Royal Canadian Regiment
A Canadian idol, 1900 vintage, Williams became a minor celebrity for sounding the charge at Paardeberg while standing to attention on an ant hill. His baby-faced good looks set female hearts aflutter across the Dominion and his media exposure for a brief while may have rivalled that of Otter; fortunately for Williams, it appears that Otter did not learn of this until well after the event. (From Gaston Labat, *Le Livre D'or,* 1900)

100-200 Highlanders and mounted infantry, and 300-400 Cornwalls, although some troops had fallen asleep as a result of a combination of stress and fatigue and literally slept through the charge, and Otter arranged to hold G and H Companies back as a reserve. Still, the number that did not charge could not have been large enough to affect the outcome, as the defenders' position was too strong for a rush to succeed. Lieutenant A.C. Caldwell, the battalion signals officer, wrote, "the charge came, and the fire was awful. I can't see how so few were hit. It is simply a wonder that the regiment wasn't wiped out to a man. …… The men dropped right and left, and the regiment on our right lost men in bunches,"[29] while in another officer's opinion, "It was a hopeless undertaking to cover 600 yards of open ground where the enemy had the exact range. When we started to move the bullets fell like a perfect hailstorm and the men fell by dozens all around me."

The main body of the charge faltered to a halt 300 yards from the Boers, although some managed to get much closer, and two Canadian bodies were recovered from within the Boer lines. Lieutenant Mason and Privates "Boss" Baugh and Richard Thompson of the RCR all later wrote that they came within 100 yards of the Boer lines. Aldworth, his adjutant and bugler and many of his Cornwalls died, while others lay groaning in agony. Dead was Private John Todd of A Company, a Spanish-American War veteran, whose last words were, "Come on boys; this beats Manila hollow." Dead too were White of B Company and Lester of E Company, the tallest soldier in the battalion. With them fell Manion of C and Lewis, seconded from the NWMP, of D, and several others. Mason, who had charged in the group that included Aldworth, was shot diagonally from left to right through the chest, but would survive to rejoin the battalion in the field. Private James Bradshaw, from Picton, Ontario, would have bled to death from a bullet wound through his neck had not Richard Thompson lain across him, applying pressure to his wound for seven hours until the regimental stretcher bearers eventually reached them. Others lay writhing and moaning until their comrades were able to creep out after nightfall and retrieve them.

Smith-Dorrien was horrified; his first impression was that the Canadians had mounted an unsupported assault. Only later did he learn that the charge had been ordered by Kitchener. Diplomatically he noted, "It was quite irregular that my troops had been ordered to execute such an important movement, except through me, as any possibility of my supporting the charge with the rest of the Brigade was effectually prevented, for by the time I realised what was happening,

Under fire

This remarkable photograph shows a left-handed Canadian soldier under fire at Paardeberg. His bandolier is clearly visible and the position of the action on his Lee-Enfield indicates that his rifle is cocked. (NAC, PA-181414)

the attack was over, since it only occupied a minute or two." Always the loyal subordinate, Smith-Dorrien told Otter no more than that he had not ordered the charge, leaving Otter in the dark as to the origin of the order. The first impulse is to blame Aldworth, but he was not the only one whose actions do not stand close scrutiny; he was the only one unable to defend himself after the event. Could the attack have succeeded? Possibly, if orders had been passed through Smith-Dorrien, and a coordinated operation mounted. There were claims that an attempt to contact him by heliograph failed because the weather was too cloudy! Otter had estimated the Boer strength at 1,200; while this may have been high, the enemy had already halted an attack by the Highland Brigade and were able to shoot down nearly 100 men in a few minutes. One of the Canadians wrote, "Of that ill fated charge of the Canadians, Cornwalls and A&S [Argyll and Sutherland] Highlanders … the less said about it the better. It was a charge that never should have been made." That was a poor epitaph for brave men.

To make a dark day darker, Boer fortunes took a turn for the better. De Wet with over 500 men appeared from the south and seized Kitchener's Kopje, unaccountably guarded by only a small party. If De Wet could resist British attempts to oust him, and if his forces were reinforced, not only might Cronje break out of the trap, but Roberts's army, already in a precarious supply situation, would be threatened.

Dead and wounded lay scattered across the field, and the Boers continued to fire at any movement. After nightfall the Canadians collected their casualties and withdrew to the area of the *drift*. Private T.H. Banton of the RCR volunteered to search for the wounded and remembered being "out all night until four the next morning, when I laid down, played out. I never want to witness such terrible sights as I saw that night again."[30] There could be no accurate assessment of the losses until daylight, but the first count was not encouraging; fully half the battalion was absent. The crowded field hospital about a mile behind the lines was already busy with the wounded from the long day spent under fire on the open *veldt* and Private F.H. Dunham from Toronto, who visited that hospital a few days later, remembered it as a terrible place:

The charge of the Canadians at Paardeberg

The artist, allowing free rein to his imagination, has ventured past the bounds of allowable licence into the realm of the sheer fantasy usually reserved for serious practitioners of recreational pharmacology. Virtually every detail of the painting is, to put it bluntly, dead wrong. (From *The Story of South Africa*, 1905)

Field hospital, Paardeberg 19 February 1900
A group of slightly wounded soldiers of the 9th Division resting by a farm house near the drift. Their more severely wounded comrades were faced with a long, uncomfortable trip by wagon and train to a general hospital back along the lines of communication. (NAC C-006097)

> Hundreds of men were lying in the worst stages … without a single nurse amongst them, with only a few ordinary privates to act as orderlies, rough and untrained to nursing & with only 3 doctors for 350 [wounded]. The patients lay in their clothes which have not been off for weeks & and they cannot get washed & they are covered with bedsores & other things, eated by flies, frozen at night, burn up in the day & got no medicine & of course died in hundreds.[31]

Through the night of 18/19 February, dead and wounded were brought in by search parties, while other men straggled back to a rationless, barren bivouac. When all were accounted for several hours later, the picture was not as dreadful as first thought – a small consolation.

Sunday, 18 February 1900, however, was still a bad day. It had cost 19 Brigade 228 casualties, including 79 Cornwalls from the three companies that had charged in the late afternoon; the RCR had fared little better, 18 dead and three more, including Captain Arnold, mortally wounded, and 60 wounded, or nearly 10 per cent of its strength. The total British casualties were some 1,300; five battalions lost more heavily than the Cornwalls and the Canadians on the first day of Paardeberg. Clearly this could not continue.

Through the next morning, 19 February, the battalion was occupied with the depressing task of searching for wounded and clearing the battlefield. The Canadians buried their dead, including 17 men in a long common grave near the banks of the Modder. Meanwhile, the news of the battle and its deadly toll brought Roberts hurrying forward with the 7th Division from Jacobsdal to take back command from Kitchener, and to change the tactic from one of frontal assaults to one of containment and siege. With the *laager* surrounded, he planned to have two brigades, one of which was Smith-Dorrien's, advance the trench lines towards it, one each from the east and west along the north bank of the Modder, while the remainder of his force maintained the cordon a safe distance from Cronje's men across the featureless *veldt*.

In the late afternoon the Canadians were ordered to occupy an outpost line some three miles away. By 6.00 P.M. the move was complete. It was not until two and a half hours later that the men had their first real meal in 36 hours, and the last meal had mostly been rum and coffee. The next day 19 Brigade occupied a line within 1,000 yards of the Boer trenches; the RCR, flanked by the Shropshires and the Gordons, spent a day under heavy fire, including the nerve-shattering experience of being on the receiving end of bursts of fire from a pom-pom automatic cannon. The firing line was protected by a ridge, but some rounds cleared the crest and dropped in on the reserves, wounding four men, the only Canadian casualties of the day. The weather was very hot and once again the men suffered from hunger, with only a single biscuit each to gnaw on, and thirst, as Boer fire drove the water cart back whenever it approached the Canadian lines. It was after 6.00 P.M. when the bone-weary soldiers fell in and trudged back to the barren plain by the Modder for another night.

That day Smith-Dorrien advised Roberts, Colvile and Kitchener that a frontal assault was out of the question. Instead, he proposed a gradual tightening of the noose, night by night, culminating in an attack when the time was right. Roberts bought the plan, but Kitchener urged Smith-Dorrien to attack immediately, suggesting he would be a "made man" if he succeeded; the brigade commander declined the opportunity.[32]

The Paardeberg battlefield resembled a large bullseye: in the centre the Boers formed the eye, with a circle of British troops deployed around them at a range of

1,200 to 2,500 yards and a larger outer circle running on the south from Paarde-berg Drift to Makow's Drift round by Kitchener's Kopje, and on the north by the Kodoesrand and Kameelfontein back to the Paardeberg. The troops in this latter circle faced outwards to defend against any Boer attempts to force a corridor through to the *laager*.

Despite the natural strength of their position, it had not been a good day for Cronje's beleagured force. The *laager* was shelled heavily, a pattern that persisted through the rest of the siege, and wagon after wagon caught fire and burned into a heap of twisted iron and ashes. The Boers could do little more than crouch in their trenches and wait until darkness provided a respite from the ordeal. The slaughter of animals, an entirely legitimate military target that effectively elimi-nated the possibility of escape from the *laager*, was incredible; if, as estimated at the time, three-quarters of the horses, and perhaps the same proportion of other animals died, then at least 3,000 animals perished in the *laager*. The Boers attacked the problem with their characteristic directness; the dead animals were dumped into the river to drift downstream towards Paardeberg Drift.

The 21st was a day of relative rest and quiet for the Canadians and there was a break in the monotony of the rations when a little fresh meat appeared in the cooking pots. During that night the battalion took its turn on outpost. Thursday morning, 22 February, the men were fresher than they had been since leaving Graspan hardly a week earlier, but all good things must come to an end, and nowhere does that saying hold more true than in the army. Nineteen Brigade marched handily out of camp to line a ridge line against the threat of a large body of Boers riding to raise the siege of the *laager*. The enemy failed to materialize; what did appear was a furious rainstorm that lashed the countryside and soaked the troops. The rain fell the rest of that day and all that night, only letting up in the morning, but then resuming and falling all night on Friday. With the regimental transport isolated on the other side of the river, the men were with-out their greatcoats and on short rations, thanks to De Wet. Blankets had been pooled to provide some extra comfort for the wounded, so many of the troops did without. That afternoon a party from A Company marched down to bury Captain Arnold, who had passed away quietly that morning; he had been uncon-scious since receiving his fatal wound and there never had been any chance of his recovery. Corporal William Hart-McHarg wrote of his passing

His death was a distinct loss to the whole regiment. He was the senior captain and was rightly looked upon as a particularly efficient officer. But it was to A

Company that the blow was most severe. He was an enthusiastic, painstaking and competent officer, and in addition to this had endeared himself to every one of his men by the careful manner in which he looked after their interests, and by the sympathy he always envinced in all matters relating to the internal economy of his company. He was exceedingly proud of A Company, and his men were equally proud of their captain, mourning his untimely death very deeply.[33]

In the meantime De Wet had been resisting all attempts to dislodge him from Kitchener's Kopje. Finally on 23 February, after five days and nights, he reluctantly left Cronje to his fate. The British cordon, however, was not airtight; brave men crept in and out of the *laager* with messages, the last actually leaving in the early hours of the 27th. When there was still a possibility of outside assistance, Cronje had discouraged any large-scale attempts to break out; by the time that he accepted that relief was impossible, it was too late for more than a handful to get away.

Meanwhile it was the Canadians' turn for some sorely needed rest in a position near the river on the 24th. Eight hundred and ninety-six Canadians had left Belmont on 12 February; this morning the battalion mustered 708 officers and men fit for duty. The combination of battle casualties, exhaustion, injury and disease had depleted the ranks by 20 per cent in less than two weeks. Heavy rain flooded the bivouac, and the troops spent another miserable night shivering in their sodden uniforms. At sunrise the battalion rescued their kit from the mud and water and carried it to higher ground, to spend the day attempting to dry equipment and clothing and enduring the horrible, sickly sweet stench of death from the carcasses bobbing in the only source of water. Otter noted that a new animal appeared every two minutes or so; the troops noted there was a distinctive taste to the tea.

The next day, 26 February, normal rotation saw the Canadians replace the Cornwalls in the forward trenches facing the west end of the *laager*. A Company crossed the Modder by a pontoon bridge near the Royal Engineers observation balloon and occupied a trench on the south side as a flank guard; C, D and E Companies moved into a long trench that was anchored on the river and extended a quarter of a mile inland; while the four remaining companies were in reserve a few hundred yards to the rear.

Twenty-seven February was the anniversary of the Boer triumph at Majuba Hill. As it happened, the brawny subaltern in the Gordon Highlanders who had fought the Boers hand to hand until subdued on the peak of Majuba Hill was now

Brigadier General Hector "Fighting Mac" Macdonald, who had been wounded leading the Highland Brigade on the 18th. He wrote Roberts from his hospital bed, asking that Majuba be avenged and the army's honour restored by forcing Cronje to surrender on the 27th. MacDonald was a national hero, especially in Scotland, and his plea must have carried particular weight with Roberts; Majuba would be exorcised. In the meantime attempts by the Boers to relieve Cronje had failed, and the slaughter of the horses effectively prevented any break-out in strength. Conditions were terrible; the din of the shelling; the shortage of rations; and, especially the stench of the carcasses that had not been dumped in the river. Shelters had been dug into the river banks, and the wounded and non-combatants were leading a safe but uncomfortable existence. There had been an attempt to build an improvised bridge, but it was destroyed by the British artillery. Cronje accepted that he must capitulate; the question was when. Every day he resisted was a day that delayed the British march. The symbolism of Majuba Day was not lost on the Boers, and Cronje finally agreed to surrender, but not on Majuba Day. However, the British bombardment on the afternoon of 26 February had badly shaken the burghers and, after a council of war, Cronje agreed to surrender at 6.00 A.M. on 27 February, a decision that was not communicated to the British.

Roberts's decision was more than a reaction to a plea by a wounded hero. Smith-Dorrien's preparations for the attack were complete. Nineteen Brigade had been reinforced by the Argyll and Sutherland Highlanders and two companies of the Black Watch as well as 7th Company, Royal Engineers. The forward Canadian companies were in trenches anchored on the river 500 yards from the Boer lines; to their left rear the Gordons, Shropshires and Black Watch lay on a north-south line threatening the *laager* from the west. Behind them facing outwards, the Argylls and the Cornwalls protected the rear of the brigade and the artillery on Gun Hill. Last, B Company of the RCR was detailed as the brigade reserve.

Smith-Dorrien appreciated the key to the *laager* was the Boer position facing him. If he could capture or dominate these trenches, his troops would be able to fire directly into the *laager* and the dugouts on both sides of the river bank. His plan was to advance and seize the Boer position by a stealthy attack; if surprise was lost before the trenches were assaulted, the troops would dig in where the advance was halted. The main attack along the bank would be mounted by the Canadians and the engineers; the Gordons were to be prepared to follow up the attacks, while the Shropshires and the Black Watch would support the attack with rifle fire from the flank when the attackers were engaged. Darkness precluded any artillery support for the attack.

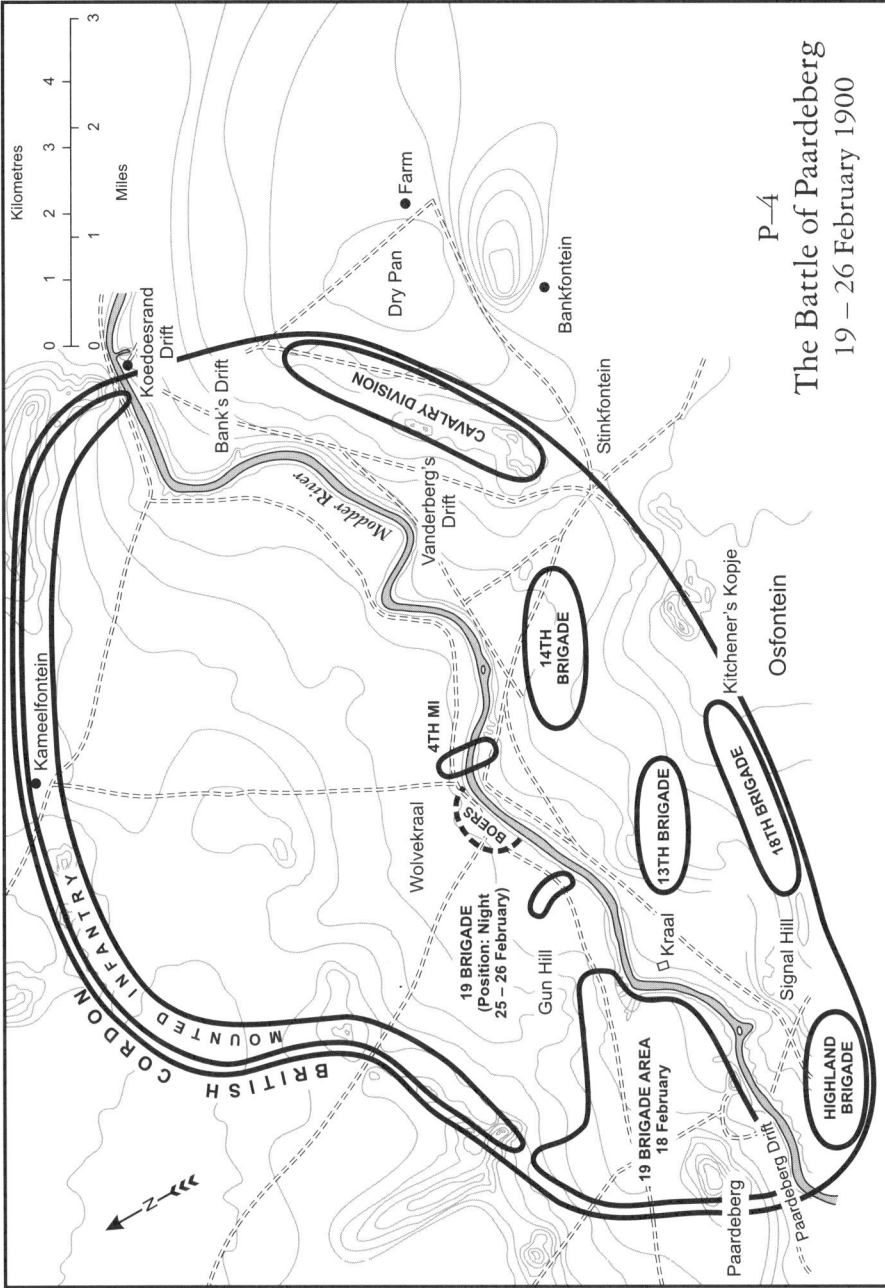

P–4

The Battle of Paardeberg
19 – 26 February 1900

The RCR would advance with six companies, C through H, in line in two ranks. The front rank would have bayonets fixed and rifles ready, prepared to cover the rear rank and the engineers, who had the vital task of digging in if the advance was halted. The rear rank were to advance with their rifles slung, carrying shovels; if surprise was lost they would drop flat and, covered by the front rank, dig in where they lay. To keep direction the ranks would advance shoulder to shoulder, with left arms grasping the rifle of the next man. Buchan would command the left flank and Pelletier the right, while Otter would move just to the rear of the left centre.

At last light the depth RCR companies, less B in brigade reserve, moved up to the forward trench. Smith-Dorrien accompanied by his brigade major and aide-de-camp joined the battalion in their trenches about 10.30 P.M. That night there was a "very heavy dew, wetting everything, but mercifully no fog, from which we had suffered on two nights lately." He would advance with his men and the engineers on the right near the river. Finally, the supporting Gordons moved forward to occupy the Canadian trenches; all were awake and at their places by 1.45 in the morning of Majuba Day. At 2.15, with a slight scuffling sound and the creak of equipment, 240 Canadians climbed from the trenches, paused sightly to set alignment, and moved off into the night; the rear rank, the engineers, the stretcher bearers and the brigade commander and his staff followed.

It was only 500 yards to the Boer trenches. At 20 yards a minute the advance would reach its objective in 25 minutes, but Smith-Dorrien found that "although I did not realize it at the moment, we were going slower than that even, and thinking over it afterwards I was not surprised, for it was a stealthy step-by-step advance in perfect silence, except for the occasional breaking of a twig or kicking of a stone – a movement most creditable to the troops."[34] By 2.45 A.M. the brigade commander was very anxious, anticipating perhaps that direction had been lost and the advance was veering across the front. Suddenly there was the rattle of rocks in cans hung on wire, followed almost immediately by a shot, a cry of pain and desperation, and then the flash and crash of a volley of rifle fire from the Boer lines. With the first shot the men dropped flat, avoiding most of the fire, and the front rank began to return fire, while the rear rank literally dug for their lives. On the left the night winked with flashes as the Shropshires and Highlanders volleyed into the *laager*.

Incredibly, casualties in this first engagement were light, except in F and G Companies, who lay closest to the trenches. Night firing is a tricky business, and the tendency is to fire high. Steadily, minute by minute and stroke by stroke, the

Canadian trench deepened. Progress was quickest on the right, where the ground provided complete protection for the engineers and H Company, who would escape without casualties that night. The battalion was in good hand and reacting properly to orders; Smith-Dorrien noted that the Canadians were firing volleys as the digging went on. Private Tweddell and his section mates in E Company were taken aback to hear a voice from their right shout out "retire." At first they thought the order was to fire, but a lieutenant leaped to his feet, repeated the order, and bolted to the rear. Men began to drop back in response to the order and the example shown by their officer. The Boers poured fire into the confusion and men fell. Panic, or at least the sense of self-preservation, spread down the line, although not all the soldiers heard the order or retired immediately.

Private Richard Thompson found himself alone while reloading his magazine during a pause in the firing and dropped back until he found the firing line a short distance to the rear. A private in C Company wrote that, once they came under fire, "we dropped flat, and gradually worked our way back to cover." This implies that some troops, perhaps most, retired under control, and G and H Companies under Lieutenant Macdonnell and Captain Stairs ignored or did not receive the word and fought on as their comrades fell back. The latter is more likely, for the heaviest casualties, 12 and 15 respectively, were suffered by F and G Companies, and a gap in the line, except for the dead and wounded, likely prevented the spread of the panic to the two right-hand companies. In the Canadian trenches the Gordons stood by, peering into the dark, wondering what was happening a quarter mile to their front, when suddenly, along with the crack of the bullets passing overhead, came the thump of boots and dark shadows leaping into the trenches. Contrary to what was later reported, the Highlanders realized it was the Canadians returning and did not resort to the use of the bayonet at close quarters, although a few Canadians apparently were injured in the confusion.

Otter returned disgustedly and set about reorganizing the battalion for the morning. He knew that two companies and the engineers were still in position, and therefore all was not lost. It was a small consolation for an officer who, for the second time in his career, had had his men break and run about him, the first being at Ridgeway in 1866. Otter and Forbes MacBean, the commanding officer of the Gordons, knew that Smith-Dorrien was still forward, though they could not know if he was alive or dead. By the time a coherent picture began to emerge it was short hours before dawn and it was clear that G and H Companies were still fighting the Boers; there was nothing to do but wait it out.

P-5

The Battle of Paardeberg
Night of 26 – 27 February 1900

When the forward trench was completed, the Maritimers of G and H Companies had gratefully moved back into it and continued the fight. Finally the sky lightened in the east over the *laager* and objects became clearer. The trench anchored on the river bank dominated the Boer trenches and, as expected, allowed fire from covered positions into the *laager* and the dugouts in the river bank. A building across the river provided cover for riflemen to shoot the length of the Canadian trench, so Smith-Dorrien hastily sent orders back, and A Company captured it without incident. Checkmate![35]

As the sky lightened, the Canadians could see huddled forms lying on the open, coverless field. From the main trench men could make out a body near the Boer lines that seemed to be gesturing for help. A corporal in the Cape Bearer Company asked for a volunteer to bring him in; Private Richard Thompson, who had saved Bradshaw's life on 18 February, lay down his rifle, lit his pipe, nodded to his comrades and drew himself out of the trench. Somehow he managed to cover the long quarter mile to the body; the Boers usually shot anyone who approached their lines, not as much from brutality as from ignorance of the conventions of war, except perhaps under a flag of truce. Inexplicably the proverbial luck was with the Irish-born Thompson, who reached the body, determined that the man was dead and made his way back to the safety of the trench.

Pausing only to retrieve some personal effects, he returned to the Canadian lines and jumped down into the protection of the trench. A short time later, Thompson left the protection of the trench again to go to the aid of another man who appeared to be in need of assistance, but who also was dead when he was reached. Thompson's bravery on 18 February and on this occasion was rewarded with one of the four scarves crocheted by Queen Victoria for presentation to the "four most distinguished private soldiers in the Colonial Forces of Canada, Australia, New Zealand and South Africa."* In an era that made a fetish of personal courage, Richard Thompson stands with the very bravest in an army of brave men.[36]

There had been attempts by some of the Boers to give up, but the troops had heard too many stories of feigned surrenders to take them seriously. Smith-Dorrien finally called to the enemy to surrender and the trenches spouted a sea of white as bitter, bearded men began to emerge and throw their rifles to the ground.

---

* Contrary to popular lore, these scarves are not the equivalent of and certainly do not rank above the Victoria Cross, and Thompson was not recommended for the VC at Paardeberg. While a highly respected mark of distinction, the scarves have no status as a gallantry award.

So many popped out of holes that the brigade commander was prompted to quip that it was just like the resurrection. Soon a large white flag was raised over the *laager* itself; Paardeberg was won.[37]

There was still, however, the matter of the unplanned Canadian withdrawal during the night of 26/27 February. Otter could not have been pleased with the retrograde movement just when it seemed that success was near. Not only had his troops broken, but he and Buchan had been unable to stem the tide. To make matters even worse, Oscar Pelletier, his other major, had returned to the Canadian lines with what Otter considered a minor wound,* leaving his two forward company commanders directly under the command of his brigade commander. The sudden blossoming of white flags surely buoyed his morale; with victory assured the retreat would soon be forgotten. With long lines of Boers despondently trudging into camp and Roberts's congratulations fresh in his ears, Otter discretely let the matter drop. He would have been even more inclined to accept the inevitable that afternoon when he received a personal note and two bottles of champagne from "Fighting Mac" Macdonald, the hero of Majuba. It is doubtful that knowledge of the withdrawal was widespread: Smith-Dorrien glossed over it in his memoirs; the Gordon Highlanders' historian barely mentioned it; and Sir Arthur Conan Doyle called it "a planned manoeuvre" in his popular history of the war. Occurrences of this type are more commonplace than one would imagine. All regiments in all armies have days they would rather not discuss; the Highland Brigade, for example, had broken and run twice at Magersfontein, so fingers were unlikely to be pointed.[38]

The mystery that will probably remain unsolved is who caused the sudden retreat. There has been speculation that the order to retire came from Boer lips, or even from a renegade Canadian in their ranks. However, at the time few suggested the withdrawal was the result of a clever Boer ruse. In an attempt to put the matter to rest, Marquis wrote that the culprit died that night. The command "Retire and bring in your wounded" appeared in Otter's formal report, submitted after the battalion returned to Canada. However it is not clear that Otter heard the order himself; his first report to Ottawa and the unit's staff diary only mention the word "retire," once with reference to a call to bring back the wounded, and the other without any mention of any such call. Private Tweddell of E Company, who heard the call, recorded it as "retire" in his diary, although there may have been other, later calls to bring back the wounded and he also noted

---

* Pelletier had also been wounded while serving under Otter's command at Cut Knife Hill in 1885.

Boer prisoners after Paardeberg. Hurry up and wait, Boer-style.
Here a group of Boer prisoners are waiting to begin their long trip into captivity on the island of Sainte Helena in the south Atlantic. (NAC, C-024559)

that one of his company officers repeated the order, and then set the example by leaping to his feet and bolting to the rear. The company was later cautioned to never mention the incident. What was the intention of the order? Perhaps it may have been for the front rank to fall back to occupy a trench, which was not yet complete. Perhaps a company officer or a section commander decided to regroup his men in an attempt to outflank the enemy trenches or to move to a less-exposed position. Perhaps someone panicked. The rear rank, lying prone and hacking at the hard ground with shovels, could not have known the order was not for them and dropped back. If the front rank could not find an obvious place to halt, the tendency would have been to keep falling back. Withdrawals under fire are notoriously difficult, especially at night, and Murphy's inexorable law invariably rules. Circumstantial evidence suggests the order came from someone in the immediate area of E or F Companies, and one may speculate that while Otter may not have considered Major Pelletier to have been the culprit, he did blame him for not maintaining tighter control over his half of the battalion. In any case, within hours it mattered not. The Boers surrendered, Roberts lavished praise on the Canadians, and the matter was discreetly dropped.[39]

There have been questions as to whether the attack mounted on 27 February was necessary, especially as Roberts had spent, or wasted if you prefer, over a week besieging the Boers trapped on the edge of the Modder River. Emotion and symbolism no doubt played a part, but there were sound military reasons for attacking. Smith-Dorrien had reported to Roberts that his preparations were complete on the 26th. While it has been suggested that Roberts knew Cronje must soon surrender, he did not know when or how much longer he could maintain his defences. Roberts, therefore, would be inclined to attack once all was ready, and that was during the early morning hours of 27 February. To attack when he did was a sound military decision.

Smith-Dorrien had reported the early surrender to Colvile* and Roberts, followed by the welcome news of a general capitulation. In return the field marshal ordered 19 Brigade to occupy the Boer *laager*. By 9.30 A.M. lines of khaki-clad infantry advanced past the Boer trenches and into the heart of the devastated *laager*. The troops who moved forward warily with bayonets fixed and rifles at the ready found a scene that defied imagination; for the first time, the effects of the concentrated shelling could be examined at first hand. Virtually all the Boer wagons and carts were shattered hulks; clustered where they fell lay the loathsome carcasses of dead animals that had not been tipped into the Modder. Altogether 4,100 Boers surrendered, including 150 wounded, along with 1,000 horses, 5,000 rifles and five guns. The Transvaalers, 18 officers and 2,593 men, came almost entirely from Western Transvaal commandos – Potchefstroom, Bloemhof, Gatsrand, etc., – while the Free Staters numbered only 18 officers and 1,327 men and were made up of small detachments from ten different commandos as well as Major Friedrich Albrecht and his staff of the Orange Free State artillery. The more perceptive noted that digging saved lives; altogether there were fewer than 300 Boer casualties.[40]

---

* Colvile claimed that he took the first Boer surrender, although it is more likely that while Smith-Dorrien did receive the first enemy to lay down their arms, the divisional commander did arrive on the scene in time to share in the glory.

It was not until 4.00 P.M. that Lord Roberts finally appeared to thank his troops. The commander-in-chief had been a busy man: since shortly after dawn he had met Cronje and accepted his surrender, issued orders for the handling of the prisoners, addressed himself to the resumption of the advance, and sent off his despatches. The first despatch, which set London agog, merely said

> PAARDEBERG, Feb. 27, 7:45 a.m. – General Cronje and all his force capitulated unconditionally at daylight and is now a prisoner in my camp. ......
> I hope that Her Majesty's Government will consider this event satisfactory, occurring as it does, on the anniversary of Majuba.

Reports from correspondents arrived in London during the day, fuelling endless speculation. Paardeberg was the first major victory of the South African War, and the world waited for a more complete report to allow a more accurate tally. Finally the following was received:

> From information furnished daily to me by the intelligence department it became apparent that General Cronje's force was becoming more depressed, and that the discontent of the troops and the discord among the leaders was rapidly increasing ...... Each night the trenches were pushed forward towards the enemy's laager so as to gradually contract his position, and at the same time I bombarded it heavily with artillery ...... At 3 a.m. today a most dashing advance was made by the Canadian regiment and some engineers, supported by the First Gordon Highlanders and Second Shropshires, resulting in our gaining a point about six hundred yards nearer to the enemy and within about eighty yards of his trenches, where our men entrenched themselves and maintained their positions until morning, a gallant deed worthy of our Colonial comrades, and which, I am glad to say, was attended by comparatively slight loss.[41]

Paardeberg was a stunning victory and perhaps the turning point of the war in South Africa; it is not too much of an exaggeration to claim that it was greater in its effect than the German surrender at Stalingrad was in the Second World War. Close to 10 per cent of the Boer forces were captured and the mercurial Boer morale was shattered. It very nearly ended the war, and if the British had not mismanaged the next battle, at Poplar Grove, the Boers might well have sued for peace. While the issue was no longer in doubt, the war dragged on for 26

Majuba avenged!
Field Marshal Lord Roberts accepts the surrender of Boer General Cronje in the British headquarters at Paardeberg. (From Amery, *The Times History of the War in South Africa,* 1905)

more long, bloody months until finally the two Boer republics signed a surrender at Vereeniging on 31 May 1902.

As for Otter and his battalion, Paardeberg was but the first in an unbroken string of victories until finally, on 5 June 1900, the regiment marched past Lord Roberts in Pretoria with a strong claim to the title as the best infantry battalion in South Africa. The Second (Special Service) Battalion, Royal Canadian Regiment of Infantry, had set a very high standard of performance that many modern battalions would be hard pressed to emulate. Regrettably Otter, who seemed prone to both toadying to his superiors and abusing his subordinates – the suck up, kick down principle – squandered the goodwill earned by his successes over the next few months and the regiment returned home bitter and divided with Otter on one side and virtually everyone else on the other.* It was both unfortunate

---

* His position was not enhanced by the actions of Major Lawrence Buchan, his second-in-command, who seldom missed an opportunity to undermine Otter's authority. In turn, Otter, who was no slouch at bureaucratic infighting, ensured that Buchan returned to Canada with him and the main body of the battalion, thus denying his disloyal subordinate any chance to tell his version of events without Otter being able to defend himself.

and perhaps demonstrative of the colonel's attitude towards his citizen soldiers that his battalion was the only Canadian unit that served in South Africa that did not have a single gallantry decoration awarded to an enlisted man.

It is not too much to suggest that the Second Anglo-Boer War (1899-1902), leading as it did to the revitalization of the moribund British army, prevented German victory in Flanders in 1914, and therefore played a part in shaping our world in the 20th century. Alongside these momentous events, the effect on the Canadian army loomed small, but the seeds of the two competing Canadian themes, national self-interest and collective defence, first cohabited in a meaningful, if uneasy way, in South Africa. One of the offspring of this joust on the *veldt* was the realization that the tiny, financially-starved Canadian army could rise above its patronage-ridden roots and fight as the qualitative equal of the British army.

The Battlefield Today

Remarkably, the battlefield at Paardeberg has escaped most of the ravages of development. To get there, the best starting point is Bloemfontein, which is a major air destination from Johannesburg. From Bloemfontein drive west on Highway R48, which becomes N8; after some 75 miles you will cross the Modder River and will be able to see the town of Perdebrug on the north shore of the river. Follow the dirt road on the north shore of the Modder in a northeast direction and you will see a prominent sign indicating a right turn towards the battlefield, which is clearly marked. There is a monument on the south side of the river dedicated to the Canadians who were killed on 18 February 1900.

Last Canadian
Cavalry Charge

When war came again to the British Empire in 1914, there was no hesitation on the part of Robert Borden's Conservative government about committing Canadian troops to the conflict. In 1914, when Britain was at war, Canada was at war, although Canada could specify the size of her military contribution. In any case, the nation's response was enthusiastic – the official declaration of war was made on 4 August 1914 and just under two months later the First Canadian Contingent, consisting of 30,000 men, was on its way overseas. In the four years that followed, they would be joined in uniform by another 589,000 Canadian men – nearly one in three of military age across the country, all of whom were, until 1918, volunteers – and of that total, 59,544 would be killed in action or die of illness and 172,950 would be wounded. By any calculation, it was a tremendous effort by a nation whose population was estimated in 1911 only to be between 8 and 9 million people.

Canadian troops fought their first their major action in April 1915 at the Second Battle of Ypres, an engagement that also witnessed the first large-scale use of poison gas, and from then until the summer of 1918 they experienced some of the most severe fighting on the Western Front – that man-made hell on earth, with its barbed wire, shell holes, mud, corpses and rats. By 1918 the Canadian Corps, with its four experienced infantry divisions and its large establishment of corps artillery, was widely regarded, along with the Australian Imperial Force, as the shock troops of the British Empire. During the great German offensives of the spring and early summer of that year, most of the Corps was held in reserve, in readiness for a counteroffensive.

That offensive began at Amiens on 8 August 1918 when the Canadian Corps punched a hole through the German lines and, from then until almost Armistice

Day on 11 November, it mounted successive attacks that gradually forced the Germans back. These successes were not gained cheaply – one fifth of all Canadian casualties suffered on the Western Front were incurred during the last three months of the First World War – but they came close to breaking the morale of the seemingly invincible German army, and by October that army was in full retreat back to its own frontiers, its withdrawal skilfully covered by rearguard units.

For the Canadian Corps, particularly the mounted units which had been waiting for years for the return of mobile warfare, this was an interesting, if costly, time. The Corps possessed, in the form of Brigadier General Raymond Brutinel's Independent Force, with its mixture of armoured vehicles, horsed cavalry and cyclist infantry, the ideal formation to pursue a withdrawing foe, and Brutinel's units harassed the Germans throughout the autumn of 1918. On 10 October, elements of the Independent Force came upon a determined German rearguard holding a ridge near the village of Iwuy in northeastern France. At the outset, this looked to be yet another rearguard skirmish but the resulting action was one of the most interesting engagements of the First World War, involving as it did one of the few cavalry charges of that conflict and the German use of tanks.

4

"My God, look at

them houses moving!"

Combined Arms

Action at Iwuy

10-11 October 1918

Fig. 8.

67. *First movements on horseback.*

Mobile warfare, 1918

As the Allied armies began their great offensive in the late summer of 1918, Brutinel's Independent Force became a very effective component in the mobile warfare that ensued. Here, the motorized infantry of the Force take a break during the advance from Arras in September 1918. (NAC, PA-3399)

"My God, look at them houses moving!"

❧ ❧ ❧

Combined Arms Action at Iwuy

10-11 October 1918

Michael R. McNorgan

The poets, since the War began,
Have written lots of things
About our gallant soldier lads
Which no one ever sings.
Although their words are very good,
The lilt they seem to miss;
For Tommy likes a tricky song,
The song that goes like this —

Here we are! Here we are! Here we are again!
There's Pat and Mac and Tommy and Jack and Joe.
When there's trouble brewing,
When there's something doing
Are we downhearted?
NO! Let them all come!
Here we are! Here we are! Here we are again!
We're fit and well, and feeling right as rain.
Never mind the weather,
Now then, all together,
Hullo! Hullo! Here we are again![1]

The Great War of 1914-1918 was far from great for any soldier who participated and especially for those in the mounted arm. The conflict occurred during a period of accelerated technological progress when 19th-century military organizations and tactics encountered 20th-century weapons systems with devastating results for all involved. For Canada's mounted troops this collision of past and future technologies was epitomized by a military engagement that took place on a ridge near an obscure hamlet in northeastern France named Iwuy. The battle of Iwuy (pronounced *E-way*) would see, almost simultaneously, the last charge made by Canadian cavalry and the first encounter of Canadian troops with enemy armour.

The story of the battle of Iwuy could be said to begin in the first week of October 1918 in the ranks of the Canadian Independent Force where, wiping off his spectacles, 22-year-old Trooper George Hambley strained to hear the news being passed along a line of resting horsemen. "The cavalry are in a cat-hole!" was what he heard and this bright young soldier recognized the meaning of the somewhat garbled phrase – British and Canadian cavalry were in Le Cateau, a small city about 12 miles southeast of Cambrai. Here, the Germans had been hounded from one delaying position to another with sequential mounted charges delivered by the Royal Canadian Dragoons, Lord Strathcona's Horse and the Fort Garry Horse, all supported by the 13-pdr guns of the Royal Canadian Horse Artillery. These units of the Canadian Cavalry Brigade, along with the brigade's machine gun squadron, were fulfilling the ambition Allied commanders had nursed since the winter of 1915-16 – a cavalry breakthrough. Le Cateau had been the scene of heavy fighting in 1914 during the retreat from Mons; now it was being recaptured in spectacular fashion by mounted troops.

To the north of Le Cateau another Allied advance was underway, this one spearheaded by the veteran and effective Canadian Corps under Lieutenant General Sir Arthur Currie. Leading the advance on the right of Currie's juggernaut was Brigadier General Raymond Brutinel's Canadian Independent Force, a mobile fighting formation quite different from the traditional mounted formation represented by the Canadian Cavalry Brigade. It consisted of a mixture of horsed cavalry (the Canadian Light Horse), armour (1st and 2nd Canadian Motor Machine Gun Brigades), bicycle infantry from the Canadian Cyclist Battalion,[2] and artillery in the form of two trench mortar sections transported in 3-ton trucks. Brutinel's Independent Force was an early example of what a modern soldier would recognize as an all-arms battle group, and in fact Brutinel had

Cavalryman, 1918

During the stalemate on the Western Front, which lasted from late 1914 to the spring of 1918, cavalry proved of little use. After the German offensives in 1918, mobile warfare returned and cavalry and armoured vehicles came into their own. Depicted here is a Canadian cavalryman as he would have been armed and equipped in 1918 (although the sword was more useful for toasting bread over a fire than for combat). Note the extra bandolier of .303 ammunition slung around his "long-nosed chum's" neck and the nose bag for the chum buckled below the soldier's canteen. (Painting by Ron Volstad, courtesy Department of National Defence).

organized its elements to create what amounted to three such battle groups.[3]

Bespectacled Trooper Hambley served in 4 Troop, A Squadron, Canadian Light Horse, an *ad hoc* unit created in 1916 when the reorganization of British, and by extension Canadian, cavalry saw the divisional cavalry squadrons removed from the order of battle; there was not much use for them when the parent divisions were serving in the trenches. Cavalrymen could, however, still have a useful role in the higher formations and so a three-squadron regiment was attached to each corps as corps troops, reporting directly to the corps commander. For the Canadians that meant the cavalry squadrons of the 1st, 2nd, 3rd and 4th Canadian Divisions were amalgamated in a new creation designated the Canadian Corps Cavalry Regiment, a cumbersome title that was soon replaced with Canadian Light Horse. Identity was always a problem with the Light Horse because each original squadron had been drawn from a different parent regiment and each, therefore, had a unit identity it was loath to lose. A Squadron, serving with the 1st Division, wore the badges of the 19th Alberta Dragoons, B Squadron those of London Ontario's 1st Hussars, and C Squadron the insignia of the 16th Saskatchewan Light Horse. Fortunately, as it turned out, the 4th Division's cavalry squadron had also been badged from the latter unit and there was no problem blending them with the 3rd Division's contribution. The sticky issue of identity was finally resolved by leaving everyone with their regimental badges and adding a common shoulder title, which read "C.L.H." According to one Light Horse wag these initials stood for Canada's Last Hope. In the final weeks of the war Lieutenant Colonel Ibottson Leonard, 36 years old and late of the 1st Hussars, was commanding the Light Horse and it was under his orders that Canadian military history was made on Thursday, 10 October 1918, when, at 2.15 P.M., the CLH mounted the last Canadian cavalry charge. This historic event took place at Iwuy, five miles northeast of Cambrai.*

Like the Light Horse, Brutinel's Canadian Independent Force was also an *ad hoc* organization first formed for the August 1918 Battle of Amiens with the title Brutinel's Brigade. The core of this force was Brutinel's own Canadian Motor Machine Gun Brigade (CMMGB) raised in Canada in 1914 using purpose-built armoured cars, called Autocars, each armed with two .303 Vickers machine guns. Weighing 3 tons and propelled by a two-cylinder gasoline engine, these vehicles could reach a top speed of 25 miles per hour on prepared roads but possessed little or no cross-country capability as their engines lacked power, while their thin, solid rubber tires had too little grip.[4] At Amiens, the role of Brutinel's armoured vehicles had been to maintain contact with the French forces operating on the Canadians' right flank – and this they did, taking many prisoners and capturing a number of machine guns in the process. That success led to the creation of 2nd CMMGB – quite a feat for the 46-year-old Brutinel but he was not an officer to rest on his laurels. Despite the success at Amiens, Brutinel had seen the limitations inherent in his brigade: trees dropped by the Germans across the roads had severely impeded the progress of his vehicles. Cavalry, of course, had the cross-country capability his vehicles lacked, as, to an extent, did the Canadian Corps Cyclist Battalion, but on their own each of these units was horribly vulnerable to machine-gun fire, which was not the case with his armoured cars.

Always creative, Brutinel realized that a mixed force of cavalry, cyclists and armoured vehicles would possess speed, mobility and robustness, and he set out to create such a force. He could not do much about the limitations of his vehi-

---

* In his excellent book *Spearhead to Victory: Canada and the Great War* (Edmonton, 1987), Daniel Dancocks makes the statement that the Canadian Cavalry Brigade was responsible for the last charge on horseback on 9 October 1918, a point he gleaned from Colonel G.W. Nicholson's official history, *The Canadian Expeditionary Force 1914-1919*, p. 462: "The Last Cavalry Action." However, the CCB's *Narrative of Operations for the Period 8th-9th-10th October 1918* notes: "At daylight (10th) the [Canadian Cavalry] Brigade withdrew to the valley E[ast] of TROISVILLES, having been relieved by the 7th Cavalry Brigade and infantry." The charge by the CLH at Iwuy took place at 2.15 P.M. on 10 October 1918, making it the last such exploit.

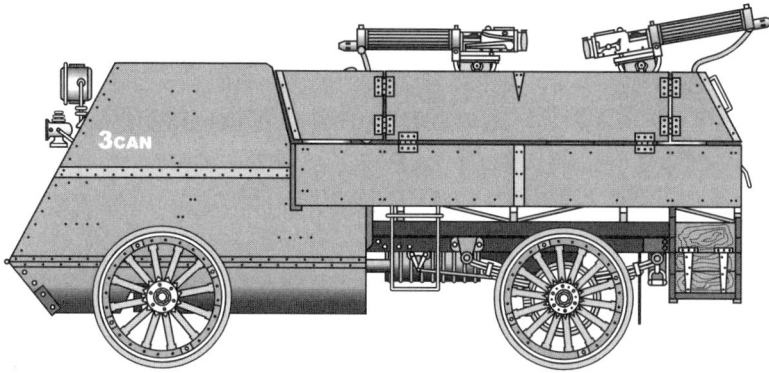

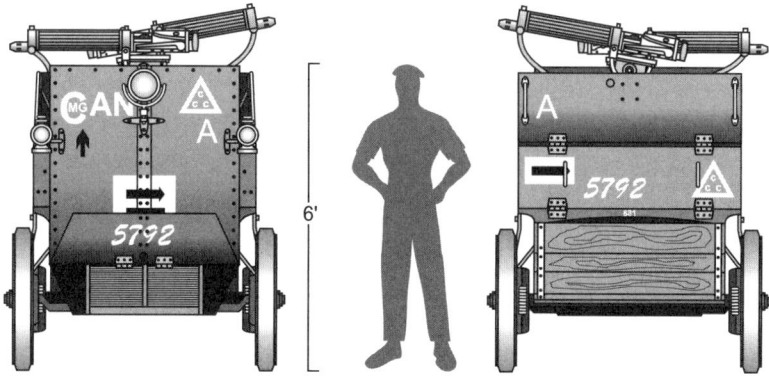

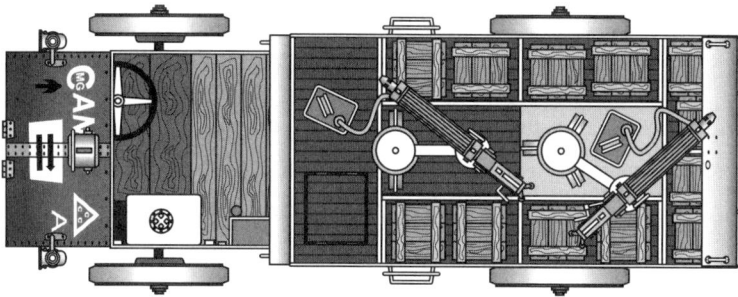

Armoured Autocar

Developed in 1914, the Autocar combined an existing delivery van chassis produced by the Auto Car Company of Ardmore, Pennsylvania, with an open-topped armoured body designed by Raymond Brutinel himself. It incorporated two pedestal-mounted Colt machine guns until 1916 when they were replaced by the more reliable Vickers .303 weapon.

Country of origin: Canada

Crew: 8 (commander, driver, 2 x Vickers .303 inch MG gun crews)

Length: 14 feet 9 inches

Width: 3 feet 7 inches

Height: 6 feet

Weight: 6,000 pounds

Engine: 2 cylinder, gasoline

Maximum speed: 25 mph

Range: Unknown

Armour – Maximum: 9.5 mm

Armament: 2 x .303 inch Vickers MGs, 1 x .303 inch Lewis MG (optional)

The dawn of armoured warfare

A soldier of the Motor Machine Gun Brigade beautifies his Autocar. Note the doll hanging from the single, central headlight, clearly a crew mascot. When mobile warfare returned to the Western Front in 1918, the Motor Machine Gun Brigade came into its own and proved very successful. (NAC, PA-2003)

cles, but he could and did get another cavalry regiment, the British 10th Royal Hussars, and more firepower in the form of the 30th Field Battery, Canadian Field Artillery, as well as additional armoured cars from the (British) Tank Corps. Finally, he obtained a wireless section to improve his communications. This new organization was tried out during the breaking of the Drocourt–Quéant Line in early September but again proved to have limitations because the old technology (horsed cavalry) was obsolescent while the new technology (armour) was immature. Still, the principles were sound and the formula would be tried again.

In this early autumn of 1918 the Allied armies were advancing on all fronts and on 5 October the German government approached the United States to discuss terms for an armistice. The German initiative was rejected, the war continued, and four days later the Canadian Corps captured Cambrai. Following that success, the Corps paused to gather strength for another push to the east. As the next offensive was readied during these early October days, the Canadian Corps operations order laid out the tasks for the Canadian Independent Force. Once again they would be on the corps right flank and their mission would be:

> to cross the Canal de l'Escaut [Schelde Canal] in the vicinity of Cambrai and to exploit success along the Cambrai – Iwuy – Valenciennes road, special attention being paid to securing the crossings over the Canal de l'Escaut between Cambrai and the Sensée....
>
> The Brigade will be free to operate on any road suitable for its purpose, but care must be taken not to block the roads over the Canal du Nord longer than is absolutely necessary, as the maintenance of a continuous flow of artillery ammunition is vital to the success of the operation.[5]

In tasking Brutinel to exploit along roads, the operations order was making a virtue of necessity.

The plan that this order was setting in motion was a probe northeastward toward the next major city, Valenciennes. First, though, the Corps had to cross the Canal de L'Escaut. Here a Canadian engineer, Captain Coulson Norman Mitchell, gained a Victoria Cross by capturing and, while still under fire, neutralizing the German demolition charges on the last remaining bridge over the canal, permitting the advance to continue with the Light Horse leading the way. Once over the obstacle, the Canadians swung to their left to follow the lines of communications – road, rail and water – toward Valenciennes. The Independent Force was now free to exploit along the main highway to Valenciennes, but crossing the Canal de L'Escaut held another significance

The father of Canadian armour

Brigadier General Raymond Brutinel, shown here as a lieutenant colonel, commanded the British-Canadian Independent Force organized in September 1918, which consisted of the two Canadian Motor Machine Gun Brigades, horsed cavalry, a cyclist battalion and light artillery, signals and supply elements. It was a proto-armoured division and the first of its kind in history. Among the officers in the force was Captain F.F. Worthington, who would become of the "father" of the Canadian Armoured Corps in the Second World War. (Directorate of History and Heritage, DND)

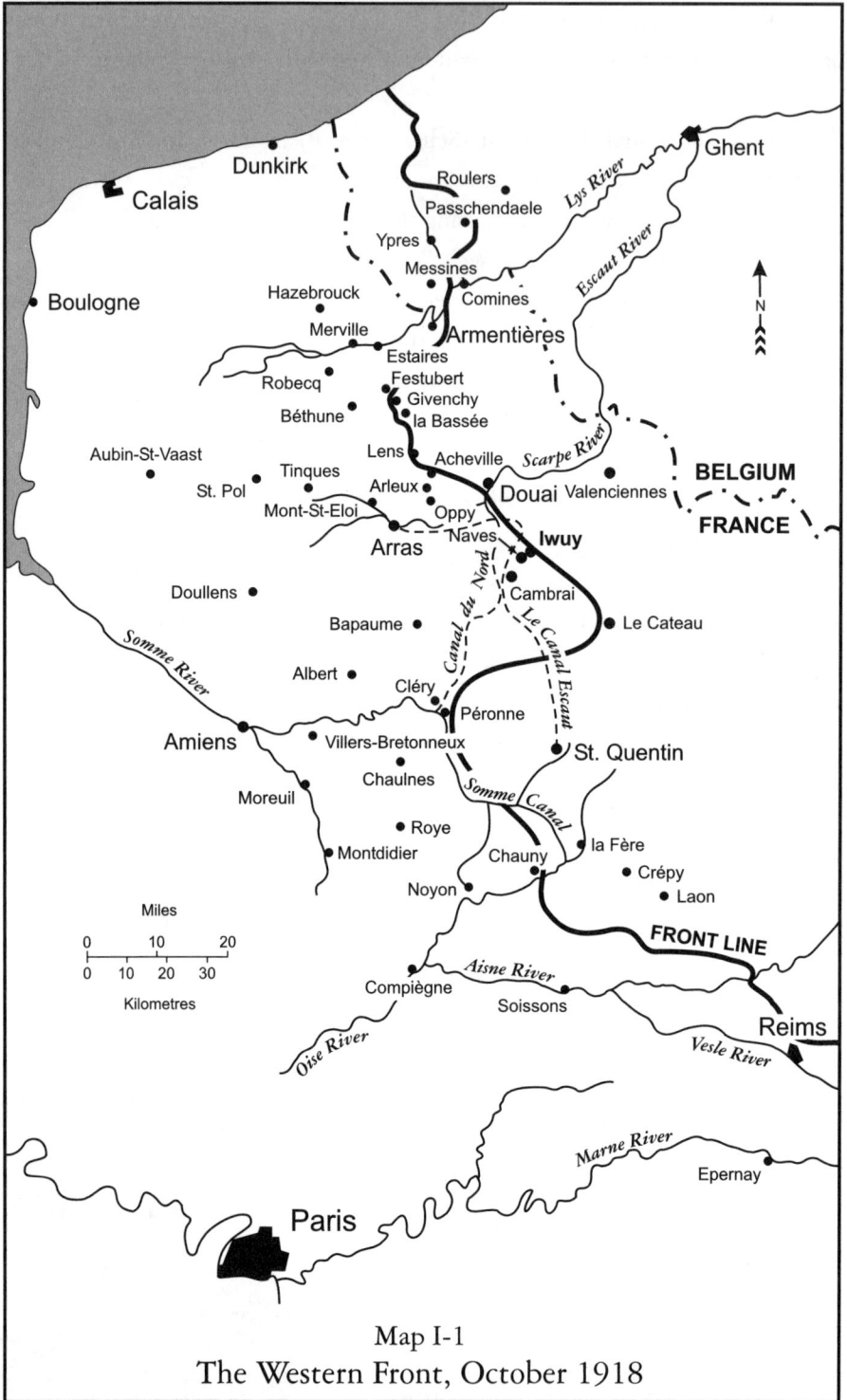

Map I-1
The Western Front, October 1918

for there were no German trenches east of that barrier and the Canadian Corps would be fighting in open country. To avoid giving the Germans time to dig new trenches, the pressure had to be maintained, and as this was one of the traditional tasks of mounted troops, Brutinel's force was ordered to do exactly that.

A withdrawing force will usually attempt to delay its pursuers by utilizing layback positions (small, isolated posts whose role is to inflict casualties and delay the pursuers before slipping away to a fresh position where they will repeat the operation) and the German weapon of choice for this role was the machine gun nest. The 1918 German infantry division was equipped with 164 machine guns in comparison to the 96 such weapons in a Canadian or the 64 in a British formation of similar size.[6] These rearguard positions (the standard size was one yard deep by two yards square) would delay an advance until they were captured or neutralized and bypassed. The German machine gunners were brave and determined men and, even though the Allied rumour mill liked to suggest that they had been chained to their guns and left behind to die by their brutal officers, they were in fact volunteers. But they were indeed left to die, for the Canadians almost invariably killed such crews whether they tried to surrender or not – as Trooper George Hambley noted in his diary on 3 October: "Last night I was taking a despatch and had to go through Bourlon Wood when our men were attacking … [a house] … the boys found two machine guns upstairs. They bayoneted both gunners and threw their bodies out the window."[7]

Throughout 9 October it was the Light Horse's B (1st Hussars) Squadron that bore the brunt of the action and in a long afternoon of fighting they advanced 2,500 yards, inflicting 20 known casualties on the enemy and capturing two of the hated machine gun nests. Doing this gained the squadron a Distinguished Conduct Medal but cost it one non-commissioned officer killed and 11 men wounded as well as 12 horses killed and 35 wounded. The Light Horse held their gains for six and a half hours before being relieved by the infantry of 2nd Canadian Division.

Meanwhile, 1st Canadian Motor Machine Gun Brigade (1 CMMGB) and the Canadian Corps Cyclist Battalion were able to cross the Canal de l'Escaut over a freshly repaired bridge at Point d'Aire. They then pushed forward to relieve the Light Horse that evening with the Cyclists moving into forward positions backed up by two batteries of machine guns, the third battery remaining in a depth position behind the village of Naves. During the night of 9/10 October,

The Cyclist Battalion at rest, 1918

The Cyclist Battalion provided the bulk of the infantry in Brutinel's Independent Force, although the utility of the bicycle in combat was a matter of debate. Nonetheless, these "mounted infantry" were able to keep up with the more mobile components of Brutinel's command. (Canadian Forces Photo, O.3195)

2nd Canadian Motor Machine Gun Brigade (2 CMMGB) concentrated north of Escadeuvers while their sister unit, 1 CMMGB, and the Cyclist Battalion located southwest of the same village. The stage was now set for the Battle of Iwuy.

Come morning, Brutinel's troops had two tasks. The first was to support the infantry assault on Naves, the second to carry out a reconnaissance of crossing sites on the Erclin River, which lay on the other side of Naves. In particular, they were to capture a bridge over the Erclin before the enemy could blow it. At 6 A.M. on Thursday, 10 October 1918, four armoured cars and four platoons of cyclists supported attacks by the 25th and 16th Battalions, Canadian Expeditionary Force (CEF), against Naves. At the same time 2 CMMGB and the remainder of the Cyclist Battalion came up behind the advance, ready to replace their comrades in the line and push on to the Erclin bridge. When the infantry took Naves, the armoured cars of A Battery, 2 CMMGB and one platoon of attached cyclists moved through the village to seize a bridgehead over the Erclin, but were stopped by heavy machine gun fire originating on the ridgeline that dominated the far or east bank of the Erclin. Unfortunately, the bridge they had hoped to capture had been destroyed and neither the armoured vehicles nor the cyclists could ford the river and so, for now, they waited.

This ridgeline, the Iwuy spur, was a natural defensive position, as not only did it dominate the surrounding countryside but just east of its crest lay a sunken road, 10 to 20 feet deep with steep sides, which provided a ready-made trench line. The road joined the villages of Iwuy to the northwest and Rieux-en-Cambrésis to the southeast. Any force attacking the ridge from west to east had to expose itself along the skyline to German fire delivered from the sunken road on the reverse slope. A finer defensive position could not be asked for.

With reports in hand to the effect that his vehicles and the cyclists had been unable to cross the Erclin, Lieutenant-Colonel Harry Meurling, commanding 2 CMMGB, went forward on a personal reconnaissance. Meurling, 43 years of age in 1918, was a Swedish civil engineer who had come to Canada during the gold rush at the turn of the century. When he enrolled in the 5th Canadian Mounted Rifles in Sherbrooke, Quebec, in 1915, he declared his previous service in the Swedish Royal Navy. Subsequently, he joined the Yukon Motor Machine Gun Battery, which had been raised in 1914 by the legendary "Klondike Joe" Boyle. (In keeping with Klondike Joe's style, the battery's original cap badges were reputed to have each contained a gold nugget.) Boyle's battery eventually became a part of Brutinel's organization – A (Yukon) Battery, 2 CMMGB – while Meurling, a forceful personality and a natural leader, rose steadily in rank and responsibility in the novel new world of armoured warfare.[8]

On his return from the reconnaissance, Meurling despatched a working party to a nearby engineer dump to obtain materials to repair the bridge over the

Lieutenant Colonel Harry Frederick Meurling

Shown here as a captain, Meurling commanded the 1st Canadian Motor Machine Gun Brigade at Iwuy. He was an aggressive and thorough commander who performed very well at Iwuy in 1918, but his postwar life would not mirror his wartime successes. (NAC, PA-2535)

Erclin, and this party also stripped the village of Naves of wire and telephone poles. Aided by six sappers borrowed from 6 Canadian Infantry Brigade (CIB), the working party set to its task at the bridge. Watching them from across the Erclin, however, were artillery observers from the 6th German Division, who had been anticipating exactly this operation, and they brought down heavy fire on the crossing site that wounded a number of Canadians, preventing work on the bridge until dark.

Brutinel himself now came on the scene and was soon busy planning an attack to get across the Erclin without the bridge. Using the eight Vickers machine guns of A Battery and additional guns from B Battery, he laid down a screen of covering fire that permitted a platoon from C Company of the Cyclists to leave behind their gas pipe chargers, as they called their Planet bicycles, and cross the shallow Erclin on foot. Running over the 1,400 yards of open ground, this platoon reached the sunken road on the ridge, where they turned left and moved along it until they were stopped at a point where a natural bend created a traverse similar to those found in a trench system. Beyond that bend was a German machine gun that pinned them in place. Private Mennill of the Cyclists' B Company, who was now approaching the ridge, recounts what happened next:

> Presently, No. 5 Platoon, "B" Coy were ordered to hit the road through Naves and get up to the sunken road where the "C" Coy platoon was engaged … As No. 5 Platoon coasted [on their bicycles] down the long grade toward Naves, "Fritz," who had us under direct observation from his high ground, stepped up his artillery fire on the village and by the time we started through it the main street was a shambles of shell holes, bricks, telephone poles and wire and coal boxes were bursting in all directions.* It was a case of riding through hell for leather and the devil take the hindmost.
>
> Clearing Naves, we continued down the road until stopped by the blown and wrecked bridge over the Erclin River, about 1.5 miles from the village. Here we left our cycles beside the road and continued on foot, fording the river, which was shallow at this point. "Fritz" had evidently kept good track of us and now cracked down with salvoes of grass cutters, that type of shell, which burst on immediate contact, without digging a crater.** We all took to

---

* Shell fire from a German 5.9 in (15 cm) howitzer, the name derived from the thick black smoke caused by the bursting round.

** These were small anti-personnel shells that burst on impact, scattering shrapnel at low levels.

the roadside ditch.… In the meantime, two Motor Machine Gun trucks had come up from Naves to the wrecked bridge. [This was a four-vehicle patrol commanded by Lieutenant T.A. Smith, who had not yet heard that the bridge was blown.] Unable to cross the river they were frantically gee-hawing around trying to get turned in the narrow road in order to get the hell out of there. Fritz now lifted his fire from us and went after the trucks and we immediately started working our way up the road once more. We arrived at the sunken road, which led to the left of the main road, toward the rear of and to the east of the village of Iwuy without further trouble.[9]

Although Merrill does not seem to have been aware of it, Lieutenant Smith's patrol, under heavy shell and machine gun fire, dismounted their own Vickers .303s and supplied the supporting fire that allowed No. 5 Platoon of the Cyclists to ford the Erclin. Smith's initiative was recognized with a Military Cross.

The Cyclists, prevented from clearing the entire ridgeline, even with the reinforcement of Mennill's platoon, waited for dark, when a composite force, composed of a company each from the 19th and 20th CEF Battalions, came to their assistance. Although their end of the sunken road was thus secured, this force decided to wait until daylight before renewing the attack.

Thanks to the capture of Naves in the early morning of 10 October, the 19th and 20th CEF Battalions of 4 CIB had a forming-up place for the follow-on phase: an advance to the dominating Iwuy spur 2,000 yards ahead, the eastern end of which had been secured by Brutinel's troops. The top of the ridge held the sunken road that joined Iwuy and Rieux-en-Cambrésis, but this road was still in dispute as the Motors and the Cyclists fought to hold on to their end of the spur. However, the 2nd Canadian Division commander's focus was on Iwuy and Lieutenant Colonel Leonard's orders were for his CLH to secure a hill on its far side, important ground that overlooked a small industrial suburb with its brick houses and winding streets.

The German troops in Iwuy came from the 10th Ersatz Division. As its name implied, it was a composite formation that drew its soldiers from Westphalia and Thuringia. Always considered a division of modest accomplishment, it was rated by Allied intelligence as being third-class and only capable of holding a sector of front line – not expected to either attack or defend, merely occupy. The relative ease with which it had been pushed out of Naves justified this assessment. The

First aid, September 1918

In the weeks preceding the battle of Iwuy, the Canadian Light Horse saw much action. Here a section corporal applies a dressing to a wounded cavalryman who, judging by the position and nature of his wound, has been struck by a fragment of shrapnel from an artillery airburst. Standing at the left is Trooper George Hambley, who recorded his impressions of the battle of Iwuy in a diary that has survived. (NAC, PA-2003)

Germans defending the Iwuy spur were another matter altogether as they were from the 6th Division, Prussian regulars, rated by Allied intelligence as one of the best German shock divisions.[10] Following the battle for Cambrai, the 6th Division had been placed in reserve but had returned to the line on 7 October after a six-day rest. While opposing the crossing of the Canal de l'Escaut there had been plenty of time for them to conduct a reconnaissance of the natural defensive position southeast of Iwuy and this included the registration of targets, such as the bridge over the Erclin at Naves, for the division's 3rd Artillery Regiment.

Great War Cavalry commanders have been frequently criticized for being reckless with the lives of their men. It is appropriate, therefore, to take a closer look at the tactical situation that resulted in the last Canadian cavalry charge. Having received his orders, Lieutenant-Colonel Ibbotson Leonard of the Canadian Light Horse considered his options, which boiled down to the traditional three: an approach from the left, centre or right. Iwuy and the hill that Leonard wanted to reach lay on the opposite side of the Erclin River, a shallow, virtually dry riverbed that was an obstacle to armoured cars, trucks and mounted cyclists, but not to cavalry. By this time the damaged bridge was under intense artillery fire, ruling it out as a crossing site, and leaving Leonard with the choice of attacking directly across the river on foot or on horseback. The ground on either side of the Erclin was open grassland and fields, with no cover for advancing infantry, except such artificial cover as could be supplied by smoke shells. The Canadian artillery, however, was still out of range. Because attacking on foot would leave the troops exposed to enemy fire for a prolonged period, Leonard decided to use the Light Horse. Since B Squadron had carried the battle throughout the previous day, it was now in reserve. C Squadron had been leading the advance since first light but had sustained no casualties and was still capable of further effort. A Squadron, including George Hambley's 4 Troop, was in support.

But which route should Leonard's Light Horse take – left, centre or right (see map I-2)? To get to the hill via the left or centre approaches would entail passing through the built-up area of Iwuy (left) or immediately past it (centre). Neither option appealed to Leonard since the village was an obvious location for machine gun nests which would be difficult to spot and even more difficult to attack. An attack on a machine gun nest in a built-up area could only be made dismounted, and dismounting involved the immediate loss of one quarter of his fighting power since one trooper in four would be detailed to hold the horses of the other three. A cavalry section of six troopers, a lance corporal and a corporal could fight dismounted as a force of two NCOs and four men. However, the inevitable consequences of soldiering meant that any body of troops was usually at less than full strength due to illness, injury, wounds, courses and/or detachments to other duties. A dismounted cavalry section would likely only have four or five men rather than the official figure of eight.

The right flank approach was the most appealing – it was open ground, ideal for horses, and the shortest, and therefore quickest, route to his objective. The major drawback was the long, smooth, sloped ridge, the Iwuy spur. The Cyclists and their infantry companions had been clearing the ridge's sunken road from southeast to northwest but the job was not yet finished, as the sounds of fighting on the ridge indicated. Still, if the defenders were occupied fighting off an assault on their left, a sharp cavalry attack over the ridge and past Iwuy to the hill behind might just be feasible. Then, with the dominating hill secured, either the 19th or 20th CEF Battalion could occupy the village.

The opening Leonard was seeking appeared when the Light Horse liaison officer attached to the 19th Battalion reported that unit's plan to attack the ridge at 2 P.M. Leonard called forward A and C Squadrons and briefed the two officers in command. With the 19th Battalion attracting the attention of the enemy toward the sunken road on the ridge, the squadrons might be able to advance to the road – a farm house would be their intermediate objective – then push on through to secure the hill behind Iwuy. C Squadron would lead on the right closely followed by A Squadron, which would come up on the left of C. B Squadron would remain in reserve.

The stage was now set for the last Canadian cavalry charge. At 2.15 P.M. Lieutenant Richard Hocken, of 1 Troop, C Squadron, led his men around Naves and up to the Erclin River, which ran parallel to the ridge along its base. As they crossed the Erclin, Hocken's troop came under shellfire; then, as they charged up the bare slope toward the sunken road, machine guns opened up, killing Hocken, seriously wounding three men and hitting all but one of the troop horses.[11]

When a horse went down, its rider, if he were unhurt, would take cover behind the horse's body and use his rifle to support his comrades. The survivors of 1 Troop reached the sunken road thanks to Trooper Stewart Thornton, who, when the remaining members of his section were shot down, charged an enemy machine gun alone, killing the crew and securing the position. Those men who had lost their horses continued forward on foot protected by the covering fire of Lance Corporal Robert Hill, who was in command of the troop Hotchkiss section. (The Hotchkiss was a light, bipod-mounted machine gun firing nine-round feed strips of .303 service ammunition. It required at least two men to use and several horses to transport.) When they finally reached the ridgeline, they encountered an isolated party of the 19th Battalion.

The C Squadron commander, Lieutenant Fred Matheson, who followed Hocken's route with 2 and 4 Troops, also came under artillery fire while crossing the river. Matheson lost Squadron Sergeant-Major George "Paddy" Aitkin and 2 men killed, 3 men wounded and 5 horses killed before reaching the sunken road on the crest where he paused, waiting for A Squadron to come up on his right.

In A Squadron, Lieutenant Robert Fyfe's 2 Troop led, followed by 4 Troop under Lieutenant Alan Sharp. In this attack, A Squadron suffered more heavily than C Squadron. At the crest line Sharp's horse was killed under him but, though dazed, he continued in command, organizing his men and the few sol-

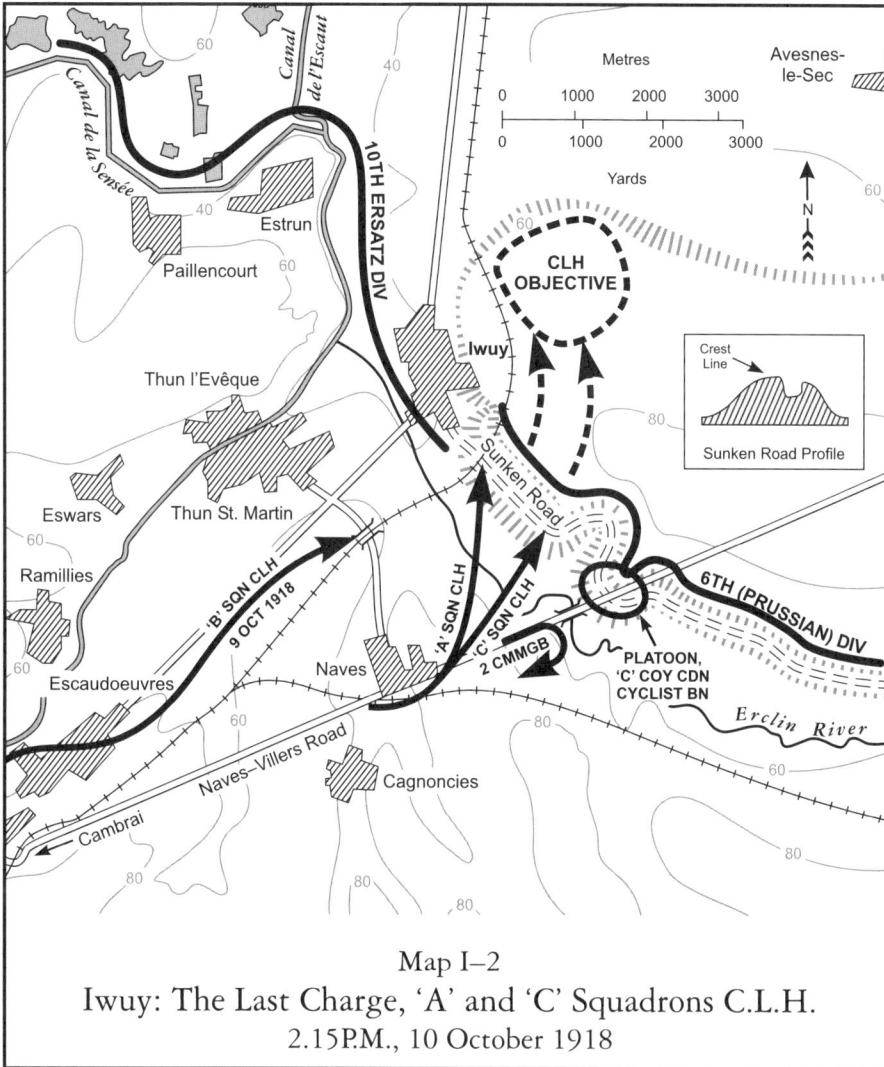

Map I–2
Iwuy: The Last Charge, 'A' and 'C' Squadrons C.L.H.
2.15P.M., 10 October 1918

diers of the 19th Battalion he found there to form a defensive position on the newly won ground.

What was it like to ride in Canada's last cavalry charge? Trooper George Hambley remembers:[12]

Our orders took us out around the village of Naves – across the railroad tracks to the east of the village and out towards the little river. We spread out into sections – Dan Reaves, Joe Scanlon, Corp[oral] Marlowe and myself on the right, Mr Sharpe [sic], Braggins – Tom Sheppard and Larry Bell in the centre and the [Hotchkiss] machine gun section on the left. While skirting the village we had been galloping along through plowed fields, turnip patches over spur railroads [and] steep embankments. Our horses were quite tired before we came to the little narrow river – at the times we would have considered it impossible to jump the stream [*sic*] – but our objective being in sight we charged it and with a heroic struggle every horse got down, jumped and up the other steep side. Then a mad gallop began. Dan and Joe got tangled up in a telephone line. Joe's old mare went down. Dan had to cut off the saddle to free him. The rest of us galloped on across the field and up the slope. The crest of the hill was lined with three or four enemy machine guns and as we galloped along they all opened up. Bullets began to plow up the dust and sizzle through the air. Every horse was doing his best. Every rider urging them on toward the farm our objective. A bullet hit old Nix [Hambley's horse] near the right temple – he went down like a stone. I came down on my head. Nix turned over right on top of me – quivered all over and never moved again. My helmet had rolled away somewhere. I attempted to get out from under my horse but had a hard struggle to free my feet. At last I raised his legs and got out. I lost no time in getting around behind the horse's body out of the hail of bullets. As I looked around I found that I had no broken bones – only a battered head and later I found I had a sprained wrist. Only a few minutes had elapsed but the rest were just mounting the objective to the road. Joe had cut off his saddle – pulled out his sword – mounted the old mare bareback and dashed up the field past me. He made the objective too. I saw the boys get to the road – then horse after horse went down and men rolled off.[13]

B Squadron of the Light Horse was about to cross the Erclin when word arrived from Leonard's command post, just northeast of Naves, not to send any more men up the ridge. During the 20 minutes that had elapsed, Leonard had watched as the hillside became littered with the bodies of 66 horses, interspersed with the dead or wounded bodies of 23 of the troopers.

Through this attack, however, Leonard had secured additional positions on the Iwuy spur, but not the hill he had set out to take. The capture of that position would have to wait; right now it was all Leonard could do to hold on to the gains made, but this was done and the position on the ridgeline was defended throughout the afternoon.[14]

Under cover of darkness, and an intense enemy artillery barrage, the surviving cavalrymen turned over the dearly won sunken road to the infantry and withdrew across the Erclin. The wounded were evacuated but the shelling was so fierce that the dead had to be left behind and were not recovered for another two days.

For their efforts in this short but intense little action, Lieutenants Sharp and Matheson would be awarded the Military Cross (MC), Trooper Thornton the Distinguished Conduct Medal (DCM), frequently referred to by the soldiers as the poor man's VC, while three additional troopers each gained a Military Medal (MM).

For Trooper George Hambley the end of 10 October 1918 brought a reckoning of the cost as he wrote up his diary that night. Keeping such a diary was illegal, since in the event of capture it could provide useful information to the enemy; diaries such as Hambley's are consequently extremely rare today. In the following entry it is clear that Hambley, as a good cavalryman should, showed as much concern for his troop's horses as for their riders.

> Larry [Bell] was shot through the right elbow he told me of the others. Dan Reeves and horse safe. Joe [Scanlon] safe, horse lost. Kennedy safe Count [Kennedy's horse] killed. Mr Sharpe [sic] safe, Bill [Lieutenant Sharp's horse] killed. Banford killed horse safe. Poor old Banford with his grotesque laugh and Roman nose. Paddy Aitkins [the much respected squadron sergeant major] killed, horse killed. Sgt McRoberts wounded through the thigh, Luke [Sgt McRobert's horse] shot. Ashcroft wounded through the knee, [his] horse Rufus killed. Bob Eley's horse lost, Bob miraculously escaped. All [Hotchkiss] machine gun [section] horses lost wounded and killed. Gillam's horse killed, he was safe. Nicholson's horse shot in foreleg, he is safe. Bill Watt's horse lost, Bill safe, in fact all M[achine] G[un] men came out safely and dragged themselves home, here one-by-one as I did. It was a happy meeting, they all thought me killed when Nix went down. But poor old [Corporal] Marlowe lies out there yet.[15] Quinton again escaped very closely as four or five bullets cut his tunic, breeches and grazed his puttee, but he is safe. Redman had his machine gun up and accounted for a few Fritzes as our objective was won. Tim Sheppard also narrowly escaped. In short it was a miracle indeed that anyone of us came out at all as such a mad adventure was never seen before.[16]

An hour before midnight, a party from the 4th Battalion, Canadian Engineers came forward with all the appropriate materials to repair the damaged Erclin bridge. Assisted by soldiers of 2 CMMGB and covered by their guns, the

Canadian Light Horse, 1918

Formed in 1916 from the divisional cavalry squadrons of the four infantry divisions of the CEF, the Canadian Light Horse was attached to Brutinel's Independent Force in the autumn of 1918. Here, a CLH squadron moves up to the front in the autumn of 1918 while German prisoners and Allied wounded move back. (Canadian Forces Photo, O.3320)

sappers completed their labours at 2 A.M. on 11 October. The armour and the Cyclists could now continue their advance mounted. Covered by the fire of A and D Batteries, E Battery and two platoons of Cyclists rode across the bridge, joined their comrades at the end of the sunken road and tried once again to roll up the German line, but this was easier said than done. The Cyclists took casualties, as the German machine gunners were not giving up easily, and by dawn on Friday, 11 October 1918, the capture of the ridgeline was still not completed.

At 9 A.M. that Friday morning, the Canadian Corps set out to secure Iwuy before turning that section of the front over to the British. The Corps had already received orders to redeploy and carry out a crossing of the Canal de la Sensée. On the night of 10/11 October the 49th (West Riding) Division had moved up on the 2nd Canadian Division's right flank, and waiting to relieve 2nd Canadian Division was the 51st (Highland) Division while on the Canadian left was the British 11th Division.

Major General Harry Burstall's 2nd Canadian Division attacked the Iwuy area on Friday, 11 October, with two brigades forward. Brigadier General Alexander Ross's 6 CIB on the left was tasked with clearing the village of Iwuy, while two battalions of 4 CIB under Brigadier General Eric McCuaig were ordered to seize the ridgeline east of Iwuy. The Canadian artillery laid down an intense bombardment on the village and fired smoke to cover the approach of the attacking troops. The German artillery retaliated and it was under heavy enemy fire that the 28th (Northwest) Battalion CEF entered Iwuy from the south to begin a house-to-house struggle. The numerous machine gun nests were, as always, the major problem. The officer commanding D Company of the 28th, Lieutenant W.J. "Pete" White, MC, distinguished himself in dealing with these impediments by several times leading "small groups of men against enemy machine guns in defended localities, overwhelming, by his dash and gallantry, the enemy resistance. On one occasion he rushed out and, single-handed, killed or captured the entire post, consisting of eight or ten men, thus ensuring the success of the operation."[17] White's recommendation for a Victoria Cross was not approved and he had to be content with the Distinguished Service Order.

The 31st (Alberta) Battalion CEF, tasked with following the 28th into Iwuy, was unfortunately caught in its assembly area, a wood, by the enemy's counter-bombardment and was soon in serious trouble:

No sooner had the advance commenced, however, than German artillery observers, watching the lines of infantry as they moved forward, signalled their batteries, and within a few minutes a devastating barrage had been brought down upon the Canadian formations.

The 31st Battalion, waiting in its assembly positions, came in for a terrific shelling with gas and high explosives. Almost immediately Lieutenant H.H. Barnes and 12 other ranks were killed, while Lieutenants A.H. Freudemacher, W. Whyte, MC, A.J. Talbourdet, and J.C. Hutchinson, with no fewer than 118 other ranks were wounded.

For a time hell was loose among the men of Alberta. The shells, as they fell, detonated off the trees that covered the Battalion's assembly area, and the wounds caused by the flying shell splinters were terrible. Enemy machine gunners, realising that the Regiment was being cut up, poured belt after belt of machine gun bullets into the area; and the deafening crash of bursting shells, the rending of riven timber and the continual stammer of the machine guns combined in an inferno of din sufficient to strike terror into the heart of the bravest.

To the lasting credit of the 31st Battalion it must be recorded that this terrible punishment at the very start of the day's operations produced neither panic nor confusion, nor did it in any way deter officers and men from proceeding to carry out their allotted tasks in the day's campaign. Quickly, but in good order, the Battalion moved to the right to get away from the zone of the German barrage, and here it proceeded to reorganize.

While the 28th and 31st Battalions were engaged in the Iwuy street-fighting, their sister unit, the 29th (Vancouver) Battalion, was tasked with supplying an evacuation party. This job entailed the collection of casualties by stretcher bearers and their removal to a Casualty Clearing Station (CCS), which had been set up in the courtyard of the chateau of Thun-St. Martin. Also in that courtyard were a growing number of German prisoners of war. The officer in charge of the stretcher bearers had determined that the prisoners represented a source of untapped manpower and so approached a young enemy officer to suggest that his men could help. The German, a medical student from Bonn, agreed and soon Germans were carrying stretchers, at first at a rate of one German to three Canadians, then two and two, and finally there were four Germans per stretcher with no Canadians assisting. After a period the Canadian officer from the 29th Battal-

Mud was everyone's worst enemy.
A cheerful infantryman of the Cyclist Battalion reverts to "Shank's mare" to defeat muddy terrain on the Western Front. Despite the extremely limited usefulness of the bicycle in modern warfare, the Canadian army persisted in issuing these items in both world wars. (NAC, PA-1581)

ion noticed that no more German casualties being brought in, only Canadians. On enquiring about this he was told that the German officer had instructed his men only to collect Canadian wounded. The matter was quickly cleared up and soon German wounded appeared again at the CCS. At this point the Canadian bearers were ordered to report to the front line to collect more wounded and this they did, arrangements being made for the Germans to come forward and take over the stretchers at an intermediate point. After about an hour the Germans stopped showing up at the rendezvous and when the 29th Battalion officer returned to the CCS to investigate what had happened to them, he discovered that

> a "lost" Canadian party of about one hundred men, commanded by an officer, had moved into the courtyard of the Chateau and had "captured" the prisoners. He saw the Germans lined up against the far wall being searched for souvenirs. A Canadian major was holding the young German officer by the throat behaving, apparently, just as his men. It was an ugly sight. The German officer was looking upward and his lips were moving in prayer, certain, no doubt, he would be killed if he resisted. Finishing his silent prayer, he looked to his left and saw the 29th officer standing in the gateway. A slow and happy smile lit the German's face. It was not a smile of satisfaction that help had arrived so much as a smile that his prayer had been answered in an instant.
>
> The 29th man promptly ordered the prisoners released and then placed the Canadian officer, who had been drinking, under arrest. Accompanied by the German, he crossed the courtyard and ordered that all souvenirs taken be returned, explaining that the prisoners were under his command and were part of the evacuating party. He then requested the German officer to ask the prisoners whether everything taken had been returned. There were shouts of "Nein, Nein!" Hands were raised and fingers pointed.
>
> Only when all prisoners were satisfied was the Canadian party marched off. The prisoners were ordered back to work and, seizing stretchers, happily resumed this new duty, which they performed speedily and well.[18]

While Iwuy was still being fought over, on the right (east) the 20th (Central Ontario) Battalion led the advance onto the ridge, but because the village was still in enemy hands they found themselves between two lines of fire and taking heavy casualties. Unable to complete their primary task of clearing the ridgeline because of the fire coming from their rear, a small force under the command of 27-year-old Lieutenant Wallace Lloyd Algie, commanding B Company, turned back to attack Iwuy:

> [Machine gun] fire from Iwuy was causing many casualties in the ranks of the 20th Battalion [and] the Germans were observed bringing additional machine guns … towards positions from which the whole 4th Brigade front could be enfiladed, a situation which Lieutenant W. L. Algie … determined to prevent.… His plan was to move to the left, well outside the Battalion's boundary and deny the east end of the village to the enemy … If successful he would threaten the enemy's occupation of Iwuy and force its evacuation …
>
> In its first rush the little party captured two machine guns … and destroyed their crews; following that the men set up the two captured guns and with those and their Lewis gun opened fire on advancing German squads … After a brief struggle the survivors of the Germans were taken prisoner, an officer and ten men.
>
> Lieutenant Algie[19] immediately disposed his men in positions which denied the enemy the use of the eastern part of the village … He then returned to the Battalion and collected reinforcements, but was killed while guiding them across the railway.[20]

The 21st (Eastern Ontario) Battalion now moved up behind the 20th, tasked with linking the 28th and 31st Battalions in Iwuy with the 20th Battalion on the ridgeline. This was done, but at 10.30 A.M. the Canadian and British troops around Iwuy came under intense artillery fire. Following the German bombardment five battalions, drawn from 370th and 371st Infantry Regiments of the 10th Ersatz Division, counterattacked.

The German attack included more than infantry. As they watched the enemy advancing toward them one Canadian soldier blurted out, "My God, look at them houses moving!"[21] Farther along the ridgeline, Captain George Stirrett of the Light Horse later recalled that one of his men asked what were the giant objects moving toward them. He replied, "Why, it's the Irish navy, can't you tell?[22] What the incredulous Canadians saw were the Germans' 1st and 13th Panzer Detachments, a force of five *Sturmpanzerwagen A7V* tanks supplemented by three captured British Mark IV tanks. The Canadians were about to be on the receiving end of their first tank attack (see map I-3).

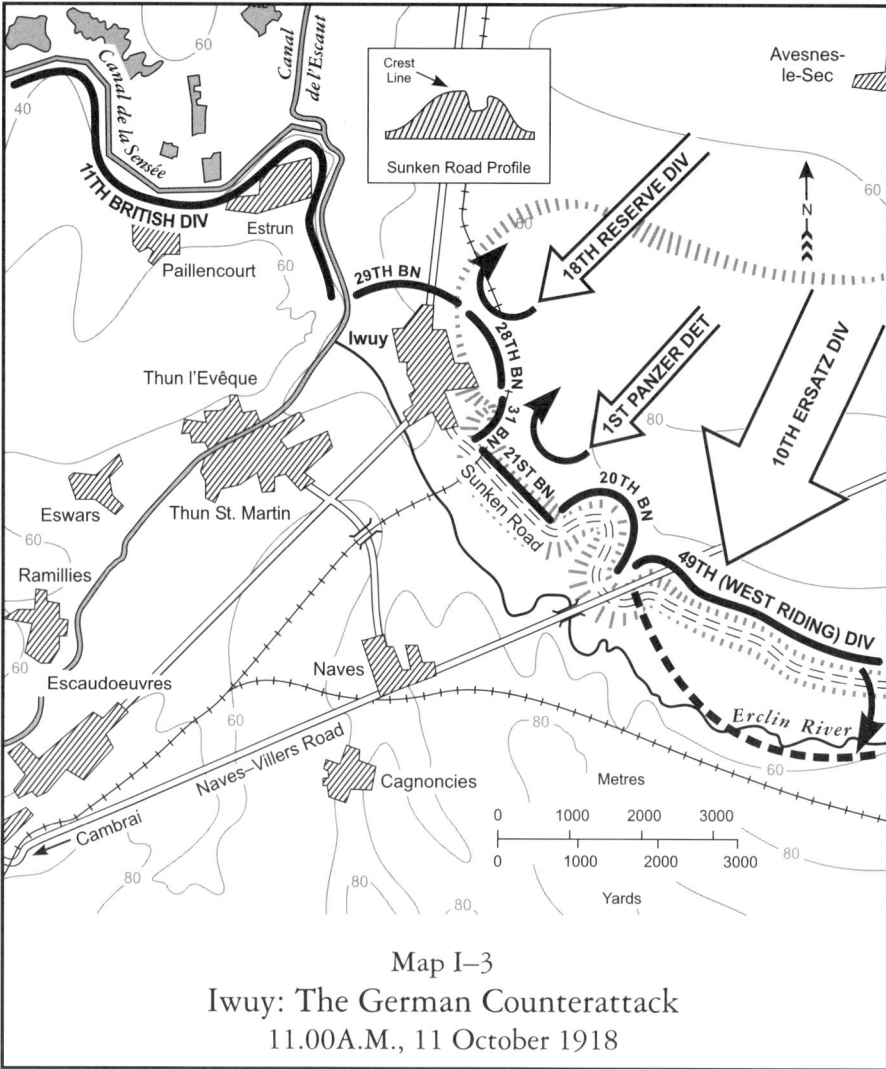

Map I–3
Iwuy: The German Counterattack
11.00A.M., 11 October 1918

The A7V Panzer Detachments were Germany's answer to the Allied tank forces. There were four such units on the Western Front in 1918, each comprising five A7V tanks with supporting vehicles. The 1st Detachment had been raised in September 1917 and saw action in the German March 1918 offensive, where it had the distinction of participating in the world's first tank-versus-tank engagement at Villers Bretonneux on 24 April 1918. Both sides took and inflicted casualties but the historic engagement proved inconclusive. Vehicle casualties here and throughout the summer caused the original four German tank units to coalesce into three and by October the 1st and 2nd Detachments were operating as a single force with eight A7Vs in total. The designation A7V,

1st Panzer Detachment (Hauptmann Greiff)

A7V 501 'GRETCHEN'
(Broke down before
the action at Iwuy.)

A7V 525 'SIEGFRIED'
LEUTNANT WAGNER
(Attacked Rieux-en-Cambrésis.)

A7V 540 'HEILAND'
VzFw LOMMEN
(Attacked Iwuy and rescued crew
of tank 560.)

A7V 541
LEUTNANT SCHÜCK
(Attacked Iwuy and tried
unsuccessfully to tow away tank 560.)

A7V 560
LEUTNANT VOLCKHEIM
(Knocked out in action
at Iwuy.)

A7V 562 'HERKULES'
LEUTNANT MULLER
(Broke down before
the action at Iwuy.)

A7V 563 'WOTAN'
LEUTNANT GOLDMANN
(Attacked Rieux-en-Cambrésis.)

13th Panzer Detachment (Hauptmann Thofern)

MARK IV NUMBER 118
(Attacked Iwuy. Tank burned.)

MARK IV NUMBER 127
(Broke down before action at
Iwuy. Destroyed by the crew.)

MARK IV NUMBER 137
(Attacked Iwuy. Tank burned.)

MARK IV NUMBER 142
(Attacked Iwuy. Tank burned.)

MARK IV NUMBER 209
(Broke down before action at
Iwuy. Tank recovered later.)

MARK IV NUMBER 213
(Broke down before action at
Iwuy. Tank caught fire.)

like the designation "tank," was a deliberately vague term used as a form of verbal camouflage – it stood for *Allgemeine Kriegsdepartment 7 Abteilung Verkehrwesen* (which translated as General War Department Division 7 Transport). Overall, the Kaiser's tanks did not make a great impression in the war, in part because they were too few in number: only 20 A7Vs were manufactured.

Although the tank was looked upon by many at the time, and by some historians since, as a wonder weapon, it was anything but. The state of tank technology in 1918 fell short by a good margin of producing a war-winning weapon. The British had pioneered the tank, closely followed by parallel French developments, but the Germans were slow to explore this new field, a deficiency that they would make up in the inter-war period. Any tank of 1918, British, French or German, was an ergonomic nightmare. A tank crew's effectiveness was measured in hours: eight was considered the maximum, as inside their vehicles the crews worked amid conditions of extreme heat mixed with gasoline fumes. There were no shock absorbers and every jolt was liable to send a crewman reeling up against a metal projection or a red-hot, unprotected engine. Claustrophobia and motion sickness were frequent problems. A tank crew was also virtually blind and navigating a tank out of action usually involved following a ground guide, while in action direction-keeping was a major problem. On the A7V the driver and commander sat on top of the vehicle, above the dual Daimler engines. Neither could observe any ground closer than 27 feet in front of the vehicle, which required the vehicle to approach its objective by driving in a zigzag pattern in order to see what was in front. From his perch the driver's controls were: a steering wheel, a speed selector set for 3, 6 or 12 kilometres per hour, clutch pedals, brake and drive levers for each track. The commander's controls included switches to relay orders to the gunner of the 57 mm weapon. A white light at the gunner's station meant "attention," a red light meant "fire" and no light meant "reload." The gunner sat in a seat that was attached to his weapon, so that as he used his elevation and traversing controls he moved along with the gun, a system that could cause the gunner to lose orientation as the vehicle moved.

All German tanks bore the black cross symbol, the majority using the traditional Maltese style with flared arms, although towards the end of the war a new form of black cross with straight arms was introduced. In addition the vehicles of the 1st Panzer Detachment were each adorned on the nose with the unit's insignia, a skull and crossbones design, a symbol later widely copied as an emblem of German armour. Some tanks carried names although these were apt to be changed if a new crew took over the vehicle.

The Canadian soldiers were not exaggerating when they thought the A7V resembled a moving house. Standing 10 feet 10 inches high, the 32-ton vehicle was propelled over the ground at a speed of 7.5 miles per hour by two Daimler 100-horsepower gasoline engines. The ground could not be too bumpy, however, as the ground clearance of the A7V was an incredible 15.75 inches. Inside was a crew of 18 who, among other tasks, operated a single 57 mm gun in the bow and no less than six machine guns – two on each side and two in the rear. The crews were an interesting mixture of infantrymen manning the machine guns, artillerymen manning the 57 mm gun, and engineers to drive and maintain the beast (each tank carried its own mechanic!).

Accompanying the A7Vs of 1st Panzer Detachment were three captured British Mark IVs belonging to the 13th Panzer Detachment under the command of *Hauptmann* Thofern. Each of these vehicles weighed 28 tons, had a speed of 4 miles per hour, 12-mm-thick armour, two 47 mm guns and four machine guns. To man these tanks a crew of eight was required, including four drivers to control the 105-horsepower Daimler engine.

The German plan called for A7V tanks, hull numbers 525 and 563, to accompany the 371st Regiment against the British forces near Rieux-en-Cambrésis, while A7V tanks 540 and 541 hit the Canadians near Iwuy. *Hauptmann* Thofern's captured Mark IVs were to assemble at a small wood northwest

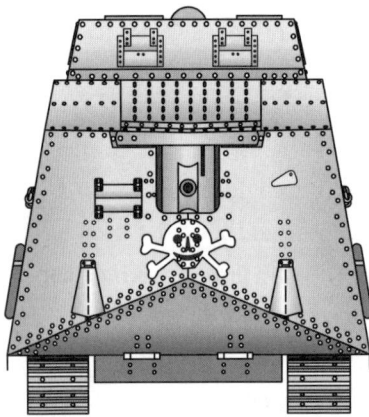

Country of origin: Germany
Crew: 18
Length: 7.35 metres
Width: 3.05 metres
Height: 3.3 metres
Weight: 60,000 pounds
Engine: 2 x Daimler 4 cylinder, gasoline
Maximum Speed: 10 km/h
Range: 35 kilometres
Armour: Maximum: 30 mm
Minimum: 10 mm
Armament: 2 x 5.7 cm Guns
6 x MGs

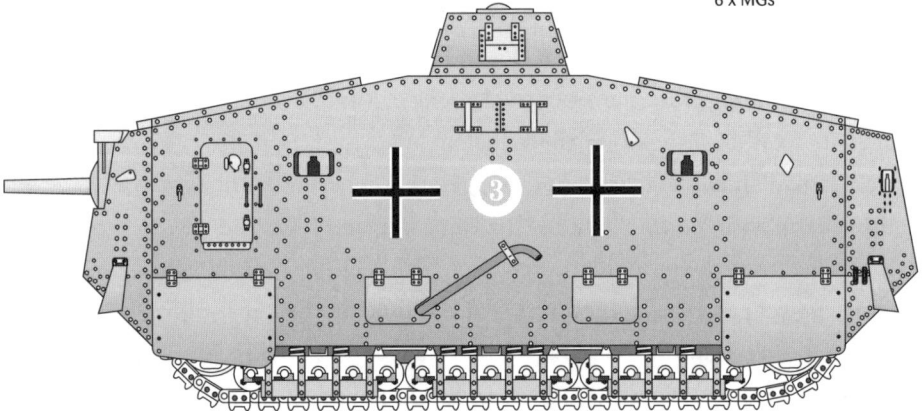

A7V

A design hurried on by the appearance of British tanks in 1916, the A7V was essentially the marriage of an existing Holt tractor suspension with a large armoured box. Limited ground clearance, insufficiently elevated sprockets and idler wheels and a suspension that was too short, resulted in severely limited mobility over broken ground for a vehicle of this size.

of Avesnes-le-Sec also for a strike against Iwuy. Of the original six vehicles under his command, number 127 soon broke down and was destroyed by its crew as being beyond repair, tank 209 broke down with an unspecified mechanical problem and tank 213 suffered from an engine fire. That meant only three vehicles arrived at the wood to prepare for the attack. As the three remaining Mark IV vehicles, hull numbers 118, 137 and 142, moved out of Avesnes-le-Sec, one immediately caught fire and had to be abandoned. A second had its engine seize and caught fire when the crew attempted to restart it. The third lost its transmission when it was about 500 yards from Avesnes and was burned by its crew to prevent its recapture.[23]

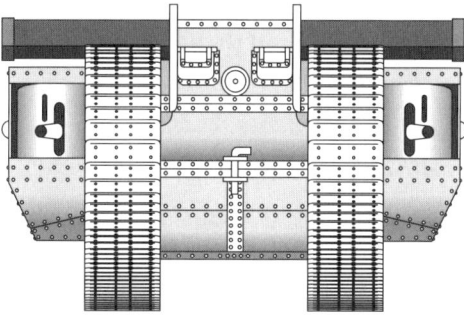

Country of origin: Great Britain
Crew: 8
Length: 26 feet 5 inches
Width: 13 feet 6 inches
Height: 8 feet 2 inches
Weight: 62,720 pounds
Engine: Daimler 6 cylinder, gasoline
Maximum Speed: 3.7 mph
Range: 35 miles
Armour: Maximum: 12 mm
          Minimum: 6 mm
Armament: 2 x 6 pdr Quick Firing in sponsons
          4 x Lewis MGs

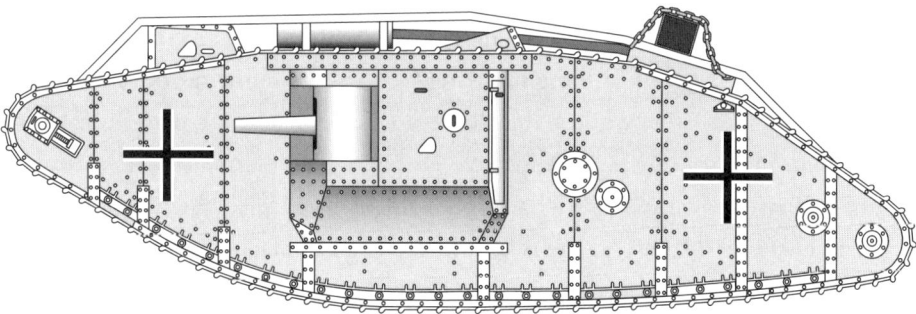

Mark IV

Entering British service in June 1917, the Mk IV was based on the original Mk I rhomboid design. It incorporated all the improvements exhibited in the Mks II and III. The Mk IV boasted increased ventilation, better armour, hinged sponsons for ease of shipment, and the elimination of a gravity feed fuel system. A total of 420 male and 595 female variants were produced during the war.

Things went no better for the German tanks in the north. This force was quickly reduced to three A7Vs, hull numbers 540, 541 and 560. As these tanks closed on the Allied lines they were joined by members of the 18th Reserve Division, who indulged in a spontaneous charge. Considered by Allied intelligence to be a second-class formation, the 18th was listed as a holding division, suitable for fighting on the defensive but not the offensive. Trained in open warfare, and not committed to action between January 1918 and the fighting east of Cambrai in early October, the soldiers of the 18th, however, were more than ready for a fight.[24]

The German counterattack struck hardest against the British troops of the 49th (West Riding) Division, who were in the process of advancing and were caught somewhat off-balance. Thus the Germans succeeded in pushing back the Yorkshiremen's front line a distance of some 2,000 yards. The battalions on the Canadian right flank conformed to the British move and fell back about 700 yards, all the while keeping up a hail of small-arms fire against the advancing German armour. The situation in the Canadian centre was not critical; the enemy's assault stalled when Lieutenant Vincent Crombie of the 21st Battalion brought a captured anti-tank rifle into action that damaged a track of A7V number 560. The tank's driver skilfully moved the vehicle into a sunken road before its track came off. From here the twice-wounded commander of 560, *Leutnant* Ernst Volckheim, summoned nearby number 541, which made an attempt to tow the disabled vehicle away. It was unable to do so and 560 was blown up to prevent its capture. Volckheim's crew, which now included eleven wounded, was picked up by tank 540 and returned to their own lines. Crombie, who gained a Military Cross for his efforts, unfortunately later died of wounds.[25]

The stopping of 560 and the destruction by fire of the Mark IVs took the steam out of the attack and the surviving German armour withdrew in the direction of Avesnes-le-Sec whence they had come, followed by the now-disheartened German infantry of the 18th Reserve Division. The Germans were assisted in their departure by the fire of a battery of Canadian artillery, which had come into action between Naves and Rieux-en-Cambrésis. The machine guns of 2 CMMG Brigade, deployed along the ridgeline, also assisted in propelling the German infantry backward. With the line restored the Canadian units were relieved by 51st (Highland) Division and went into reserve. The action had cost 4 CIB some 700 casualties, but they had succeeding in blunting the counterattack. The Germans, however, regarded the counterattack as a success since they credited it with stopping the British/Canadian advance from Iwuy. Success or failure, it was also the last hurrah for both the 1st and 13th Panzer Detachments, which although re-plenished with replacement vehicles and crews, would see no more action. Thus ended the only occasion during the Great War when Canadians fought German armour, an experience their successors in the Second World War would come to know only too well.[26]

Although Iwuy was a relatively insignificant action compared to the great events of October 1918 on the Western Front, there would be a direct link between it and the armoured battles of the next global conflict. One of the protagonists in particular was to be a key figure in the development of this new form of warfare. The commander of A7V number 560, *Leutnant* Ernst Volckheim (1898-1962), had fought during the first tank-versus-tank battle at Villers-Bretonneux in March and had seen more armoured combat in the last year of the war than most of his peers on either side. Immediately after the war, he was assigned to teach armoured and motorized tactics at the Infantry Officer School and it was during his service here that he wrote a book titled *The Tank in Modern Warfare*, a work that was well received and was issued as a pamphlet throughout the German army. In all Volckheim would write three books and he has been credited with having originated the concept of placing radios in tanks to permit all-arms cooperation – the genesis of *blitzkrieg*.

Thus, it can be said that the sharp little action at Iwuy was the precursor of things to come.

The Battlefield of Iwuy Today

To reach Iwuy and Naves from Cambrai, take the D-114 highway. The two villages are once again quiet rural communities and there are no monuments to the events of 1918, but unlike many other battlefields of the First World War, this one is virtually unchanged. Driving east along the D-114, you will come to the bridge over the Erclin that is a modern replacement for the one destroyed during the 1914-18 conflict, and just beyond is the Iwuy spur with its sunken road. If you climb the spur there is a scenic view to be had from the ridgeline with its smooth green slope down to the river, behind which lies sleepy Naves. The red-brick cluster that is Iwuy is on the right. You have only to shut your eyes to hear the pounding of horses' hooves and the clatter of the machine guns; if you face the other direction, the mind's eye can easily picture the clanking charge of the German armour against the Canadian positions on 11 October 1918. This ridge, the Iwuy spur, is indeed an important location because it lies on a hinge of history.

A Successful

Small Unit Action

When Canada went to war again in September 1939, the actions of Prime Minister Mackenzie King's Liberal government were a study in contrasts to those of his First War Conservative predecessor, Robert Borden. King wanted to wage a war that would not only be financially profitable for Canada but would also see fewer casualties, as the high losses of the First World War and the resultant imposition of conscription had almost torn the country apart along linguistic lines. It was King's hope that the Canadian navy and air force would bear the burden of the new struggle and that Canadian troops would not suffer the heavy losses experienced on the Western Front in 1915-1918. Public opinion in English Canada forced the dispatch of troops overseas to Britain but the government hedged their ultimate deployment with so many restrictions – the main one that they would only be committed to action as a complete army under Canadian generals – that Canadian troops were forced to spend years twiddling their thumbs in Britain. The Canadian army saw limited action in the French campaign of 1940, in a raid on Spitzbergen in 1941 and at the disastrous raid on Dieppe in 1942, but mostly it waited, and waited …

By late 1942, the Canadian troops had trained for more than two years but had gained little practical combat experience. As the First Canadian Army was to be part of a planned invasion of mainland Europe to take place in 1943 or 1944, its higher commanders, their staffs and soldiers needed experience. It was also somewhat embarrassing that in 1942 Canada was the only major Commonwealth country without any troops fighting and it seemed odd that its soldiers were sitting in England while the Americans, relative newcomers to the war, were in combat in North Africa. By early 1943, public opinion forced King to revise his policies and look for active employment for the Canadian army, which by this time had grown to three infantry divisions and two armoured divisions, as well as two independent armoured brigades. With some reluctance, the British War Office agreed that the 1st Canadian Division would become part of the force destined for the invasion of Sicily in July 1943.

When Sicily fell, Allied leaders planned to tie down German forces by pushing Fascist Italy out of the war. King and other senior Canadian leaders and officers supported an expansion of Canada's role in the Mediterranean theatre and offered Britain additional troops, including a corps headquarters. Told there was insufficient shipping to move them, the government persisted until finally it received agreement from the War Office that the headquarters of 1st Canadian Corps, its corps troops and the 5th Canadian Armoured Division would be exchanged for British formations scheduled to return to Britain to prepare for the invasion of France. Beginning in October 1943, the first of 39,000 Canadian soldiers moved to the Mediterranean, and by early 1945 92,757 Canadians would be serving in the Italian theatre.

While these deliberations were going on, 1st Canadian Division landed on the Italian mainland on 3 September 1943 and advanced up the east coast of the "boot," undertaking two major operations, including Ortona, and earning a reputation for fighting in built-up areas. By the early spring of 1944, 1st Canadian Corps, with the 1st Canadian Infantry Division and 5th Canadian Armoured Division, was concentrated south of Rome to prepare for the first Canadian corps operation since 1918. This operation, codenamed CHESTERFIELD, was part of an even more ambitious operation, DIADEM, to be mounted by the 5th United States Army and the 8th British Army in May 1944 which was intended to bring the Italian campaign to a swift and successful conclusion.

As is often the case – particularly when fighting against the highly professional German army – these operations did not achieve the desired results. But, as far as Canada is concerned, they led to one of the most hard-fought and successful small unit actions waged by Canadian soldiers during the Second World War – the struggle to seize and hold a bridgehead over a nearly dry, little Italian waterway called the Melfa River.

5

"A perfect example of teamwork:" The Battle for the Melfa Crossing

24-25 May 1944

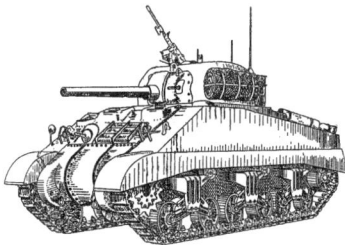

Waiting to move up – Canadian Shermans, May 1944

A heavily camouflaged column of Sherman tanks from 1 Canadian Armoured Brigade waits to move up in the Liri Valley in May 1944. Despite the attempts at concealment, German observers from the high ground around the valley could spot any major movement below and bring down artillery and mortar fire. (NAC, PA-139891)

> "A perfect example
> of teamwork"
> � � �
>
> The Battle for the
> Melfa Crossing
>
> 24-25 May 1944
>
> John R. Grodzinski

We are the D-Day Dodgers
Out in Italy
Always on the vino,
Always on the spree
Eighth Army codgers and their tanks,
We live in Rome, among the Yanks
For we are the D-Day Dodgers
In sunny Italy.[1]

In the offensive planned for May 1944, codenamed Operation DIADEM, the "codgers" of Eighth Army would play a major role by advancing up the Liri Valley, cracking the enemy's Gustav and Hitler Lines, and pushing the German 10. *Armee* north. At the same time, the American Fifth Army would mount a powerful offensive thrust from the Anzio beachhead and drive northeast through the Alban Hills to block Highway 6, closing the escape route of 10. *Armee*. The aim of the offensive, as explained by General Sir Harold Alexander, the Allied commander in Italy, was to accomplish "the destruction of the German Tenth Army and the withdrawal of the remnants of the Tenth and Fourteenth armies north of Rome," and, ultimately, "to wipe out" enemy "forces in Italy." Unfortunately, in the event, Lieutenant General Mark Clark, commanding Fifth Army, had different ideas – he chose not to cut Highway 6 and prevent the supply and withdrawal of 10. *Armee*, which would have accelerated "the dogged but slow advance of the Canadians and 13th [British] Corps," but decided instead to swing north to take Rome. The British and Canadians were thus left to fight a battle of attrition up the Liri Valley. Such are the pitfalls of coalition warfare.[2]

Lieutenant General E.L.M. Burns's 1 Canadian Corps was part of the Eighth Army. This formation, famous for its victories in North Africa was, despite its nominally British title, a heterogeneous collection of Commonwealth and Allied formations including British, Canadian, Greek, Indian, Italian, Jewish, New Zealand, Polish and South African, most of which were organized, armed and equipped along British lines. It was commanded by Lieutenant General Sir Oliver Leese, who had five corps – 5, 10 and 13 British, 1 Canadian and 2 Polish – deployed along a 55-mile front. The British 5 and 10 Corps held the line on the eastern half of the Italian peninsula, while the other three corps with eight infantry and three armoured divisions were concentrated along a 10-mile front along the south edge of the Liri Valley on the western side. Leese's plan for Operation DIADEM called for 10 Corps to conduct a feint to deceive the Germans into thinking that the main effort would be in the centre of Italy, while 13 Corps attacked across the Gari below Cassino and, in conjunction with an attack by the Poles farther north, isolated the strongpoints of Cassino and Monastery Hill. Burns's 1 Canadian Corps was to be held in reserve, ready for one of two missions – if 13 Corps was successful, the Canadians would exploit up Highway 6 towards Rome; if that formation proved less successful, it would cross the Gari and advance north to the left of 13 Corps.[3]

The natural avenue of approach to Rome from the south – the valley of the Liri and Saaco Rivers – lies to the west of the Appennine Mountains. About 20 miles long and 4 to 7 miles wide, this valley is flanked by mountain ranges – along its southern edge are the Aurunci and Ausoni Mountains and to the north the dominant feature is Mount Cairo, 5,500 feet above sea level. In 1944, the Liri Valley was flat and open at its eastern end and extensively cultivated with vine and grain, but as one moved westward, the terrain became rolling and thickly wooded, with small poplars and scrub oak. The valley is cut at its opening by the Gari (also known as the Rapido in the vicinity of Cassino) and Liri Rivers, which run parallel to the mountain ranges. Six miles from the southern end, a series of transverse gullies run southwest into the Liri: the first is a deep feature with a pair of semi-canalized streams known as the Forme d'Aquino; farther west is the wider but more shallow Melfa River. The upper Liri Valley begins near

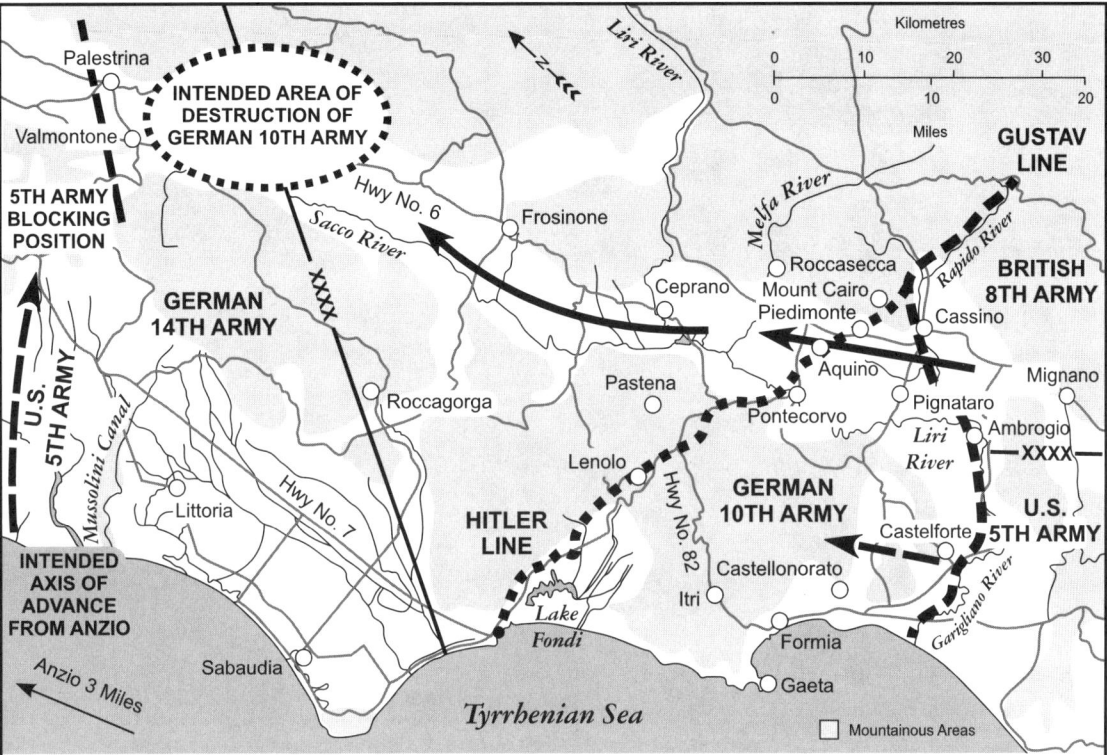

M–1
The Allied Operational Plan,
Operation DIADEM as Conceived Spring 1944

Ceprano, where the river it is named after turns north into the mountains, while its tributary, the Sacco, continues to the northwest. In 1944, the railway from Naples ran along the northern edge of the valley through Cassino to Rome.[4]

The terrain in the Liri Valley presented problems for Eighth Army. The mountains along its northern edge dominated its entrance, like "ramparts to deny any hope of progress." Advancing troops were under continual observation from both the abbey atop Cassino and the Piedimonte heights – and, in 1944, observation meant enemy artillery fire. The limited road network was not designed for the heavy traffic of modern war. Highway 6, the main route from Naples, which ran through both valleys to Rome, followed the path of old Roman roads and there were at least four secondary roads running north-south between the Gari and the Melfa, as well as other smaller tracks and trails. The key town of Ceprano lay at the junction of Highway 6 and Highway 82 (running north-south). Generally the main roads were well constructed and surfaced with asphalt, but during the forthcoming operations, 1 Canadian Corps was forced

Gridlock, 1944 vintage

While appearing wide and flat in panoramic photos, the Liri Valley was actually hilly with many natural obstacles, thick vegetation and few roads, resulting in horrific traffic jams throughout the battle. (NAC, PA-140208)

to make do with narrow, poorly surfaced and improperly-founded secondary roads blocked in many places by German demolition which required considerable work to render them usable. Those roads running near waterways were often not well founded and heavy traffic often caused them to collapse. Nor was the Naples-Rome railway bed any better as vehicles moving along it or near it were vulnerable to fire. As if all this was not bad enough, to cross the Gari and Liri Rivers, bridging was required but the Germans controlled the San Giovanni

Dam upstream on the Liri and constantly opened it to change water levels, thus making bridge construction difficult. There were, however, useable fords on the Melfa, although that waterway, about 100 yards wide, had steep embankments and a swampy course that limited movement.[5]

Terrain such as this affected not only mobility but also tactics. Prevailing British and, by derogation, Canadian armour doctrine in 1944 held that "good tank country" was the "type of country which offers good going, and contained successive features, permitting good fields of fire from hull down positions and support tank by tank or troop by troop." Such terrain allowed "fire and movement," the key characteristics of modern tactics, because tanks moved in bounds from fire position to fire position, always under the watchful eye of other tanks, which improved their survivability and ability to engage targets. After they moved past supporting tanks to a fire position, the lead tanks would take up a "turret down" position, allowing the commander to peer over a crest while the remainder of the vehicle remained under cover. After studying the ground, the tank might move to a "hull down" position, exposing only the turret and gun so as to be able to engage targets.[6]

The terrain in the Liri Valley hampered the use of these tactics as open areas were rare, and those that did exist were "covered by carefully sited Panther or Tiger tanks, or Anti-Tank guns of various types" making movement costly. Successful tank movement was only made possible by "careful study of the ground and skilful driving." Initially, armour operating in this area tried to avoid "close country" and follow established doctrine, but the olive groves, vineyards, grain fields, broken ridges, walled cemeteries and other features provided excellent cover for enemy infantry employing hand-held anti-tank weapons placed to fire into killing zones along choke points that were strewn with mines. Tank-infantry cooperation could overcome these obstacles, but the wheeled and half-tracked infantry-carrying vehicles of 1944 were largely limited to the roads, making it easy for armour to be separated from its supporting infantry.[7]

The Germans had put great effort into constructing fixed positions in this area, although the need for camouflage cover and a shortage of troops meant that "thick and abundant" crops were often left uncut "and fields of fire were therefore very restricted" so that Allied soldiers could use this natural growth to provide cover during the advance – although soldiers under fire may not have appreciated it at the time. In the end, experience in Italy showed that "the more difficult the tank going, the better the tank country, so long as drivers were skilled, vehicles camouflaged, infantry present and sappers available." But time and again, terrain confounded all efforts to concentrate armour – more often than not, tanks fought in small groups and could not exploit the massed effects of speed and violence. As the coming battle would demonstrate, however, when the openness of the terrain along the riverbanks in the Liri made concentration possible, open ground proved deadly. Dispersion was thus necessary and this increased the significance of small unit battles, making the actions of junior leaders very important.[8]

The German commander in Italy, *Feldmarschal* Albert Kesselring, skilfully utilized the terrain to confound Allied offensive operations. He defended by using fixed positions with small mobile reserves ready to launch immediate local counterattacks. The German defences south of Rome were based on these principles and consisted of three lines. The first, known as the Gustav Line, was anchored on Monte Cassino and followed the west bank of the Rapido-Gari-Garigliano rivers to the Gulf of Gaeta on the Tyrrhenian coast. It was strongest on the anticipated axis of advance up the Liri Valley and its forward zone was swept by machine gun fire from concrete emplacements and semi-mobile steel pillboxes. In this sector, 40 shellproof shelters were spaced at 150-yard intervals, each large enough for eight to ten men and interconnected by tunnels with fire pits, to protect the defenders from artillery and air bombardment. There were also 18 specially-constructed pillboxes mounting revolving Panther tank 75 mm turrets, interspersed between the bunkers. Throughout was an extensive network of field fortifications and minefields and there was much camouflage, including "extremely realistic" dummy tanks positioned so that Allied tanks "in manoeuvring to engage them presented enfilade targets to enemy anti-tanks guns." The mountain heights afforded excellent vantage points for calling down artillery on advancing troops.[9]

Backing up the Gustav Line was the *Führer Riegel* or *Führer* "Switchline." Although later renamed the *Senger Riegel* after a senior German officer, to Allied soldiers it was always the Adolf Hitler Line. This position lay eight miles west of the Gari and hinged on Mount Cairo, from where it stretched across the valley, past the villages of Piedimonte, Aquino and Pontecorvo. South of the Liri, it swung southwest through Sant'Oliva into the Aurunci Mountains. As it had no water barrier to its front, a continuous line of concrete and steel fortifications like those in the Gustav Line was built along this position with anti-tank ditches located at likely approaches, designed to channel movement into killing zones or to force vehicles to expose themselves. Although the Hitler Line's anti-tank defences were sited in depth, there was not enough infantry to defend it – when 1 Canadian Infantry Division advanced against it on 23 May 1944, it was held by less than a thousand enemy troops. The Germans planned to hold this line "primarily as a delaying position, but with a proviso that if the impetus of the British advance was lost or the line held for a few days, the delaying position might be turned into a permanent defensive position." Should the situation in the Liri Valley or a breakout from the Anzio beachhead force their withdrawal, the Liri Valley would be defended along the Melfa River long enough to allow a retreat to the third German defensive belt, known as the Caesar Line, immediately south of Rome.[10]

The regrouping of Allied forces for the forthcoming Operation DIADEM coincided with similar moves initiated by Kesselring. Hampered by poor intelligence and confused by a successful Allied deception plan, Kesselring believed his opponents would not attack the Gustav Line directly but attempt to outflank it by means of an amphibious landing. The German commander faced tremendous disadvantages in numbers – in May 1944, 670,000 Allied soldiers were opposed to 303,000 Germans, with about 67,000 riflemen against 24,000, while 1,900 tanks faced 450 German, and there were 4,000 Allied aircraft against just 450 German. Defending the Liri Valley was 14. *Panzerkorps*, with a panzer grenadier division and two infantry divisions, which held a narrow line from Terracina on the coast to the Liri River. Next to it, *General der Gebirgstruppen* Valentin Feuerstein's 51. *Gebirgskorps* of four divisions covered the sector north of the Liri River. Holding Cassino itself was the 1. *Fallschirmdivision*, with two more divisions to its north stretching across central Italy. Kesselring also had a mobile reserve consisting of the 15. *Panzerdivision*, and 29. and 90. *Panzergrenadierdivisione*. German armour included the Mk IV and Panther tanks, the latter being the new medium tank of the *Wehrmacht* which, at 45 tons, weighed more than a Sherman, had the advantage of sloped armour and carried a long 75 mm gun, making it a dangerous opponent. However, the main threat faced by Allied armour in the forthcoming operation in the Liri Valley was posed by German self-propelled and towed anti-tank guns.

Fortunately, the beginning of Operation DIADEM found many German units moving to new positions, leaving the entrance to the Liri only lightly defended by the machine gun battalion of the 1. *Fallschirmdivision*, two battalions of *Panzergrenadierregiment* 115 and two battalions from *Grenadierregiment* 576. A successful Allied deception plan had thus resulted in the concentration of 13 Allied divisions against four German.[11]

Operation DIADEM commenced on 11 May 1944 when 13 British and 2 Polish Corps attacked the German defences south of Rome. On that day, 8th

Indian Division, supported by 1 Canadian Armoured Brigade, penetrated the Gustav Line, but progress on the fronts of both 13 and 2 Polish Corps was slow at first. Once bridging across the Gari was completed on 13 May, however, Allied armour pushed in and Sant'Angelo, the keystone of German resistance in 13 Corps sector, fell, allowing the bridgehead to be enlarged. Bitter fighting continued, but by the end of the day the Gustav Line was smashed, leaving Monte Cassino as its sole remnant in German hands. Leese now decided to exploit the success of 8th Indian Division and release his reserve, 1 Canadian Corps, so as to continue the battle on a three-corps front. On the evening of 15 May, Burns's 1 Canadian Corps was instructed to relieve 8th Indian Division and advance up the southern half of the Liri Valley, and 1st Canadian Infantry Division entered the line that night. At this point, events were happening fast and, by the late afternoon of 16 May, 13 Corps had cut the new German defensive line along the road running Esperia–Pignataro–Cassino, forcing Kesselring to order a general withdrawal to the Hitler Line.[12]

As the lead brigades of 1st Canadian Division advanced north, they encoun-

Planning is always important.

Major-General B.M. Hoffmeister, General Officer Commanding, 5th Canadian Armoured Division, giving orders just prior to Operation CHESTERFIELD. As the forthcoming operation required careful coordination of armour, artillery, infantry, engineers and other services, several such Orders Groups, involving commanders and staff officers, were held. (NAC, PA-189920)

tered mixed resistance. On 18 May, while the Poles took Monte Cassino, the Canadians reached the fringes of the Hitler Line but an attempt that day to make a quick breakthrough failed and Leese became convinced that only a major assault could overcome the new German position. He ordered Burns to break the line between Pontecorvo and its junction with the Forme d'Aquino, giving him a pause of 48 hours for reconnaissance, planning and the necessary regrouping. Early on the morning of 21 May, Burns issued orders to his two divisional commanders, Major General Christopher Vokes of 1st Canadian Infantry Division and Major General Bertram Hoffmeister of 5th Canadian Armoured Division. Vokes was allotted the task of breaching the Hitler Line, while Hoffmeister was to be prepared to support Vokes and then seize crossings over the Melfa River, before taking Ceprano. Over the next three days, from 21 May to 23 May, while infantry and engineer patrols probed the German positions, these plans were further developed and H Hour for Operation CHESTERFIELD, the Canadian part of the next phase, was set for 6.00 A.M. on 23 May.[13]

During the initial stages of the forthcoming attack, Hoffmeister placed his 5th Canadian Armoured Division behind the Forme d'Aquino, awaiting the codeword "PUNCH" to begin their advance. During the first four days of DIADEM, the division had remained in reserve but tension in the formation was palpable as all ranks pondered the immediate future. In the camp of Lord Strathcona's Horse, one of the armoured regiments in the division, there was a feeling "hard to define …… It reminds one of that awful hush that precedes a Saskatchewan hailstorm. Without being told, we know the Strathconas will be going in soon."[14]

Burns's orders to Hoffmeister were that 5th Canadian Division was to first secure a bridgehead over the Melfa River, about 5 miles northwest of Pontecorvo, and then exploit to Ceprano, another 5 miles beyond. The crossing operation was assigned to the division's 5 Armoured Brigade, while its 11 Infantry Brigade received the task of seizing Ceprano. The division faced a difficult task as, if 13 Corps was delayed or stopped, it might have to penetrate 5 miles into enemy territory on a relatively narrow front with an open right flank. With this in mind, the forthcoming operation was further subdivided. In the first phase, a firm base would be established between the Hitler Line and the Melfa, and then a crossing would be secured over that river. To accomplish this objective in the face of determined German resistance, strong supporting forces would be necessary and armour, artillery, engineers and infantry would have to be properly coordinated to achieve success.

This coordination would be done at the divisional level, the lowest level where all these capabilities were combined, and it would be wise at this point to examine in detail the organization of 5th Canadian Armoured Division. By the mid-20th century, due to the range and lethality of weaponry, advances in mine defences and obstacles, and the advent of mechanized warfare, the complexities of military operations had increased. These factors had brought greater dispersion to the battlefield and increased difficulty in commanding and controlling forces spread over a large area. These challenges were overcome by the development of wireless (radio) communication systems that permitted commanders to control the battle and maintain the tempo of operations but the increased technical nature of war also meant that these same commanders had to understand the capabilities and limitations of all arms, while trusting both their subordinates and other arms and services to complete their assigned tasks. Detailed planning and familiarity between units was critical to success, for once a battle commenced, uncertainty increased, making coordination difficult. Even in 1944, running a battle remained very much an art but the personal bravery, skill and efforts of those fighting were still important.[15]

Hoffmeister's division contained an armoured brigade and an infantry brigade and there were important differences between the employment and command of these two different arms. While infantry units operated on relatively narrow fronts and in close proximity to one another, the proper employment of armour required a careful balance of speed, concentration, surprise, cooperation, initiative and control. Although it was structured with these elements in mind, the Commonwealth armoured division of 1944 was often employed as two distinct elements owing to the mixed protection and mobility of its armoured brigade, the "chief hitting force" of the division, and its truck-borne infantry brigade.

An armoured brigade headquarters was fully mobile to keep pace with its subordinate units – because armour fought on the move – and to exploit mobility and protection to win fights at extreme range. The role of the infantry brigade was to maintain mobility by acting as a "pivot of manoeuvre" for the division or to lead it if the country was less suitable for armour, such as close terrain or built up areas, where anti-tank weapons could play havoc with tanks. Infantry remained the only arm capable of seizing and holding ground, while the artillery provided indirect fire support and engineers aided mobility and protection. Generally, the supporting units within an armoured division were organized and equipped to support either its armour or its infantry brigade – one of the divi-

5 Canadian Armoured Brigade
Operation CHESTERFIELD, May 1944

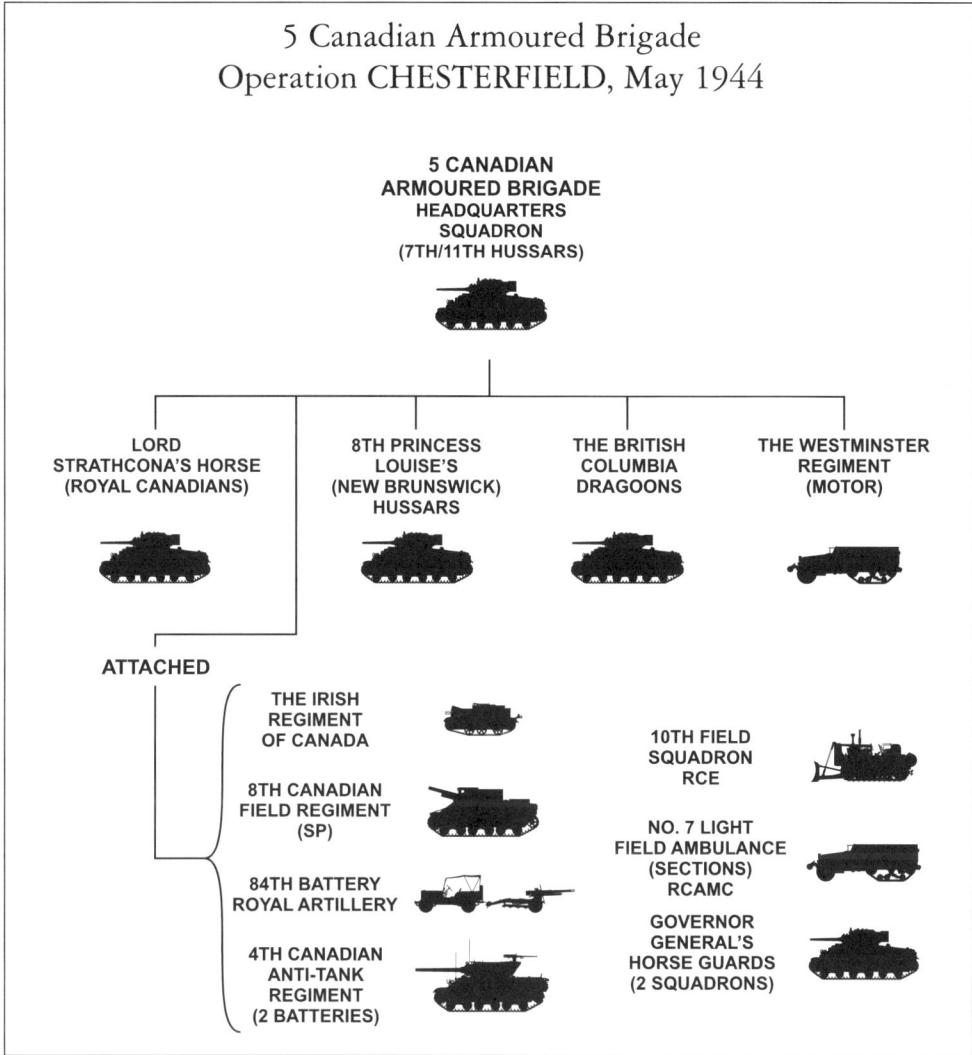

**5 CANADIAN
ARMOURED BRIGADE
HEADQUARTERS
SQUADRON
(7TH/11TH HUSSARS)**

**LORD
STRATHCONA'S HORSE
(ROYAL CANADIANS)**

**8TH PRINCESS
LOUISE'S
(NEW BRUNSWICK)
HUSSARS**

**THE BRITISH
COLUMBIA
DRAGOONS**

**THE WESTMINSTER
REGIMENT
(MOTOR)**

ATTACHED

**THE IRISH
REGIMENT
OF CANADA**

**8TH CANADIAN
FIELD REGIMENT
(SP)**

**84TH BATTERY
ROYAL ARTILLERY**

**4TH CANADIAN
ANTI-TANK
REGIMENT
(2 BATTERIES)**

**10TH FIELD
SQUADRON
RCE**

**NO. 7 LIGHT
FIELD AMBULANCE
(SECTIONS)
RCAMC**

**GOVERNOR
GENERAL'S
HORSE GUARDS
(2 SQUADRONS)**

sion's artillery regiments was self-propelled, while the other, which had towed guns, usually worked with the infantry brigade.[16]

The "heavy punch" of the Commonwealth armoured division was its armoured brigade with its three armoured regiments. In 5 Armoured Brigade, these units were organized according to the Mediterranean Theatre of Operations War Establishment. Taking one of these units, Lord Strathcona's Horse, as an example, it consisted of an RHQ (Regimental Headquarters) with four command tanks, a regimental reconnaissance, or "recce," troop of 11 Stuart light tanks, an inter-communication troop of six scout cars, and three fighting squadrons, each with 16 Sherman tanks, organized in a four-tank squadron headquarters and four troops, each of 3 tanks. A major commanded a squadron and was assisted by two captains, one as second-in-command and the other as a "battle captain" who provided the rear radio link to RHQ, allowing the squadron commander to "fight" the squadron. A lieutenant led a tank troop and was responsible not only for fighting it but also for commanding his own tank, while within the troop a sergeant commanded the second tank and a corporal the third. Behind the fighting squadrons came the A Echelons or logistical elements which supplied the fighting squadrons. The echelons included recovery tanks, maintenance vehicles, transport vehicles, to carry petroleum, oil and lubricant, or POL, ammunition, supplies and medical vehicles and they frequently came under fire in the discharge of their duties. Overall, a 1944 Commonwealth armoured regiment consisted of about 54 officers and 600 other ranks with 52 Sherman tanks, 11 Stuart light tanks and 2 recovery tanks.[17]

The main armoured fighting vehicle of 5th Canadian Division was the American Sherman M4A4 tank. It weighed 35 tons and was armed with a 75 mm gun capable of firing a variety of explosive, armour-piercing or smoke rounds, a .50 machine gun and two .30 calibre machine guns, one in the bow and another mounted co-axially with the main gun. The Sherman had a crew of five: commander, gunner, operator (or loader), driver and co-driver. The crew commander was responsible for directing the driver to tactically move the vehicle and for indicating targets to the gunner. Mechanically, the Sherman was very robust but it was under-gunned and more lightly armoured than its German counterparts, particularly the Panther and Tiger.

Operating ahead of an armoured regiment's fighting squadrons was its recce troop, which employed stealth and guile to collect detailed information about the enemy and ground to assist in the deployment of the squadrons. This troop was equipped with the Stuart M3A3 Light Tank, or as it was known in the Mediterranean, the "Honey." Normally a Stuart weighed over 15 tons and was armed with a 37 mm gun, but in Italy the turret of most Stuarts had been removed and their firepower reduced to a .30 calibre machine gun in the bow and a .50 calibre machine gun on a flexible mount on the top of the hull. The four men in a Stuart crew – commander, gunner, driver and assistant driver – were also trained to conduct dismounted foot patrols if necessary. Accordingly, the recce troop carried infantry weapons including PIATs (Projectile, Infantry, Anti-Tank – the Commonwealth equivalent to the American bazooka), grenades and other small arms. Finally, the armoured regiment's intercommunication troop of six scout cars assisted with liaison, communication, movement control and other duties.[18]

For combat, an armoured regiment was normally formed into a battle group

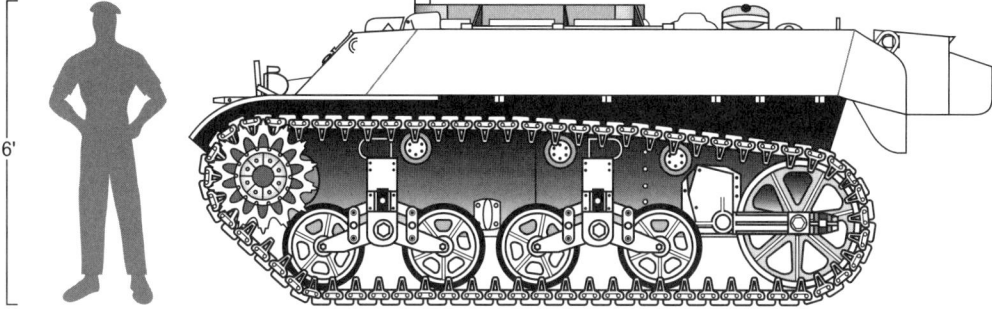

6'

Honey – regimental recce vehicle

The American M3 Light Tank, known in British service as the Stuart or by its nickname "Honey," was used by the British, Commonwealth and many Allied armies for reconnaissance and other roles. Each Canadian armoured regiment employed a reconnaissance or "recce" troop of 11 Stuarts. Normally equipped with a 37 mm gun, recce Stuarts were stripped of their turrets and main armament, giving them a lower silhouette and greater speed but restricting armament to a single .50 calibre gun and miscellaneous weapons employed by the crew. Three Stuarts of the Strathcona recce troop spearheaded the advance of the 5th Canadian Armoured Division to the Melfa River.

based on the unit itself, combined with a company of motorized infantry, a platoon of anti-tank guns, attached engineers, and a self-propelled artillery battery in support. One of the key steps made by divisional and brigade commanders before an operation was to decide the proper mix of these supporting elements so that the armoured battle group had the capabilities to accomplish its mission. As often as possible, training exercises were held to ensure the armour, artillery, infantry and engineers became familiar with each other's capabilities, doctrine and procedures. In the two months leading up to Operation DIADEM, for example, 5th Division organized demonstrations and training on a number of subjects, including combined attacks by armour and infantry, artillery and small arms, camouflage, tank driving, recce schemes, sand table exercises and wireless communications.

This training was to pay dividends. On 16 May 1944, in anticipation of operations in the Liri Valley, Lieutenant Colonel Patrick ("Paddy") Griffin, commanding officer of Lord Strathcona's Horse, informed his subordinate commanders and probable supporting units that it was "possible that during the course of present ops a Regimental Group may be formed on LdSH(RC). This g[rou]p if formed will be known as STRATHFORCE." The next day, Griffin held a full O Group (Orders Group) "to discuss the operations of 'the armoured regimental group,'" which was followed by a TEWT (Tactical Exercise Without Troops) on sand tables.[19]

As armour required infantry support, various methods had been developed by 1944 to keep the infantry with the tanks. One method was to actually carry the "flat feet" (as armoured troopers termed their infantry comrades) on the tanks, but this required careful coordination, for the infantry could become dispersed if the tanks spread out, while riding on tanks offered little protection against enemy fire. The best solution and the one that left armour free to manoeuvre but kept infantry close at hand was the motor battalion. Whereas a standard infantry battalion moved mainly on foot or "soft-skinned" vehicles, a motor battalion was the closest thing in the Commonwealth armies to the American concept of mechanized or armoured infantry. It was a specialized unit equipped with 15 cwt.* American-built halftracks. Despite having the appearance of an armoured vehicle, these trucks were actually soft-skinned and not designed to operate in the thick of battle. Each Commonwealth armoured division had one motor battalion and this unit had three motor companies, each with three rifle platoons and a scout platoon for reconnaissance. The main fighting elements in the battalion were the motor platoons, comprising one officer and 20 other ranks, carried in four halftracks. With 21 men, a motor platoon was half the size of a conventional infantry platoon, which limited its employment and time in combat. The battalion's scout platoon had two officers and 41 other ranks divided in three 12-man sections and was mounted on fully-tracked Universal Carriers.

The motor battalion relied on firepower rather than manpower in action and it possessed a considerable range of firepower. Subtracting vehicle crews and those needed to operate heavy weapons, the motor battalion, with a total complement of 38 officers and 816 other ranks, could only put 348 riflemen into action but it had a powerful support company. This sub-unit consisted of three anti-tank platoons, each with four 6-pounder (57 mm) guns, and two medium machine gun platoons, each with four Vickers .303 heavy machine guns. These weapons were usually distributed among the three motor companies, making each a self-contained fighting unit designed to support armour against light opposition and to seize, deny or hold vital ground. Also distributed throughout the battalion were a number of PIATs and 2-inch mortars. The motor battalion could be employed in the advance against enemy anti-tank gun screens and lightly-held obstacles, such as a river, where its manual stated that, "having captured a crossing," it "will hold it until either relieved by infantry from the lorried infantry brigade or the armour

---

* A reference to the carrying capacity of the vehicle measured in long hundredweights or "cwt," an Imperial unit of weight equal to 112 lb, so the load-carrying capacity of these vehicles was 1,680 lb.

Calm and cool in action.

Lieutenant Colonel George Corbould of the Westminster Regiment with Lieutenant Colonel Patrick Griffin, commander of Griffin Force. Both officers were well liked by their men and responded well to the difficult challenges they faced during their first major action. (Author's collection)

has passed through." The Westminster Regiment, the motor battalion of 5th Armoured Division, would put this doctrine to a thorough test at the Melfa.[20]

Considerable artillery support was also planned for the forthcoming operation. Initially, each of the three armoured regiments in 5 Armoured Brigade would be supported by one regiment of field artillery, increasing to three by the end of the barrage program. Accompanying each armoured battle group would be a self-propelled artillery battery of eight 105 mm howitzers, a jeep battery with eight 75 mm pack howitzers, and there would be further support from the rest of the self-propelled artillery regiment. Detailed lists of opportunity targets, potential enemy locations such as road intersections or concentrations, were compiled in advance by the gunners. One of these lists included "Possible Turrets or Turret Reference Points" and 47 potential "Uncle" targets (divisional artillery targets), with a detailed description of each including map reference, type of fire desirable, bearing and length of linear concentration.

Artillery fire would be delivered either by a "stonk," or one round per gun, or by "murder" – continual fire on the target until ordered to stop. Fire was called down by Forward Observation Officers or FOOs, riding in armoured observation posts (tanks with their main armament removed), who identified targets and submitted requests for fire up the gunner's radio net, probably the most efficient communications system in the field. The FOOs recommended the type of fire and the number of guns as some targets required only a few rounds while others needed greater concentration. Standard code words designated fire to be brought down by a single regiment ("Mike"), divisional artillery ("Uncle"), corps artillery ("Victor"), artillery group ("Yoke") and all artillery in Eighth Army ("William") on targets. Fire could also be called down by 654 Air Observation Post Squadron, an RAF unit equipped with light planes flown by artillery officers who func-

tioned as airborne FOOs, and one flight was allocated to 5th Division for the forthcoming attack.[21]

The artillery also provided a battery of twelve M-10 self-propelled anti-tank guns, armed with high-velocity 3-inch guns, to deal with enemy armour and anti-tank guns. While it was the job of the tanks to destroy these targets, the M-10 provided additional support from the battery assigned to each battle group.

Finally, there were the long-suffering and often-overlooked engineers, without whose efforts, modern warfare would be impossible. For the forthcoming operation, Griffin of the Strathconas was allotted a sapper troop of one officer and 71 other ranks which possessed a great variety of stores and equipment to enhance mobility and protection by clearing obstacles and improving defensive positions. To improve response time, engineer recce parties were assigned to each squadron in the Strathconas, riding in Honey tanks provided by the regimental Recce Troop.

A famous military proverb holds that no plan survives first contact with the enemy, but in the case of Operation CHESTERFIELD the plans changed even before the enemy was encountered. At 9.30 A.M. on Sunday, 21 May 1944, Brigadier J.D.B. Smith, commander of 5 Armoured Brigade, held an O Group with his unit commanding officers to pass on instructions. Commanding the brigade since February 1944, Desmond Smith was described as a "young, very dynamic person" (which might account for his nickname of "Sixteen Cylinder") and took a keen interest in what would be his formation's first major operation. After this O Group, the remainder of the day was spent working out final details. Lieutenant Colonel Frederick Vokes of the British Columbia Dragoons (brother of the general officer commanding 1st Division), whose unit would lead the attack, conferred continuously with Smith. At noon, Lieutenant Colonel Griffin of the Strathonas held his own O Group with representatives from the supporting units: 64 (Jeep) Field Battery, Royal Artillery; 82 Anti-Tank Battery; 1 Field Squadron, RCE; and 7 Light Field Ambulance.

Griffin's plan for CHESTERFIELD was for Lieutenant Edward Perkins to lead with the Strathconas' Recce Troop, followed by A Squadron under Major Lee Symmes. Moving to the right of Symmes's squadron would be Major William ("Bill") Milroy's B Squadron with C Squadron, commanded by Major Jack Smith, on the left. Behind the tank squadrons would come A Company of the Westminster Regiment, under Major Jock Mahony (pronounced "Manny"), followed by the

"Sixteen-Cylinder" Smith

Brigadier J.D.B. ("Sixteen-Cylinder") Smith, Commander 5 Canadian Armoured Brigade. Noted for his energy and drive, Smith demanded careful planning for the Liri Valley operation, perhaps realizing that once the battle commenced, he would exert little influence on it. (Author's collection)

anti-tank battery and the British jeep field battery. Six Honeys were detached from Perkins's troop to carry engineer recce parties and two of these vehicles were attached to each tank squadron. Each squadron also had a FOO party while the commander of 61 Battery, 8 Field Regiment, Major George Ward, and a liaison officer from the medium artillery, would accompany the Strathconas' RHQ. The artillery, engineer and infantry attachments, less 64 (Jeep) Battery, arrived in the Strathconas' assembly area at 6.00 P.M. that Sunday.[22]

As a result of the successful advance to the Hitler Line, Brigadier Smith held another O Group at 1.30 P.M. on 22 May to inform his commanders that things had changed and the operation would now be conducted in three phases. During Phase I, the British Columbia Dragoons, with the Irish Regiment of Canada (from the 5th Division's 11 Infantry Brigade) and C Squadron of the 8th New Brunswick Hussars would pass through 1st Division and take an objective code-named GIN. In Phase II, the Strathconas with A Company of the Westminsters and the three Westminster scout platoons would seize a crossing over the Melfa, and during Phase III, the 8th New Brunswick Hussars, the brigade reserve, and the remainder of the Westminster Regiment would expand this bridgehead and take Ceprano (see map M-2). Smith stressed that his battle groups would have "all possible backing; flanks secured; all div[isional] resources and air support." He emphasized that speed and the bold use of armour were essential as 1st Division would commence its major attack on the Hitler Line at 6.00 A.M. the following day while 5th Armoured Division would move on order.[23]

Everything looked "good to go" but on 23 May events occurred that were to affect these plans. During the day, the 1 Division attack made good progress although the natural cover from trees, vegetation, tall grain and mist, combined with dust from artillery fire, made it increasingly difficult to move units and control the battle. Late in the afternoon, the division reached its objectives but supporting tanks and anti-tank guns were held up by wire, mines and fire. To 2 Infantry Brigade's left, 3 Infantry Brigade advanced well and by 1.00 P.M., Major General Vokes realized that the 2 Infantry Brigade attack was unlikely to succeed. With the concurrence of Burns, he reinforced the more successful penetration by 3 Brigade thus making another attempt to capture objectives northeast of Pontecorvo. By 4.50 P.M., these were secure and by nightfall, the lead elements were firmly in their new positions and 1st Canadian Division had broken through the Hitler Line. [24]

Later that day, due to the continued fighting, Smith was again forced to change his own plan and, at 4.30 P.M., he held his second O Group of the day to finalize details for CHESTERFIELD. Its Phase I had been accomplished by Vokes's infantry and the enemy sent "reeling back towards the Melfa" and the Hitler Line breached, but in the "wrong place" and farther south than intended, towards Pontecorvo. While a battalion of paratroopers from 1. *Fallschirmdivision* and two companies from 5. *Gebirgsdivision* were "wiped out," Smith was concerned about further German reinforcements and in particular their armour, which Canadian intelligence estimated as being 96 tanks, including 24 of the new Panthers, as well as anti-tank guns. Smith told his subordinates that 1st Division would now consolidate its position, while 5 Armoured Brigade would pass through it and proceed to the Melfa, again in three phases. During Phase I, the British Columbia Dragoons, with the Irish Regiment of Canada and an anti-tank battery, would form a battle group known as Vokes Force, after its commanding officer, Lieutenant Colonel Frederick Vokes. Two infantry companies would follow in carriers, while the third would ride on the reserve squadron of tanks. The objective of Vokes Force was to establish a firm base known as BRANDY which, once secure, would be handed over to 11 Canadian Infantry Brigade, while the Dragoons continued to their Phase II objective, a feature known as KUMMEL near Mancini. Once KUMMEL was secure, Griffin Force (Lord Strathcona's Horse and attached troops) would then commence Phase III and capture BENEDICTINE, a crossroads just east of the Melfa, before gaining a bridgehead over that river. This bridgehead would be formed "by the motor company and if possible by the armour of the group," and the remainder of the Westminster Regiment would follow, their flanks covered by two squadrons from the Governor General's Horse Guards, to enlarge it. Finally, the 8th New Brunswick Hussars, in reserve, would proceed through the bridgehead and exploit towards Ceprano.[25]

The delays, change of axis and new commitments brought inevitable changes to the artillery fire plan. Artillery from Eighth and Fifth Armies was no longer available, reducing the number of tubes available for the forthcoming operation from 480 to 236, to be now provided exclusively by 1 Canadian Corps. Two series of "stonks" codenamed LAGER and BASS were to be fired by the corps artillery but the direct support planned for each battle group was unchanged.* There were also twenty-four 105 mm self-propelled, and eight 75 mm jeep-drawn guns that would move forward with 5 Armoured Brigade to "give it close observed support during the arm[oure]d attack."

At 5.30 P.M., the divisional commander, Hoffmeister, called Burns to report he believed conditions were favourable for Phase II of CHESTERFIELD to commence. Burns agreed and ordered that H-Hour would be 6.30 A.M. on the following day. As a result, the "Mighty Maroon Machine" – as its men called 5th Armoured Division after the colour of its shoulder patch – began to move to its start lines.[26]

From the outset, this movement ran into trouble. The division first regrouped east of the Forme d'Aquino before advancing to its forward assembly areas. Originally these areas had been located behind 3 Canadian Infantry Brigade, but the recent changes of plan required the assignment of new areas, and movement into them would have to be conducted by a series of road moves. In modern warfare, road movement and traffic control are carefully orchestrated operations designed to ensure units arrive at the right place at the right time and in the correct order. During the Melfa campaign, these movements were organized, coordinated and controlled by brigade and divisional staffs who determined the order of march based on the overall plan and who also assigned control measures, such as assembly areas, start and release points, route names (card suites were normally used, such as HEART, SPADE or CLUB), traffic control points and timings. The actual signage of routes and control of movement was the responsibility of the Provost Corps, or military police.[27]

Based on these plans, units then issued their own movement instructions. As an example of how this was done, take the overnight move on 17/18 May 1944 made by the Strathconas to Mignano. The regiment used a typical order of

---

* The staff officer who selected the codenames for Operation CHESTERFIELD was clearly a man who enjoyed his tipple as is indicated by his choice of such terms as BASS (a beer), BRANDY, BENEDICTINE, GIN, KUMMEL (a liqueur), LAGER and VERMOUTH.

Griffin Force Battle Group Organization

REGIMENTAL HEADQUARTERS

RHQ TROOP

CO   2IC   Tp Ldr   Tp Sgt

61 Bty Comd

ARMOURED O.P.

INTER-COMMUNICATION TROOP

Med Bty Comd

ARMOURED O.P.

RECONNAISSANCE TROOP

ARMOURED O.P.

"X" – Casualty on 24 May1944

'A' SQUADRON

SQN HEADQUARTERS   FOUR TROOPS – THREE TANKS PER TROOP   WESTMINSTER RIFLE COY RECCE PLATOON

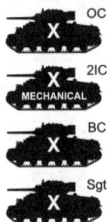  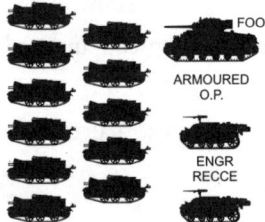

OC   Tp Ldr   Tp Sgt   Cpl   FOO

2IC   MECHANICAL   ARMOURED O.P.

BC   ENGR RECCE

Sgt   LOST– JOINED 'B' SQN

'B' SQUADRON

'C' SQUADRON

Sgt

ARMOURED O.P.

Griffin Force: The armoured battlegroup in detail

Griffin Force was one of three armoured battlegroups formed by 5 Armoured Brigade for Operation CHESTER-FIELD. It was based on Lord Strathcona's Horse (Royal Canadians) and included elements from its parent brigade and 5 Canadian Armoured Division, including a motor company and other elements from the Westminster Regiment (Motor), a battery of self-propelled artillery, an anti-tank battery and a troop of field engineers. This combination of assets was determined by the divisional, brigade and regimental commanders to ensure that each fighting element had sufficient strength and capabilities to meet a variety of anticipated scenarios. Given the difficult terrain, considerable reconnaissance assets from both the Strathconas and the Westminster Regiment were allocated to give early warning of enemy positions and information on routes, crossings and other vital details.

SP BATTERY M7 "PRIEST" R.C.A. (TWO TROOPS), 61 (PETER) BATTERY

Tp Comd — GPO

ARMOURED O.P.   ARMOURED O.P.

Tp Comd — GPO

ARMOURED O.P.   ARMOURED O.P.

82ND A/Tk BATTERY, 4 ANTI-TANK REGT, R.C.A.

Tp Comd   Tp Sgt

Bty Comd

FIELD TROOP, 1ST FIELD SQUADRON R.C.E.

'A' COMPANY WESTMINSTER REGIMENT (COY HQ AND THREE PLATOONS)

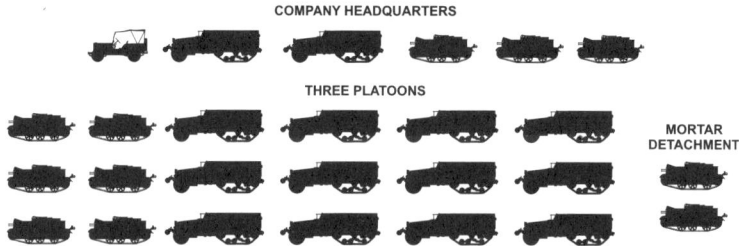

COMPANY HEADQUARTERS

THREE PLATOONS

MORTAR
DETACHMENT

ONE MMG PLATOON [(6 CARRIERS WITH 4 MMG) (SUPPORT COY, WESTMINSTER REGT.)]

THREE ANTI-TANK PLATOONS (SUPPORT COY, WESTMINSTER REGT.)

Once deployed, the battlegroup occupied an area, depending on the terrain, equivalent to the size of several football fields, making radio communication vital to its success during operations. At the Melfa, communications proved difficult and despite mechanization, well-sited enemy defences resulted in the equivalent of one of the two assaulting tank squadrons being lost or destroyed and only three small recce vehicles crossed the river during the initial battle, while most of the soldiers that defended the bridgehead during 24/25 May 1944 arrived there on foot. This chart also depicts vehicle casualties suffered by the Strathconas just east of the Melfa, while the losses suffered by the Westminster motor company are unconfirmed, although at least three of their White scout cars are known to have been destroyed. Not shown are the artillery guns and vehicles "in support" and the logistic vehicles that provided supply, maintenance, medical and other services.

march, with the commanding officer leading, followed by the intelligence officer, Recce Troop, RHQ, after which came B, C and A Squadrons in that order and, bringing up the rear, the recovery tanks, signals vehicles and the squadron logistical vehicles. The next night, another move from an assembly area behind Mount Trocchio and across the Gari River to an area just northeast of Pignataro demonstrated the difficulties involved in road moves, particularly at night and during a period of intense operations where recce and control measures might not have been as well conducted as they should have been. To get his units onto the designated route, Brigadier Smith found it "necessary to put a tank across the road to stop all traffic" while each unit in his brigade was moving out. Congestion forced traffic to move at one mile per hour, causing Smith to request a delay in the road move until morning. The Strathconas, for example, found that a stream crossing point was actually unsuitable for tanks, which caused "a large scale traffic jam." About a mile farther north, Lieutenant Colonel Griffin found an alternate route that was "entirely clear" but he first had to extricate his regiment from the mess on the other road, in the reverse order, before they could continue. Conditions were bad and congestion even worse during this move and Squadron Sergeant Major Richard Cunniffe of Headquarters Squadron remembered the road being "choked with vehicles" and the men "choked with dust" as four infantry and three armoured divisions were moving about with more than 20,000 vehicles in an area of not more than 25 square miles. The result was that a move of some seven to ten miles commencing at 12.30 A.M. on 19 May took 12 hours to complete.[28]

Similar problems occurred during the night of 23/24 May as the units of 5 Brigade struggled to reach their forward assembly areas. HEART Route, the primary divisional route, was blocked by "the poor condition of the roads, exercise traffic and insufficient traffic control," and matters were complicated by a rearward movement by 25 British Armoured Brigade, which was coming out of the line. HEART Route was used by both 1 Canadian and 13 British Corps, and although Eighth Army controlled the route, and should have assigned priority of movement "in accordance with the course of battle," it appears that "no preference was necessarily give to army or corps vehicles." To add to the congestion – and the confusion – large numbers of Italian civilians also began to appear "literally out of the very earth." Rain made the crossing of the Forme d'Aquino difficult and the roads became practically impassable to armour. By 9.00 P.M. on 23 May, Vokes Force had barely reached the 3 Infantry Brigade gap in the Hitler Line, while the Strathconas and Westminster Regiment had made a road move "in pitch darkness that took all night to complete and we were all dead tired

Sherman moving up, May 1944

A Canadian tank moves up in the Liri Valley. Note the dust. When thousands of vehicles moved along such roads, concealment was impossible and German artillery observers could bring down artillery fire. In the Liri in May 1944, the saying was, "Dust means Death." (NAC, PA-139890)

when we arrived at our destination about 3 in the morning." The British Columbia Dragoons' assembly area was not only crowded, it was dangerous – while waiting for Operation CHESTERFIELD to begin, they were "shelled, mortared and machine gunned," and one tank was lost to a mine. First light on 24 May found the Strathconas still east of the Gari River "with no sign of improvement in the congestion." The wheeled vehicles got over the Gari at OXFORD Bridge at 10.30 A.M., followed by the tracked vehicles 30 minutes later and within an hour the move was completed.[29]

1 Canadian Corps had demonstrated difficulty in planning and executing road moves during this operation, not surprising given its lack of experience. Poor discipline resulted in excess casual traffic on the assigned routes, which overloaded their capacity, and the forward route maintenance troops, established to improve routes as units tore up roads, could not keep up with the damage. The

combined effects meant that the move to the forward areas "was delayed by the congestion on the roads and by a necessary last minute change in assembly areas." Hoffmeister therefore informed Burns that he had postponed H Hour until later in the morning of 24 May, and this meant that, once again, the gunners had to revise their fire plans.[30] The "Mighty Maroon Machine" was discovering that, in modern warfare, getting to battle was almost as difficult as fighting it.

It was entirely fortunate for 5th Division, struggling forward, that the Germans were in no position to seriously hinder their laborious progress because the *Wehrmacht* had taken a beating since the commencement of Operation DIADEM on 11 May 1944. The prestigious 44. *Reichsgrenadierdivision Hoch und Deutschmeister*, an elite formation raised in the former Austria, had suffered such heavy casualties that it had to pulled out of line and replaced by the 90. *Panzergrenadierdivision*. That formation occupied the enemy sector opposite 1st Canadian Division at 6.00 A.M. on 16 May, the first day the Canadians entered the line, and suffered from the massive Allied artillery fire, which proved devastating and contributed to the 1 Canadian Corps' initial successes. The war diaries of the German 10. *Armee* and 51. *Gebirgskorps* noted that 23 May was a "critical" day because of the

> unprecedented artillery bombardment ... the ceaseless air attacks; the blinding of our battle stations with phosphorus and the attacks by armour and infantry occurring immediately thereafter, have depleted the formations and exhausted the troops, who have been fighting for eleven days.[31]

Combined with the "rather deep penetration" by Canadians north of Pontecorvo, senior German commanders gave some thought to "a fighting withdrawal to the 'C' Position" (the Caesar line referred to above). The operations of the American Fifth Army assisted those of the British Eighth Army since "no added support could be given to the defensive front against Eighth British Army. On this front our troops were protected by the defence works of the Senger Riegel, and by strong artillery concentrations. Here the battle in itself was not without hope." However, the "great weight of armour and artillery employed by the enemy" meant the "defence was soon worn down" and as a result, on 24 May 14. *Panzerkorps* "had to begin to withdraw, in the first instance behind the sector of the River Melfa."[32]

The German formations most concerned with the forthcoming 5th Division attack were the 90. *Panzergrenadierdivision* and its neighbouring formation to the north, the 1. *Fallschirmdivision*. Although it was not clear to the Canadians, their planned advance would bring them squarely against the boundary line dividing these formations. Canadian intelligence reports made repeated references to German units being under strength, poorly equipped and suffering from "low morale," creating a mood "certain of German defeat" and there was some element of truth to these assessments. The 90. *Panzergrenadierdivision*, commanded by *Generalleutnant* Ernst-Günther Baade, had been in the line since 14 May and had suffered considerable losses inflicted by 1st Canadian Division. The division's *Aufklärungsabteilung* (reconnaissance battalion) 190 and two panzergrenadier battalions were continually flanked and surrounded, resulting in their destruction between 17 and 24 May, while *Grenadierregiment* 200, described as the division's "sole element of any substance," had only 300 men in the Ceprano area. Other units of the division were still at fighting strength, including *Panzerabteilung* 190, a battalion of *Artillerieregiment* 190, *Panzerjägerabteilung* 190 and *Pioneerbataillon* 190 and Baade had received reinforcements from the 44. *Reichsgrenadierdivision*, 5. *Gebirgsdivision*, 114. *Jägerdivision* and other formations. These reinforcements increased his strength but also turned his division into an *ad hoc* grouping of separate infantry, artillery, tank and engineer units.[33]

Baade's divisional armoured unit, *Panzerabteilung* 190, was equipped with assault guns, not tanks – in this case 30 vehicles with a 75 mm gun on a Mark IV tank chassis – which would prove very effective in the defensive role. German assault gun tactics, first developed in 1940 and refined on the Eastern Front, had become quite sophisticated by 1944 and emphasized the strong points of this type of armoured vehicle: its powerful main armament, thick armour and low profile which rendered it easily concealed. Generally, assault guns moved forward with

An opponent to be respected

Generalleutnant Ernst-Günther Baade, commander of 90. *Panzergrenadierdivision* from December 1943 to December 1944, was a veteran commander, having fought in Poland, France, North Africa, Sicily and Italy. Both he and his troops were no strangers to fighting Canadians and his formation was responsible for destroying many Canadian tanks at the Melfa. Baade died on 8 May 1945, the day the war in Europe ended, after being wounded in an attack by British fighter-bombers. (Author's collection)

assaulting infantry, engaging targets until the objective was reached, after which they fell back about 1,000 yards to await further orders. Due to their vulnerability – the fact that they did not have a turret that would provide all-around defence – the assault guns never stayed forward.[34]

Panzerjägerabteilung 190 was also capable of delivering a strong punch with its 36 towed 75 mm Pak 40 anti-tank guns, low-slung, high-velocity weapons that could penetrate the frontal armour of a Sherman at long range. Intelligence

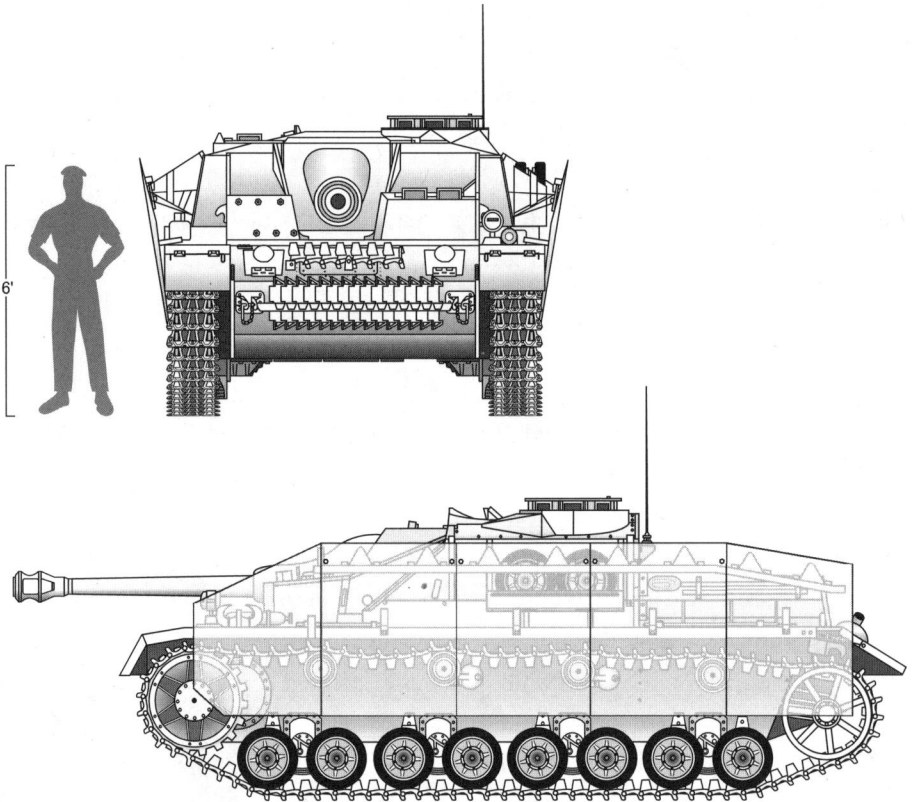

6'

Sturmgeschütze IV: The devil at the Melfa

The main anti-armour threat faced by Canadians at the Melfa was not from tanks but assault guns or *sturmgeschütze,* consisting of large-calibre guns mounted on a variety of armoured self-propelled chassis. The guns had limited traverse, making it necessary to turn the entire vehicle when aiming. First developed in the late 1930s, German assault gun forces were expanded in 1940. The *Sturmgeschütze IV* shown here was armed with a 75 mm Pak 39 gun and fired both high-explosive and anti-armour shells. The metal skirts were added in the field to afford greater protection from enemy fire. Other variants included 88 mm guns and even more armour. Known for their crafty and aggressive employments, *sturmgeschütze* destroyed almost half of the assaulting Sherman tanks at the Melfa River, making it a feared and respected weapon. In this illustration, the side skirt is shown as semi-transparent so as not to obscure the detail behind it.

A feared weapon

The Nebelwerfer, or "Moaning Minnie," was a multi-barrelled rocket launcher that harassed the defenders of the bridgehead throughout 24 and 25 May 1944. Taking only 90 seconds to load, it could hurl several 150 mm rounds in six seconds to a range of 7,000 yards. Here members of the 4th Anti-Tank Regiment, RCA, examine a projector captured during the battle. (NAC, PA-169111)

reports from early May indicate the Germans had about 300 anti-tank guns in the Liri Valley, including the Panther Turret Company *Panzerjägerabteilung* 114 with 75 mm guns, and ten 88 mm Hornet tank destroyers of *Schwere Panzerjägerabteilung* 525 as well as vehicles of *Sturmgeschützbrigade* 907. While many of these weapons had been eliminated in the recent fighting, no one knew how many were still around. Just to make things worse, Baade received two powerful reinforcement elements, a tank company from the 26. *Panzerdivision* and another from *Panzerabteilung* 1 of *Panzerregiment* 4. This latter company, which was equipped with Panthers and had been fighting since 15 May, joined the 90. *Panzergrenadierdivision* in time to face Canadian armour.[35]

Finally, Baade deployed another weapon that was feared by Allied soldiers. By the afternoon of 22 May, *Werferregiment* 71 had two battalions in the Pontecorvo-Aquino sector and another covering Highway 6. Each battalion had 18 five- or six-barrelled 15 cm rocket *Nebelwerfer* projectors, which could be loaded and fired in about 90 seconds. Fire from these weapons, nicknamed "Moaning Minnies" from the sound of their projectiles, was "cordially hated especially by the infantry" and would almost continually harass the Canadians during the forthcoming battle.[36]

By midnight on 20/21 May, Baade's 90. *Panzergrenadierdivision* was under command of 51. *Gebirgskorps*, led by Feuerstein. Throughout 23 May, 10. *Armee* received repeated appeals from that officer to withdraw his corps from Pontecorvo and a "battle that could not restore the situation," but was so preoccupied with the Anzio front that there was only time to reply with a communiqué praising the corps "at the very moment they were being beaten by the Canadians." Faced with an impossible situation, Feuerstein pulled back to a new defensive line running from San Giovanni on the Liri to Ponte-Regno, with 1. *Fallschirmdivision* north of Ponte-Rego and 90. *Panzergrenadierdivision* to the south.[37]

They would not be there for long.

I t was cold and misty when the British Columbia Dragoons, supported by the Irish Regiment of Canada, set off at 5.30 A.M. on 24 May 1944 to commence Phase II of Operation CHESTERFIELD. Their progress was immediately delayed when they discovered that a bridge being constructed over a gully that constituted a tank obstacle had not been completed, forcing the Dragoon Recce Troop to locate an alternate route farther north. This forced H-Hour to be delayed several times, but it was finally set for 8 A.M. Ten minutes before, a modified "laager"* stonk commenced and several targets were eliminated. The Dragoons set out again at 7.57 A.M., crossing their start line, known as VERMOUTH, with two squadrons "up" (that is, moving side by side in the advance), each followed by an infantry company in carriers (see map M-2).

The approach march met with severe shelling and fire from enemy infantry and anti-tank guns in the Aquino area, which resulted in the loss of one Honey. The terrain was very close, with "scrub trees, vineyards and copses intermingled with olive groves which at times gave partial protection to the tanks but also concealed the enemy defences." Vegetation also hindered navigation and crew commanders were unable to observe much beyond their tanks. Cement posts strung with wire were embedded throughout the vineyards at a height that could

---

* A laager or leaguer was an administrative formation used by armoured units that permitted quick resupply or regrouping. Since laagers were generally formed in open ground, they were not as secure as a harbour, which was usually formed in a woodline, and not normally used for prolonged periods.

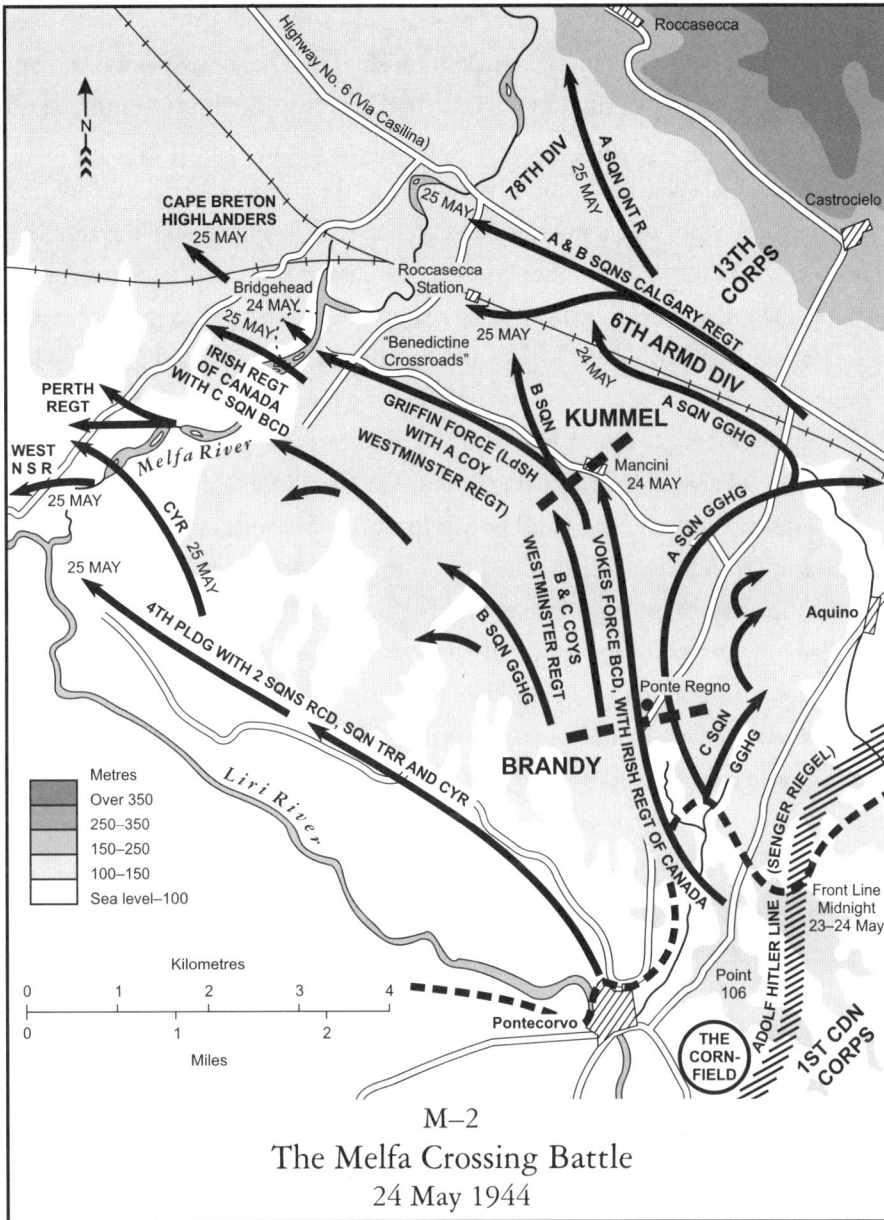

Roccasecca

Highway No. 6 (Via Casilina)

N

Castrocielo

CAPE BRETON HIGHLANDERS 25 MAY

78TH DIV 25 MAY

A SQN ONT R 25 MAY

A & B SQNS CALGARY REGT

13TH CORPS

Roccasecca Station

Bridgehead 24 MAY 25 MAY

"Benedictine Crossroads" 25 MAY

6TH ARMD DIV 24 MAY

IRISH REGT OF CANADA WITH C SQN BCD

B SQN

KUMMEL

A SQN GGHG

PERTH REGT

GRIFFIN FORCE (LdSH) WITH A COY WESTMINSTER REGT)

Mancini 24 MAY

WEST N S R

Melfa River

A SQN GGHG

25 MAY

CYR 25 MAY

25 MAY

WESTMINSTER REGT

VOKES FORCE BCD, WITH IRISH REGT OF CANADA

Aquino

B & C COYS

B SQN GGHG

Ponte Regno

C SQN GGHG

4TH PLDG WITH 2 SQNS RCD, SQN TRR AND CYR

BRANDY

Liri River

Metres
Over 350
250–350
150–250
100–150
Sea level–100

(SENGER RIEGEL)

Front Line Midnight 23–24 May

Kilometres
0 1 2 3 4
0 1 2
Miles

Pontecorvo

Point 106

THE CORN-FIELD

ADOLF HITLER LINE

1ST CDN CORPS

M–2
The Melfa Crossing Battle
24 May 1944

decapitate an unwary crew commander with his head and shoulders out of the turret, and as a result many tanks had wire and branches trailing behind them. This difficulty in moving, combined with sniper fire, slowed the infantry who became separated from the tanks. One result of the heavy enemy shelling was that Vokes Force moved to the right of the 1 *Fallschirmdivision* and into the sector of *Grenadierregiment* 361, deployed along their front. During this initial encounter, they destroyed elements of *Gebirgsjägerbataillon* 85.[38]

The Dragoons reached BRANDY "well ahead of the infantry" at 10.30 A.M. and the enemy withdrew after a brief skirmish. The Dragoons paused to consolidate but, without waiting for 11 Infantry Brigade to catch up, continued on to KUMMEL, on high ground about 2,000 yards to the northwest near Mancini. Although it was a shorter distance than that to their first objective, it took the tanks longer to reach as enemy resistance was intensifying. KUMMEL was reached, however, at 12.20 P.M. but Vokes Force immediately "came under intense heavy shelling and encountered enemy Panther tanks and self-propelled guns." On the left, B Squadron faced several Mk IV and Panther tanks. Lieutenant Nigel Taylor, a troop leader in that squadron, remembered encountering "the most enormous tank I had ever seen … I promptly reported this beast as a 'Tiger.' It turned out of course to be a PzKw V Panther. My gunner, Tpr Cecil D. Shears was a crack shot … Two quick shots and the Panther was finished." Seconds later, Taylor's Sherman was hit and Shears killed. The Dragoons lost three tanks but knocked out one Panther, two Mark IVs and seven anti-tank guns. Dismounted Germans still milled about, and as the infantry had not yet come up, members of the Dragoon Recce Troop dismounted to consolidate the position.[39]

This was the first action for the British Columbia Dragoons and it had gone well: for a loss of four tanks and five men, they had secured their objectives, destroyed several German armoured vehicles, rocket launchers and other equipment, and captured about 50 prisoners. Their engagement against the Panthers was particularly noteworthy and the Dragoon war diarist recorded that these were "a new type of tank, and to the best of our knowledge only one had previ-

British Columbia's victory
During their advance up the Liri Valley on 24 May 1944, the British Columbia Dragoons had what was likely the first encounter between Allied amour and German Panther tanks on the Western Front. A Sherman tank belonging to 4 Troop, B Squadron destroyed this particular Panther on 24 May 1944. (Courtesy The British Columbia Dragoons)

ously been knocked out by the British Army." On the debit side, resistance had intenified as the Dragoons advanced up the Liri Valley, and the Germans were already withdrawing to new defensive positions on their next objective, the Melfa, which lay 4,000 yards ahead.[40]

Shortly after Vokes Force had moved off, Lieutenant Edward Perkins and his five vehicles from the Strathcona Recce Troop followed them to monitor their progress. Earlier, Perkins and the Strathconas' commanding officer, Griffin, had carefully studied air photographs to select possible crossing sites along the Melfa. They decided on two sites – one that C Squadron would attempt and the other for Perkins's Recce Troop to cross. Perkins's site was deliberately chosen as "the most difficult since it was far less likely to be defended." As his troop moved forward, Perkins sent radio reports describing the opposition being encountered and the obstacles slowing the rate of advance. The destructiveness of the Dragoons' battle was apparent by the number of trees blasted by shellfire and the damaged equipment scattered about, but the close terrain made it difficult to see and navigation proved more difficult than anyone could have predicted. The aerial photos and panoramic photos they had studied had distorted the true nature of the ground in the valley, but Perkins did find them useful for navigation. Shortly after crossing the start line at 1.40 P.M., however, Perkins's tank broke down and he moved to Sergeant Clifford Macey's vehicle, while another sergeant remained behind to repair the immobilized Honey.[41]

Ten minutes later, Perkins cleared KUMMEL and his four Honeys with 20 men were now leading 5th Division. About 1,000 yards past the Dragoon position, the troop opened fire at a German halftrack and infantry near a building. They had moved another 2,000 yards when they spotted a Panther 300 yards ahead. Perkins opened up on the German crew commander, visible in the turret, who slumped "forward out of the cupola." The German tank did not engage Perkins, who continued moving as fast as he could. Shortly thereafter, he observed two more enemy tanks that apparently could not see him and, as the troop approached the river, they also spotted a house near the bank with some Germans in it. They fired on it, a white flag quickly appeared and eight Germans emerged, who were turned over to the crew of a scout platoon vehicle that had just came up. At 3.00 P.M. Perkins reached the Melfa River.[42]

As his other vehicles came up, Perkins discovered that one had strayed – his three Honeys and 16 men were now the lead element of 5 Armoured Brigade

Honeys en route to the Melfa

Each armoured regiment in 5th Canadian Armoured Division had a troop of American-built Stuart ("Honey") light tanks for reconnaissance. Three of these lightly armed vehicles and a handful of men charged ahead of 1 Canadian Corps, gained a bridgehead over the Melfa River and held it against significant opposition. (NAC, PA-204157)

but they were on their objective. The Honeys were parked under cover while Perkins and Sergeant Macey dismounted to recce for a crossing site while being covered by the troop. Perkins carefully studied the site he had previously selected from aerial photos. It was about 2,000 yards south of the railway; to the south the bank was impassable but about 75 yards to the north was a ledge leading down to the river that was steep but appeared usable by tanks. The river itself was some 50 yards wide at this point but with little water running in it. A number of prepared enemy positions were observed "all along the river bank," but they appeared to have been vacated in "great haste." Perkins and Macey crossed the river and immediately came under not only enemy fire, which they returned, but also machine gun fire from a Strathcona A Squadron tank which had reached the east bank of river. Perkins noted this friendly misunderstanding was "extremely nervewracking, not only because the fire was close but because we did not know how soon it would be followed by a high explosive round" from the "enemy" Sherman's 75 mm main gun. Fortunately, he recalled, "the Squadron leader saw what was happening and ordered the tank to stop" firing.[43]

Continuing his recce, Perkins found a spot that, with some improvements, would be passable as a crossing site. With a 20-foot bank and tangled with saplings and under bush, it was not perfect but would have to do. While Perkins remained on the far bank to guide his tanks, Macey returned to the other bank. The troop's three Honeys now crossed the river one at a time and went into hulldown positions just below the far bank. They were all across by 3.20 P.M. Two men were deployed to provide cover, while the remainder of the troop set about improving the crossing using explosives to remove obstructions, although most of the work was done with pick and shovel. The track was also widened, a retaining wall built out of tree trunks and a gap filled with dirt. Speed was critical as the enemy were nearby.[44]

About 100 yards south of the crossing position was a house that appeared occupied by the Germans. It had to be cleared and, accompanied by Macey and three other men, Perkins crept toward it under cover of the bank. Rushing into the courtyard, he saw eight German paratroopers through the windows facing towards the planned crossing site for C Squadron farther to the south. Perkins remembered the Germans as "big well-built men armed to the teeth" and that "for a moment I did not know what was going to happen." Perkins shouted "drop it" and the Germans turned around in considerable astonishment. Although his "trigger finger itched," Perkins did not open fire and finally one German "dropped his rifle to be instantly followed by all the others and their hands rose in sullen astonishment." While watching the expected crossing site, the Germans had been surprised by an attack from the other direction.[45]

With the immediate area secure, Perkins moved his three surviving Honeys up to the house and deployed them to provide all-around defence while the prisoners were sent back over the Melfa along with Macey, who would guide A Squadron across. Almost immediately Perkins's men came under fire from a German sniper who proved to be "an astonishingly poor shot," and two rounds from the PIAT removed this threat. Perkins was pleased with what he and his troop had accomplished in such short time and awaited the arrival of A Company of the Westminster Regiment, "on whose heels would be the remainder of the battalion," and the tanks of A Squadron of the Strathconas.[46]

The Strathconas were on the way. Knowing that speed was essential and wishing to take advantage of the somewhat disorganized enemy resistance met thus far, Brigadier Smith ordered the Strathconas to move from their assembly area at 11.30 A.M. The British Columbia Dragoons had not yet established a firm base "but it was considered that this was a legitimate risk ... and that bold action was necessary." In the Strathcona assembly area, the crews made last minute preparations on their vehicles, "giving everything the once over. Guns, ammo, petrol, rations, nothing can be left to chance at a time like this." Before moving out, Griffin held a final O Group and then the tanks lined up in formation on HEART Route. Some men had a last "brew up"; for most it would be their last food or drink for 36 hours. Then came the order to move and as Sergeant Major Dick Cunniffe, who remained behind, recalled:

> the tank engines start up, and amid the noise we wish the boys good luck. As the Shermans roll by, the crew commanders, head and shoulders out of the turret, wave and give the OK sign. The drivers, peering through their goggles, give a grin which is hard to see through the dust which has already started to come up in billows.[47]

Two hours later, the Strathconas were at Mancini, where Vokes Force was digging in.[48]

The three Strathcona squadrons and their supporting elements crossed the start line behind Perkins's troop, just after 1.40 P.M., using the road running from Mancini to the BENEDICTINE crossroads as their centre line. Griffin Force advanced in a wedge formation with A Squadron at the tip, B Squadron on the right rear and C Squadron to the left, with A Company of the Westminster Regiment between the two rear squadrons. Each squadron moved in a diamond formation with squadron headquarters in the middle and the four troops at each point around it, with the distance between each vehicle varying from 50 to 150 yards depending on conditions. Screening the movement of the tanks, were the scout platoons of the three Westminster motor companies. Capable of swift movement in their fully tracked and armoured Loyd carriers, they "did an excellent job in spotting enemy armour and infantry and sending the information back for the more heavily armed tanks to deal with." Also moving ahead of the tanks were the two Recce Troop Honeys carrying the engineer recce parties while following the tanks were the gunners' M-10s with their powerful 3-inch guns and the M-7 Priest 105 mm self-propelled guns, which moved as directed

The Gunners' Sunday punch

The M-10 tank destroyer was the main weapon of the self-propelled anti-tank regiments of the Royal Canadian Artillery. A battery of these vehicles accompanied each armoured battlegroup during the Liri Valley operations and their powerful 3-inch gun was responsible for destroying several German vehicles at the Melfa. (Author's collection)

by their parent regimental headquarters. On the flanks were two squadrons of the Governor General's Horse Guards, the armoured reconnaissance unit of 5th Division.

It was a powerful force but, despite the best efforts by the squadron commanders to keep it together, the difficult terrain made observation between vehicles difficult and the formation soon fell into disarray with several vehicles becoming separated from the group. The force also experienced the same navigational problems as Perkins, and actually moved north of its intended line of advance, but did succeed in reaching the crossing site, albeit farther north than planned.[49]

Lieutenant Colonel Griffin knew that reaching the Melfa quickly was essential to success. Abandoning caution and normal tactical movement, therefore, all three squadrons advanced as quickly as the terrain allowed. Major Bill Milroy, commander of B Squadron, thought the risks acceptable as the swift pace placed the Strathconas "on the Germans before they knew we were in the vicinity." Moving tactically, particularly where the ground was more open, could have resulted in a protracted battle, the result of which might have been "our not reaching the river when we did, or at all." Approximately a mile east of Perkins's position, Milroy's squadron moved to the right of the Strathconas' centre line and swung north towards the Roccasecca railway station, then westward to the river with its right resting some 50 yards from the railway line. The railway station backed onto both the river and a railway bridge, and to the front was a good-sized open field ringed with trees and bush. Milroy halted B Squadron under cover at the edge of the woodline and "waited to see what we might be required to do." As there was little opposition to the squadron's front, Lieutenant Jack ("Jock") Burton suggested he move his 4 Troop farther to the north, using a nearby road, as he suspected there might be Germans on the flank. Milroy agreed and Burton set off at 4.40 P.M., to discover that his instincts were entirely correct.[50]

Major Lee Symmes's A Squadron then advanced towards BENEDICTINE crossroads with its 1 Troop, under Lieutenant Robert Gartke, in the lead, close behind Perkins (see map M-2). Behind A Squadron was RHQ, then C Squadron. As it approached BENEDICTINE, Gartke's troop came under fire from enemy tanks and self-propelled guns, while C Squadron engaged other targets to the left. The

Canadian Shermans in the Liri Valley, May 1944

This photograph gives a good impression of the close terrain in the valley floor, with small farms, olive groves, crops and hedges. While this terrain made it easier for German defence positions to be concealed, it also meant that their fields of fire were limited and Allied armour could take advantage of it to move forward. (NAC, PA-204153)

Strathconas' navigational difficulties proved a blessing in disguise as the "enemy AT defences were sited as if armour had been expected from the south and not the south east," which made it possible "to engage the defences at least partially from the rear." For over an hour, both squadrons were involved in a sniping battle with enemy vehicles on both sides of the Melfa. Some cleverly-positioned dummy tanks misled the Canadians and they also encountered dismounted infantry and a *Nebelwerfer* battery. Restricted visibility made this largely a squadron-level action and seriously affected their ability to identify targets.[51]

Realizing the tank commanders were having difficulty in identifying targets, Perkins turned command of the far bank area over to Corporal F.G. McLean, moved back across the river and tried indicating targets to the A Squadron second-in-command, Captain Jack Whittle, and then Lieutenant Angus MacKinnon of 4 Troop, with no success because the German positions were obscured by vegetation or out of range. Perkins then returned to the far bank. Despite their difficulties, Lieutenant Colonel Griffin repeatedly ordered his tank squadrons to continue moving with all possible speed, and the three squadrons assisted each other by communicating their bearings or the location of supporting elements.[52]

This tank action near the Melfa resulted in heavy casualties. In A Squadron Gartke saw Major Lee Symmes's tank approach the river, then suddenly become enveloped in smoke. Symmes and three crew members were wounded, while Trooper Thomas Hately was killed. Just past the BENEDICTINE crossroads, Captain J.B. Windsor, the A Squadron battle captain, was moving near Symmes when his tank took a hit. Four of the crew scrambled out of the tank, while the fate of the fifth crewman remained unknown until he was later reported in hospital. In 1 Troop, Sergeant Scott's tank was hit and as the crew bailed out, it exploded in flames, killing three men. Casualties continued to mount, bringing a hurried call from Griffin to Callsign 16 (spoken as "one-six"), Captain Samuel Vaisrub, the Strathcona medical officer: "Hello 16, we want you badly." When Vaisrub inquired as to the number of casualties, he was told, "I haven't the slightest idea but they are heavy."[53]

Rather than assigning different frequencies to each squadron, the radios on every Strathcona tank were tuned to the same frequency, allowing personnel to follow the entire action. The traffic over the radio net was fast and to the echelons coming behind, it provided information of the battle. Dick Cunniffe, who was coming behind with HQ Squadron of the Strathconas, recalled that

Whenever we halted there is a rush to the signals lorry to get the latest news. Between flashes of gunfire we hear the crew commanders giving orders and passing messages … Messages and scraps of conversation come over the wireless. Major Jack Smith of "C" Squadron has been wounded, but is carrying on with the job – someone has taken 15 prisoners – 4th Troop of "B" Sqn is shooting up vehicles as the enemy tries to make a getaway on Highway Number 6 – "Get off the set" – our Recce Troop, under Lieut. E.J. Perkins, have got across the Melfa and are calling the Westies to come up – and all through the din of war, we hear the voice of our Colonel [Griffin], "Push On", "Push On."[54]

While 1 Troop of A Squadron stayed on the centre line of the advance, Lieutenant G.C. Catton's 2 Troop, moving on its southern flank, became separated from the squadron and then received orders to move to the right flank. The

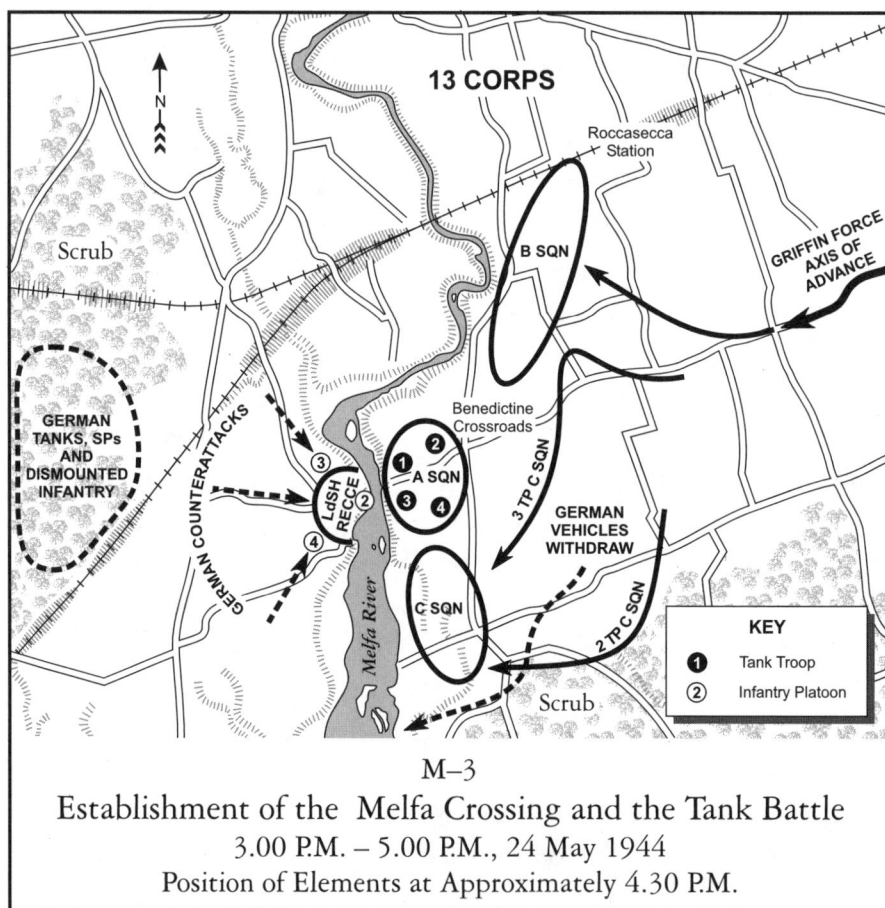

M–3
Establishment of the Melfa Crossing and the Tank Battle
3.00 P.M. – 5.00 P.M., 24 May 1944
Position of Elements at Approximately 4.30 P.M.

squadron's 3 and 4 Troops moved along its right or northern flank, with the squadron second-in-command, Captain Jack Whittle, leading them to the cross-roads. At this point 3 Troop was ordered to "approach river bank to left of centre line with 4 Troop to assist Major Symmes" (see map M-3). As the troop came up to the river, Corporal Tall's tank was hit and burst into flame. A few minutes later, the tank of the troop leader, Lieutenant Kenneth Philip, burst into flame. Philip and two of the crew were killed but Trooper Fraser managed to get out, and despite having half a leg shot away, crawled nearly 100 yards before being picked up by a first aid carrier from the Westminster Regiment.[55]

Lieutenant Angus MacKinnon's 4 Troop of A Squadron, initially in reserve, continued to the river where MacKinnon received a wound to his left arm, and his tank was immobilized. Suffering shock from the loss of blood, MacKinnon nevertheless remained in position, attempting to guide the remainder of 4 Troop down to the water. Corporal L.D. McNeil became lost and eventually joined B Squadron farther to the right. The third and last tank in the troop, under Sergeant Norris Eby, was unable to reach the crossing. MacKinnon's tank took two more hits and, unable to fight the vehicle, the crew took their troop leader back to the Regimental Aid Post. Captain Jack Whittle had no better luck. His tank experienced mechanical problems so he shifted to a 2 Troop tank, but sometime between 4.30 and 4.45 P.M. received a shrapnel wound. A Squadron had begun the day with 16 tanks and after about an hour of heavy fighting had lost nine of them. Most of the squadron's officers were dead or wounded, leaving Lieutenant Bob Gartke of 1 Troop in command. It was now about 4.30 P.M. and he attempted to reorganize the squadron.[56]

As A Squadron battled the enemy, the three engineer recce parties reached the Melfa, dismounted from their Honeys and searched for tank crossing sites. In their vehicles was equipment to lift mines, cover small gaps and mark routes as well as some demolitions. At one crossing, Lance Corporal George Chidley of 10 Field Squadron, RCE, found five derelict vehicles blocking the route and, like everywhere else along the river, this site was well covered by enemy guns. Despite enemy fire, Chidley laid charges on each vehicle, clearing the way, although one sapper was killed and two wounded doing this dangerous job. A sapper Caterpillar D-7 bulldozer allocated to Griffin Force to clear routes does not appear to have made it forward.[57]

The Strathconas' C Squadron, meanwhile, had continued behind A Squadron after B Squadron had pulled off to the north. Its two leading troops became widely separated, with 3 Troop becoming intermingled with B Squadron and 2

Troop being momentarily diverted southward before it rejoined. The remaining two troops and squadron headquarters made it to the river and pulled up to the south of A Squadron only to receive a severe pounding. After scoring a hit on a Panther, Major Jack Smith, the squadron commander was wounded. An 88 mm round wrecked the barrel of the Sherman of Captain Richard Crimes, the battle captain, so he moved to another squadron headquarters tank being used by the FOO, but it too was hit and Crimes and three of the crew killed. Captain Len Payne, the squadron second-in-command, was also wounded at this time.

Tank–infantry cooperation, May 1944

As the fighting in the Liri Valley proved, it was essential that the two arms cooperate. The infantry protected the tanks from enemy anti-tank guns and the armour took out the German machine-gun positions that held up the infantry. Note that the crew commander of the Sherman is manning the .50 calibre machine gun mounted on his turret. Also note the terrain, which provided some concealment, and the mountain heights in the background, ideal German OP positions that negated the advantages of the terrain. (NAC, PA-177096)

Sergeant R.J. Forrest's tank in 1 Troop was hit and two of the crew died of their wounds. Sergeant William Turk of 2 Troop was credited with the first Panther kill by the Strathconas, only to die along with another crew members shortly thereafter. The tank belonging to his troop leader, Lieutenant C.R. Gilliat, was hit in the suspension and Gilliat was killed after he bailed out. In 3 Troop, Lieutenant William Reade's tank took two direct hits from a German anti-tank gun but the crew managed to scramble from the burning Sherman, put the fire out, remount their now-immobile vehicle and knock out a self-propelled gun. Four Troop lost two tanks, one commanded by Sergeant D. Armstrong and the other by Corporal W. Nichol. In a few minutes, C Squadron had suffered nearly 50 per cent vehicle casualties and none of the surviving vehicles were able to cross the Melfa as planned.[58]

On the extreme right, B Squadron encountered soft-skinned vehicles, motorcycles and infantry, and was able to engage the enemy without receiving any damage itself. Meanwhile, 4 Troop of this squadron, under Lieutenant Jock Burton, which had earlier moved to the north, had a successful engagement against German targets near the river, destroying one self-propelled gun and four multi-barrelled anti-aircraft guns, before moving back to the main squadron position.[59]

The tank fight at the approaches to the Melfa was ferocious but the Strathconas managed to take out many of the German armoured vehicles on both banks. Several surviving enemy vehicles on the eastern side retired across the river at a point 1,000 yards to the south of Perkins's position. RHQ and A and C Squadrons of the Strathconas had destroyed at least five German tanks or self-propelled guns but lost 17 tanks, half their combined strength, getting to or attempting to cross the Melfa River.

Their subsequent attempts were no more successful "because of the steepness of the river banks and also because the river bank on our side of the Melfa was dominated by enemy anti-tank guns from the opposite bank." Forced to remain on the east side, the weakened Strathcona squadrons occupied the best possible positions to support the men on the other side. The remnants of A Squadron covered the approach to the crossing site and C Squadron watched the open ground southwest of the crossing, while farther to the north, B Squadron deployed to defend against counterattacks from that direction. At the crossing site itself, Sergeant Macey returned to Perkins's position and informed him that the Strathconas' A Squadron would be unable to cross." [60]

As bad as the situation appeared for the Canadians, it was worse for the Germans. At 3.40 P.M., 51. *Gebirgskorps* reported that "enemy tanks had earlier broken through south of Stazione Roccasecca and were moving towards the Melfa." German attempts to block this penetration faltered in the face of Allied artillery and air attacks while the destruction of roads and bridges slowed and finally stopped reinforcements ordered to the area. By 4.20 P.M., Allied tanks were reported "at the Melfa southwest of Stazione Roccasecca," and this was shortly followed by pleas for reinforcements, as the 1. *Fallschirmdivision* commenced withdrawing to the far bank of the river. In front of the Strathconas, in unprepared positions, were the remnants of *Grenadierregiments* 200 and 361. The situation however, was not regarded as completely lost since the operations officer of 51. *Gebirgskorps* reported that, despite heavy artillery fire, the loss of 10 assault guns, the destruction of several infantry battalions and continued attacks from 20 to 30 tanks, the defending positions could "be held for a few days," but only at "the cost of very heavy casualties."[61]

At this critical point, Perkins and Macey concluded that none of the A or C Squadron tanks would be able to cross the river. Earlier, as the tank battle had raged, Perkins felt "there was no doubt that if the enemy chose to employ his tanks and infantry … he could have driven us out of the bridgehead." To be held, this position had to be reinforced and expanded but the only reinforcement available was Perkins's broken-down Honey, which, now repaired, was brought over the river and "placed some distance below the crest as a rallying point in case we were forced from our position." Should it prove necessary, Perkins was ready to withdraw. He reported his situation to Griffin, who responded that "the tanks were fighting hard on the near bank" and unable to give much support.[62]

The Westminster Regiment, which was to consolidate and expand the bridgehead, was still nowhere in sight, and although Griffin requested they be pushed forward, it would clearly be some time before reinforcements would be available. Griffin therefore authorized Perkins to pull back if necessary, but Perkins refused as his ruses to make the enemy

Hero of the Melfa battle
Lieutenant Edward Perkins led an aggressive defence of the bridgehead, refusing to withdraw when ordered by his commanding officer. (Courtesy Lord Strathcona's Horse (Royal Canadians) Regimental Museum)

believe his force was larger than it really was appeared to be working. For now, his Recce Troop would hold the bridgehead until A Company of the Westminsters came up.

But where were they? At 4.45 P.M., Griffin asked over the command net, "where is flatfeet [A Company] there is no sign of them yet." Then, from A Squadron of the Strathconas came the welcome news that the infantry, "are coming up immediately they are near BENEDICTINE."[63]

The approach march of A Company of the Westminster Regiment to the Melfa had been difficult and the actual time of their arrival at the crossing site is still a matter of debate. For this operation, the 80 men of the company had been reinforced with three anti-tank platoons, totalling 12 6-pdr guns, and a Vickers machine gun platoon from the Westminster Support Company. Quartered in "the inevitable olive grove across the road from the Strathconas," the Westminsters had advanced in two groups. A Company, led by Major Jock Mahony and under command of Griffin Force, had moved from its assembly area at 11.30 A.M. Mahony and his men were happy to fight alongside the Strathconas again as they had exercised with "the Strats in the training days in England" and respected them "for the great team they were." Mahony had also worked with Griffin before and had great respect for the tank officer. His company was to follow the tanks in their carriers, de-bus a quarter mile from the river, move across it in extended line and then expand the bridgehead. The roads were bad and cross-country movement was extremely difficult, but the infantry appear to have kept up with A Squadron and the Strathcona RHQ although their vehicles, despite being halftracks, performed no better than wheeled vehicles and, when they tried to move off road, became stuck in the drainage ditches. The drivers, however, did a wonderful job in keeping the column rolling close behind the tanks.

The Westminsters' progress was not without incident. Three vehicles were lost from shelling and during a halt on a narrow road the mortar truck, stacked with 3-inch rounds, took a direct hit, which resulted in a "very good 4th of July display." Before reaching the river, one of the carriers spotted a German self-propelled gun and the infantry dismounted and engaged it with a 2-inch mortar. The first two shots missed, but the third was a direct hit, knocking the gun out and killing the crew. Mahony later stated the company arrived at 2.45 P.M. although the Westminster War Diary records that, at "1500 hrs the company reached the Melfa," about when the tank battle commenced, and found the Strathconas "heavily engaged by enemy tanks, A/Tk and SP guns." Mahony and his men admired the efforts of the Strathconas on their behalf: "the LdSH tanks stuck right on the job and the crews displayed great courage and devotion to duty, sacrificing themselves in carrying out their orders to get A Company across the river." Griffin, in turn, was pleased with the work of the carriers cooperating with the tanks, particularly because they assisted in the evacuation of casualties.[64]

One Westminster Scout Platoon vehicle crossed the river (although Perkins does not mention this in his account) but the remainder of A Company were forced to de-bus farther from the crossing than planned because a knocked-out tank blocked the way and dismounted about a half mile away. Mahony's plan was for his company to cross the river in extended line and then form a semi-circular arc with 3 Platoon, under Lieutenant Heber Smith, on the right and 4 Platoon, under Lieutenant Ross Douglas, on the left, with 2 Platoon, led by Lieutenant Ken Harrison, in reserve. Heavy machine guns were to be posted on the flanks to cover the area of the crossing.

Just as the first infantry splashed through the shallow Melfa, German mortar fire began to come down on the river. The records are not clear as to when the first infantry crossed – Perkins remembered that the first platoon was over at 5.00 P.M. but two other reports state that the lead elements crossed at 3.30 P.M., while the Westminster War Diary has the entire company over the river by 4.15 P.M. The differences may result from the added time required for the infantry to move up from their vehicles and delays caused by enemy fire and confusion. As the Westminsters moved up, Mahony remembered, "our eyes met with a terrible sight of burning tanks every way we looked … the [tank] fight was still going on and we could see Strath tanks still firing." The natural cover helped conceal the approach to the river, but once this was traversed, A Company came under fire and one man was lost during the crossing.[65]

On reaching the west bank, the infantry fanned out (see map M-4). Perkins's troop supported the Westminsters, but as their vehicles were only armed with .50 calibre machine guns, this limited the distance the infantry could exploit beyond the river bank. Mahony focussed on getting his 3 Platoon's position on the right established, but quickly became aware of a crisis on the left, where Douglas's 4 Platoon came under fire from enemy infantry in nearby houses and a tank. A section was pinned down by this fire and "the only thing they could do was to lie down and hope the folds in the ground would conceal them." Mahony obtained smoke grenades from the Recce Troop tanks and threw them in the area where the men lay and once the smoke was thick enough, they pulled back, except for

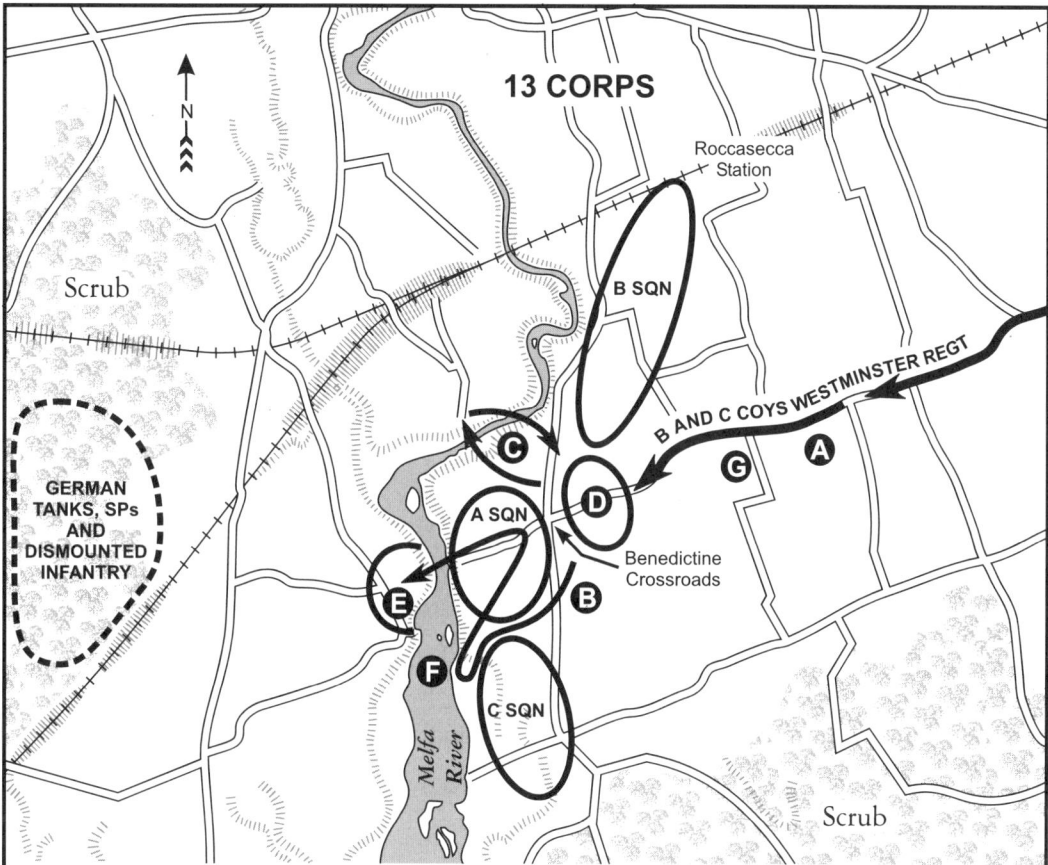

13 CORPS

Roccasecca
Station

Scrub

B SQN

B AND C COYS WESTMINSTER REGT

GERMAN
TANKS, SPs
AND
DISMOUNTED
INFANTRY

C

A SQN

D

G

A

Benedictine
Crossroads

E

B

F

C SQN

Melfa River

Scrub

(A) B and C Companies of the Westminster Regiment arrive at the Benedictine Crossroads at approximately 4:45 P.M., 24 May and begin moving to reinforce and expand the Melfa bridgehead.

(B) C Company continues by vehicle and is unable to cross the Melfa near "F". The company moves back to Benedictine Crossroads, then attempts crossing at (F) again, after which it returns to the crossroads, dismounts, and moves into the bridgehead at "E" at about 10:00 P.M., 24 May.

(C) B Company dismounts and crosses the Melfa 1,300 yards north of the bridgehead but due to its exposed position is ordered to "D" and arrives there at 2:00 A.M. on 25 May.

(D) Position of C Company at 2:00 A.M., 25 May.

(E) By 5:30 A.M., 25 May, the bridgehead consists of the LdSH(RC) Recce Troop and A Company, C Company and three 6 pdr A/Tk guns from the Westminster Regiment.

(F) Canadian engineers recce a new crossing point during the night of 24–25 May.

(G) The Irish Regiment of Canada and the Perth Regiment of 11 Infantry Brigade move up during the night of 24–25 May in preparation for the breakout attack scheduled for 6:00 A.M., 25 May.

M–4

Attempts to Reinforce and Expand the Bridgehead
3.00 P.M., 24 May – 5.00 A.M., 25 May 1944
Position of Elements at Approximately 2.00 A.M., 25 May 1944

two men who were pinned in the position. Perkins and Mahony then went forward to rescue them only to find one man dead but the two officers brought the other back to safety. The enemy had by now reoccupied the house to the south of the crossing site cleared earlier by Perkins but the remainder of Douglas's platoon, augmented by a section from 2 Platoon, still in reserve, secured it quickly and took 20 prisoners. Things, however, shortly got worse. A German self-propelled gun, hull down in a small re-entrant, was observed about 250 yards away from company headquarters, engaging the Strathcona tanks on the far bank. Corporal J.A. Thrasher of the Westminsters fired at it with a PIAT. His first round fell about 30 yards short but the second hit the vehicle's track, immobilizing it. The crew bailed out only to be cut down by rifle and Bren fire from 2 Platoon.[66]

Trooper Jacob Funk of Perkins's troop and two Bren gunners from A Company volunteered to take out another self-propelled gun that was spotted in a nearby area. Funk crept along the riverbank with a PIAT until he was within 150 yards of the target and fired but the round hit foliage and exploded. Funk moved to a better position and prepared to fire again, although loading and firing a PIAT from a prone position was not an easy task. First, the launcher was heavy, some 34.5 lb., and difficult to handle. Second, to load, the operator had to rest the projector on his chest, and while holding the weapon in place by placing his

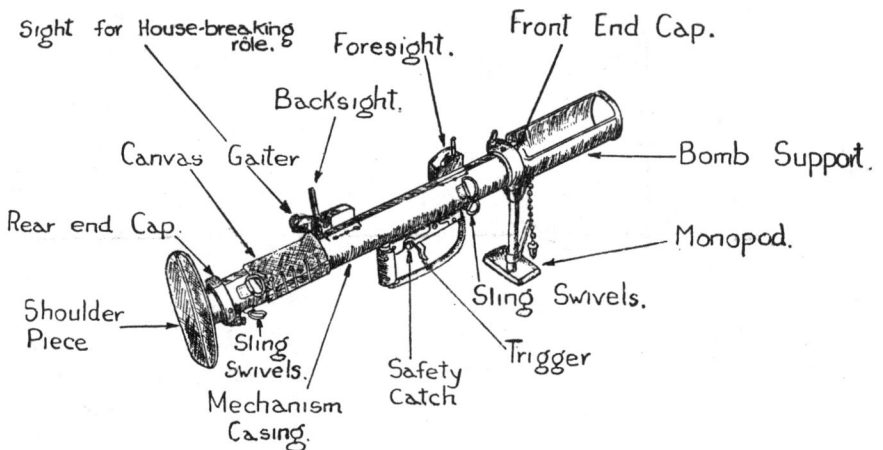

The PIAT, a weapon that required a good sense of humour to use properly

For more than eight hours, the Projector, Infantry, Anti-Tank, or PIAT, was the sole anti-tank weapon in the Melfa bridgehead. Employed by both the Strathconas and the Westminster Regiment, the spring-loaded PIAT fired a 2.5 lb. bomb with a hollow charge and was officially listed as being effective against light armour out to a range of 115 yards and against bunkers up to 350 yards. At the Melfa, it was used at considerably shorter ranges. Loading this weaon required considerable physical effort. (Author's collection)

It is not what it appears to be.
German defences included many realistic-looking dummy tanks that would force Canadian tanks to expose themselves to German anti-tank guns as they manoeuvred to engage these decoys. (Author's collection)

instep on the shoulder piece and keeping one hand on the trigger guard, push a 2.5 lb. bomb against the tension of the mainspring until the weapon was cocked. To do this required considerable effort as normally two men served this weapon. Handling it alone, Funk managed the difficult task of reloading. Moving to within 100 yards of his target, Funk fired a second shot which went high, then another that was low but, finally, on his fourth attempt, hit the suspension of the self-propelled gun and the crew bailed out, and were cut down or captured. At this, German armour, which had approached within 300 yards of Mahony's position, withdrew.[67]

Up to this point most of the action had been southwest of the bridgehead but a patrol north of it reported enemy tanks massing in that direction. This sector was held by 3 Platoon, now under command of Sergeant Samuel White, who had replaced the wounded Lieutenant Heber. White, described as "a stout soldier," was an older man fighting his second war. As the platoon came under fire and began to take casualties, Mahony told him to hold his position until reinforcements from C Company, expected sometime in the hour, arrived. Around this time, two carriers from 1 Platoon, back from its screening mission, arrived and their soldiers were put into the line, while the carriers took prisoners back. There were now some 90 Canadians, armed only with small arms, machine guns and PIATS, holding the bridgehead against enemy tanks and infantry.[68]

At this moment, a runner from White arrived at Mahony's position to again report armour massing to the right front of the bridgehead. Unable to confirm over the radio whether the approaching tanks belonged to the Strathconas or the *Wehrmacht,* Mahony warned his men of this new threat. It soon became clear that the vehicles were German as four tanks, spread some 30 to 40 feet apart and supported by about 50 to 100 infantry, began forming for an attack against the centre of the position, occupied by Mahony's company headquarters and Perkins's vehicles. Mahony ordered the flanking platoons to hold their ground no matter what happened and then the Honeys and every other weapon in the Company Headquarters opened up – Perkins recalling that "we fired everything we had from point fives (machine guns) to tommy-guns. We also fired the PIATs ... with the object of persuading the enemy that we had A/Tk weapons." Under this hail of small arms fire, the German tanks advanced cautiously and their fire clipped the aerials off two of the Honeys. Then, at about 200 yards and without any apparent reason, the enemy tanks turned away. Perkins's ruse had again succeeded.[69]

A few minutes later, four more German tanks, possibly the same four that had just turned back, made a sweep around to the north against the Canadian right flank. They went too far and missed 3 Platoon but on their return trip came near a forward section of that platoon. One vehicle stopped near a slit trench occupied by Private John Culling, who lobbed a No. 36 fragmentation grenade at it, killing the commander, who had rather unwisely exposed himself from out of his hatch. Alerted, the surviving crew prepared to fire in Culling's direction but the intrepid Culling threw another grenade, which went down the open hatch, killing the driver and forcing the remainder of the crew to bail out. Culling cut down two of them with his rifle and took the lone survivor prisoner.

At this point Mahony asked Perkins if he could support the infantry on the right flank with his Honeys but Perkins pointed out "that the firepower of a cut-down Stuart against a Panther was inconsiderable" and that exposing them "to fire would be virtual suicide." Nonetheless, the young armoured officer found it "extremely hard to deny this request" and decided that, if the Honeys were kept under cover, he "might succeed in bluffing the enemy as to our true strength."

By this time, the three remaining German tanks had overrun the forward section of 3 Platoon, now down to four men. After a brief struggle, one Canadian was severely wounded and the others were taken prisoner. The enemy tanks again withdrew but continued to harass the Canadians from the area of a nearby house. The remainder of 3 Platoon consolidated their position but Sergeant Samuel White, who had been badly wounded in this action, had to be evacuated. What was needed to hold the bridgehead were anti-tank guns but, despite valiant efforts, steep banks and enemy fire had halted all attempts to manhandle the 6-pdr anti-tank guns, each weighing 22½ cwt or 1,900 lb., across the Melfa.

It was now about 6.00 P.M. and the situation was not good. It shortly got worse when interference jammed the radio net, interfering with command and communication, forcing orders to be passed by runners. As if all this was not bad enough, Mahony now learned that the arrival of the Westminster's C Company would be delayed as it was pinned down on the far side and would be unable to get across for at least two more hours. The battle for the bridgehead had reached a critical point.[70]

Brigadier Desmond Smith of 5 Armoured Brigade had been closely following reports of the battle for the bridgehead. When he learned that it had been established, although very tenuously, he moved quickly. He had left his headquarters at 4.30 that morning with his tactical headquarters or "Tac"" to "control

Squadron echelon, Liri Valley, May 1944

Behind the fighting squadrons of the armoured regiments came the often-unsung heroes of their A Echelons, or support elements, whose job was to replenish the tanks with ammunition and fuel. This photograph shows a number of echelon vehicles – a Priest self-propelled 105 mm gun, a White "scout car" or halftrack (probably carrying ammunition), a replacement tank and another halftrack – on a secondary road, little better than a track in the Liri Valley. Judging by its nature, the smoke results from smoke shells, not burning vehicles. (NAC, PA-177098)

the initial part of the battle" before returning in the afternoon to his main head-quarters, which had moved to the Mancini area. At 2.20 P.M., Smith ordered his staff to "bang the whole of the Westminsters up" and to "proceed with all speed" to the BENEDICTINE crossroads just east of the Melfa. The Westminster Battalion Headquarters led, followed by B and C Companies, but their progress was "seriously handicapped by the traffic milling about in all directions." For the first half hour of the move, the Westminster commanding officer, Lieutenant Colonel Gordon Corbould, moved at the front of the convoy, pushing people out of its way. The road then came under artillery fire and an ammunition carrier was hit, resulting is another splendid display of pyrotechnics, while small groups of Germans who had been bypassed were also encountered. At 3.00 P.M., Corbould heard from Griffin of the Strathconas that the forward troops were heavily engaged and that his reinforcements were urgently needed. He reached Mancini at 3.40 P.M., but it still took another hour to clear the traffic and get up to the Strathconas' position.

At 4.45 P.M., the battalion arrived near BENEDICTINE, only to find the tank battle still raging and the entire area under enemy artillery fire. Corbould had learned A Company had crossed the river, but knew nothing of their situation. Still some 1,000 yards from the river, he ordered the two companies with him to de-bus and cross the waterway, with C Company on the left and B on the right. They were to seize objectives about 2,000 yards apart, and then link up on either side of A Company. The battalion tactical headquarters was set up at the crossroads.[71]

Although the tank battle was now over, Griffin of the Strathconas remained forward, coordinating the efforts of his battle group to defend the bridgehead and Corbould's attempts to expand it. Enemy artillery fire was intense and the Westminsters suffered accordingly. A scout vehicle from the Westminster B Company, carrying Lieutenant Ketcheson and nine scouts and snipers, received four direct hits, killing Ketcheson and five men and wounding the remainder. A vehicle in 7 Platoon was hit by an armour-piercing round that went right through it but only wounded a single soldier. Leaving the BENEDICTINE crossroads, the Westminster C Company, under Major Ian Douglas, fanned out as ordered to the left and approached the intended crossing site, about a half mile to the south of A Company. Douglas moved along a road that "was a wagon trail, narrow, sunken and lined fairly heavily with trees," and it soon became clear that this route was impassable to vehicles as at least two burning German Mk IV tanks blocked it.[72]

Finding "cross-country work on ... the company's halftracks ... was out of the question," and with the river still too far away, Douglas wheeled C Company north and at top speed attempted to catch up to B Company. They managed to find the tail vehicles from that company near the Westminster Regimental Aid Post east of BENEDICTINE. Unable to reach Corbould by radio, Douglas decided to try the same crossing site once more. He ordered 12 Platoon under Lieutenant Cruise to dismount and proceed directly to a farmhouse near the crossing site which would act as a company rendezvous. The remainder of the company was then collected in an effort to drive closer to the rendezvous. As they advanced towards BENEDICTINE, the carnage along the riverbank came into view.

After passing battalion headquarters at the crossroads, C Company turned left, but as the road paralleling the Melfa was blocked, Douglas ordered his men to dismount and move southward to the rendezvous by foot. Finding the farmhouse occupied by 12 Platoon, the members of C Company also discovered that Cruise and several of his men were wounded. Further investigation located a path running from the road along the river that offered a route to it. To the right of this path was an open field offering no cover except for a few burning tanks, while to the left was a screen of trees and foliage, beyond which were three German Mark IV tanks, which had likely wounded Cruise and his men, forming an arc around the farmhouse. PIAT teams moved forward and lobbed several bombs at the tanks to no effect and the Germans responded with their machine guns and main armament, which pinned down C Company. Although C Squadron of the Strathconas was still in this area, it was unable to offer C Company support, but Major George Wattsford, the second-in-command of the Strathconas, operating a spare command tank, was. While not required to be in the fight, Wattsford moved to within 400 yards of the Germans, where his gunner, Sergeant Lovelock, "reported he had an almost perfect shot when a branch obscured his view." Lovelock fired at a German self-propelled gun just as it fired at him. The Sherman took a direct hit, wounding Wattsford and Lovelock, and killing the co-driver and loader/operator.[73]

With his C Company unable to cross south of the bridgehead, Corbould decided to reinforce success and move it into Mahony's position. At about 8.00 P.M. Douglas received the order to move C Company into the bridgehead. Pulling back to the center line road near the BENEDICTINE crossroads, they then approached the A Company crossing site. Douglas's men feared they might bump into the enemy, but once across the river they were greeted by their comrades of A Company and Perkins's Honey crews, who were hugging the crest of the river bank. Throughout the bridgehead, "exhaustion and strain were evident, but a sense of triumph and confidence was also plain." Douglas found Mahony and after a brief discussion, they agreed that C Company should "thicken up" the bridgehead, "mostly on the flanks" and "hold what we had and not attempt to take any more now that it was dark." A platoon under Lieutenant Miller proceeded to the far left of the position and another under Lieutenant Forman went to the right. The shelling and barrages from the "Moaning Minnies" were increasing as "Jerry began to get the position really taped." Unable to hold as large a perimeter as planned, Mahony drew back his 40 or so remaining men into a "small but tight bridgehead in the general area of company headquarters," and they began digging in, "with considerable enthusiasm" as the enemy "started to put over a large number of *Nebelwerfer* bombs." The ground was so hard that No. 25 grenades, designed for blowing the tracks off tanks, were used to break it up.[74]

To the right, meanwhile, Major George Johnson's B Company of the Westminsters searched for a ford away from the main crossing site. Reaching a position north of the bridgehead, Johnson's 7 Platoon came under small arms fire from across the river, wounding Lieutenant Coe, the platoon commander, and several men. At this place the bank "was very steep and about 50 feet high, with little or no cover" while "the river itself at the pre-arranged crossing place ... was

Panther turret, Liri Valley, May 1944

German defence works in the Liri Valley included concrete shelters, steel pillboxes and machine gun positions. Interspersed between these positions were a number of Panther *Ausführung* D turrets with high-velocity 75 mm guns, mounted on a fabricated steel box. Once sited, earth was banked up around the box, the position concealed and an effective anti-tank threat established that proved difficult to spot by tank crews. (Courtesy The Tank Museum, Bovington)

quite wide and exposed." Unable to dislodge the enemy from the caves on the opposite bank and in an exposed position, Johnson sent a small scouting party to the north while he looked for an alternate crossing to the south. Meeting with no success, he then returned to his original position to find the other recce party waiting with three prisoners. They had found a crossing site about 300 yards north of the gully, moved over, encountered several Germans in a cave and cleared a number of Italians from a nearby house.

Based on the patrol leader's report, Johnson decided to cross at the same point and, leaving 7 Platoon to protect the company rear and the nearby 3-inch mortar section, he led 6 and 8 Platoons and five men from company headquarters across the stream in line abreast. His orders were for 8 Platoon to take the south side of the gully and for 6 Platoon to then cross and occupy a position to the north. After clearing another cave and a house, 8 Platoon crossed, covered by 6 Platoon. Sporadic firing was heard, but no enemy was seen. 6 Platoon then moved up and took position as planned, with their front dug in a low embankment by a railway track. Several minutes later the platoon observed about 30 Germans to the right of 6 Platoon, moving towards them. The Canadians opened fire and "several were seen to fall and remain and others scattered." Nothing was heard of 8 Platoon until Corporal Foster reported that it had come under fire from a tank, which had withdrawn, but not before the company second-in-command, Captain E.V. Ardagh, was wounded. Johnson ordered 6 Platoon to dig in. It was now about 9.00 P.M.[75]

While Johnson's men were "busy digging in and tying up fields of fire … a very heavy stonk fell right on top of the whole area" which "caught practically everyone in the open." His radios were not working, so Johnson sent a runner to Corbould to report the shelling and request reinforcements. The heavy fire delayed the arrival of B Company's 7 Platoon and the mortars until the situation stabilized and casualties could be collected. Then came three more enemy mortar stonks in quick succession that partially buried several soldiers with dirt from the embankment. At about 1600 hrs, instructions were finally received from Corbould, who, after visiting the company position some 1,300 yards north of the main bridgehead, found it too exposed and difficult to support. Johnson concurred, reporting further that he could neither support A Company from his present location and had insufficient manpower to extend the position and link up with Mahony. Corbould therefore ordered him into Mahony's bridgehead to take position with A and C Companies.

Collecting their equipment, ammunition and wounded, B Company started back but it took them nearly four hours to reach their vehicles, which they did at about 2.00 A.M. on 25 May. With planning for a breakout later that day now well underway, Corbould decided to hold the company on the east side of the Melfa.

Meanwhile, in the bridgehead, Perkins's Recce Troop and Mahony's infantry completed digging in, while No. 7 Light Field Ambulance carried out the difficult task of moving casualties to its advanced field dressing station, near the BENEDICTINE crossroads. Surprisingly, traffic congestion had little effect on ambulance movements. At the Melfa, Corporal Arneson of B Company was placed in charge of the stretcher bearers, who made several trips over the waterway that successfully accounted for all casualties.[76]

The coming of night brought no reduction of activity on the east side of the Melfa or in the bridgehead itself. With Major Wattsford wounded, the duties of second-in-command of the Strathconas fell to Major Bill Milroy of B Squadron, the only fighting squadron commander still on his feet (Major Jim McAvity continued to lead Headquarters Squadron). After handing over his squadron to Captain G.L.A. Clarke, Milroy commenced the difficult task of reorganizing the Strathconas by visiting each squadron position in turn, determining what personnel and vehicles were left, appointing acting squadron commanders, and then giving instructions for organization and night routine.[77]

Across the river, meanwhile, at about 10.00 P.M., one of the forward positions reported movement to its front. Two flares were launched but nothing was observed. During the night, the Westminsters were finally able to move their 6 pdr anti-tank guns over the river. It was laborious work, taking almost a full platoon of infantry for each gun, who lowered every weapon down the near bank by ropes and then hauled it through the stream and finally up onto the far bank. The first gun was across just after midnight, and by first light at about 5.30 A.M. on 25 May 1944, three of the battalion's 12 guns were in position.[78]

At almost the same time the guns came into position, a new enemy threat appeared from the south. Two mortar flares revealed two or three German tanks and about a dozen dismounted infantry some 500 yards away from the bridgehead. The left platoon was reinforced with another PIAT and Mahony, Douglas and Perkins braced for an attack, but nothing happened. Enemy shelling continued in and around the bridgehead throughout the night, while behind the position, friendly and enemy tanks and self-propelled guns burned, presenting a grim spectacle of an action that had now raged for about 15 hours. For the time being, the bridgehead seemed secure.[79]

B ut what of the gunners? Dismounted infantry and armour personnel had fought much of the bridgehead battle because artillery support proved difficult to provide. Despite having priority of movement, the guns supporting 5 Brigade had been unable to keep pace during the afternoon of 24 May with the rapid advance of the forward troops and as the day wore on the number of artillery pieces within range of the bridgehead declined. As early as 11.30 A.M., artillery recce parties had gone forward to locate new gun positions but heavy traffic on the assigned routes impeded all attempts of the gunners to get into these positions. By 4.00 P.M., two field regiments had reached the limits of their range and were ordered to move up, but despite their movement priority and every effort to clear the roads, they could not begin moving until 8.00 P.M. and after an hour had only progressed a mile.[80]

This meant that from 4.00 P.M. on 24 May fire support for the bridgehead was limited to the guns of 8 Canadian Field Regiment (Self Propelled), the British 64 (Jeep) Battery, and a few long-range guns of the corps and army artillery. In addition, road congestion restricted the fire from 8 Canadian Field Regiment to one battery and that unit was unable to bring fire across the Melfa until last light. It also suffered a heavy blow when one of its gun detachments lost nine soldiers and 16 wounded to shelling. Still worse, the fluid nature of the fighting on the far side meant the forward edge of the perimeter or "Foremost Defended

Half-track scout car
The rifle companies of the Westminster Regiment were equipped with the White Scout Car (so called in the official Canadian manuals, but actually a halftrack), the only Canadian infantry battalion in the Italian theatre to be so equipped. Although designated as an armoured personnel carrier, the protection afforded to the passengers was limited and none of these vehicles crossed the Melfa during the initial bridgehead battle. (Author's collection)

Line," changed frequently, affecting the "no fire" limit, a control measure designed to ensure fire did not come down on friendly troops. This made artillery coordination very difficult and most shoots required direct observation through aerial observation posts or FOO parties. Another problem was that many of the vehicles used by the FOOs had been destroyed, reducing the available fire.[81]

Perkins was determined to bring artillery fire down on the enemy and tried in vain to call it down himself. A break came when Lieutenant Robert Sutherland, the Stratchonas' intelligence officer, came across Captain Robert Martin of 64 Battery of the Royal Artillery, who was more than ready to assist. Only one radio in Martin's observation tank was working, so Sutherland parked his scout car next to it and relayed messages from Perkins and Mahony to Martin. To observe the shoots, Martin regularly exposed his observation tank, which, to allow room for additional radios, was armed only with a dummy gun. For most of the night, this single battery, equipped with 75 mm pack howitzers, was the only indirect support available to the defenders of the bridgehead and it fired more than 1,000 rounds. At 5.00 A.M. on 25 May, additional artillery support was provided by a FOO whose regiment was actually supporting the British 6th Armoured Division.[82]

Another element of the artillery was 82 Battery, 4th Anti-Tank Regiment, RCA, equipped with M-10 Tank Destroyers whose role was to destroy enemy armour. While the M-10 looked similar to a tank, it was employed differently. The lightly armoured open top turret offered limited crew protection from small arms fire and splinters from shell bursts. Normally, each vehicle remained out of sight until a target appeared within pre-arranged arcs of fire and would then run up to a pre-selected position from where it would engage the targets – ideally in defilade. Surprise was key to the success of the M-10. After firing, the tank destroyer would quickly move back under cover and where possible occupied an alternate position, 50 to 100 yards away. In the advance to the Melfa, this was done on the move and coordinated with the commander of Griffin Force. During the battle of the bridgehead, 82 Battery moved continually about the battlefield, staying "well up" and engaging whatever targets it could from five different positions. They experienced the same difficulty as the Strathconas in locating targets, but were fortunate not to lose any vehicles and destroyed at least two enemy tanks, one of them a Panther, which was hit from a range of 400 yards.[83]

Throughout 24 May, two squadrons from the Governor General's Horse Guards had provided protection to the flanks of Griffin Force. On the right A Squadron moved forward on the inter-divisional boundary along Highway 6, while B Squadron proceeded along the north bank of the Liri River, about 2,000 yards to the south. B Squadron of the Horse Guards was in almost continual contact with the enemy, but found no significant threat to the left flank of Griffin Force. The Horse Guards' A Squadron reached the Melfa during the late afternoon from where it protected the right flank of the weakened Strathcona battle group. C Squadron, originally assigned as reserve, now moved north, along the rear of the Hitler Line, much of which had not yet been cleared. Enemy probes from the south prompted the Strathconas to appeal for assistance and soon B Squadron of the Horse Guards was posted to cover the left rear, successfully preventing the enemy from infiltrating that direction.[84]

The Strathconas and Westminsters were not the only Allied troops trying to get across this shallow little Italian waterway. In both the Canadian and British sectors, several other efforts were made to seize crossings, but all ended in failure. On 24 May, Adams Force, a large battle group based on the 4th Princess Louise Dragoon Guards from 1st Canadian Division, with two squadrons from the Royal Canadian Dragoons, one squadron from the Three Rivers Regiment and the entire Carleton and York Regiment, a battalion of 3 Infantry Brigade, made some headway, but by last light on 24 May was still two miles short of the Melfa. To the north of the Canadians, 13 British Corps was plagued by bad roads, congestion, water obstacles, enemy sniping and "unexplained delays" that left it short of the river. Two regiments from 1 Canadian Armoured Brigade with that corps came within 1,000 yards of the river, but advanced patrols at the bank encountered "heavy opposition in the form of machine gun positions and self-propelled guns on the opposite bank," and all possible crossing sites "were found to be well covered by both Machine Gun and Anti-Tank weapons."[85]

The Strathcona/Westminster bridgehead was therefore the only crossing secured by Eighth Army on 24 May 1944 – and it was only weakly held. Around BENEDICTINE, the battered Strathcona squadrons formed laagers, dug slit trenches and sited weapons for all-round defence. A Squadron's six remaining Shermans were huddled in a woodline to the rear of the crossroads, while the nine surviving tanks of C Squadron took up defensive positions near it. Now across the Melfa in the bridgehead were four Honey tanks, two weak infantry companies and a few 6-pdr. anti-tank guns. It was clear that "the bridgehead would not be sufficiently strong by day and so it was decided to attack forward at first light with a view to getting at least a two-battalion bridgehead." At 6.00 P.M. on 24 May, Burns

Circling the wagons

Armoured regiments often formed a "leaguer" or "laager" when out of contact with the enemy. Tanks would tuck themselves into woodlines or use natural cover to adopt this loose formation, which provided all-round protection and an opportunity to refuel, resupply, reorganize crews, pass orders and rest. The Strathconas were in laager on 25 May 1944 when German artillery hit them hard, resulting in more casualties than suffered during the Melfa Crossing battle. This image shows Canadian replacement tanks in a laager in Italy during 1943. (Author's collection)

ordered 5th Division to strengthen the bridgehead before the move on Ceprano planned for the following day. Hoffmeister's division was also ordered to cover the crossing to the south used by the enemy and to develop a proper crossing for Canadian armour. Another large-scale operation was therefore necessary, which would be supported by Vokes's 1st Division.[86]

In response, Smith of 5 Brigade planned an early morning attack, but traffic difficulties delayed the arrival of supporting arms. The Irish Regiment of Canada was ordered up from Mancini at 6.00 P.M. on 24 May but only reached the Strathconas' area at 11.00 P.M. where it dug in on the east side of the river. Traffic problems were so bad that the War Diary of the Cape Breton Highlanders of 11 Infantry Brigade records "that quicker progress would have been made if the troops had moved by foot rather than trucks." The late arrival of 8 Canadian Field Regiment required additional coordination of the artillery plan for the attack. Two field artillery regiments would conduct the prearranged fire plan, while 8 Canadian Field Regiment was left free for close fire. Corbould of the Westminsters spent most of the night supervising planned movements by his regiment and the Irish Regiment into the bridgehead.[87]

Just before first light on 25 May 1944, Mahony was informed that the attack of the Irish Regiment would be delayed by an hour. Then, some 30 minutes after first light, he received warning of German infantry moving to the front of the bridgehead. Mahony ran forward to observe 15 Germans about 500 yards away, running diagonally across his position and ordered the Bren guns and rifles to open up, causing the Germans to go to ground. A PIAT and 2-inch mortar also engaged and the German defenders of a nearby farmhouse responded by firing on the wood where the Irish were forming up. Mahony collected a PIAT, two or three Bren guns and a few riflemen and led this group forward until they were in range and lobbed a couple of PIAT bombs into the house. Two Germans scrambled out, one carrying a machine gun tripod. Rifle fire stopped both in their tracks.[88]

During the night engineer recce parties had studied the riverbank to determine the most suitable places for the crossings scheduled for the following day. Multiple crossing sites were needed to get units over the river. At 2.24 A.M. on 25 May, the sappers reported the area near the original crossing was "not suitable [as] banks too steep" but one just to the south, "running across river in Northerly direction used by the Germans until this afternoon [i.e. 24 May]. Deep water 2 ft, type of bottom gravel, solid," was "very favourable." Just to the south of this was another potential site spanned by a shaky timber bridge where, once this area was cleared, a Bailey bridge could be constructed. Surveying for crossing sites and improving them was not the sappers' only work – they had to deal with mines on the roads, approaches and crossing sites. Bridging equipment, however, was ordered to be brought into forward assembly areas to prepare fords across the Melfa.[89]

The Germans were also assessing the situation. Kesselring, believing the battle had "reached its decisive phase," forbade any retreat but he was torn between his orders to resist any enemy attacks and his own professional understanding of

The infantry's Sunday punch, Italy 1944

During the night of 24/25 May 1944, three 6-pdr anti-tank guns of the Westminster Regiment were manhandled into the Melfa bridgehead. This weapon had a calibre of 2.24 inches or 57 mm and fired a solid shot weighting 6 lb. 4 oz., with a maximum range of 1,200 yards and effective range of some 800 yards. It was crewed by five men. Shown here is a Canadian gun in action at Ortona in December 1943. (NAC, PA-169111)

298 ~ MORE FIGHTING FOR CANADA

the need to withdraw. Von Vietinghoff, commanding the 10. *Armee,* had told his subordinate Feuerstein of 51. *Gebirgskorps* that the river line "must be held for several days" and the "enemy elements that have crossed the river [i.e., the Canadians] must be thrown back." Although he passed on the order to Baade of 90. *Panzergrenadierdivision,* Feuerstein did not believe it was possible as "the enemy has already crossed the Melfa in two places and that no further forces are available to rectify the situation."[90]

H-Hour for the renewed attack, originally slated for 6.00 A.M. on 25 May, was delayed pending the arrival of a squadron from the British Columbia Dragoons. During the wait, artillery fire – the war diary of the Westminster Regiment claims these were friendly rounds – landed in the middle of the combined headquarters of A and C Companies, wounding Mahony and two of his platoon leaders, Lieutenants Ross Douglas and Bill Delaney. The two junior officers were evacuated but Mahony refused to leave. He patched a shrapnel wound to his leg and continued leading the defence of the bridgehead.[91]

The attack finally went in at 11.30 A.M. with B and C Companies of the Westminster Regiment on the right and three companies of the Irish Regiment on the left, the latter supported by the British Columbia Dragoons (see map M-5). Perkins's troop and the Westminsters in the bridgehead covered them as best they could. Captain Martin of 64 Battery, acting as a FOO, also went forward with a manpack radio to call down artillery fire. C Squadron of the British Columbia Dragoons was ordered to "hold the bridgehead perimeter at all costs." Earlier, Major J. Turnley, the squadron commander, had examined the crossing site with Griffin, but had no "opportunity to reconnoitre the area to be attacked." Given the lack of information on the area immediately in front of the bridgehead, Turnley instructed his troop leaders to limit their advance to 1,000 yards beyond the river, or less depending on the situation. Two tank troops were ordered to position themselves on the near bank to attract enemy fire, while the other two crossed the river, after which the first two troops would cross. As the last two Dragoon troops were crossing, four or five tanks became casualties in a matter of moments. Enemy anti-tank guns and tanks proved quite effective and demonstrated that, despite the previous day's heavy fighting, the Germans were still resisting stoutly. Of the 14 British Columbia tanks that crossed, seven were lost to anti-tank fire and three of four troop leaders became casualties in exchange for one Panther, one Mk IV and four anti-tank guns. The infantry attack was successful and within an hour the bridgehead was established on a two-battalion front and the remainder of the day was spent consolidating on the objective.[92]

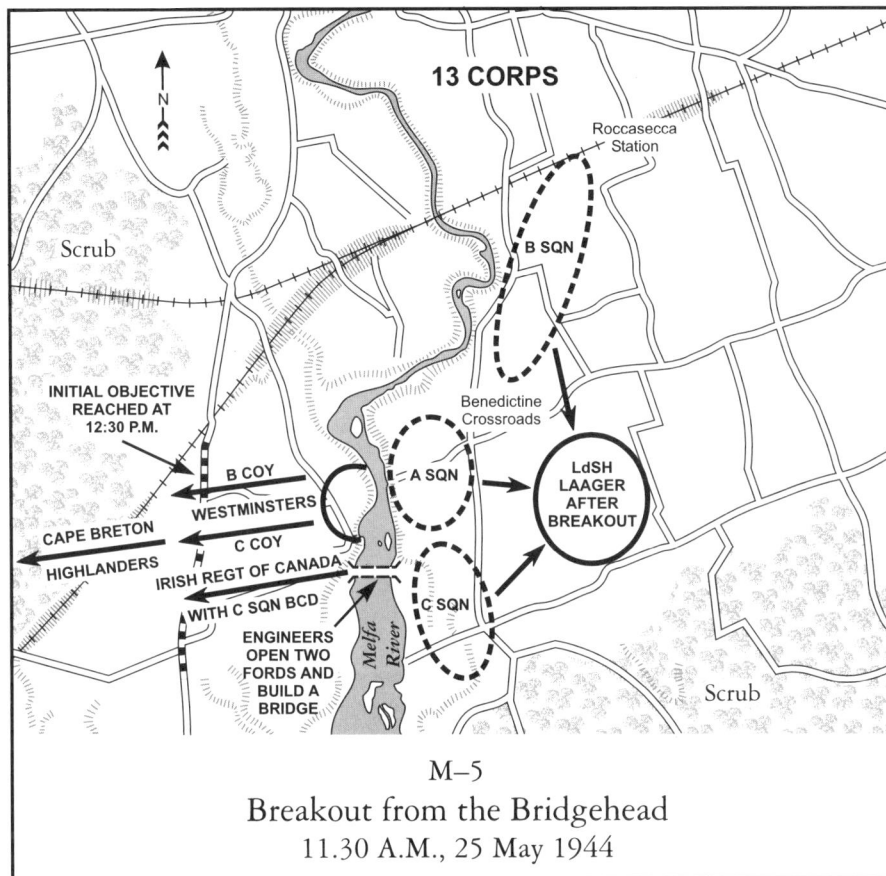

13 CORPS

Roccasecca Station

Scrub

B SQN

Benedictine Crossroads

INITIAL OBJECTIVE REACHED AT 12:30 P.M.

B COY

WESTMINSTERS

A SQN

LdSH LAAGER AFTER BREAKOUT

CAPE BRETON HIGHLANDERS

C COY

IRISH REGT OF CANADA

WITH C SQN BCD

C SQN

ENGINEERS OPEN TWO FORDS AND BUILD A BRIDGE

Melfa River

Scrub

M–5
Breakout from the Bridgehead
11.30 A.M., 25 May 1944

Beginning at 4.30 P.M. on 25 May, Hoffmeister's 11 Infantry Brigade pushed through the bridgehead and by evening was 1,000 yards beyond it. In the 1st Infantry Division sector, Adams Force, the Princess Louise Dragoon Guards battle group, reached the river but the banks were too steep to allow a crossing, while farther north the Carleton and York Regiment achieved a foothold on the far bank, but came under heavy fire during their crossing, which kept the unit pinned down for the rest of the day. Additional troops from other units also crossed, and by evening Canadians held the west bank of the Melfa from the Liri River to the railway line. Farther north, 13 British Corps reached the river but was unable to get over in strength. Movement in the Canadian sector improved through the day as the engineers opened one ford to wheeled traffic at noon and another ford at 3.00 P.M. A 40-foot-long Bailey Bridge was erected by 11.30 P.M. and by nightfall the engineers also opened a "down" route (a one-way route away from the bridgehead). By 5.00 P.M., vehicle traffic was rolling smoothly, although problems persisted as the Provosts "were not marking routes and the general discipline by M[otor] T[ransport] drivers [was] deplorable." The lack of traffic control placed a "tremendous burden on sapper resources" as did the decision to move 11 Infantry Brigade forward by two routes. By nightfall, however, the Melfa was bridged in each divisional sector, artillery and other supporting arms were moving up, and Hoffmeister reported to Burns that these new crossing sites were "good and secure."[93]

In the enemy camp, the situation was worse. Confronted with multiple "deep penetrations over a wide front" by British and Canadian forces, German commanders concluded that "the complete collapse of the sector" could only be prevented by a withdrawal and, at 11.50 P.M. on 25 May, 51. *Gebirgskorps* ordered a retreat to the Caesar Line. After two days of heavy and costly fighting, the battle for the Melfa was over.[94]

Throughout 25 May, the three Strathcona squadrons were gradually withdrawn into reserve. At 10.30 A.M., Griffin ordered his Recce Troop out of the bridgehead but Perkins requested permission to remain and even asked for additional ammunition. By 11.20 A.M., the three tank squadrons were in a harbour area south of BENEDICTINE, where they began the process of reconstitution. The regiment had suffered heavily in the fighting of the previous day. Seventeen tanks had been lost (7 from C Squadron, 9 from A Squadron and 1 from RHQ) with 2 officers and 20 other ranks killed, 7 officers and 27 other ranks wounded. Many squadron, troop and vehicle commanders had to be replaced and the surviving crews reformed, even as supplies were distributed and preparations made for further operations. Major Bill Milroy was now acting second-in-command while A Squadron was led by its only remaining officer, Lieutenant Robert Gartke, and C Squadron by Lieutenant W.M. Reade. During the morning, five replacement Shermans arrived, along with more supplies, and just after noon Perkins's Recce Troop finally pulled out of the bridgehead and returned to the regimental harbour, where they received "a rousing welcome."[95]

Sadly, during the early afternoon of 25 May, the Strathconas suffered what one termed the regiment's "greatest tragedy" during its wartime service when, with no warning, the harbour came under heavy artillery fire. Before any orders could be issued, one tank and five trucks were hit, fuel caught fire and ammunition exploded. Griffin quickly directed his squadrons to scatter, while soldiers from Headquarters Squadron tended to the wounded. It was not until 3.30 P.M. that the dispersed elements were reunited in a new harbour about 1,000 yards to the southwest and the task of regrouping commenced once again. That was not all. German artillery maintained observation on B and C Squadrons, who were forced to move twice during the afternoon and at 11.00 P.M., the entire harbour area was bombed by enemy aircraft killing another 13 officers and men, while 37 were wounded or reported missing. Although the squadrons were by now well dispersed, the effects of these attacks were devastating and more Strathconas were killed and wounded on 25 May than during the battle for the bridgehead.[96]

Overall, the Strathconas paid a heavy price for their victory. In two days the regiment lost 18 of its 52 tanks and 13 of its 37 officers for a total of 102 casualties, mostly from the 260 men who made up the tank crews. More than one third of the fighting soldiers in the unit had to be replaced and by the time this was done, the Strathconas were a very different regiment from the unit that had gone into battle on 24 May. For the survivors, triumph was tainted with anguish. Lieutenant Colonel Griffin, who had trained his regiment and commanded it in its first action was observed at the Regimental Aid Post, watching the dead and wounded being collected, "patently stunned with grief, as though bereft of his own flesh and blood." Still leading through this adversity, Griffin, however, prepared for future action by directing his subordinates to study and analyze the results of the recent fighting. Members of the unit and headquarters staff inspected damaged or destroyed enemy vehicles to assess what had taken place and early on the morning of 27 May Griffin took his officers to the Melfa to draw lessons from the fighting, because he knew there were more battles were to come.[97]

The Westminster Regiment had also suffered grievously. On 26 May, a memorial ceremony was held near their Regimental Aid Post and the remains of the fallen were wrapped in blankets and buried. At the head of each grave was a wooden cross stamped with the Regimental Crest prepared by the battalion's pioneers with a tin can containing each fallen man's particulars. Captain L.W. Owen, the regimental padre, conducted a brief service after which the graves were filled in and covered with stones. There, as one member of the regiment recorded, "on the north side of the Melfa, exactly on the objective, the bodies of twenty Westminsters lay quiet." After the unit left the area, the local inhabitants painted the stones on the graves white and placed flowers on each.[98]

Determining the exact losses suffered by 5th Canadian Armoured Division during the battle of 24-25 May 1944 is difficult as not every unit submitted accurate casualty returns, and some of the returns that were compiled have since gone missing. The records of the divisional assistant-adjutant and quartermaster general, responsible for maintaining personnel statistics, provide daily records of losses, but these show the date a casualty was reported, not when it was suffered, and therefore do not accurately reflect the intensity of the fighting. For example, the reports show the division suffered 23 casualties for 24 May, which is actually fewer than the losses suffered by the Strathconas alone. Over the next three days, however, there was a sharp rise as the casualty returns came in: 43 casualties on 25 May, 138 the next, 133 on 27 May and 97 for 28 May. Between 21 and 31 May, total casualties of 5th Armoured Division amounted to 670, including 171 killed, 441 wounded and 58 missing, and at least a third of these occurred during the Melfa battle. Officially, between 15 May and 4 June 1944, 1 Canadian Corps lost 789 killed, 2,463 wounded and 116 taken prisoner, nearly a quarter of the total losses it sustained during the first eleven months of the Italian campaign.[99]

On the German side, Baade's 90. *Panzergrenadierdivision* was reported "destroyed," although its actual losses are unknown. It would soon be reconstituted, however, and again be facing Canadians. The German 10. *Armee*, came out of the battle for Rome as "a skeleton force still capable of organized manoeuvre but in need of complete overhaul and rejuvenation." It had suffered 16,885 casualties during May 1944 and materiel losses were considerable: the Strathconas alone captured or destroyed 7 Panthers, 4 Mark IV tanks, 9 self-propelled guns, 1 field gun, 5 *Nebelwerfers*, 4 multi-barrel anti-aircraft guns, 21 motor vehicles and 3 motorcycles.[100] Further losses were inflicted by the Westminster Regiment, the British Columbia Dragoons, the Governor General's Horse Guards, and supporting artillery, aircraft and other units. After the battle, investigation teams from 5th Division confirmed the destruction of 11 Panthers, 11 self-propelled guns, seven 88 mm guns, fifteen 75 mm guns, 10 *Nebelwerfers* and a variety of other guns and vehicles. In 90. *Panzergrenadierdivision*, a lack of reinforcements and equipment left many units were under strength, "non-existent or no longer a consideration."[101]

While the Allies had chewed up several German divisions and made some spectacular gains, the words of the French General Alphonse Juin rang true. Speaking before the battle for Rome had commenced, he had predicted that its outcome would find "weary fighting troops still facing twenty or so German divisions, more, that is, than they would need to make a stand in the Tuscan mountains." These words proved to be entirely accurate and the Italian campaign ground on for another year.[102]

The day after the crossing was secured, 11 Infantry Brigade advanced to Ceprano, which fell on 27 May. They then continued to Frosinone and then Colleferro, the limit of 1 Canadian Corps' advance. In six days, between 24 and 30

May, 5th Canadian Armoured Division advanced 21 miles, through very difficult terrain, but by this time the American Fifth Army had moved towards Rome and on 4 June, triumphantly entered the Italian capital. On that same day, 30 miles away, the men of 1 Canadian Corps went into reserve, disappointed that they could not say they "drove to Rome," but happy that they would now enjoy rest, recuperation and reorganization. Two days later, the Normandy landing took place and the Italian theatre quickly became of secondary concern. Nonetheless, the units of 1 Canadian Corps continued fighting, performing brilliantly at the Gothic and Rimini Lines in late 1944 before the corps was transferred to Northwest Europe in early 1945.[103]

In the aftermath of the battle, the men of 5th Armoured Division had every right to be proud of their fight at the Melfa. Writing a congratulatory letter to the Strathconas, Brigadier Smith confidently predicted that the action "will long be remembered in the history of the Canadian effort in this war. By the gallant action of the Regiment, it was possible to seize and gain our bridgehead over the Melfa" which "was what really broke the German resistance and turned his defence into a rout." Hoffmeister also acknowledged the "brilliant actions" of the Strathconas, the Westminster Regiment and the Governor General's Horse Guards. Further praise came from Alexander, Burns and Leese. Several officers and men involved in the battle received awards of decorations including the tenacious Trooper Jacob Funk, the grenade-lobbing Private John Culling, Lance-Corporal George Chidley of the engineers and Corporal Arneson, who led the stretcher-bearers, all received the Military Medal.

For Valour: The Commonwealth's Highest Award

Major Jack Mahony with King George VI following the Sovereigns's presentation of the Victoria Cross, the highest award for valour in the British Empire, to the Canadian. Described as a quiet, almost shy man, Mahony showed strong leadership during the bridgehead battle despite being wounded several times. (Courtesy, The Royal Westminster Regiment Museum)

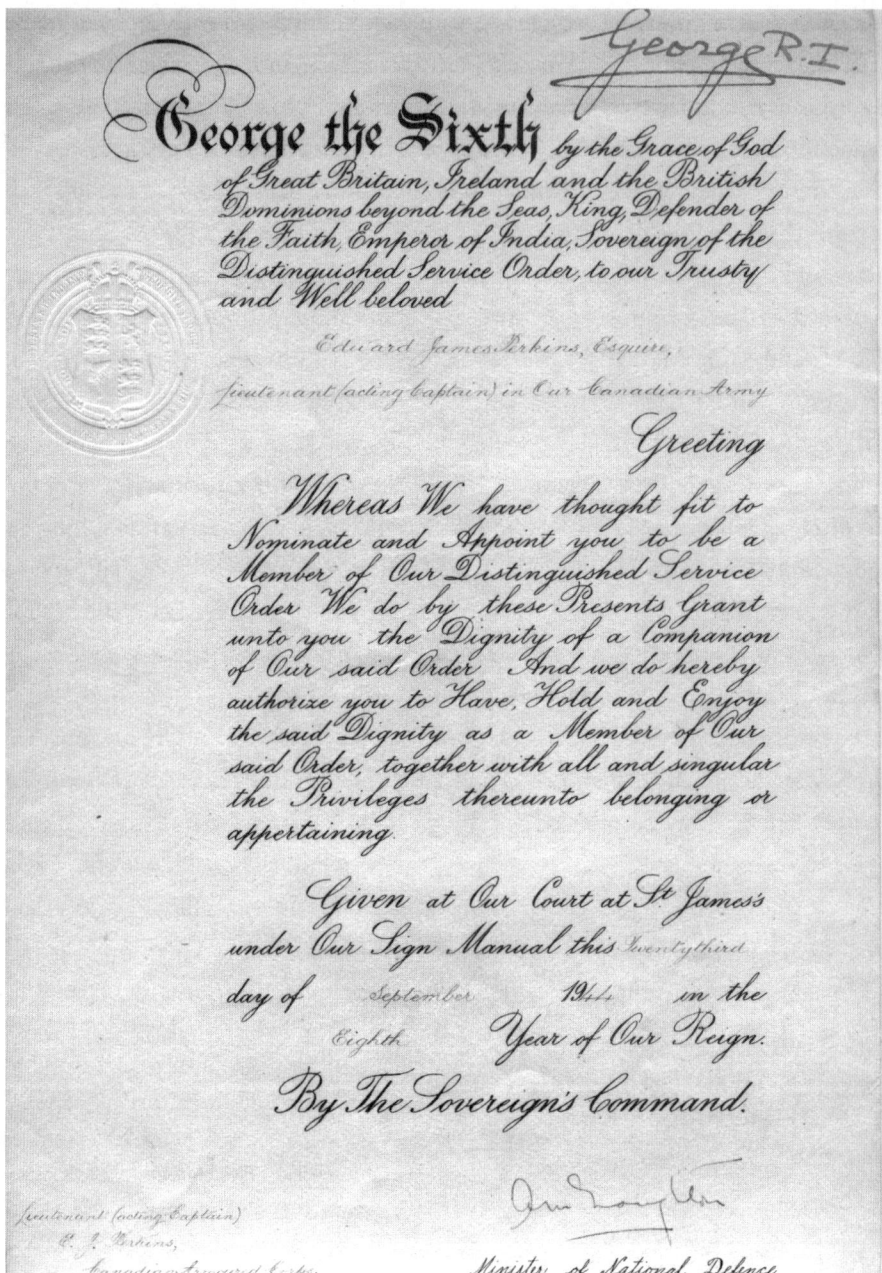

"Perky," DSO

For his service at both the Melfa and the Torrice Crossroads, Captain Edward Perkins, leader of the Strathcona Recce Troop, was awarded the Distinguished Service Order, a decoration normally reserved for more senior officers. This certificate, signed by King George VI and the Canadian Minister of National Defence, acknowledging Perkins's appointment to the Distinguished Service Order, was given to Perkins along with his decoration by the King in later 1944. (Courtesy Lord Strathcona's Horse (Royal Canadians) Regimental Museum)

Sergeant Samuel White, who continued to command his platoon despite serious wounds, received the Distinguished Conduct Medal as did Sergeant Clifford "Chum" Macey, Perkins's tenacious troop sergeant. Captain Robert Martin, the British gunner who commanded 64 (Jeep) Battery, received a Military Cross. Lieutenant Edward "Perky" Perkins was promoted to captain and, for his "gallantry and power of leadership" not only at the Melfa but also in a hard-fought action at the Torrice crossroads on 30 May 1944, received the Distinguished Service Order,[104] a rare award of this decoration to a subaltern officer.[105] Perkins received his DSO from King George VI at Buckingham Palace. Lieutenant Colonel Paddy Griffin of the Strathconas also received the Distinguished Service Order for his brilliant handling of the battle.

Perhaps the most significant award for the battle was made on 31 July 1944 at an airfield in the Volturno River valley. Before 4,000 men from 5th Armoured Division, Major John Keefer Mahony, the stoic 31-year-old former newspaper editor from New Westminster, British Columbia, and the "soul of the defence" of the bridgehead, received the Victoria Cross, the highest award for valour in the British Commonwealth, from the hands of King George VI. This was one of only three such awards made to Canadian soldiers in the Italian theatre. Mahony, still recovering from his wounds, wobbled unsteadily as the King pinned the crimson ribbon to his tunic.*

The German 10. *Armee* also praised the efforts of its troops. On 26 May 1944, the troops that defended the Melfa were commended with a simple notation in that formation's War Diary: "During the defensive battles of the last few days at the focal point of the large-scale enemy attacks 90 Pz Gren Div and attached formations have again proven and distinguished themselves by bravery."[106]

Many lessons were learned from Operation CHESTERFIELD and the battle for the Melfa River crossing. At the lowest levels, newfound experience resulted in modified procedures, which appeared in publications such as the *Reports from Overseas* series of pamphlets. Among these lessons was that preparation and

---

* Mahony's award created some controversy that continues to this day. Near the end of the war, an article about Mahony appeared in *Liberty* magazine that has been interpreted by some commentators as suggesting that Perkins should have received the VC rather than Mahony. There is no evidence to support this view. When Lieutenant Colonel James McAvity, who replaced Griffin as commander of the Strathconas in July 1944, announced Mahony's award to that regiment, "the feeling of pride that surged through the Strathcona's must very nearly have equaled that felt by his own [Mahony's] kin." See J.M. McAvity, *Lord Strathcona's Horse (Royal Canadians): A Record of Achievement*, (Toronto, 1947), 43-44. In conversation with the author, Lieutenant General (Retd.) William Milroy, the former commander of B Squadron of the LSH, agreed that "everyone was proud of Perky and his accomplishment and no one saw any reason to question either his award or Mahony's."

training was generally well conducted and units were about as ready as they could be. Canadian tactics were adapted quickly to the close terrain, while commanders and leaders at all levels demonstrated both aggressiveness and great initiative. Employing a single radio net for a battle group, however, was regarded as a mistake because it made it nearly impossible to pass orders and instructions, but a more serious error, noted particularly by the Strathconas, was in not following LOB or "left-out of battle" policies. This involved leaving a portion of the officers and non-commissioned officers in the rear area, to assist replacement during battle and reconstitution afterwards. Both the Strathconas and Westminsters had viewed LOB with derision and chose not to use it this one time "with rather awkward results." The limited anti-tank capability of the infantry had proved fairly effective against local counterattacks but confidence in the employment of 6 pdr anti-tank guns, particularly against Panthers, was mixed. Road movement was identified as the major problem because continual traffic congestion, faulty control and poor discipline seriously affected the conduct of operations. In 1 Canadian Corps, a special traffic control office was created as a result but these difficulties were never entirely overcome. There were also a host of changes in the employment of artillery, passage of information, employment of field ambulances, engineers, air support, speculative shooting and rations that are too numerous to recount.[107]

Since the war, controversy over the battle for Rome – both its conduct by senior Allied leaders and its contribution to the general victory in Europe – has continued to occupy historians. Unlike the Normandy campaign, the performance of Canadian troops has not drawn the same critical, almost damning, literature. In each campaign, a Canadian corps and an armoured division fought their first major battle and advanced on narrow fronts, often with only one or two units leading. However conditions in each theatre were quite different. In Normandy, 4 Canadian Armoured Division advanced in rolling, open terrain that invited long-range engagement from the defenders whereas in Italy the close terrain favoured concealed movement. There was also considerably more armour in Normandy than in Italy but the defences in Italy were more developed and based on fixed positions. In Normandy Lieutenant General Guy Simonds, commanding 2 Canadian Corps, emerged with his reputation intact, if not enhanced, whereas in Italy, Lieutenant General E.L.M. Burns found himself in a "devilish situation," facing criticism from both his superior, Leese, and his subordinate, Vokes, that would eventually lead to his being replaced. Hoffmeister of 5th Division was also mildly criticized but proved a quick learner, eventually emerging as the finest

The lads beneath, they slumber on.

After the battle, most of the fallen were buried in small cemeteries near the Melfa. The remains were later moved to the Commonwealth War Graves Commission Cemetery at Cassino. (Courtesy Lord Strathcona's Horse (Royal Canadians) Regimental Museum)

Canadian divisional commander of the Second World War. Brigadier Desmond Smith of 5 Armoured Brigade received praise and was shortly appointed as BGS (Brigadier, General Staff) or chief of staff to 1 Canadian Corps. It takes time and experience to produce good brigade, divisional and corps commanders and staffs but the breaking of the Hitler Line and the Melfa crossing demonstrated that Canadians were "equal as soldiers to any of the Allies" and, perhaps more importantly, "reckoned formidable by the Germans."[108]

Nearly a decade after the war, a battle honour, "Melfa Crossing," was awarded to the Strathconas, the British Columbia Dragoons, the Royal Westminster Regiment (the regiment gained the title "Royal" in 1966), the Irish Regiment of Canada and other units. Annually on 24 May, Lord Strathcona's Horse celebrate "Melfa Day" with a commemorative parade, a retelling of the battle and a sports competition.[109]

It is entirely fitting that this engagement is marked by a battle honour as it was a combined arms action that required careful planning, manoeuvre, tenacity and audacity. In 1948, Major Jock Mahony VC attributed victory at the Melfa to discipline, training, hard work and, above all, *esprit de corps* and teamwork. He stressed that "at times the situation looked pretty grim … but our orders were to hang on, and we hung on … not a man questioned that order." Dozens of "acts of individual daring and self-sacrifice" took place, but in the final analysis the Melfa Crossing "was not a one-man job," it was " by "a team that knew its job and was confident of its ability."[110]

Mahony, the recipient of a Victoria Cross, was in a position to evaluate this ferocious action but most of the Canadian servicemen who fought at the Melfa and in the Italian campaign (the "D Day Dodgers," as they ironically called themselves) received only the single campaign star given for participation in that theatre. And there were many who received a more sober decoration – a simple cross. For those Strathconas so grimly rewarded at Melfa, it was provided by Trooper Lloyd Lynch of Headquarters Squadron on 28 May 1944 when he carefully painted on each of the white wooden crosses that marked the graves of the men of the unit that had fallen in the recent fighting, their name, rank and service number.

These graves were clustered in a small, makeshift cemetery created on the outskirts of the village of Melfa. As Lynch worked, he was watched by the curious villagers, who had wisely abandoned their homes for caves in the surrounding hills during the fighting but had slowly filtered back to view with sorrow the ruins of their community. Close by the cemetery was a house that had served as the location of the Regimental Aid Post during the battle. It was the home of a Scots woman who had spent most of her life in Italy and she promised Lynch that, once the Strathconas moved on, her family would tend the graves of his fallen comrades.[111] The crosses in that little cemetery were but a few of the large many such monuments, 5,735 to be exact, that mark the resting place of the Canadians who fought and died in Italy during the Second World War – a fact so aptly described in their favourite song:

> *Look around the hillside,*
> *In the falling rain*
> *See the scattered crosses*
> *Some that have no name.*
> *Toil and pain and suffering gone,*
> *The lads beneath they slumber on.*
> *For they are the D-Day Dodgers*
> *In sunny Italy.*

The Liri Valley and Melfa Today

To visit the Melfa, take Highway A1 south from Rome or north from Naples. Follow the traffic signs for Cassino and take Highway 6 (Via Casilina). Any visit to the military history of this area must commence at the heights of Monte Cassino, 86 miles south of Rome, where the monastery is home to the Bendictine Monks and was a pivotal point of the Gustav Line in 1944. The impressive abbey is open year round to visitors (note there is a dress code) and offers a wonderful vista of the Liri Valley. From there, the A2 takes you to the Cassino War Cemetery and Memorial, which is maintained by the Commonwealth War Graves Commission. Among the tall pines and acacias, are 4,266 graves, including the remains of 855 Canadians who died in the Liri Valley during the advance to Rome. At the base of the heights is the impressive Polish Military Cemetery as well.

From the Cassino War Cemetery, drive north along Highway 6. The terrain to the left is that over which the Canadians advanced in May 1944. There are few signs of the battle today but despite the modern development, one can easily get a sense of the difficulties both sides faced, particularly in moving and fighting through the cultivated fields. The railway line is still there, and once at the Liri you are roughly at the northernmost point of the positions occupied by Griffin Force. Approximately 1½ miles south is the area of the crossing battle. Here one can almost hear the sounds of Perkins and Mahony's troops trying to hold the bridgehead. There are several crossings nearby, although Highway 6 offers an opportunity to follow the operations of the Canadian Corps past the Melfa.

APPENDIX A

Orders of Battle and Strengths,
British and French Armies at
the Battle of Sillery, 1760

BRITISH ARMY AND ROYAL NAVY

Note: Those killed or died of wounds are noted thus: +. Those wounded are noted thus: *.
Those taken prisoner during battle are noted thus: x.

STAFF

General Officer Commanding & Governor of Quebec	Brigadier General James Murray
Aide-de-Camp	Lieutenant Thomas Mills*
Second-in-Command & Lieutenant Governor of Quebec	Colonel Ralph Burton*
Deputy Quartermaster-General	Major Aemilius Paulus Irving
Assistant Deputy Quartermaster-General	Captain Matthew Leslie
Chief Engineer	Major Patrick Mackellar*
Assistant Engineers	Captain Samuel Hollandt
	Lieutenant J.W.F. des Barres
	Lieutenant L.F. Fuser
Commander, Royal Artillery	Major John Godwin, RA*
Chief Medical Officer	Dr. William Russell
Adjutant General & Town Major	Major Richard Maitland
Judge Advocate General	Lieutenant Colonel John Young*x
Provost Marshal	Mr. Zachariah Flitner

RIGHT BRIGADE (1132)

Commander	Colonel Ralph Burton*
48th Foot (Webb's) (307)	Major William Sparke
15th Foot (Amherst's) (325)	Major Paulus Irving
58th Foot (Anstruthers) (309)	Major James Agnew
2nd Battalion, 60th Foot (Royal Americans) (191)	Captain Thomas Oswald

LEFT BRIGADE (1077)

Commander	Colonel Simon Fraser of Lovat*
43rd Foot (Kennedy's) (169)	Lieutenant Colonel Demetrius James
47th Foot (Lascelles') (264)	Major John Hussey+
78th Foot (Fraser's) (370)	Major John Macpherson
28th Foot (Bragg's) (274)	Lieutenant Colonel Hunt Walsh*

RESERVE (517)

35th Foot (Otway's) (285)	Major Roger Morris
3rd Battalion, 60th Foot, Royal Americans (232)	Lieutenant Colonel John Young[*][X]

ARMY TROOPS (743)

Ranger Company (78)	Captain Moses Hazen[*]
Dalling's Light Infantry (339)	Major John Dalling[*]
Volunteers' Company (110) (Note 1)	Captain Donald Macdonell[+]
Merchants' Militia Company (est. 100) (Note 2)	Lieutenant John Grant
Royal Artillery (116)	Major John Godwin[*]
Yorke's Company	Captain John Yorke[X]
James' Company	Captain Thomas James

ORDNANCE

18 x 6-pdr. guns
2 x 12-pdr. howitzers

RECAPITULATION OF LAND FORCES

Infantry of the Line	
Right Brigade	1132
Left Brigade	1072
Reserve	517
Light Infantry	339
Rangers	78
Volunteers	110
Royal Artillery	116
Total	3364 troops with 22 pieces of artillery

ROYAL NAVY (Note 3)

Ships stationed at Quebec, Winter 1760.

Armed Schooner *Lawrence* (Sailed 23 April to find relief fleet)	Lieutenant Fortye, 35th Foot
HMS *Racehorse*, 12 guns (Sailed 1 May 1760 to find relief fleet)	Captain John Macartney, RN
HMS *Porcupine*, 16 guns (Attacked French squadron 16 May 1760)	Master Henry Guy, RN

Ships from Swanton's squadron arriving before 17 May 1760 to help lift siege

Commander	Commodore Robert Swanton, RN
HMS *Lowestoft*, 28 guns (Arrived 9 May 1760 and attacked French squadron on 16 May)	Captain Joseph Deane, RN
HMS *Vanguard*, 70 guns (Arrived 16 May 1760 and bombarded Foulon supply depot and batteaux)	Commodore Robert Swanton, RN
HMS *Diana*, 32 guns (Arrived 16 May 1760 and attacked French squadron)	Captain Alexander Schomberg, RN

FRENCH ARMY AND NAVY

STAFF

General Officer Commanding	François Gaston, *Chevalier* de Lévis, *marechal-de-camp*
Aide-de-Camp	Jean-Nicolas Desandrouins, *capitaine d'ingenieurs*
Second-in-Command	François-Charles de Bourlamaque, *brigadier**
Adjutant-General	Pierre-André de Gohin, *Chevalier* de Montreuil, *lieutenant-colonel*
Deputy Quartermaster-General	Plantivit de Margon de Lapause, *lieutenant-colonel*
Chief Engineer	Nicolas Sarrebource de Pontleroy, *lieutenant-colonel d'ingenieur*
Artillery Commander	F.-F. Potot de Montbelliard, *capitaine d'artillerie*
Inspector-General, troupes de la marine	Jean-Daniel Dumas, *major des troupes de la marine*
Senior Naval Officer	Jean Vauquelin, *capitaine de fregate**

LEFT BRIGADE (BRIGADE DE LA SARRE) (710/241) (Note 4)

Commander	Jean d'Alqier de Sarrian,* *lieutenant-colonel*
2e Bataillon, Régiment de Bearn (371/221)	Jean d'Alqier de Sarrian,* *lieutenant-colonel*
2e Bataillon, Régiment de la Sarre, (339/230)	F-C. Bertrand de Palmerolle,+ *lieutenant-colonel*

INNER LEFT BRIGADE (BRIGADE DE BERRY) (727/519)

Commander	Jean-Baptiste de Trivio,* *lieutenant-colonel*
2e Bataillon, Régiment de Berry (360/269)	Jean-Baptiste de Trivio,* *lieutenant-colonel*
3e Bataillon, Régiment de Berry (367/250)	M.-J.-T. de Carnay du Trecesson,+ *lieutenant-colonel*

CENTRE BRIGADE (BRIGADE DE LA MARINE) (898/246)

Commander	Jean-Daniel Dumas, *major des troupes de la marine*
1er Bataillon, troupes de la marine (450/123)	Chevalier de la Corne,* *capitaine des compagnies franches de la marine* and *commandant du bataillon*
2e Bataillon, troupes de la marine (448/123)	Jean-Baptiste Mutigny de Vassan,* *capitaine des compagnies franches de la marine* and *commandant du bataillon*

INNER RIGHT BRIGADE (BRIGADE DE LA REINE) (650/508)

Commander	Jean-Georges Dejean de Roquemaure, *brigadier*
2e Bataillon, Régiment de la Reine (370/223)	J.-G. Dejean de Roquemaure, *brigadier*
2e Bataillon, Régiment de Languedoc (280/285)	M.-A. de Privat,* *lieutenant-colonel*

RIGHT BRIGADE (BRIGADE DE ROYAL-ROUSILLON) (625/540)

Commander	Médard de Poulariez, *lieutenant-colonel*
2e Bataillon, Régiment de Royal-Rousillon (305/279)	Médard de Poulariez, *lieutenant-colonel*
2e Bataillon, Régiment de Guyenne (320/261)	J.-B. Le Porquier de Launay,* *lieutenant-colonel*

RESERVE (287)

Milice de Montreal et Quebec (287)	Chevalier de Repentigny

ARMY TROOPS

Left wing Grenadier Battalion (est. 300) (Note 5)	Charles de Nevaire d'Aiguebelle, *capitaine de grenadiers*
Centre Grenadier Battalion (est. 200) (Note 5)	J.-R. de Montreuil de Lachaux,+ *capitaine de grenadiers*
Cavalry (200)	Sieur de la Rochebeaucourt, *capitaine de cavalrie*
Aboriginal warriors (270)	Corne Ste-Luc, *capitaine des compagnies franches de la marine*
Artillerie de la marine (est. 30)	Jean de Louvicourt, *capitaine d'artillerie*

ORDNANCE

3 x 6-pdr. guns

RECAPITULATION OF FRENCH LAND FORCES

Troupes de terre	2712
Troupes de la marine	898
Milice	2551
Artillery	30
Cavalry	200
Aboriginal Warriors	270
Total	6661 troops with 3 pieces of artillery

NAVY

Commander	Jean Vauquelin, *capitaine de frégate*
l'Atalante, 22 guns (Destroyed 16 May 1760)	Jean Vauquelin, *capitaine de frégate*
Pomone, 22 guns (Destroyed, 16 May 1760)	Sieur de Sauvage, *capitaine*
Marie, flute, transport (Escaped 16 May 1760)	Sieur de Cornille, *capitaine*
La Pie, transport (Destroyed 16 May 1760)	Unknown
L'Amitie, transport (Destroyed 16 May 1760)	Unknown
Le Sioux (Destroyed,16 May 1760)	Unknown

NOTES

1. Lieutenant John Knox recorded that on 24 April 1760, "A company of volunteers are to be ordered to be formed instantly, to consist of one Captain, four Subalterns, six Serjeants, six Corporals, four Drummers, and one hundred privates." Knox, *Journal*, 288-289.

2. Lieutenant John Knox recorded that on 27 April, the day before battle, "All the British merchants were reviewed and, at their own request, formed into an independent company of volunteers, to be commanded by Lieutenant Grant of the fifty-eighth regiment." Whether they actually fought on the battlefield is unknown, but most likely were used to guard the city gates and ramparts. Knox, *Journal*, 291.

3. Ships that arrived to help lift the siege are listed (despite not having been present for the battle).

4. The first number in unit strength denotes regulars, the second incorporated militiamen. Totals not known exactly are noted "est." for estimated.

5. The grenadiers of the French army were divided into two detachments for the start of the battle, but around 9 A.M. Lévis sent the four grenadier companies from the centre of his line to Dumont's Mill on his left flank, where they remained for the rest of the battle.

SOURCES

British: "A Return of the Number of Officers and Men that Marched into the Field and theNumber of Killed & Wounded the 28th April 1760,"; "State of the Garrison of Quebec, 24 April 1760;" and "List of British Officers Killed, Wounded and Prisoners at Quebec, From April 27 to May 21, 1760," all in John Knox, *An Historical Journal of the Campaigns in North America. 1769.* A.G. Doughty, ed., Vol.III, (Toronto, 1914-1916); Public Record Office, War Office 71/68, Marching Regiments, October 1760-July 1761; M.E.S. Laws, *Battery Records of the Royal Artillery* (Woolwich, 1951); Dictionary of Canadian Biography, vos 3 and 4; William Wood, ed., *The Logs of the Conquest of Canada* (Toronto, 1909); Murray to Pitt, 25 May 1760, in Gertrude Selwyn Kimball, ed., *Correspondence of William Pitt when Secretary of State with Colonial Governors and Military and Naval Commissioners in America, Vol.II*, (1906; reprint New York); R.H. Mahon, *Life of General The Hon. James Murray* (London: 1921).

French: Jean-Yves Bronze, *Les Morts de la guerre de Sept Ans au Cimitière de l'Hôpital-General de Quebec*, (Quebec, 2001); *Rapport de l'Archiviste de La province de Quebec pour 1931-34*, "Papiers La Pause;" H.R. Casgrain, ed., *Collections des manucrits du Marechal de Lévis*, 12 vols (Montreal & Quebec, 1889-1895); P.B. Casgrain, *Les Batailles des Plaines d'Abraham et de Sainte-Foye [sic]*, (Quebec, 1908); Pierre Pouchot, *Memoirs on the Late War in North America between France and England*, B.L. Dunnigan, ed. (Youngstown, 1994).

APPENDIX B

Order of Battle and Strengths, Opposing Forces at the Battle of Cut Knife Hill, 1885

CANADIAN MILITIA AND MOUNTED POLICE FLYING COLUMN

COMMAND AND STAFF

Commander	Lieutenant-Colonel W.D. Otter, C Company, Infantry School Corps
Chief of Staff	Superintendent W.M. Herchmer, NWMP
Brigade Major	Lieutenant J.W. Sears, C Company, Infantry School Corps
Brigade Quartermaster	Captain W.G. Mutton, Queen's Own Rifles
Brigade Surgeon	Dr. F.W. Strange, MP and 5 men of C Company, ISC, attached as stretcher bearers (5)
Scouts	Constable Charles Ross, NWMP, Josie (Joseph) Alexander, Peter Ballendine, Adam Ballendine, John Todd, and John Pambrun (6)
Transport	48 wagons used for carrying dismounted personnel as well as ammunition, rations and other stores. They carried no water (est. 48 teamsters)
War Correspondents	H.A. Kennedy, *Montreal Daily Witness,* and A. Harkin, *Montreal Star,* and W.W. "Billy" Fox, *Toronto Daily Mail*

UNITS AND DETACHMENTS

Listed in the order they moved behind the scouts on 1-2 May 1885

NWMP Mounted Detachment	Superintendent P.R Neale (50)
B Battery, Royal Canadian Artillery	Major C.J. Short (88)
C Company, Infantry School Corps	Lieutenant R.L. Wadmore (46)
Governor General's Foot Guards	Lieutenant H.H. Gray (21)
Queen's Own Rifles	Captain Thomas Brown (62)
Left Half	Lieutenant H.J. Brock
Right Half	Captain P.D. Hughes
NWMP Dismounted Detachment	(Probably commanded by an NCO) (23)
Battleford Rifles	Captain E.A. Nash (43)

NOTE ON CANADIAN FORCES

The militia used the term "brigade" when several units, however small, were grouped together. Thus, Otter's Flying Column, although with a strength of under 400, was organized as for a "brigade," with the appropriate terms used.

Flying column unit strength figures contained in the reports and newspaper accounts differed slightly as some authors rounded off the figures. The acknowledged total figure for the column was 325 but, as noted in the text of the study, the fighting strength, including armed teamsters and medical staff, was closer to 400, a figure that did not include the commander, his staff and retinue, or the war correspondents. The most important figure, however, was the number of longarms and it was about 375 rifles or carbines.

PLAINS CREE, ASSINIBOINE, SAULTEAUX AND MÉTIS PEOPLES

(Either participating in the battle or in the Indian camp)

PLAINS CREE PEOPLES

Wah-wee-kah-oo-tah-mah-hote (Strike-Him-On-The- Back) Band, Reserve No. 113
There were probably 51 men involved. Of 27 women, 79 boys, and 90 girls who were considered participants in the rebellion, an unknown number were in the camp. Fine Day was from this band. Only two men from this band did not participate.

Thunderchild Band, Reserve No. 115
A small band, and only two men and their families possibly were at the battle: 2 men, 2 women, 1 boy, and 2 girls.

Pitiwahnapiwiyin (Poundmaker) Band, Reserve No. 114
There were 36 men, 56 women, 61 boys, 58 girls, one other male, and 10 other females - total 222 who probably were in or near the camp and at the battle. One of them, Fred Napasis or Fred Ballendine, was related to the two Ballendine men in Constable Charles Ross's scout section.

Min-a-he-quo-sis (Little Pine) Band, Reserve No. 116
There were 31 men, 54 women, 108 boys, 104 girls, 7 other females, totalling 304 members who possibly were involved.

Pap-a-way-napayo (Lucky Man) Band, Shared the Little Pine Reserve No. 116
Lucky Man and a group of followers joined Big Bear at Frog Lake. Only a small group probably were involved: 7 men, 16 women, 29 boys, 29 girls.

CREE AND MIXED BLOODS PEOPLE

Pee'yahn-kah-nichk-soo-sit (Red Pheasant) Band, Reserve No. 108
This band had 25 men, 31 women, 29 boys, 16 girls, for a total of 101 band members who were at or near the battle.

CREE-SAULTEAUX PEOPLES

Moosomin or Mooseberry Band, Reserve No. 112
A small band with only 16 participants at the battle: 5 men, 3 women, 3 boys, and 5 girls.

Napahase (The Slayer) Band, Shared the Thunderchild Reserve No. 115
Probably close to 90 members were involved: 9 men, 21 women, 34 boys, and 25 girls.

Es-pem-ick-kah-ki-toot (Young Chipewayan) Band, Reserve No. 107
In 1885 the chief and only a few followers moved onto the Thunderchild reserve, and 2 men, 3 women, 4 boys and 9 girls, totalling 18, possibly were involved.

STRAGGLERS AND MIXED-BLOODS

These were Indians and Métis who did not belong to any particular band. It is not known how many of the men participated in the battle. There were 16 men, 50 women, 44 boys, and 72 girls in this group.

ASSINIBOINE PEOPLES

Whostahkah (Lean Man) Band, Reserve No. 111
A small band with 37 members probably involved at Cut Knife Hill: 6 men, 13 women, 11 boys, and 7 girls.

Mahtopah (Grizzly Bear's Head) Band, Reserve No. 110
One hundred and four members were probably involved: 22 men, 39 women, 22 boys, and 21 girls.

Sakimayo (Mosquito) Band, Reserve No. 9
Almost all band members were possibly involved: 29 men, 45 women, 26 boys, and 18 girls, for a total of 188 members.

PLAINS MÉTIS

Robert Jefferson the Indian agent and Father Cochin reported that there were a significant number of Métis fighters in the large Cut Knife camp, but no one gave an estimate of numbers. There may have been as many as 40 Métis in the action.

NOTE ON INDIAN AND MÉTIS STRENGTHS

The above estimates for Indians at, or near the battle, were calculated by Douglas W. Light in his work *Footprints in the Dust*, pages 294-295 and 305-330. Light based his figures on Indian Department records but pointed out that many names were misspelled and that, in many cases, it was difficult to make a positive identification because some people received several different names during their lifetime and family names had disappeared.

Light estimated that more than 1500 men, women and children were in the Cut Knife Hill camp at the time of the battle but one cannot be sure how many Indian or Métis combatants were in the ravines or at the west end of the battlefield.

SOURCES

Militia and NWMP: Superintendent W.M. Herchmer to Lieutenant Colonel A.G. Irvine, Commissioner of the NWMP, 27 July 1885, contained in Appendix B to "Report of the Commissioner of the [NWMP] 1885," Ottawa, 1886, in *Settlers and Rebels Being The Official Reports To Parliament of the Activities of the Royal [NWMP] from 1882-1885 by the Commissioners of the RNWMP*, (reprint, Ottawa, 1973); General Sir Fred. Middleton, "Suppression of Rebellion in the North-West Territories of Canada, 1885," *United Service Magazine*, January 1894; NAC, MG 30 G 14, Otter Papers, Correspondence, Vol I, File # III, Jan 1885–Dec 1890; DHH 500.0009 (D32), Otter's Despatch to Middleton, 5 May 1885; Ernest J. Chambers, *The Queen's Own Rifles of Canada*, (Toronto, 1901); Desmond Morton, *The Last War Drum: The North West Campaign of 1885*, (Toronto, 1885); Charles Pelham Mulvaney, *The History of the North-West Rebellion of 1885*, (Toronto, 1885).

Indian and Métis: Douglas W. Light, *Footprints in the Dust*, (North Battleford, 1987).

APPENDIX C

Orders of Battle and Strengths, Opposing Forces, Paardeberg, February 1900

IMPERIAL FORCES

SOUTH AFRICA FIELD FORCE – WESTERN FRONT (SEE NOTE 1)

STAFF

Commander in Chief:	Field Marshal Lord Roberts
Chief of Staff:	Major General H.H. Kitchener
Deputy Adjutant General:	Major General W.F. Kelly

1ST DIVISION (See Note 2)

General Officer Commanding:	Lieutenant General Lord Methuen

Divisional Troops

20, 38 Batteries, RFA (Royal Field Arty)	12 x 15-pdr guns
37 Battery, RFA	4 x 5-inch howitzers
Detachment, Naval Brigade	2 x 4.7-inch guns
17 Field Company, RE	
Balloon Section, RE	
1st Division Field Hospital	

1 (Guards) Brigade

	Major General R. Pole-Carew
3rd [Battalion] Grenadier Gds	915
1st Coldsteam Guards	965
2nd Coldstream Guards	921
1st Scots Guards	953
18th Bearer Company	
18th Field Hospital	

9 Brigade

	Brigadier General C.W. Douglas
1st Northumberland Fusiliers	617
1st Loyal North Lancashire	447
2nd Northamptonshire Regiment	850
2nd King's Own Yorkshire Lt Infy	840
1st Bearer Company	
19th Field Hospital	

6TH DIVISION
General Officer Commanding: Lieutenant General T. Kelly-Kenny

Divisional Troops

76, 81 Batteries, RFA	12 x 15-pdr guns
Detachment, Naval Brigade	2 x 12-pdr guns
6 Division Ammunition Column	
38 Field Company, Royal Engineers	
Field Hospital	

13 Brigade   Major General C.E. Knox

2nd East Kent Regiment	786
2nd Gloucestershire Regiment	735
1st West Riding Regiment	750
1st Oxfordshire Light Infantry	614
7th Bearer Company	
Field Hospital	

18 Brigade   Brigadier General T.E. Stephenson

2nd Royal Warwickshire Regiment	850
1st Yorkshire Regiment	936
1st Welsh Regiment	970
1st Essex Regiment	787
6th Division Fd Hosp Bearer Company	
No. 3 Section, Cape Field Hospital	

7TH DIVISION
Commander: Lieutenant General C. Tucker

Divisional Troops

18, 62, 75 Batteries, RFA	18 x 15-pdr. guns
Ammunition Column	
9 Field Company, RE	
Field Hospital	

14 Brigade   Major General H. Chermside

2nd Norfolk Regiment	814
2nd Lincolnshire Regiment	858
1st King's Own Scottish Borderers	950
2nd Hampshire Regiment	700
Bearer Company	
Field Hospital	

15 Brigade   Major General A.G. Wavell

2nd Cheshire Regiment	830
1st East Lancashire Regiment	910
2nd South Wales Borderers	961
2nd North Staffordshire Regiment	900
Bearer Company	
Field Hospital	

9TH DIVISION

General Officer Commanding: Lieutenant General Sir H.E. Colvile

Divisional Troops

82 Battery, RFA	6 x 15-pounder guns
65 Battery. RFA	6 x 4.5-inch howitzers
Detachment, Naval Brigade	2 x 4.7-inch guns, 2 x 12-pounder guns
7th Field Company, RE	(less one section with Kimberley Garrison)

3 (Highland) Brigade   Brigadier General H.A. Macdonald

2nd Black Watch	649
1st Highland Light Infantry	950
2nd Seaforth Highlanders	703
1st Argyll and Sutherland Hdrs	819
Cape Volunteer Bearer Company	
3 Co. Field Hospital	

19 Brigade   Brigadier General H. Smith-Dorrien

2nd Duke of Cornwall's Lt Infy	836
2nd King's Shropshire Lt Infy	886
1st Gordon Highlanders	900
2nd Royal Canadian Regiment	925
7th Division Field Hospital Bearer Company	
No. 1 Section, Cape Field Hospital	

CAVALRY DIVISION

General Officer Commanding: Lieutenant General J.D.P. French

1 Cavalry Brigade

Commander:	Colonel T.C. Porter
2nd Dragoon Guards	438
6th Dragoon Guards	464
Squadron, 6th Dragoons}	
Squadron, 14th Hussars}	464
Squadron, New South Wales Lancers}	
Q, T and U Batteries, RHA (Royal Horse Arty)	each 6 x 12-pounder guns
Ammunition Column	

2 Cavalry Brigade

Commander:	Colonel R. Broadwood
Composite Regiment, Household Cavalry	625
10th Hussars	458
12th Lancers	500
P and G Batteries, RHA	each 6 x 12-pounder guns
Ammunition Column	

3 Cavalry Brigade

Commander:	Colonel J.R.P. Gordon
9th Lancers	418
16th Lancers	540
Q and R Batteries, RHA	each 6 x 12-pounder guns
Ammunition Column	

9 and 12 Bearer Companies
6 and 9 Field Hospitals

Mounted Infantry Brigade

Commander:	Colonel E.A.H. Alderson
1st Battalion, Mounted Infantry	413
3rd Battalion, Mounted Infantry	460
Roberts's Horse	550
Two squadrons, Kitchener's Horse	200
Queensland Mounted Infantry	275
Two companies, New Zealand Mtd Rifles	204
Rimington's Guides	150

Regular Mounted Infantry (See Note 3)

Commander:	Colonels O.C. Hannay and C.P. Ridley
2nd Battalion, Mounted Infantry	440
4th Battalion, Mounted Infantry	450
5th Battalion, Mounted Infantry	430
6th Battalion, Mounted Infantry	460
7th Battalion, Mounted Infantry	450
8th Battalion, Mounted Infantry	430

OTHER MOUNTED UNITS (See Note 4)

Nesbitt's Horse	250
Two squadrons, Kitchener's Horse	200
City Imperial Vols Mounted Infantry	250
1 Grahamstown City Volunteers	200
New South Wales Mounted Infantry	120

TRANSPORT (See Note 5)

Commander:	Colonel W.D. Richardson

21 Mule Companies with 1,134 wagons, 11,000 mules and 2,700 drivers
Six Oxen Companies with 600 wagons, 9,600 oxen and 1,320 drivers

Approximate Strengths, including Non-combatants

First Division	7,400
Sixth Division	6,700
Seventh Division	7,900
Ninth Division	7,400
Cavalry Division (including Alderson's Mtd Infy)	8,000
Other Mounted Troops	3,600
Transport	4,000
Total	45,000 (of which 37,000 with 30,000 combatants, took part in the invasion of the Orange Free State)

KIMBERLEY GARRISON (See Notes 6 and 7)

Commander:	Lieutenant Colonel R.G. Kekewich
23rd Company, RGA (Royal Garrison Arty)	Maxim machine gun battery
Section 7th Field Company RE	
Half, 1st Loyal North Lancashire Regt	422
Detachment, Loyal North Lancashire Regt	22

MOUNTED INFANTRY

Regular Cape Volunteers	840
Kimberley Regiment of Volunteers	881
Cape Police	478
Town Guards	2,824

NOTES ON IMPERIAL FORCES

1. The organization and strengths are taken from the table on pages 375-378 of Volume III of *The Times History of the War in South Africa 1899-1900.*

2. Remained on Western Front.

3. These battalions, especially the higher-numbered ones, were created by ordering every infantry battalion in South Africa to provide a company for conversion to mounted infantry. Hastily formed, their quality varied, but most had not yet reached a satisfactory standard of training in tactics and horsemanship. The story of the neophyte mounted infantryman who climbed into the saddle after placing his wrong foot in the stirrup, and found himself facing to the rear wondering whatever had happened to his horse's head, is not a military myth.

4. Probably employed as escorts to transport columns.

5. This transport was supplemented by brigading unit transport wagons.

6. "No reliable numbers are available as to the forces employed in the Defence of Kimberley." These words opened the section titled "Kimberley Garrison Strength" in Donald R. Forsyth's monograph *Defenders of Kimberley.* He then listed the various compilations, which ranged from 4,730 to 5,664, and concluded that, despite some duplications, the figure of 5,664 given in the roll of recipients of the Defence of Kimberley bar to the Queen's South Africa Medal must be accepted as the best approximation of the strength of the garrison.

7. Only major combatant units shown.

BOER FORCES

Overall Commander	Assistant **Commandant General** P.A.Cronje

TRANSVAAL FORCES

Commander:	Assistant **Commandant General** J.H. (Koos) De La Rey

Commando	Commanding Officer/s	Strength
Potchesfroom	*Commandant* M.J. Wolmarins	1249
Heidelberg	*Commandant* R.C. Spruyk	2375
Bloemhof	*Commandant* J.F. De Beer	680
Zoutspanberg?	Adjutant J.C. Albert	1017
Wolmaransstaad	*General* S.P. Du Toit	838
Pretoria?	Field Cornet M. Marass	2832
Scandinavian Corps	Captain J.J. Friis	100
Scout Corps	Captain Danie J.S. Theron	

ORANGE FREE STATE FORCES

Commander	*Vechtgeneral* C.R. De Wet

Commando	Commanding Officer/s	Strength
Kroonstad	*Commandant* S.W. Meintjes	2068
Bloemfontein	*General* W.J. Kolbe	1253
Winburg	*Commandant* H. Theunissen	1616
Ladybrand	*Commandant* R.J. Snijman	749
Hoopstad	*Commandant* J.C. Greyling	494

Jacobsdal	*Commandant* J.S. Lubbe	139
Bethlehem	*Commandant* D.J. Steyn	1142
Fiksburg	*Commandant* J.C. De Villiers	235
Boshof	*Commandant* R. Diedrichs	780
Fauresmith	*Commandant* P.J. Visser	988
Philippolis?	*Commandant* J.A.M. Hertzog	209
Wepener	*Veld Cornet* T. Spiller	253

Orange Free State Artillery
Commander

Major R.F.W. Albrecht
4 x Krupp 75mm guns, 1 x 37mm Pom-Pom

GRIEKWALAND WES KOMMANDO (CAPE REBELS FROM KIMBERLEY DISTRICT)
Commander

Veld Cornet W.C. Steyn

RECAPITULATION OF STRENGTH

Transvaal Forces	8,991
Orange Free State force	9,926 (plus State Artillery)
Other forces	100-150 (est.)
Total	19,017–19,067 (see below)

NOTES ON BOER FORCES

The organization and list of officers was provided by the Anglo-Boer War Museum in South Africa. The strength figures are from the tables on pages 513-514 of Volume IV of *The Times History of the War in South Africa* and represent the total of men "registered for the field" at the beginning of the war. The actual number present on the western front would have been much smaller. For example, a detachment of the Heidelberg Commando led by Cornelius Spruyt was sent north to assist in forcing a way open for the Boers trapped at Paardeberg to escape, while the majority of their comrades remained on the central front. Two members of this commando were killed while Spruyt and thirteen others were captured, although Spruyt later escaped from the train taking him to captivity when his guards fell asleep and he eventually rejoined the Boer forces. *For this reason, the total given above for Boer forces can not be taken as the number of men who fought at Paardeberg; it was probably only about 10,000 combatants.*

A detachment of the Scandinavian Corps lost 43 of 50 men at Magersfontein whien it was overrun by the 2nd Seaforth Highlanders of the Highland Brigade.

The ordnance listed for the Orange Free State Artillery were the pieces captured when Cronje surrendered at Paardeberg.

Orders of Battle,
Canadian and German Forces,
Action at Naves–Iwuy, October 1918

CANADIAN

CANADIAN INDEPENDENT FORCE
Commander   Brigadier General R. Brutinel

Canadian Light Horse
Commander   Lieutenant Colonel I. Leonard
A Squadron
B Squadron   Major C.F. McEwen
C Squadron   Lieutenant F. Matheson

1st Canadian Motor Machine Gun Brigade
Commander   Lieutenant Colonel W.K. Walker
A Battery
B Battery
C (Borden) Battery
D (18th Company Canadian Machine Gun Corps) Battery
E (18th Company Canadian Machine Gun Corps) Battery

2nd Canadian Motor Machine Gun Brigade
Commander   Lieutenant Colonel H.F.V. Meurling
A (Yukon) Battery
B (Eaton) Battery
C (19th Company Canadian Machine Gun Corps) Battery
D (17th Company Canadian Machine Gun Corps) Battery
E (17th and 18th Machine Gun Companies) Battery
Note: Each battery had 1 captain, 2 lieutenants, 1 warrant officer, 4 sergeants, 16 rank and
file for a total of 3 officers and 21 men

Canadian Cyclist Battalion
Commander   Major A.E. Humphrey

2ND CANADIAN DIVISION
Commander   Major General Sir H.E. Burstall

4th Infantry Brigade   Brigadier General G.E. McCuaig
18th (Western Ontario) Battalion

19th (Central Ontario) Battalion
20th (Central Ontario) Battalion
21st (Eastern Ontario) Battalion

6th Infantry Brigade   Brigadier General A. Ross
27th (City of Winnipeg) Battalion
28th (Northwest) Battalion
29th (Vancouver) Battalion
31st (Alberta) Battalion

GERMAN

6. INFANTERIEDIVISION
Note: each German infantry regiment contained three battalions invariably numbered I, II and III
Infanterie-Regiment 24
Infanterie-Regiment 64
Infanterie-Regiment 396
Feldartillerie Regiment 3

10. ERSATZ DIVISION
Infanterie-Regiment 369
Infanterie-Regiment 370
Infanterie-Regiment 371
Feldartillerie Regiment 95

18. RESERVE DIVISION
Reserve-Regiment 31
Reserve-Regiment 84
Reserve Regiment 86
Reserve Feldartillerie Regiment 18
Artillerie Bataillon 126

1. PANZERABTEILUNG
Commander: *Hauptmann* Greiff
A7V 501 "Gretchen": broke down before the action at Iwuy
A7V 525 "Siegfried" (*Leutnant* Wagner): attacked Rieux-en-Cambrésis
A7V 540 "Heiland" (*Vizefeldwebel* Lommen): attacked Iwuy, rescued crew of tank 560
A7V 541 (*Leutnant* Schück): attacked Iwuy, tried unsuccessfully to tow away tank 560
A7V 560 (*Leutnant* Volckheim): knocked out in action at Iwuy
A7V 562 "Herkules" (*Leutnant* Muller): broke down before the action at Iwuy
A7V 563 "Wotan" (*Leutnant* Goldmann): attacked Rieux-en-Cambrésis

13. PANZERABTEILUNG
Commander: *Hauptmann* Thofern
Mark IV 118: attacked Iwuy, tank burned
Mark IV 127: broke down before action at Iwuy, destroyed by crew
Mark IV 137: attacked Iwuy, tank burned
Mark IV 142: attacked Iwuy, tank burned

Mark IV 209: broke down before action at Iwuy, vehicle later recovered
Mark IV 213: broke down before action at Iwuy, tank caught fire

SOURCES

Maxwell Hundleby and Rainer Strasheim, *The German A7V Tank and the Captured British Mark IV Tanks of World War I* (Somerset, 1990); G.W.L. Nicholson, *The Canadian Expeditionary Force, 1914-1919*, (Ottawa, 1962); ; War Department, *Histories of the Two Hundred and Fifty-One Divisions of the German Army which participated in the War* (1914-1918) (Washington, 1919); War Office, *Official History of the War - Military Operations, France & Belgium, 1918*, (London, 1931).

Orders of Battle and Strengths, Battle of the Melfa Crossing, 24-25 May 1944

CANADIAN

5TH CANADIAN ARMOURED DIVISION

General Officer Commanding:	Major General B.M. Hoffmeister

5th Canadian Armoured Brigade

Commander:	Brigadier J.D.B. Smith

"Strathforce"

2nd Canadian Armoured Regiment (Lord Strathcona's Horse (Royal Canadians))

Commanding Officer:	Lieutenant Colonel P. Griffin
Second in Command:	Major George Wattsford
Recce Troop:	Lieutenant Edward Perkins
A Squadron:	Major Gordon Symmes
B Squadron:	Major William Milroy
C Squadron:	Major Jack Smith
HQ Squadron:	Major James McAvity
Medical Officer:	Captain "Sammy" Vaisrub
Padre:	(Hon.) Captain R.W. Brundage

The Westminster Regiment (Motor)

Commanding Officer:	Lieutenant-Colonel G.C. Corbould
Headquarters Company:	Captain Hoskin
Medical Officer:	Captain Edward Wilder
Padre:	(Hon.) Captain Owen
Intelligence Officer:	Lieutenant J. Biggs
A Company:	Major John Mahony
Second in Command:	Captain J. Hughes
1 Platoon (Scout)	Lieutenant William Delaney
2 Platoon:	Lieutenant Ken Harrison
3 Platoon:	Lieutenant Heber Smith
4 Platoon:	Lieutenant Ross Douglas
B Company:	Major George Johnson
5 Platoon (Scout)	
6 Platoon	
7 Platoon	
8 Platoon	
C Company:	Major Ian Douglas
Second in Command:	Captain William Neill

9 Platoon (Scout)	
10 Platoon	
11 Platoon	
12 Platoon:	Lieutenant Cruise
Support Company:	Major Donald MacKenzie

61st (Peter) Battery, 8th Field Regiment, RCA

Commander:	Major George Ward

82nd Battery, 4th Anti-Tank Regiment

5TH CANADIAN ARMOURED DIVISION DIVISIONAL UNITS

3rd Armoured Reconnaissance Regiment (The Governor General's Horse Guards)

Commanding Officer:	Lieutenant-Colonel K. Jordan
A Squadron:	Major Frank Classy
B Squadron:	Major Timothy Hugman
C Squadron:	Major Alan Burton

1st Field Squadron, Royal Canadian Engineers

10th Field Squadron, Royal Canadian Engineers

4th Field Park Squadron, Royal Canadian Engineers

No. 7 Field Ambulance, Royal Canadian Army Medical Corps

D Section	Captain O.E. Morehouse

OTHER 8TH ARMY UNITS

64th Battery, 165 Field Regiment (Jeep Artillery), Royal Artillery

Battery Commander:	Captain Robin Martin

GERMAN

Note: Throughout this period, German units were continually and quickly moved between quieter and busier sectors and were then amalgamated with other units as casualties were suffered, making the compilation of a completely accurate order of battle difficult. Units listed below division level are based on units recorded as having been present in the Melfa River area on 24 and 25 May 1944 rather than the divisional establishment.

It is nearly impossible to construct an accurate picture of the strength of German units at the battle of the Melfa Crossing. The 5th Canadian Armoured Division Intelligence Summaries for this period provide general details of 90. *Panzergrenadierdivision* but, given the pace of operations, they are not entirely accurate. The Summaries contain frequent comments such as "short of equipment," or "believed eliminated" but little else.

Among the reinforcements, *Panzerregiment* 4 was a unit of Army Troops assigned to 10. *Armee* on 19 May 1944. Its No. 1 Company was equipped with Panthers and joined 90. *Panzergrenadierdivision* on 20 May 1944. *Feld-Ersatz Bataillon* 96 was a "replacement" unit but the 10. *Armee* order of battle contains only one unit in 44. *Infanteridivision* with this number and that was the reconnaissance battalion although the *Feld-Ersatz* battalion had the same number but was also sometimes identified by the divisional number.

51. GEBIRGSKORP: GENERAL DER GEBIRGSTRUPPEN
VALENTIN FEUERSTEIN

1. FALSCHIRMDIVISION
Commander   General der Falschirmjaeger Richard Heidrich

90. PANZERGRENADIERDIVISION
Commander   Generalleutnant Ernst-Günther Baade
Grenadierregiment 200
Grenadierregiment 361
Aufklärungsabteilung 190
Panzerabteilung 190 (12 assault guns)
Artillerieregiment 190 (one battalion)
Panzerjägerabteilung 190 (approximately 36 guns)
Pioneerbataillon 190

UNITS THAT REINFORCED 90. PANZERGRENADIERDIVISION
FROM 11 TO 24 MAY 1944:
1 company, *Panzerregiment* 4 (Panther)
1 tank company from 26. *Panzerdivision*
Panzergrenadierregiment 115 (two battalions) from 15. *Panzergrenadierdivision*
Grenadierregiment 576 (two battalions, from *Sperrverband Bode*)
Gebirgsjägerbataillon 85 (three companies) from 5. *Gebirgsjägerdivision*
Panzerjägerabteilung 85 from 5. *Gebirgsjägerdivision*
Panzerjägerabteilung 114 from 114. *Jägerdivision*
Company, *Pioneerbattaillon* 114 from 114. *Jägerdivision*
III Battalion, 721 *Jägerregiment* from 114. *Jägerdivision*
Feld-Ersatz Bataillon 96 from 44. *Infanteriedivision*
Werferregiment 71 (*Nebelwerfer*)
Schwere Panzerjägerabteilung 525

SOURCES
Allied: The Strathconas' order of battle was constructed from NAC, RG 24, vol 14192, WD LdSH, 9 Jan 44, and App 25, "Organization LdSH (RC)," App A to "STRATHFORCE – Planning Note, May 1944." This document provides detailed informaiton on the number of personnel and weapons system just prior to the battle. Also consulted were H.F. Joslin, Orders of Battle: Second World War, 1939-1945, (London, 1990), 142; J.M. McAvity, Lord Strathcona's Horse (Royal Canadians): A Record of Achievement (Toronto, 19i47), 43-44. Order of battle and key appointments of the Westminister Regiment are from Infantry Battalion WEII/233/2, Motor Battalion, August, 1944, and J.E. Oldfied, The Westminsters' War Diary: An Unofficial History of The Westminister Regiment (Motor) in World War II, (New Westminster, 1964), 77-96.

German: The order of battle present is drawn from DHH, AHS Report No. 20, "Information from German MIlitary Documents in General and Canadian Operations in Particular," 19 July 1948, 4n, 19, 71n, 77n, 81-82.

Endnotes

Abbreviations Used in Endnotes

AHS   Army Historical Section
ALFF   Army Land Forces College, Fort Frontenac, Kingston
BCD   British Columbia Dragoons
CAB   Canadian Armoured Brigade
CAD   Canadian Armoured Division
CHR   *Canadian Historical Review*
CLH   Canadian Light Horse
CMHQ   Canadian Military Headquarters
DCB   *Dictionary of Canadian Biography*
DHH   Directorate of History and Heritage, Ottawa
GHQ   General Headquarters
JSAHR   *Journal of the Society for Army Historical Research*
LdSH   Lord Strathcona's Horse
MG   Manuscript Group
NAC   National Archives of Canada, Ottawa
NWFF   North West Field Force
PAM   Public Archives of Manitoba, Winnipeg
PRO   Public Record Office, Kew, Britain
RCA   Royal Canadian Artillery
RCE   Royal Canadian Engineers
RG   Record Group
RFA   Royal Field Artillery
RGA   Royal Garrison Artillery
RHA   Royal Horse Artillery
WD   War Diary
WestR   Westminster Regiment (Motor)
WO   War Office

1. Sillery

The author takes this opportunity to acknowledge his gratitude to Directorate of History & Heritage Librarian Madeleine Lafleur-Lemire, for her gracious assistance; his colleague Major Leo Regimbal, for his assistance in translation of French texts; and Dr Stephen Brumwell, for sharing research gathered for his book *Redcoats: The British Soldier and War in the Americas 1755-1763* (Cambridge: 2002).

1. The title, taken from a plea uttered by Lieutenant Charles Stewart of the 78th Foot, Fraser's Highlanders, after the Battle of Sillery, 28 April 1760, links the action with a more famous battle fought some 14 years previously. Stewart was a Jacobite who had fought for Bonnie Prince Charlie at the Battle of Culloden, 16 April 1746, under the command of Lord George Murray. Both April battles, despite their being fought in different years and different places, shared similar sleet and mud conditions which bogged down soldiers and artillery alike, and resulted in serious wounds on both occasions for Stewart and disastrous defeats for his respective Murray commanders. Stewart quote in J.R. Harper, *The Fraser Highlanders* (Montreal, 1979), 103-104.

2. The Battle of Sillery, 1760, is also known as the Battle of Sainte-Foy or the second Battle of the Plains of Abraham. Contemporary French accounts of the action merely referred to it as "*l'affaire de 28 avril*" while John Knox gave the battle a subheading "The Battle of Sillery" in his original 1769 book, *An Historical Journal of the Campaigns in North America…*, (London, 1769), 292 (hereafter *Knox's Journal*). The actual battle was fought nowhere near Sainte-Foy but along the western edges of the Plains of Abraham and the *Bois de Sillery* in the parish of Sillery. For this reason I have chosen to use the earliest published account of the battle's name.

3. This song was composed by a soldier of the 78th Fraser's Highlanders shortly after the Siege of Quebec, probably during the cold winter months of 1759-1760. Collected from

the oral tradition, it first appeared in print in 1822 and was attributed to Iain Campbell. For the full song and other 18th century Gaelic songs celebrating the Highlanders on campaign in North America during the Seven Years' War and American Revolution, see Michael Newton's excellent book *We're Indians Sure Enough: The Legacy of the Scottish Highlanders in the United States*. (Auburn, NH: 2001). Also see collected 18th century military songs relating to Quebec in "Appendix J" to C.P. Stacey, *Quebec, 1759* , Donald E. Graves, ed., (Toronto, 2001).

4. Lévis, *DCB*, III, 477-73.

5. See Ian McCulloch, "Like Roaring Lions Breaking From their Chains: The Battle of Ticonderoga, 1758" in Donald E. Graves, ed., *Fighting For Canada: Seven Battles, 1758-1945* (Toronto, 2000), 23-80.

6. *DCB*, III, 478.

7. Strong posts guarding the approaches to Montreal were established at Île aux Noix at the northern end of Lake Champlain on the Richelieu River commanded by *Colonel* Louis-Antoine de Bougainville and at Fort Lévis situated on an island in the Saint- Lawrence River near Prescott, Ontario, commanded by *Capitaine* Pierre Pouchot.

8. Le Comte de Maurès de Malartic, quoted in Abbé H.R. Casgrain, *Wolfe and Montcalm*, (Toronto, 1911), 241. For French strengths see Major General R.H Mahon, *Life of General the Hon James Murray*, (London, 1921), 219-22; and Martin L. Nicolai, "A Different Kind of Courage: The French Military and the Canadian Irregular Soldier during the Seven Years' War," *CHR*, LXX, (1989), 72-73.

9. The Chevalier de Lévis' "Instructions concernant l'ordre dans lequel les milices attachée à chaque bataillon seront formées pour camper et servir pendant la campagne" in *Collections Des Manuscrits du Maréchal de Lévis: Journal des Campagnes du Chevalier de Lévis en Canada de 1756 à 1760*, H.R. Casgrain, ed., I, (Montreal, 1889), 248. For an excellent article on *Canadien* militiamen see Nicolai, *A Different Kind of Courage*, 53-75.

10. Lévis quoted in Casgrain, *Wolfe and Montcalm*, 241-2.

11. For details on uniforms and units see René Chartrand, *The French Soldier in Colonial America*, (Bloomfield, 1984), 36.

12. "Journal of the Battle of Sillery and Siege of Quebec," *Documents Relative to the Colonial History of the State of New York*, X, 1080 (hereafter *Lévis' Journal*). François-Charles de Bourlamaque, of Italian ancestry, was born 1716, Paris, died 23 June 1764 at Guadeloupe. Entered *Régiment du Dauphin* as a gentleman volunteer 1739; second-lieutenant, 1740; lieutenant, 1742; adjutant and captain in 1745; he was reputedly an excellent engineer though no records survive to prove he belonged to the corps of engineers. He took part in the battles of Fontenoy and Rocourt during the War of the Austrian Succession and in 1755 received an award for rewriting and improving the standard army drill book. In 1756 he received the *Croix de Saint-Louis*, was promoted *colonel d'infantrie* in Canada and accompanied Montcalm to New France as his third-in-command. He directed the sieges of Oswego, 1756, Fort William Henry, 1757 and Quebec, 1760, the latter from a camp bed as he was seriously wounded in the leg. He also fought at the battles of Ticonderoga, 1758, and Sillery, 1760, but missed the Plains battle as he was guarding the southern approach to Montreal against Amherst. Promoted brigadier general prior to the battle of Sillery, Bourlamaque returned to France on the capitulation of New France, was promoted to major-general in 1763 and appointed as governor of Guadeloupe, which he took back in a formal handover from the British. He died the following year of fever. *DCB*, III, 84-86.; James Johnstone, *The Campaign of 1760 in Canada. A Sequel attributed to Chevalier Johnstone*, (Quebec, 1868), 17, [hereafter *Johnstone's Memoirs*].

13. Lévis quoted in Casgrain, *Wolfe & Montcalm*, 249.

14. *Lévis' Journal*, 1081.

15. *Knox's Journal*, 290.

16. François Bernier to Vaudreuil, September 1759, quoted in Casgrain, *Wolfe & Montcalm*, 254-55; *DCB*, III, 569-78.

17. Anonymous journal , NAC: MG 18, N 54, Microfilm reel A-652. This anonymous officer may be one of Wolfe's ADCs, probably Captain Hervey Smythe of the 15th Foot, who was wounded at the Plains battle and returned home with Wolfe's body. The NAC alleges the journal to be the work of Major

Irving, but this cannot be, as existing copies of Irving's handwriting do not match that of the unknown staff officer.

18. James Murray to George Murray, October 1759, quoted in Mahon, *Murray*, 200.

19. Mahon, 25; *DCB*, III, 569-78.

20. James Miller, "Memoirs of an Invalid," U1350/Z9 & Z9A, Centre for Kentish Studies, Maidstone (hereafter "*Invalid Memoirs*").

21. Bernier to Vaudreuil, September 1759, quoted in Joseph Lister Rutledge, *Century of Conflict: The Struggle Between the French and British in Colonial America*, (New York, 1956), 504; Patrick Mackellar, *A Short Authentic Account of the Expedition Against Quebec in the year 1759,"* (Quebec, 1872), 36; *Knox's Journal*, 328.

22. John Johnson, "Memoirs of the Quarter-Mas'r Sergeant" in A.G. Doughty & G.W. Parmalee, eds., *The Siege of Quebec and the Battle of the Plains of Abraham*, eds., V (Quebec, 1901) 115, [hereafter *QM Memoirs*].

23. For examples of French and British accounts: see *Knox's Journal*, 289-90 and *Lévis' Journal*, 1081.

24. Brigadier-General James Murray, *Journal of the Siege of Quebec from 18th September to 25th May 1760*, (Toronto, 1939), 24 (hereafter *Murray's Journal*); Murray quoted in Gertrude Selwyn Kimball, ed., *Correspondence of William Pitt when Secretary of State with Colonial Governors and Military and Naval Commissioners in America*, II, (New York, 1906), 292 (hereafter *Pitt Correspondence*).

25. *Murray's Journal*, 25.

26. "A Return of the Officers and Men that marched into the Field and the Number of Killed and Wounded the 28th April 1760" in *Townshend Papers*, Vol.XII, NAC, Microfilm Reel C-369. "Plan of the Battle fought the 28th of April 1760..." by Major Patrick Mackellar, in *Report Concerning Canadian Archives for the year 1905*, vol.I, (Ottawa, 1905) facing p. 4 (hereafter *Battle Plan*).

27. Murray to Pitt, 25 May 1760, in Kimball, *Pitt Correspondence*, 291-97.

28. Letter, Ensign John Désbruyêres to George Townshend, 19 May 1760, in *Townshend Papers*, 426-29. Ensign John Désbruyêres was commissioned from the ranks of the gentlemen volunteers serving with Wolfe's army the year before, 27 July 1759. He fought at

the battle of the Plains of Abraham and on 15 September 1759 was named Secretary in charge of vetting all prisoners' letters and captured enemy documents as a member of Murray's staff. In post-Conquest years he served as the Secretary of the Governor of Trois Rivières, Colonel Ralph Burton, and accompanied Burton when he was transferred to the Governorship of Montreal.

29. *Murray's Journal*, 26; *Knox's Journal*, 290.

30. *Knox's Journal*, 291.

31. *Knox's Journal*, 291.

32. *Knox's Journal*, 291; *Murray's Journal*, 26; Murray's biographer, R.H. Mahon, notes that the parish records of Sainte-Foy show that the British commander sent £25 the following month to assist in the rebuilding of the church destroyed by his orders. Mahon, *Murray*, 227n.

33. *Murray's Journal*, 26; *Knox's Journal*, 291.

34. *Knox's Journal*, 291.

35. *Murray's Journal*, 26.

36. *Lévis' Journal*, 1081.

37. *Lévis' Journal*, 1081.

38. *Lévis' Journal*, 1081.

39. Lieutenant-General le Comte de Maurès de Malartic, *Journal des Campagnes au Canada de 1755 a 1760.*, Paul Gafferel, ed. (Paris, 1890), 315, (hereafter *Malartic's Journal*).

40. *Malartic's Journal*, 315.

41. *Lévis' Journal*, 1082.

42. *Lévis' Journal*, 1082.

43. Writing to Pitt on 25 May 1760, Murray reiterated his intended plans for the defence of Quebec thus: "My plan of defence was, to take the earliest Opportunity of entrenching myself upon the Heights of Abraham, which entirely commanded the ramparts of the place at a distance of eight hundred yards, and might have been defended by our Numbers against a large Army: But the Chevalier de Lévis did not give me time to take the Advantage of this Situation, The 23rd, 24th and 25th I attempted to execute the projected lines, for which a Provision of Fascines and every necessary Material had been made, but found it impracticable, as the Earth was still covered with Snow in many places, and every where impregnably bound up with frost."; Kimball, *Pitt Correspondence*, 292; *Murray's Journal*, 25.

44. Malcolm Fraser, "The Capture of Quebec. A Manuscript Journal Relating to the Opera-

tions Before Quebec From 8th May, 1759, to 17th May, 1760. Kept by Colonel Malcolm Fraser. Then Lieutenant in the 78th Foot (Fraser's Highlanders), *JSAHR*, XVIII (1939) (hereafter, *Fraser's Journal*), 166; *Murray's Journal*, 26.

45. *Knox's Journal*, 292.

46. *Lévis' Journal*, 1082.

47. *Malartic's Journal*, 22.

48. *QM Memoirs*, 120.

49. For a complete account of this Highland regiment see J.R. Harper, *The Fraser Highlanders* and Harper, *A Short History of the Old 78th Regiment or Fraser's Highlanders, 1757-1763*, (Laval, 1966) [hereafter cited as *"Old 78th"*]. James Thompson's Memoirs, MG 23, K2, Microfilm Reel M-2312 (hereafter *Thompson's Memoirs*); *Fraser's Journal*, 164.

50. *Fraser's Journal*, 164.

51. John Prebble, *Culloden*, (Harmondsworth, 1967), 80-1; John Godwin started in a Miner's Company in 1740, and served as the officer in charge of the Royal mortars in Flanders. He served at Culloden in 1746 and came to America as a captain in 1757. He was the Commander Royal Artillery at the commencement of the siege of Gibraltar in 1779 with the rank of Colonel. W.H. Askwith, *List of Officers of the Royal Regiment of Artillery*, (London, 1900), 3a, 197; M.E.S. Laws, *Battery Records of the Royal Artillery*, (Woolwich, 1951).

52. Stephen Brumwell, "Rank & File: A Profile of One of Wolfe's Regiments," *JSAHR*, 79 (2001) 14-15. In another twist of irony, Brumwell points out that the Kingston Light Horse "had recruited amongst the butchers of Nottingham" and thus "echoed their civilian calling by leading the slaughter of the Jacobite wounded" at Culloden.

53. Harper, *The Fighting Frasers*, 3 -10.

54. Prebble, *Culloden*, 99-102.

55. *Fraser's Journal*, 164; *Murray's Journal*, 27.

56. Mackellar, *Battle Plan* Notes.

57. *Murray's Journal*, 26.

58. Murray's Dispatch to Amherst, 30 April 1760, quoted in Mahon, *Murray*, 238.

59. *Murray's Journal*, 27.

60. Ensign John Désbruyêres to Colonel George Townshend, *Townshend Papers*, 426-29.

61. *Knox's Journal*, 294. *Fraser's Journal*, 164.

62. *QM's Memoirs*, 121; Mackellar, *Battle Plan* Notes.

63. Mackellar, *Battle Plan* Notes.

64. While certainly not present on this part of the battlefield, Johnson must have heard the story secondhand from a 58th Foot volunteer who survived the ordeal; *QM Memoirs*, 127. Of the Volunteer Company officers listed in Knox, only Macdonell was listed as killed in the casualty returns. Lieutenant Alexander Grant, 3/60th Foot is listed as wounded while Lieutenant Farqhuar, 47th Foot, Lieutenant Crofton, 48th Foot and Ensign Crank Maw of the 43rd, are not listed as casualties in the battle, an indication that all survived the alleged ambush. Maw, however, was wounded and captured two nights later leading a sortie of 22 men against French working parties in the siege lines. *Knox's Journal*, 289, 298.

65. *Lévis' Journal*, 1084.

66. Not unlike Bourlamaque, Murray had two horses shot from underneath him with no apparent injury as well as "his clothes riddled by the enemy's musketry." James Murray to George Murray, 19 October 1760, quoted in Mahon, *Murray*, 271-2. Colonel Simon Fraser of Lovat commanding the left forward brigade was also mounted for the battle and "was touched at two different times; the first took him in the right breast, the second he got in the retreat, striking against the cue of his hair," noted Malcolm Fraser in his *Journal*, 165.

67. *Lévis' Journal*, 1084.

68. *Knox's Journal*, 293-4.

69. The Dumont Mill site was purchased from the Jesuits in 1741 by Jean-Baptiste Dumont, a Quebec trader. The transaction included a house, a tannery and its fittings, a small adjoining house, a grange, and a stone mill ten metres high. Dumont in turn put the property up for sale in 1779 and by the middle of the following century, all that remained of it were its foundations. In 1855 a monument designed by the famous architect-engineer Charles Baillairgé and dedicated to Levis and Montcalm was erected on the site. It was inaugurated 19 October 1863 by Lord Monck, Governor-General of Canada and consists of a large column surmounted by the Roman goddess of war, Bellona. It stands at the end of the *Avenue des Braves* which follows the final line of the battle. Jacques Mathieu & Eugen Kedl, *The Plains of Abraham: The Search for the Ideal*, (Montreal, 1992), 100.

70. Dumas to Vaudreuil, 12 April 1760. "Letters of Vaudreuil, Lévis and Dumas in 1760," NAC *Sessional Papers No. 18*, (Ottawa, 1906), 26.

71. *Lévis' Journal*, 1084.

72. *QM Memoirs*, 121. At the Battle of Sillery, Sergeant John Johnson was 40 years of age, 5 feet 9 inches in height, of fair complexion, "long visage," grey eyes and brown hair. When recruited by John Montague, Fourth Earl of Sandwich, at Huntingdon on 26 March 1756, Johnson had already served five years in the 36th Foot and another four in the 4th Foot. Discharged on 2 January 1784 at the age of 64, Johnson was recommended and accepted to the Royal Chelsea Hospital as a pensioner. Brumwell, *"Rank & File,"* 14-15.

73. Murray's Journal, 27.

74. Lieutenant Thomas Mill's testimony in "General Court Martial held at Quebec, 1 June 1761," General Court Martial Proceedings, WO71/68, Marching Regiments October 1760 to July 1761, PRO, London (hereafter, *GCMQ*).

75. Private John Maxwell's testimony, *GCMQ*.

76. Lieutenant George Weld's, Lieutenant Ormsby's and Private John Stone's testimonies, *GCMQ*.

77. Lieutenant George Fraser's testimony, *GCMQ*.

78. *Knox's Journal*, 294.

79. *Fraser's Journal*, 164

80. Fraser is mistaken. There were three 6-pdrs but Fraser may have only seen two personally. *Fraser's Journal*, 164; *Murray's Journal*, 27; *Thompson's Memoirs*. Sergeant Thompson's memory is also faulty regarding his company commander, for the Fraser officer he refers to is most certainly Captain Alexander Fraser of Culdathel whom Lieutenant Malcolm Fraser describes as "wounded in the right temple and thought [to be] very dangerous." Gazetted a captain 15 September 1758, Alexander Fraser commanded the 14th company of the 78th that arrived before Quebec on 4 September 1759. There were a total of 26 Fraser officers serving during Sergeant James Thompson's service with the regiment so he can be excused the rank mistake, but perhaps not for standing on his Captain when he was still alive! There were three Lieutenant Frasers (all named Alexander) wounded at the battle though none in

the temple and all three recovered. *"Old 78th,"* 86-89. *"List of British Officers Killed, Wounded and Prisoners at Quebec, From April 27 to May 21, 1760"* in John Knox, *An Historical Journal of the Campaigns in North America*. 1769. A.G. Doughty, ed. Vol. III (Toronto, 1914-1916), 135-42.

81. *Knox's Journal*, 294.

82. *Johnstone's Memoirs,* 11.

83. *Johnstone's Memoirs*, 11-12.

84. *Johnstone's Memoirs*, 12. Malartic tells the same story noting that Dalquier said for all to hear: "Major, I'm taking sole responsibility to contravene the General's order. Let us profit from out soldiers' fighting spirit. Let us not fire, but instead fall on our enemy with our bayonets and we shall vanquish them." *Malartic's Journal*, 317.

85. *QM Memoirs*, 121.

86. Mackellar *Battle Plan* Notes; *Knox's Journal*, 317.

87. *Malartic's Journal*, 319. Lieutenant Malcolm Fraser recorded: "It appears they allowed the savages to scalp all the killed and most part of the wounded." Days later, when the siege was lifted, British soldiers traversing the 28 April battlefield "found a great many scalps on the bushes." *Fraser's Journal*, 168.

88. Thomas Mante, *The History of the Late War in America*, (London, 1772), 281. The steadiness of the 58th Foot is not surprising as its commander, though not present at the battle of Sillery, was none other than Lieutenant Colonel William Howe and the unit had drawn the admiration of James Wolfe the year before as "the best trained battalion in all America." R. Wright, *The Life of Major-General James Wolfe*, (London: 1864), 468.

89. James Murray to brother George Murray, quoted in Mahon, *Murray*, 272.

90. *Invalid Memoirs*.

91. *Fraser's Journal*, 164-5; *Thompson's Memoirs*.

92. *Fraser's Journal*, 164-5.

93. *Malartic's Journal*, 318.

94. Quoted in Casgrain, *Wolfe and Montcalm*, 265-6.

95. *Knox's Journal*, 294-5.

96. *Knox's Journal*, 295; *"List of British Officers Killed, Wounded and Prisoners at Quebec, From April 27 to May 21, 1760"* in John Knox, *An Historical Journal of the Campaigns in North America*. 1769. A.G. Doughty, ed., Vol. III,

(Toronto, 1914-1916), 135-42.

97. Quoted in Mahon, *Murray*, 236.

98. Pierre Pouchot, *Memoirs on the Late War in North America between France and England*, B.L. Dunnigan, ed. (Youngstown, 1994), 255.

99. *Malartic's Journal*, 318-19.

100. *Knox's Journal*, 296-8.

101. *Knox's Journal*, 301.

102. *Lévis' Journal*, 1087.

103. Désbruyêres to Colonel George Townshend, 19 May 1760, *Northcliffe Collection*, 428.

104. *Knox's Journal*, 309-10.

105. A weak fleet of French transports with troops, guns and ammunition had also been dispatched on 15 April 1760 from France under the protection of the frigate *Machault* which arrived in the Saint Lawrence on 15 May 1760. When the French naval commander, François Chenard Giraudais, learned that Commodore Robert Swanton's squadron had preceded him up the River, he directed his fleet to the Bay of Chaleur on the other side of the Gaspe peninsula to hide. The small convoy took refuge in the mouth of the Restigouche River where it was discovered and destroyed by Commodore Byron's squadron in July 1760. For a more complete account of this naval action see George F. Stanley, *New France: The Last Phase, 1744-1760* (Toronto, 1968), 259-62.

106. *Lévis' Journal*, 1087.

107. *Lévis' Journal*, 1088.

108. William H. Wood, ed., *The Logs of the Conquest of Canada* (Toronto,1909), 331, (hereafter *Logs*).

109. *Logs*, 331.

110. *Logs*, 324.

111. *Johnstone's Memoirs*, 15-16. Jean Vauquelin (1728-1772) born at Dieppe, France, son of Jean Charles Vauquelin, captain of a merchant vessel. He first entered the merchant marine as a boy and by age 22 was commanding his own ship. At the outbreak of the Seven Years' War in 1755, Vauquelin was given command of the frigate *Aréthuse* which was the only ship to escape the British blockade at Louisbourg in 1758. In 1759, he was appointed commander-in-chief of the French flotilla in the St Lawrence until his defeat in May 1760. He was cleared of negligence on his return to France and continued to serve in the French Navy with increasing rank and responsibilities, serving overseas in the Indian Ocean and dying in 1772 of ill health. *DCB*, II, 751-2.

112. Mackellar, *Battle Plan* Notes.

113. *QM Memoirs*, 123.

114. Horace Walpole, quoted in Parkman, *Montcalm & Wolfe*, II, 371-72; Walpole to Sir Horace Mann, 28 June 1760, quoted in Mahon, *Murray*, 269.

115. Anonymous, *Annual Register*, 1760, quoted in Mahon, 237.

116. Mackellar, *Battle Plan* Notes.

117. James Murray to George Murray, 19 October 1760, quoted in Mahon, 271-2.

118. François Bernier to Vaudreuil, September 1759, quoted in Casgrain, *Wolfe and Montcalm*, 254-55. Murray would face one more siege in his lifetime as the Governor of the small island of Minorca off the east coast of Spain in 1782. Severely outnumbered, with a garrison smaller than the one he commanded at Quebec, he surrendered after a spirited resistance reminiscent of his 1760 siege. However, he is best known in Canadian history for his six tempestuous years as Quebec's first peacetime British Governor, making his greatest impact as one of the first champions of French-Canadian rights. No matter what his failings as a military commander might have been, he was a generous, compassionate man of principle who was ultimately recalled from Canada never to return again, a victim of New England and British interest groups who engineered a series of false charges to be levelled against him. A fighter to the end, Murray left his true legacy to Canadian history with these parting words:

"I glory in having been accused of warmth and firmness in protecting the King's Canadian subjects and of doing the utmost in my Power to gain to my Royal Master the affection of that brave hardy People; whose Emigration, if it shall ever happen, will be an irreparable Loss to this Empire, to prevent which I declare I would cheerfully submit to greater Calumnies & Indignities if greater can be devised, than hitherto I have undergone."

2. Cut Knife Hill
Author's Note and Acknowledgements
This work is rooted in my studies with Profes-

sor Jean Friesen at the University of Manitoba in 1981. She taught me that there was a distinct Indian and Métis experience and to look for it in non-traditional evidence. Since that time my understanding of the North West Rebellion has benefitted from the knowledge and advice of countless other people. Of particular importance were the late John Foster and Gerhard Ens (University of Alberta); John Milloy (Trent); Bill Waiser (University of Saskatchewan); the late Barry Hunt and Don Schurman, Ron Haycock, Jane Errington, Benoit Cameron and Ross Mackenzie (Royal Military College); Steve Harris, Mike Whitby, Warren Sinclair and Madelaine Lafleur-Lemire (Directorate of History and Heritage); present and former staff of Parks Canada in Ottawa and Winnipeg, Walter Hildebrandt, and Glen Ebert and staff at the Fort Battleford site; and the staff at the National Archives and National Library in Ottawa and the Saskatchewan Archives Board, Tim Novak (Regina) and Nadine Charabin (Saskatoon); Plains Cree descendents, elders and local historians of the Poundmaker Reserve, including Vera Kasakeo and the Tootoosis family and especially Jim Senior, who had been adopted by Blue Horn, who himself had been adopted by Poundmaker; and other supporters including Patrick Niesink, who provided computer support; Sandy Lynch, who provided critical artistic assistance; and the eclectic staff of O'Brien's Eatery and Pub, Ottawa.

Two people, Sharon Babaian of the Canada Science and Technology Museum in Ottawa, and Professor Jack English, late of the United States Naval War College in Newport, R.I., have supported me throughout. So did Flashy. To them I owe the greatest debt.

1. Douglas W. Light, *Footprints in the Dust*, (North Battleford, 1987), 315-316.

2. *Toronto Mail*, 24 Aug 1885.

3. Peter Erasmus, *Buffalo Days and Nights*, (Calgary, 1976), 244-245.

4. Alexander Morris, *The Treaties of Canada with the Indians of Manitoba and the North-West Territories ...* (Toronto, 1971), 184-186.

5. Light, *Footprints*, 316; and Norma Sluman, *Poundmaker*, (Toronto, 1967), 19-88.

6. Sluman, *Poundmaker*, 145-159; Light, *Footprints*, 316.

7. Gerald Friesen, *The Canadian Prairies – A History*, (Toronto, 1984), 150.

8. Friesen, *Canadian Prairies*, 162-194.

9. John L. Tobias, "Canada's Subjugation of the Plains Cree, 1979 – 1885," *Canadian Historical Review*, LXIV, 4, (1983), 520.

10. Tobias, "Canada's Subjugation of the Plains Cree," 525, 531; Hugh A. Dempsey, *Big Bear: The End of Freedom*, (Vancouver, 1984), 120-149.

11. W.B. Cameron, *Blood Red the Sun*, (Edmonton, 1977), 35. This work was first published in 1926.

12. Light, *Footprints*, 72.

13. Light, *Footprints*, 80. Light cites the *Saskatchewan Herald*, 18 Aug 1883.

14. Light, *Footprints*, 75.

15. Dempsey, *Big Bear*, 146-149; Tobias, "Canada's Subjugation of the Plains Cree," 532-533.

16. Sluman, *Poundmaker*. Sluman concentrates the first two parts of her book on the Poundmaker-Crowfoot relationship.

17. Light, *Footprints*, 75, quoting the *Saskatchewan Herald*, 18 Aug 1883.

18. Light, *Footprints*, 76.

19. Light, *Footprints*, 76-80.

20. Light, *Footprints*, 81.

21. *Saskatchewan Herald*, 26 Jan 1884.

22. Friesen, *Canadian Prairies*, 149-152; Dempsey, *Big Bear*, 135.

23. *Saskatchewan Herald*, 4 May 1884.

24. Light, *Footprints*, 88, 323-324.

25. Friesen, *Canadian Prairies*, 151; Dempsey, *Big Bear*, 126-134. See also *The Cree Rebellion of '84*, Battleford Historical Society Publication, Vol. I, No. I, 1926, for a compilation of accounts. Friesen described the great Indian rendezvous in June 1884 as "probably the greatest assembly of plains chiefs in [Canadian] history,", see Friesen, 151.

26. Dempsey, *Big Bear*; Friesen, *Canadian Prairies*, 151; John Peter Turner, *The North-West Mounted Police 1873-1893*, Vol II, (Ottawa, 1950), 59-67.

27. G.F.G. Stanley, *Louis Riel*, (Toronto, 1963), 270-272. Riel arrived in the Saskatchewan country on Dominion Day, 1 July 1884.

28. Light, *Footprints*, 81-82.

29. Bob Beal and Rod MacLeod, *Prairie Fire*, (Edmonton, 1985), 111-113; 122-127.

30. Walter Hildebrandt, *The Battle of Batoche*, (Ottawa, 1985), 89.

31. Desmond Morton, *The Last War Drum:*

The North West Campaign of 1885, (Toronto, 1885), 3-5; Charles Pelham Mulvaney, *The History of the North-West Rebellion of 1885*, (Toronto, 1885), 29-45.

32. Friesen, *Canadian Prairies*, 154; Morton, *Last War Drum*, 28-41; Light, *Footsteps*, 165-279.

33. Tobias, "Canada's Subjugation of the Plains Cree," 542.

34. Light, *Footsteps*. This book represents a life time of work on the part of Douglas W. Light, who was raised and lived in the Battleford area.

35. Bill Waiser and Blair Stonechild, *Loyal Till Death: Indians In The North-West Rebellion*, (Canada, 1997), Chapters 5 to 7.

36. Waiser and Stonechild, *Loyal Till Death*, 96-104.

37. Waiser and Stonechild, *Loyal Till Death*, 99.

38. Waiser and Stonechild, *Loyal Till Death*, 105.

39. Waiser and Stonechild, *Loyal Till Death*, 103.

40. Light, *Footprints*, 356.

41. Friesen, *Canadian Prairies*, 152-153. On page 153 of this work Friesen explores the effect of Frog Lake on North-West Rebellion history: "The terror among white settlers and the coincidence of the Métis skirmish at Duck Lake, with the Cree action at Frog lake have combined to influence historical interpretations ... The political goals of Dewdney, the panic of white settlers, and the assumptions of historians have created a concerted Indian-Métis war where, in fact, sporadic raids for food and violent acts by a few young Indian rebels happened to coincide with the Métis uprising." See also Dempsey, *Big Bear*, 153-162; and a compilation of views in Stuart Hughes, *The Frog Lake "Massacre": Personal Perspectives on Ethnic Conflict*, (Ottawa, 1976).

42. Morton, *Last War Drum*, 31-33.

43. DHH, 500.009 (D32), Sir John A. Macdonald to General F.D. Middleton, 29 Mar 1885, in "Extracts from Correspondence of Sir John A. Macdonald bearing on the North West Rebellion of 1885."

44. William D. Otter, *The Guide – A Military Manual of Interior Economy, Discipline, etc.* (Toronto, 1880).

45. T.C. Willett, *Canada's Militia: A Heritage at Risk*, (Canada, 1990), 56-60; Morton, *Last War Drum*, 30-31.

46. Richard Scougall Cassels, "The Diary of Lieutenant R.S. Cassels," in R.C. Macleod, (ed), *Reminiscences of a Bungle by One of the Bunglers*, (Edmonton, 1983), (hereafter Cassels), 132.

47. Charles Ross had been a scout with the United States Army before joining the NWMP in Aug 1884 at age 27. See Neil G. Speed, *Born To Fight: Major Charles Joesph Ross DSO*, (Melbourne, 2002), 8-10.

48. Superintendent W.M. Herchmer to Lieutenant Colonel A.G. Irvine, Commissioner of the NWMP, 27 Jul 1885, contained in Appendix B to "Report of the Commissioner of the [NWMP] 1885," Ottawa, 1886, in *Settlers and Rebels Being The Official Reports To Parliament of the Activities of the Royal [NWMP] from 1882-1885 by the Commissioners of the RNWMP*, reprint, (Ottawa, 1973) (hereafter Herchmer Report) 50-51.

49. Four 7-pdr. guns, all in the service of the NWMP, saw action during the 1885 campaign: one was at Prince Albert and was deployed at Duck Lake; one remained at Regina; and two were moved from Calgary to Regina in March 1885. These two pieces were retained by Superintendent Herchmer throughout all his operations that year. For further information, see H.M. Gilbey, "Seven-Pounders of the Force," *The RCMP Quarterly*, Vol 37, No 3, (July 1972), 7. The author is indebted to Glen Eberts of Fort Battleford National Historic Sites for providing this information.

50. Herchmer Report, 51.

51. Waiser and Stonechild, *Loyal Till Death*, 129; Hugh A. Dempsey, *Crowfoot, Chief of the Blackfeet* (Norman, 1972), 168-172.

52. Thomas B. Strange, *Gunner Jingo's Jubilee*, (London, 1893), 406.

53. For a compilation of *Saskatchewan Herald* articles on the Battleford experience, see William L. Clink, *Battleford Beleaguered: 1885*, (Willowdale, 1984).

54. Herchmer Report, 51.

55. Desmond Morton, *The Canadian General Sir William Otter*, (Toronto, 1974), 92.

56. Light, *Footprints*, 586.

57. Cassels, 133.

58. Cassels, 133; R.H. Roy, "The Diary of Rifleman Forin," *Saskatchewan History*, Vol XXI

(1968), No. 3, Autumn, 102. Forin had previous service in the rural Ontario militia unit of the 49th battalion (Hastings Rifles), where he had attended the week-long summer militia camp in eastern Ontario in 1880 (hereafter Forin).

59. Light, *Footprints*, 586.

60. Cassels, 133.

61. J. Elton Prower, "With Otter's Column in the North-West, *United Service Magazine*, V, (Apr 1895), XI, New Series, (hereafter Prower), 495.

62. Light, *Footprints*, 73.

63. Colonel Oscar C. Pelletier, *Mémoires Souvenirs de Famille Recits*, (Quebec, 1940) (hereafter Pelletier), 225-226. This important book was published only in French. The translation for this work was done by a competent Carleton University student.

64. Cassels, 136-137.

65. Pelletier, 226-227.

66. Prower, 496.

67. Cassels, 138-139.

68. Prower, 496.

69. George T. Denison, *Soldiering in Canada: Recollections and Experiences*, (Toronto,1900), 315.

70. *The Riel Rebellion 1885*, (Montreal, n.d., c. 1885), 20. This was a special edition produced without reference to the parent paper, which was probably either the *Daily Witness* or the *Daily Star*.

71. The *Montreal Daily Star* reporter W.A. Harkin telegraphed his newspaper, from Battleford, that, on Sunday 26 Apr 1885, Otter's scouts had found Poundmaker's main camp, and that "every day the long delayed order from Middleton to advance on Poundmaker, who is reported to be wantonly slaughtering the stolen cattle, is expected to arrive." "How Poundmaker's camp was Discovered," *Montreal Daily Star*, 16 May 1885.

72. Herchmer Report, 51.

73. Pelletier, 8.

74. NAC, MG 30 G 14, Otter Papers, Correspondence, Vol I, File # III, Jan 1885 – Dec 1890 (hereafter, NAC Otter Papers).

75. Desmond Morton and Reginald H. Roy, *Telegrams of the North-West Campaign 1885*, (Toronto, 1972), 210. Morton also summarized the factors that had suddenly turned against Middleton, demonstrating how quickly late

19th century war could change, which in turn changed attitudes and plans. Morton, *Canadian General*, 112.

76. NAC, Otter Papers, Middleton to Otter, 26 Apr 85, Otter to Middleton, 26 Apr 85.

77. NAC, Otter Papers, Middleton to Otter, 26 Apr 85,

78. NAC, MG 27 I, C4, Vol 5, Dewdney Papers, Otter to Dewdney, 26 Apr 1885.

79. NAC, Dewdney Papers, Dewdney to Otter, 26 Apr 1885.

80. Morton, *The Canadian General*, 13.

81. NAC, Otter Papers, Otter to Middleton, 29 Apr 1885; Middleton to Otter, 1 May 1885; Otter to Middleton, 1 May 1885, Middleton to Otter, (date uncertain).

82. Cassels, 149.

83. Prower, 499.

84. The principle source for this table and the strength figures was Light, *Footprints*, 586. Light reproduced diagrams for the order of march on pages 363-366 of his work. Other sources used to calculate these figures will be found in Appendix B.

85. Otter's Despatch to Middleton, 5 May 1885, copy in DHH 500.0009 (D32), DHH, NDHQ, Ottawa, (hereafter Otter Despatch), 1.

86. Prower, 499,

87. Prower, 499.

88. W.W. Fox, *Toronto Dail Mail*, 19 May 1885.

89. Cassels, 150. Neither the Otter Despatch nor the Herchmer Report mention the signal fires and thus the apparent loss of surprise.

90. Prower, 499.

91. Cassels, 150.

92. Prower, 499.

93. Prower, 499.

94. Cassels, 151.

95. Cassels, 151.

96. Cassels, 151.

97. D.S.C. Mackay, ed., "The North-West Rebellion, 1885. A Memoir by Colour Sergeant (later Major-General) C.F. Winters," *Saskatchewan History*, vol 35, no 1 (Winter, 1982) (hereafter Winter), 9.

98. Waiser and Stonechild, *Loyal Till Death*, 140-141.

99. The Dominion of Canada's Surveyor-General map of 1919 describes the ground as "rolling country with poplar and willow scrub."

Saskatchewan Archives Board (SAB), Saskatoon, A113, IV, a, 8, Surveyor General Map, 20 May 1919.

100. Denison, *Soldiering in Canada*, 284.

101. Prower, 499.

102. "An Indian had a Treaty medal in his war bonnet band and this was struck." Author's interview with Mr. Jim Tootoosis (Junior), 9 Jan 2003, Poundmaker Reserve, Saskatchewan.

103. Ernest J. Chambers, *The Queen's Own Rifles of Canada*, (Toronto, 1901), 101.

104. William A. Oppen, *The Riel Rebellions: A Cartographic History/Le récit cartographique des affaires Riel* (Toronto, 1979), 52-53.

105. Cassels, 151.

106. Chambers, 101.

107. Cassels, 152.

108. Prower, 500.

109. Herchmer Report, 52.

110. Only one horse was hit during the action.

111. Cassels, 152.

112. Prower, 500.

113. Winter, 9.

114. Light, *Footprints*, 356, 358, 367.

115. Author's interview with Mr. Jim Tootoosis (Senior), 9 Jan 2003, Poundmaker Reserve, Saskatchewan.

116. SAB Saskatoon, A113, II, b, 4, Cutknife Hill, Coming Day's Speech, 26 Jul 1935.

117. SAB Saskatoon, A113, II, b, 4, Cutknife Hill, Speech of Basil Favel (Junior), 26 Jul 1935.

118. A field dressing stations is the first level of medical care on a battlefield, where wounded soldiers are taken, cared for and protected from enemy fire.

119. Pelletier, 233-234.

120. From the term *paniers de pensement* used in French military ambulances.

121. Pelletier, 234-235.

122. Pelletier, 235-236.

123. R.W. Rutherford Diary, 25 Mar–31 Dec 1885, SAB, University of Regina, mfm R-E133, (hereafter Rutherford Diary), 14-15.

124. Prower, 500.

125. Although the Indians knew of the potential effect of the breech-loading rifle in a battle, when they began to settle on reserves in the late 1870s and mid-1880s, many sold these weapons for more practical weapons like smoothbore shotguns – breech and muzzle-loading – because those weapons were best suited to hunting migratory and upland birds, as well as small game, deer-sized animals at short ranges and trapline work. In the Indian world, guns were tools designed to meet specific needs, and there were no military demands in the early 1880s. See Light, *Footprints*, 420.

126. Rutherford Diary, 15.

127. Cassels, 153.

128. Cassels, 152-153.

129. Cassels, 153.

130. Prower, 501. Although there were many suggestions of a trap or an ambush, this was the *only* evidence from anyone in the column that there were prepared rifle pits. There is a reference to a missing historical photograph at the SAB Saskatoon captioned "Cutknife Hill – Rifle Pits," and as we will see, Father Louis Cochin, a captive priest, also claimed that there were "excavations."

131. Prower, 501.

132. Cassels, 153.

133. Cassels, 154.

134. Rutherford Diary, 15-16.

135. Rutherford Diary, 16.

136. Prower, 502.

137. Prower, 502.

138. Forin, 103.

139. NAC, Otter Papers, McKell Account, 18.

140. SAB Saskatoon, A113, II, b, 4, Cut Knife Hill, Sapostokun's Speech, 26 Jul 1935.

141. Prower, 502-503; Winter, 10; Cassels, 154-155.

142. Otter Despatch, 2.

143. Winter, 11.

144. Prower, 503.

145. Prower, 503-504.

146. Cassels, 155.

147. *Montreal Daily Star*, 7 May 1885, 1.

148. W.W. Fox, *Toronto Daily Mail*, 7 May 1885, 1.

149. G.H. Needler, *Louis Riel – The Rebellion of 1885*, (Toronto, 1957), 44.

150. Howard A. Kennedy, *The North-West Rebellion*, (Toronto, 1935), 26.

151. Otter Despatch, 2.

152. Cassels, 156.

153. C.P. Mulvaney, *The History of the North-West Rebellion of 1885*, (Toronto, 1885), 171.

154. Light, *Footprints*, 608.

155. Jefferson had been a school teacher on the Red Pheasant reserve, but in April 1884 there

was change in white staff on the reserves, and Jefferson went to Poundmaker's reserve as a Farm Instructor. This was commensurate with the government policy that only married men would be employed as Instructors, in order that their wives could teach indian women in "household management". Light, 85. Jefferson was an englishman who, while on the Red Pheasant reserve, had married Phoebe Little, the daughter of Shooting Eagle, of Poundmaker's band. As Poundmaker and Fine Day, a war leader, had also married daughters of Shooting Eagle, Jefferson was a brother-in-law to these two powerful Cree leaders. *Footprints*, 90.

156. Robert Jefferson, *Fifty Years on the Saskatchewan*, (Battleford, 1929) (hereafter Jefferson), pp. 140-141.

157. Jefferson, 141.

158. Jefferson, 146.

159. Jefferson, 141-2.

160. Jefferson, 142. Rutherford's note number 10 on his sketch on p. 120 confirmed that the "fire was most destructive" from that location.

161. Jefferson, 142.

162. Jefferson, 143.

163. Jefferson, 143.

164. Jefferson, 143.

165. Louis Cochin, OMI, *The Reminiscences of Louis Cochin, OMI, A Veteran Missionary of the Cree Indians and A Prisoner in Poundmaker's Camp in 1885*, (Canadian North West Society Battleford Publication, 1926) (hereafter Cochin), 32.

166. Cochin, pp. 32-33.

167. Cochin, pp. 32-33.

168. Cochin, 34. Lt. Prower had mentioned "rifle pits" in his account.

169. Cochin, 34-35. The soldier left on the battlefield had been Private William B. Osgoode, 43rd Battalion, attached to the Sharpshooter Company of the Governor General's Foot Guards. This information was provided to the author by Dr. Kenneth Reynolds, regimental historian of the Cameron Highlanders of Ottawa, 14 July 2003.

170. Otter's Despatch, 1.

171. Herchmer Report, 1885, 52.

172. W.W. Fox, *Toronto Daily Mail*, 7 May 1885.

173. *The Montreal Daily Star*, 7 May 1885, 1.

174. Howard Angus Kennedy, *The North-West*

Rebellion, 24. He misread "finish", because the original was "punish".

175. The four versions of the plaque that have replaced each other over the past seventy-five years are a separate story, and the evidence remains available from Parks Canada records in Ottawa.

176. Howard Angus Kennedy, *The North-West Rebellion*. Historian Douglas Light researched Kennedy's life. He was born in England on 27 December 1861. He emmigrated to Canada in 1881, and worked for the *Daily Witness* until 1890. He lived in the west, and wrote extensively about it all his life. Light, *Footprints in the Dust*, (North Battleford, 1987), 587.

177. Howard Angus Kennedy, "Memories of '85", *Canadian Geographical Journal*, Vol LXX, No 5, May 1965, 154. This was a reprint of the original article in the *Journal* in Aug 1935.

178. Needler, *Louis Riel The Rebellion of 1885*, 43-4.

179. Lieutenant-Colonel Grasett to George F. Hagarty, 7 June 1885, "Misc 1885", 3. Provided to the author by Walter Hildebrandt from his NW Rebellion file. Parks Canada office, Winnipeg, Aug 1985.

180. General Sir Fred. Middleton, "Suppression of Rebellion in the North-West territories of Canada, 1885", *United Service Magazine*, Jan 1894, 380-1.

181. Author's interview with Allan McCullough, retired Parks Canada official, Ottawa, 17 Dec 2002.

182. The author agrees with this argument, because if we remove the battle from the events of the Rebellion, the outcome probably would still have been the same.

183. Waiser and Stonechild, *Loyal Till Death*, 144. Because "native studies" as a branch of historical scholarship only bloomed in the late twentieth century, historians were stuck with no satisfactory explanation of the native experience in the north-west rebellion until recently.

184. NAC, RG 10, Vol 3584, File 1130, Pt. 1A, H. Reed to E. Dewdney, 5 May 1885.

185. Beal and Macleod, *Prairie Fire*, 306, 315; Dempsey, *Big Bear*, 195.

3. Paardeberg

1. "Goodbye Dolly Gray," by Will D. Cobb was sold as sheet music in at least two separate

versions featuring illustrations of American soldiers during the Spanish-American War. With the outbreak of the South African War, a version with images of men in khaki-drill and stetsons appeared for the British and Canadian markets. Cobb was a prolific composer whose works included "School Days" as well as a number of patriotic songs in the First World War.

2. Sir George Pomeroy Colley (1835-1881) was born in Dublin, educated at Sandhurst and was commissioned in the 2nd Foot in 1852. He served in South Africa, leading the expedition which killed the Xhosa chief Tola in 1858, China in 1860, the Ashanti campaign 1873-1874 under Wolseley, India 1876-c.1879, South Africa again as chief of staff to Chelmsford in the 1879 Zulu War and was promoted major general in 1880. In April 1880 he became governor of Natal and High Commissioner of SE Africa. When the Boers invaded Natal, Colley took command of the British forces in the colony. Ian Uys, *South African Miltary Who's Who, 1452-1992*, (Germiston, 1992), 47-48.

3. Unless noted otherwise, much of this section on the battle of Majuba Hill is based on Byron Farwell's short epistle on the First Anglo-Boer War. Byron Farwell, *Queen Victoria's Little Wars*, (New York, 1972), 243-251.

4. James Birch and Henry Northop, *History of the War in South Africa*, (London, 1900), 179.

5. The figures in the *Times History* are 92 killed and 134 wounded for the British and one killed and one died of wounds for the Boers, while Birch and Northop put the figures as 90 killed, 133 wounded and 58 taken prisoner. Leo Amery, (ed) *The Times History of the War in South Africa*, Vol I, (London, 1900), 66; Birch and Northop, *History of the War in South Africa*, 192.

6. According to Donald E. Graves, eleven Hunters were hanged, while the others were either released for lack of evidence or sentenced to be transported to a penal colony for life. Donald Graves, *Guns Across the River: The Battle of the Windmill, 1838*, (Toronto, 2001), 180.

7. Castell Hopkins and Murat Halstead, *South Africa and The Boer-British War, Comprising a History of South Africa and Its People, Including the War of 1899 and 1900*, Volume I, (Toronto, 1900), 170-171.

8. Stephen Harris, *Canadian Brass: The Making of a Professional Army, 1860-1939*, (Toronto, 1988), 12.

9. George Stanley, *Canada's Soldiers: The Military History of an Unmilitary People*, (Revised edition), (Toronto, 1960), 209.

10. Stanley, *Canada's Soldiers*, 210-210.

11. Brian Reid, *Our Little Army in the Field: The Canadians in South Africa, 1899-1902* (St. Catharines, 1996), 24.

12. Reid, *Our Little Army*, 24.

13. Leo Amery, (ed.), *The Times History of the War in South Africa*, Vol. III, (London, 1905), 369-370.

14. William Hart-McHarg, *From Quebec to Pretoria With the Royal Canadian Regiment*, (Toronto, 1902), 90-91.

15. Private Chester McLaren of B Company put the time the battalion left Belmont as sundown, which would have been a few minutes before seven p.m., while Corporal (later Sergeant) William Hart-McHarg of A Company wrote "that evening we went up to Graspan by train." McLaren letter quoted in Birch and Northop, *War in South Africa*, 530; Hart-McHarg, *From Quebec to Pretoria*, 90.

16. Hart-McHarg, *From Quebec to Pretoria*, 95.

17. Amery, *Times History*, Vol. III, 390-391.

18. My copy of Hart-McHarg's book was owned by Lieutenant Reginald Temple, one of the battalion officers, who wrote in the margin beside the passage on this event, "I was in charge of our men." Hart-McHarg, *From Quebec to Pretoria*, 95-96.

19. Birch and Northop, *War in South Africa*, 531.

20. Birch and Northop, *War in South Africa*, 531.

21. Hart-McHarg put the number of wagons at 180, while De Wet claimed 200 wagons, and Otter reported the number lost as "some 200 supply wagons." Hart-McHarg, *From Quebec to Pretoria*, 97; Christiaan De Wet, *Three Years War*, (English edition), (London, 1902), 47-48; William Otter, "Report A" in *Supplementary Report: Organization, Equipment, Despatch and Service of the Canadian Contingents in South Africa, 1899-1900*. Sessional Paper No. 35a, (Ottawa, 1901), 15.

22. Hart-McHarg, *From Quebec to Pretoria*, 97; C. Grennhill-Gardyne, *The Life of a Regiment: The History of the Gordon Highlanders, Vol. 3*,

From 1898 to 1914, (London, 1922), 124-125.

23. Amery, *Times History*, Vol III, 401-402.

24. Birch and Northop, *War in South Africa*, 531.

25. Russell Hubly, *G Company, or Every-day Life of the R.C.R.*, (Montreal, 1902), 65.

26. Kingsley Brown, Sr., Kingsley Brown, Jr., and Brereton Greenhous, *Semper Paratus: The History of the Royal Hamilton Light Infantry (Wentworth Regiment) 1862-1977*, (Hamilton, 1977), 112.

27. Amery, *Times History*, Vol. III, 421-422.

28. Horace Smith-Dorrien, *Memories of Forty-Eight Years Service*, (London, 1925), 150-152.

29. Gaston Labat, *Le Livre d'Or (The Golden Book) of the Canadian Contingents in South Africa*, (Montreal, 1901), 148.

30. Quoted in George W. Beal, *Family of Volunteers: An Illustrated History of the 48th Highlanders of Canada* (Toronto, 2001), 37.

31. Quoted in Beal, *Family of Volunteers*, 40.

32. Smith-Dorrien, *Memories of Forty-Eight Years Service*, 155.

33. Hart-McHarg, *From Quebec to Pretoria*, 121-122.

34. Smith-Dorrien, *Memories of Forty-Eight Years Service*, 159.

35. Hart-McHarg, *From Quebec to Pretoria*, 130.

36. Reid, *Our Little Army*, 65-66.

37. Smith-Dorrien, *Memories*, 60-61.

38. Reid, *Our Little Army*, 66.

39. Reid, *Our Little Army*, 67-68.

40. Amery, *Times History*, Vol. III, 484; Hart-McHarg, *From Quebec to Pretoria*, 131.

41. William Harding, *War in South Africa and the Dark Continent from Savagery to Civilization*, (Chicago, 1902), 466, 468-469.

4. Iwuy

1. "Here we are! Here we are again!" composed in 1914 by Charles Knight and Kenneth Lyle, remained a popular tune with Canadian troops throughout the war.

2. In 1914 each Canadian division had contained an independent cavalry squadron and a cyclist company, both of similar organization and size. The cyclists in the pre-war period had specialized in intelligence matters, the location and identity of enemy units, the prepara-tion of operational maps and the carriage of despatches. In 1916 they were reorganized as a battalion and made corps troops, in exactly the same way as the divisional cavalry squadrons were formed into a regiment, also as corps troops.

3. Raymond Brutinel (1882-1964) was in many ways the father of Canadian armour and indeed a pioneer in the development of armour internationally. His largely unknown story will be the subject of a forthcoming biography by Dr. Yves Tremblay of Ottawa.

4. Today there is a surviving example of the Autocar left, at the Canadian War Museum in Ottawa.

5. *Official History of the War – Military Operations France & Belgium, 1918*, Vol V, Appendix V, p. 630 (HM Stationery Office, London, 1947).

6. *History of the Canadian Machine Gun Corps, Vol I Organization 1914-1918*, p. 188. Unpublished manuscript held by DHH.

7. Public Archives of Manitoba, (PAM) MG 7 H 11 Box 1A, Diary # 10, Hambley Diary (hereafter Hambley Diary).

8. Lieutenant Colonel Harry Frederick Victor Meurling, DSO, MC (1875-1954). Meurling's postwar career was not so successful. A drinking problem and mental instability kept him from using his obvious talents profitably, and although his many famous connections, such as Brutinel and General Sir Arthur Currie, tried to assist, he slowly sank into decline.

9. *Saga of the Cyclists in the Great War 1914 1918.* (Canadian Corps Cyclist Battalion Association, Toronto, 1965) pp. 75, 76.

10. *Histories of Two Hundred and Fifty-One Divisions of the German Army which participated in the War (1914-1918)* (US War Office, 1920).

11. Lieutenant Richard Henry Hocken (1892-1918) was the son of a Member of Parliament and cabinet minister. He is buried in Drummond Cemetery, Raillencourt Nord, France.

12. George Henry Hambley (1896-1983) survived the war to become a United Church minister. His extensive diaries are held by the Manitoba Archives.

13. Hambley Diary.

14. Ibottson Leonard (1882-1974) left the CLH just a few weeks before the Armistice to return to his family business in London, Ontario, which, it seems, had fallen into difficulties in

his absence.

15. Corporal H.G. Marlow and Sergeant Major George Taylor Aitkin, MM, both lie in Drummond Cemetery, Raillencourt Nord, France.

16. Hambley Diary.

17. DSO Citation for Lieutenant William James White, MC and Bar, *London Gazette*, 10 April 1919.

18. H.R.N. Clyne, *Vancouver's 29th: A Chronicle of the 29th in Flanders Fields*, (Vancouver, 1964), 77.

19. Lieutenant W.L. Algie, VC (1891-1918) is buried at Niagara Cemetery, Iwuy Nord, France.

20. John Swettenham, ed., *Valiant Men* (Toronto, 1973), 159.

21. Quoted in Daniel Dancocks, *Spearhead to Victory: Canada and the Great War*, (Edmonton, 1989), 178.

22. DHH 74/633, George Stirrett, "A Soldier's Story, 1914–1918."

23. Information on the A7V from Maxwell Hundleby and Rainer Strasheim, *The German A7V Tank and the Captured British Mark IV Tanks of World War I*, (Somerset, 1990).

24. *Histories of Two Hundred and Fifty-One Divisions of the German Army.*

25. Lieutenant V. Crombie, MC, is buried at Etaples Military Cemetery, Pas de Calais, France

26. A single example of an A7V survives in Australia. Hull number 506, named *Mephisto*, is today on display in the Queensland Museum, Brisbane.

5. Melfa

1. The "D-Day Dodgers," sung to the ever-popular tune of "Lili Marlene," was "the song" of the Commonwealth troops in the Italian theatre in 1944-1945. It had many verses, including one that harpooned the left-wing British MP, Nancy Astor, who, it is claimed, invented the phrase, "D-Day Dodgers":

> *Dear Lady Astor*
> *You think you know a lot*
> *Standing on a platform*
> *And talking Tommy rot*
> *You're England's Sweetheart and her pride*
> *But we think your mouth's just too bloody wide*
> *From the D-Day Dodgers*
> *In sunny Italy.*

2. Carlo D'Este, *Fatal Decision: Anzio and the Battle for Rome* (New York, 1989), 332, 334, 339-340, 410-411; G.W.L. Nicholson, *The Canadians in Italy* (Ottawa, 1956), 387-389; Shelford Bidwell and Dominick Graham, *Tug of War: The Battle for Italy, 1943-1945*, (London, 1986), 334-337; Harold Alexander, *The Allied Armies in Italy, Despatch by His Excellency Field Marshal The Viscount Alexander of Tunis*, 53. The best studies on the overall background of the battle for Rome are D'Este, *Fatal Decision*; Bidwell and Graham, *Tug of War*, and John Ellis, *Cassino: The Hollow Victory, The Battle for Rome, January-June 1944* (New York, 1984). The Canadian perspective is well presented in Daniel Dancocks, *The D-Day Dodgers: The Canadians in Italy, 1943-1945* (Toronto, 1986) and W.J. McAndrew, *Canadians and the Italian Campaign, 1943-1945* (Montreal, 1996).

3. G.W.L. Nicholson, *Canadians in Italy*, 341-342, 346, 681; Bidwell and Graham, *Tug of War*, 401.

4. Nicholson, *Canadians in Italy*, 394; DHH, CMHQ Report No. 179, "Canadian Operations in the Liri Valley, May–June 1944," (hereafter, CMHQ, "Liri Valley"), 18.

5. A.J. Kerry and W.A. McDill, *The History of the Corps of Royal Canadian Engineers; Vol. II, 1936–1946*, (Ottawa, 1966), 202, 206; *Engineers in the Italian Campaign*, (GHQ, Italy, 1945), 30, 64; Ellis, *Cassino*, 67; G.R. Stevens, *Princess Patricia's Canadian Light Infantry, Vol. III*, (Edmonton, 1957), 148.

6. "In the Liri Valley: An Account of Operations 1 Canadian Armoured Brigade, Italy, April–May 1944," (hereafter "1 CAB, Liri"), Part I, Section (d), "What is Tank Country?", 1-3, copy in author's possession.

7. *Current Reports from Overseas*, No. 47 (22 July 1944), "A Description of the Hitler Line," 8-9.

8. *Current Reports from Overseas*, No. 47 (22 July 1944), "A Description of the Hitler Line," 8-9; "Armour Troops Precis, Camberley Course No. 14, August 1944," (hereafter "Camberley 14"), "Armoured 5: Armoured Regiment, Employment," 1-3.

9. NAC, RG 24, vol 14229, WD BCD, App 10, "Enemy Defences–Adolf Hitler Lines," 154A, 155-156; D'Este, *Fatal Decision*, 43-44; Nicholson, *Canadians in Italy*, 394-395; War

Department, *Handbook on German Military Forces, United States War Department Technical Manual, 15 March 1945*, (Washington, 1944), IV-20; Alexander, *Allied Armies in Italy*, 18; *Current Reports from Overseas*: No. 47 (22 July 1944) 7- 8; No. 53, (2 Sep 1944), "Notes on the Pursuit Beyond the Liri Valley," Section 2. "Armour in the Advance and the Pursuit, 5."

10. NAC, RG 24, vol 14229, WD BCD, App 10, "Enemy Defences–Adolf Hitler Lines," 154A, 155-156; D'Este, *Fatal Decision*, 43-44; Nicholson, *Canadians in Italy*, 394-395; War Department, *Handbook on German Military Forces, United States War Department Technical Manual, 15 March 1945*, (Washington, 1944), IV-20; Alexander, *Allied Armies in Italy*, 18; *Current Reports from Overseas*: No. 47 (22 July 1944) 7- 8; No. 53, (2 Sep 1944), "Notes on the Pursuit Beyond the Liri Valley," Section 2, "Armour in the Advance and the Pursuit, 5."

11. Nicholson, *Canadians in Italy*, 397-399; Ellis, *Cassino*, 463n; Bidwell, *Tug of War*, 266, 269; Wolfgang Schneider, *Tigers in Combat, Volume 1* (Winnipeg, 1994), 376-377; DHH, AHS Report No. 20, 19 Jul 1948, "The Italian Campaign (4 Jan 44-4 Jun 44), Information from German Military Documents Regarding Allied Operations in General and Canadian Operations in Particular," (hereafter AHS "German Documents,"), 101.

12. Nicholson, *Canadians in Italy*, 407; Lord Strathcona's Horse Museum, Calgary, Richard Cunniffe, "Melfa River 1944: A Sixteen Day (Account) of A Echelon, 2nd Armoured Regiment (LdSH (RC))," (hereafter Cunniffe, "Melfa"), entry for 16 May 1944.

13. Nicholson, *Canadians in Italy*, 410-412. .

14. Cunniffe, "Melfa," entry for 16 May 1944.

15. "Camberley 14": Armoured 1, 3; Armoured 2, 1.

16. "Camberley 14,": Armoured 1, 3; Armoured 2, 1, 2.

17. NAC, RG 24, vol. 14192, WD LdSH, 9 Jan 1944 and App 25, "Organization LdSH(RC)," App A to "STRATHFORCE – Planning Note May 1944;" H.F. Joslin, *Orders of Battle: Second World War, 1939 – 1945*, (London, 1990), 142; J.M. McAvity, *Lord Strathcona's Horse (Royal Canadians): A Record of Achievement*, (Toronto, 1947), 43-44. See Nicholson,

Canadians in Italy, 355–362, for a detailed discussion of the problems in equipping the new Canadian units arriving in Italy.

18. "Camberley 14," Armour 5, Armoured Regiment, Employment, 3; Canadian Military Headquarters, *Vehicle Data Book (Restricted) Canadian Army Overseas*, (London, 1944), 17, 23.

19. "Camberley 14," Armour 5, Armoured Regiment, Employment, 1; NAC, RG 24, vol 14192, WD LdSH, App 25, "Planning Notes, May 1944," dated 16 May 1944; McAvity, *Record of Achievement*, 61-62; NAC, RG 24, vol 14056, file 564, WD 5 CAD, App 12, "Notes on Exercise Chesterfield," 2 Jun 1944, 940.

20. "Camberley 14," Transport of Infantry on Tanks, and App 1; Armour 2, Outline Organization of an Armoured Division, 1; Infantry Battalion WE II/233/2, Motor Battalion, WE II/233/2, August 1944; CMHQ, *Vehicle Data Book*, 52; "Camberley 14," Student Notes on Armour, August 1944, Serial 4, Organization and Employment of a Motor Battalion; Armoured 8: Motor Battalion, Employment; NAC RG 24, vol 14192, file 1100, WD LdSH, App 25, "STRATHFORCE Planning Notes, 16 May 1944," Organization of an Infantry Battalion, WE II/233/2, 1944.

21. ALFF, Artillery Precis Package, Canadian Army Staff College, 1950 Course, Artillery 3: Artillery Organization; NAC, RG 24, vol 14229, WD BCD, App 11, "Notes from 5th Canadian Armoured Brigade O Group, 22 May 1944 at 1330 hrs," 163-164; G.W.L. Nicolson, *The Gunners of Canada, Volume II*, (Ottawa, 1972) 113n; NAC, RG 24, vol 14334, file 578, WD RCA 5 CAD, May 1944, "Order of Battle, 1 Canadian Corps Artillery, 20 May 1944, 292.

22. NAC, RG 24, vol 14292, WD LdSH, 21 May 1944; author's interview with Lieutenant General (Retd) William Milroy, Kingston, 3 Feb 2003; McAvity, *Record of Achievement*, 69.

23. NAC, RG 24, vol 14229, file 1104, WD BCD, 25 May 1944, and App 11, "Notes from O Group, 221330 May 1944," 162-163; Anonymous, War Diary 8th New Brunswick Hussars, (privately published), entry for 23 May 1944; Ellis, *Cassino*, 389-390.

24. DHH, CMHQ Historical Report No. 121,

"Canadian Operations in the Liri Valley (Italy) May – June 1944," 8 August 1944, 21-22; NAC, RG 24, vol 13796, WD HQ 5 CAB, 21 May 1944.

25. NAC, RG 24, vol 14229, file 1104, WD BCD, 23 May 1944, App 10 "Adolf Hitler Line," 22, and App 12, "Notes on Orders Group, 1630 hrs, 23rd May 1944"; DHH, CMHQ Historical Report No. 121, "Canadian Operations in the Liri Valley (Italy) May – June 1944," 25-26; Reginald H. Roy, *Sinews of Steel: the History of the British Columbia Dragoons*, (Brampton, 1965), 245, 253; Nicholson, *Canadians in Italy*, 423-425, 428.

26. NAC, RG 24, vol 14229, file 1104, WD BCD, 23 May 1944, 7; App 10, "Adolf Hitler Line," 22, and App 12, "Notes on Orders Group, 1630 hrs, 23rd May 1944;" CMHQ "Canadian Operations," 25-26; Roy, *Sinews of Steel*, 245, 253; Nicholson, *Canadians in Italy*, 423-425, 428; War Office, *German Weapons Illustrated, 1943, Amended to May 1944*, 70; *Handbook on German Military Forces*, VII-88; NAC, RG 24, vol 14056, file 564, WD 5 CAD, App 12, "Notes on Exercise Chesterfield," 2 Jun 1944," 941; Nicholson, *Gunners of Canada*, II, 205-206; NAC, RG 24, vol 14334, WD RCA 5 CAD, "Report on Operations 24-30 May 1944," 385-386.

27. CMHQ "Canadian Operations," 26, and App, "HQ 1 Canadian Infantry Division Orders for Operation Chesterfield,". 6, para 18, and App D, "Factors Slowing the Advance," 1; NAC, RG 24, volume 14292, WD LdSH, App 30, "Movement Order Tracked Convoy LdSH, 17 May 1944."

28. CMHQ "Canadian Operations," 26, and App B, "HQ 1 Canadian Infantry Division Orders for Operation Chesterfield," 6, para 18, and App D, "Factors Slowing the Advance," 1; NAC, RG 24, vol 14292, WD LdSH, App 30, "Movement Order Tracked Convoy LdSH(RC), 17 May 1944: Stevens, *Princess Patricia's Canadian Light Infantry*, 153-154; Cunniffe, "Melfa," entry for 19 May 1944; NAC, RG 24, vol 14056, file 564, WD5 CAB, 19 and 29 May 1944, and App 11, "The Crossing of the Melfa and the Securing of a Bridgehead by 5 Canadian Armoured Division," (hereafter "Crossing of the Melfa") 929.

29. McAvity, *Record of Achievement*, 67; NAC, RG 24, volume 14292, WD LdSH, 19 May 1944; CMHQ, "Liri Valley," 141; DHH, file 145.2W1011(D3), "The Melfa Crossing Address recorded by Lt-Col J.K. Mahony, VC for delivery at reg dinner, Westminster Regt, 1948," (hereafter "Melfa Address"). 3; *Current Reports from Overseas*, No. 48 (29 July 1944), Section 3, "Notes on Traffic Control," 10; Roy, *Sinews of Steel*, 246; NAC, RG 24: vol 14056, WD 5 CAB, 23 May 1944; vol 13686, WD 1 Cdn Corps, May 1944, "1 Canadian Corps, Security Intelligence Report No. 15, Period 20 to 26 May 1944," 619.

30. McAvity, *Record of Achievement*, 67; NAC, RG 24, volume 14292, WD LdSH, 19 May 1944; CMHQ "Liri Valley,", 141; "Melfa Address," 3; *Current Reports from Overseas*, No. 48 (29 July 1944), Section 3, "Notes on Traffic Control," 10; Roy, *Sinews of Steel*, 246; NAC, RG 24: vol 14056, WD 5 CAB, 23 May 1944; vol 13686, WD 1 Cdn Corps, May 1944, "1 Canadian Corps, Security Intelligence Report No. 15, Period 20 to 26 May 1944," 619.

31 Nicholson, *Canadians in Italy*, 409; DHH, CMHQ "Liri Valley," 132-133; AHS "German Documents," 73, 81.

32. Nicholson, *Canadians in Italy*, 409, 426; DHH, CMHQ Report 179, "Canadian Operations in the Liri Valley, May–June 1944," 132-133, Statement by General Wentzell, Chief of Staff, 10th German Army; AHS "German Documents, 73, 81."

33. Nicholson, *Canadians in Italy*, 423-425, 428, 429n, 430; Ellis, *Cassino*, 550, 532; NAC, RG 24, vol 13796, file 5621/65, WD 5 CAD, "5 Canadian Armoured Division Intelligence Summary No. 7, 25 May 1944," 153; AHS "German Documents," 58, 64, 71, 82, 83.

34. NAC, RG 24, vol 14229, file 1104, WD BCD, 23 May 1944, 7 and App 10, "Adolf Hitler Line, 22; App 12, "Notes on Orders Group, 1630 hrs, 23rd May 1944;" CMHQ "Canadian Operations," 25-26; Roy, *Sinews of Steel*, 245, 253; War Office, *German Weapons Illustrated, 1943, Amended to May 1944*, 70; *Handbook on German Military Forces*, VII-88; NAC, RG 24, vol 14056, file 564, WD 5 CAD, App 12, "Notes on Exercise Chesterfield, 2 June 1944," 941; AHS "German Documents," 71, 75, 76

35. Nicholson, *Canadians in Italy*, 423-425,

428, 429n1, 430; Ellis, *Cassino*, 532, 550; NAC, RG 24, vol 13796, file 5621/65, WD 5 CAD, "5 Canadian Armoured Division Intelligence Summary No. 7, 25 May 1944," 153; AHS "German Documents," 58, 64, 71, 82-83; NAC, RG 24, vol 14229, file 1104, WD BCD, 23 May 1944, 7, and App 10, "Adolf Hitler Line," 22, App 12, "Notes on Orders Group, 1630 hrs, 23rd May 1944"; CMHQ "Canadian Operations," 25-26.

36. NAC, RG 24, volume 13796, file 5621/65, WD 5 CAD, "5 Canadian Armoured Division Intelligence Summary No. 7, 25 May 1944," 153; AHS "German Documents," 58, 64, 71, 82-83; War Office, *German Weapons Illustrated*, 70; *Handbook on German Military Forces*, VII-88.

37. AHS "German Documents," 71, 75-76.

38. NAC, RG 24, vol 14229, file 1104, WD BCD, 23 May 1944; Reginald H. Roy, *Sinews of Steel; the History of the British Columbia Dragoons*, 247-250; DHH, CMHQ Report No. 20, 80-81, 83; NAC, RG 24, vol 14056, WD 5 CAB, 24 May 1944; NAC, RG 24, vol 14334, WD RCA, 5 CAD; "In the Liri Valley: An Account of Operations 1 Canadian Armoured Brigade, Italy, April-May 1944," 392-393, copy in author's possession; author's interview with Major General (Retd.) George Wattsford, 25 Sep 2003.

39. NAC, RG 24, vol 14229, file 1104, WD BCD, 23 May 1944; Roy, *Sinews of Steel*, 247-250; DHH, CMHQ Report No. 20, 19 July 1948, 80-83; NAC, RG 24, vol 14056, WD 5 CAB, App 11, "Crossing of the Melfa".

40. NAC, RG 24, vol 14229, file 1104, WD BCD, 23 May 1944; Roy, *Sinews of Steel*, 247-250; DHH, CMHQ Report No. 20, 19 July 1948, 80-83; "Crossing of the Melfa."

41. McAvity, *Record of Achievement*, (Toronto, 1947), 68; E.J. Perkins, "Account of Action, 24 May 1944," (hereafter Perkins, "Account"), 1-2; DHH, file 145.2W1011 (D3), "The Melfa Crossing Address," 3 (hereafter "Melfa Address").

42. McAvity, *Record of Achievement*, 68; E.J. Perkins, "Account," 1-2; DHH, "Melfa Address," 3.

43. Perkins, "Account," 3-4; McAvity, *Record of Achievement*, 70.

44. Perkins, "Account," 4; "Crossing of the Melfa."

45. Perkins, "Account," 5.

46. Perkins, "Account," 6.

47. Perkins, "Account," 3; Cunniffe, "Melfa," (hereafter Cunniffe, "Melfa"), entry for 23 May 1944; "Crossing of the Melfa."

48. NAC, RG 24, vol 14292, WD LdSH, 24 May 1944, App 41, "Wireless Notes, 24 May 1944 (hereafter "LdSH Wireless Notes"); McAvity, *Record of Achievement*, 69.

49. LdSH, "Wireless Notes;" McAvity, *Record of Achievement*, 69; DHH, "Melfa Address," 4; 5 CAB, "Crossing of the Melfa"; P.G. Griffin, "Italian Interlude, Third Installment," *Tank-Canada*, (Jan-Feb 1945), 6.

50. Author's correspondence with Lieutenant General (Retd.) William Milroy, 19 July 2003; Richard Cunniffe, *The Story of a Regiment*, (Lord Strathcona's Horse, 1995), 74-75.

51. Author's correspondence with Lieutenant General (Retd.) William Milroy, 19 July 2003; LdSH, "Wireless Notes" 6; McAvity, *Record of Achievement*, 69; DHH, "Melfa Address," 4; NAC, RG 24, vol. 14056, WD 5 CAB, 24 May 1944.

52. Author's correspondence with Lieutenant General (Retd.) William Milroy, 19 July 2003; LdSH, "Wireless Notes," 6; McAvity, *Record of Achievement*, 69; DHH, "Melfa Address," 4; NAC, RG 24, vol 14056, WD 5 CAB, 24 May 1944.

53. McAvity, *Record of Achievement*, 262; NAC, RG 24, vol 14229, WD LdSH, "'A' Squadron War Diary," 312-314; LdSH, "Wireless Notes," 6; App 35, "Recommendation for the Distinguished Service Order Major George James Harrison Wattsford." Despite the recommendation, Wattsford never received the award, but was Mentioned in Despatches.

54. Cunniffe, "Melfa," entry for 24 May 1944.

55. NAC, RG 24, vol 14229, WD LdSH, "'A' Squadron War Diary," 315-316.

56. NAC, RG 24, vol 14229, WD LdSH, "'A' Squadron War Diary," 317. MacKinnon was recommended for the Military Cross for this action, but the recommendation was not approved. See "Recommendation for the Military Cross, Lieutenant Angus MacKinnon," WD LdSH, App 40. MacKinnon died of wounds on 17 Apr 1945.

57. Kerry and McDill, *History of the Corps of Royal Canadian Engineers*, 207; 5 CAB, "Crossing of the Melfa," 928.

58. McAvity, *Record of Achievement*, 78-79, 264-266; NAC, RG 24, vol 14292, WD LdSH, 24 May 1944, 7.

59. McAvity, *Record of Achievement*, 78-79, 264-266; NAC, RG 24, vol 14292, WD LdSH, 24 May 1944, 7.

60. 5 CAB, "Crossing of the Melfa," 929.

61. CMHQ Report No. 20, 19 July 1948, 80-82, 85.

62, Perkins, "Account," 6; LdSH, "Wireless Notes," 6.

63. Perkins, "Account of Action," 6; LdSH, "Wireless Notes," 6.

64. NAC, RG 24 C3, vol 15283, WD WestR, May 1944; DHH, "Melfa Address," 2, 4; War Office, *Small Arms Training, Volume 1, Pamphlet No. 24, Projector, Infantry, Anti-Tank (PIAT)*, (London, 1943) and Amendments No. 4, 1, 6, 12;. Frederick C. Painton, "What it Takes to Win the V.C.," *Liberty* (21 April 1945) 9.

65. NAC, RG 24, vol 15283, WD WestR, May 1944, 3; Perkins, "Account," 7; CMHQ "Liri Valley," 143; DHH, "Melfa Address," 6-7; J.E. Oldfield, *The Westminsters' War Diary: An Unofficial History of The Westminster Regiment (Motor) in World War II*, (New Westminster, 1964), 77-78; 5 CAB, "Crossing of the Melfa," 929.

66. NAC, RG 24, vol 15283, WD WestR, 24 May 1944; DHH, "Melfa Address," 6-7; CMHQ "Liri Valley," 143; Oldfield, *Westminsters' War Diary*, 77-78; 5 CAB, "Crossing of the Melfa," 929.

67. NAC, RG 24, vol 15283, WD WestR, 24 May 1944; DHH, "Melfa Address," 6-7; CMHQ "Liri Valley," 143; ; Oldfield, *Westminsters' War Diary*, 77-78; 5 CAB, "Crossing of the Melfa," 929.

68. NAC, RG 24, vol 15283, WD WestR, 24 May 1944; Perkins, "Account," 7; DHH, "Melfa Address," 9.

69. NAC, RG 24, vol 15283, WD WestR, 24 May 1944; Perkins, "Account," 7; DHH, "Melfa Address," 9.

70. NAC, RG 24, vol 15283, WD WestR, May 1944; Perkins, "Account," 7; DHH, "Melfa Address," 10; McAvity, *Record of Achievement*, 72; Cunniffe, "Melfa," entry for 24 May 1944. The latter two sources mention the net jamming but do not describe the effects. 5 CAB, "Crossing of the Melfa," 929; War Office, *Infantry Training, Part VI: The Anti-Tank Platoon*, (London, 1943), 1.

71. RG 24, vol 14669, file 562, WD HQ RCE, 5 CAD, 24 May 1944, Sheet 17.

72. Ellis, *Cassino*, 403; NAC, RG 24, vol 15283, WD WestR, 24 May 1944; Perkins, "Account," 8; DHH, "Melfa Address," 11; Painton, "What it Takes to Win the V.C.," 47; Oldfield, *Westminsters' War Diary*, 81, 83-84, 89-90; NAC, RG 24, vol 14056, WD 5 CAB, 24 May 1944.

73. NAC, RG 24, vol 15283, WD WestR, 24 May 1944; Perkins, "Account," 8; DHH, "Melfa Address," 11; McAvity, *Record of Achievement*, 77; Oldfield, *Westminsters' War Diary*, 83-84, 89-90.

74. NAC, RG 24, vol 15283, WD WestR, 24 May 1944; 3; Perkins, "Account," 8; DHH, "Melfa Address," 11; McAvity, *Record of Achievement*, 77; Oldfield, *Westminsters' War Diary*, 83-84, 89-90.

75. NAC, RG 24, vol 15283, WD WestR, 24 May 1944; Perkins, "Account," 8; DHH, "Melfa Address," 11; Oldfield, *Westminsters' War Diary*, 84, 89-90.

76. NAC, RG 24, vol 15283, WD WestR, 24 May 1944; Perkins, "Account," 8; W.R. Feasby, *Official History of the Canadian Medical Service, 1939–1945: Volume One, Organizations and Campaigns*, (Ottawa, 1956), 183; Oldfield, *Westminsters' War Diary*, 85-86.

77. DHH, "Melfa Address," 12; author's interview with Lieutenant General (Retd) William Milroy, 19 July 2001.

78. DHH, "Melfa Address," 12.

79. DHH, "Melfa Address," 12.

80. NAC, RG 24, vol 15283, WD WestR, 24 May 1944; Perkins "Account," 7; NAC, RG 24, vol 14292, WD LdSH, 24 May 1944, "Citation Military Cross, Capt. Robert Martin, 165 Field Regiment (Jeep Artillery), R.A.,";. NAC RG 24, vol 14451, WD 8 Canadian Field Regiment (Self Propelled), 24 May 1944; McAvity, *Record of Achievement*, 78; G.W.L. Nicholson, *Gunners of Canada* II, 205.

81. NAC, RG 24, vol 14292, WD LdSH, May 1944, "Citation Military Cross, Capt. Robert Martin, 165 Field Regiment (Jeep Artillery), R.A."; NAC, RG 24, vol 14451, WD 8 Canadian Field Regiment (Self Propelled), 24 May 1944; McAvity, *Record of Achievement*, 78;

Nicholson, *Gunners of Canada* II, 205; NAC. RG 24, vol 14334, WD RCA 5 CAD, June 1944, "Report on Operations 24-30 May 1944," 386-387.

82. NAC, RG 24, vol 15283, WD WestR, 25 May 1944; Perkins, "Account," 7; NAC, RG 24, vol 14292, WD LdSH, May 1944, "Citation Military Cross, Capt. Robert Martin, 165 Field Regiment (Jeep Artillery), R.A.;" NAC, RG 24, vol 14451, WD 8 Canadian Field Regiment (Self Propelled), 24 May 1944; McAvity, *Record of Achievement*, 78; Nicholson, *Gunners of Canada* II, 205; NAC, RG 24, vol 14334, WD RCA, 5 CAD, June 1944, "Report on Operations 24-30 May 1944," 386-387.

83. Canadian Army Staff College, Kingston, Artillery Precis, 1950, "Artillery 13, Anti-Tank Artillery;" Nicholson, *Gunners of Canada* II, 206; NAC, RG 24, vol 14334, WD RCA, 5 CAD, May 1944, "Report on Operations 24-30 May 1944," 387; vol 13686, WD 1 Canadian Corps, May 1944, General Staff Log, 1 Canadian Corps, Sheet 128, Serial 964, 744.

84. NAC, RG 24, vol 15283, WD WestR, 24 May 1944; DHH, CMHQ "Liri Valley," 147; Cunniffe, "Melfa," entry for 24 May 1944.

85. CMHQ "Liri Valley," 150-151; Nicholson, *Canadians in Italy*, 434; "In the Liri Valley: An Account of Operations 1st Canadian Armoured Brigade, Italy, April–May 1944," Part I, 9.

86. CMHQ, "Liri Valley," 156; NAC, RG 24, vol 14229, WD BCD, 25 May 1944; DHH, "Melfa Address," 14; 5 CAB, "Crossing of the Melfa," 930.

87. CMHQ, "Liri Valley," 156; NAC, RG 24, vol 14229, WD BCD, 25 May 1944; DHH, "Melfa Address," 14; 5 CAB, "Crossing of the Melfa," 930. Alex Morrison and Ted Slaney, *The Breed of Manly Men: The History of The Cape Breton Highlanders*, (Toronto, 1994), 184.

88. CMHQ, "Liri Valley," 156; NAC, RG 24, vol 14229, WD BCD, 25 May 1944; DHH, "Melfa Address," 14; 5 CAB, "Crossing of the Melfa," 930; Morrison and Slaney, *Breed of Manly Men*, 184. Letter from Robert Gartke to William Milroy, 21 February 1996. The author is indebted to Lieutenant-General (Retd) Bill Milroy for providing a copy of this correspondence.

89. NAC, RG 24, vol 13686, WD 1 Canadian Corps, May 1944, General Staff Log, 1 Canadian Corps, 25 May 1944, Sheet No. 135 Serial 967 and Sheet No. 139, Serial 1, 751, 755; Kerry and McDill, *History of the Royal Canadian Engineers*, 207.

90 CMHQ Report No. 20, 19 July 1948, 85-86.

91. CMHQ, "Liri Valley," 156; NAC, RG 24, vol 14229, WD BCD, 25 May 1944; DHH, "Melfa Address," 14; Roy, *Sinews of Steel*, 258-260; NAC, RG 24, vol 13686, WD 1 Canadian Corps, May 1944, General Staff Log, 1 Canadian Corps, 25 May 1944, Sheet No. 141 Serial 25, 757.

92. CMHQ, "Liri Valley," 156; NAC, RG 24, vol 14229, WD BCD, 25 May 1944; DHH, "Melfa Address," 14; Roy, *Sinews of Steel*, 258-260, 260; NAC, RG 24, vol 13686, WD 1 Canadian Corps, May 1944, General Staff Log, 1 Canadian Corps, 25 May 1944, Sheet No. 141 Serial 25, 757.

93. NAC, RG 24, vol 14229, WD BCD, 25 May 1944; CMHQ, "Liri Valley," 157; CMHQ Report No. 20, 19 July 1948, 87; NAC, RG 24. vol 14334, WD RCA 5 CAD, May 1944, "Report on Operations 24-30 May 1944," 388; vol 13686, WD 1 Canadian Corps, May 1944, General Staff Log, 1 Canadian Corps, 25 May 1944, Sheet No. 142 Serial 34 and Sheet No. 145, Serial 51, 760, 763; vol 14669, file 562, WD HQ RCE 5 CAD, 25 May 1944, Sheet 18.

94 CMHQ, "Liri Valley," 157; NAC, RG 24, vol 13686, WD 1 Canadian Corps, May 1944, General Staff Log, 1 Canadian Corps, 25 May 1944, Sheet No. 142 Serial 34 and Sheet No. 145, Serial 51, 760, 763.

95. NAC, RG 24, vol 14292, WD LdSH), 25 May 1944.

96. NAC, RG 24, vol 14292, WD LdSH, 25 May 1944; McAvity, *Record of Achievement*, 85-86.

97. NAC, RG 24, vol 14292, WD LdSH, 25 May 1944; McAvity, *Record of Achievement*, 85-86.

98. Oldfield, *Westminsters' War Diary*, 96-97; CMHQ Report No. 20, 19 July 1948, 101-102.

99. CMHQ Report No. 20, 19 July 1948, 101-102.

100. CMHQ Report No. 20, 19 July 1948, 101-

102; NAC, RG 24, vol 13700, WD Assistant-Adjutant and Quartermaster General, 5 CAD "Daily Returns of Losses, May 1944," 1250-1261. The return for 26 May is missing from the records, so the figures for that day have been extrapolated.

101. McAvity, *Record of Achievement*, 79; NAC, RG 24, vol 13796, file 562.65, WD 5 CAD, May 1944, Intelligence Summary No. 7, Part I, 25 May 1944, 151; 5 CAB, "Crossing of the Melfa," Annex A, 929.

102. Ellis, *Cassino*, 466.

103. CMHQ, "Liri Valley," 162-163, 175, 181, 185-186; NAC, RG 24, vol 14334, WD RCA 5 CAD, May 1944, "Report on Operations 24-30 May 1944," 398.

104. The DSO was awarded for "acts of gallantry of a high order under fire for distinguished services in actual combat with the enemy" and was "intended to reward commissioned officers below field rank for distinguished service in time of war, and for which the VC would not be appropriate," while the Military Cross was a gallantry award for captains, lieutenants and warrant officers "when performing acts of bravery on the ground." See John R. Grodzinski, "Summary of Awards," in *The Operational Handbook for First Canadian Army: Formation Organization, Staff Technique and Administration*, (Kingston, 1998), 108; and *Medal Yearbook, 1997*, (1996), 59, 63.

105. Nicholson, *Canadians in Italy*, 301, describes the award of the DSO to Lieutenant J.F. McLean of the Seaforth Highlander of Canada, following an action at San Leonardo in December 1944. Nicholson writes "McLean won the DSO, one of the very few junior officers to receive this award in the Italian Campaign."

106. Letter from Smith to McAvity, 1 June 1944, reprinted in McAvity, *Record of Achievement*, 81; Nicholson, *Canadians in Italy*, 446, "Recommendation for Award, Lieut (A/Capt) Edward James Perkins, 12 July 1944;" Oldfield, *Westministers' War Diary*, 86. The name "Arneson" may not be correct as there is no record of an award of a Military Medal to a sol-

dier by that name. CMHQ Report No. 20, 19 July 1948, 72n. Frederick C. Painton, "What It Takes to Win the V.C.," *Liberty Magazine*, 21 April 1945, p. 8.

Painton's article includes an overview of the Melfa action and is rife with errors. It shows the Strathconas as having lost 31 tanks and the enemy "many more" (p. 8), claims the defenders employed Tiger tanks, which they did not, and contains other errors of fact. As a product of wartime journalism, the article focuses on the need for leadership and bravery in war.

107. *Current Reports from Overseas*, No. 52, Part 2, "Six Pounders versus Panthers," 7-8; Oldfield, *Westminsters' War Diary*, 47; author's interview with Lieutenant General (Retd) William Milroy, 19 July 2001; NAC, RG 24, vol 14056, WD 5 CAD, June 1944, App 12, "Notes on Exercise Chesterfield," 2 June 1944, 942.

108. Ellis, *Cassino*, 261-263. See also Nicholson, *Canadians in Italy*, 451n, 606, and Dancocks, *D Day Dodgers*, 288-290, for a discussion of E.L.M. Burns and his supposed shortfalls as a corps commander.

109. War Office, *The Official names of the Battles, Actions and Engagements fought by the Land Forces of the Commonwealth during the Second World War, 1939–1945* (London, 1956), 35; Canadian Army Orders, Part "A": Issue 508, 10 September 1956; Issue 611, 1 September 1958.

110. DHH, "Melfa Address," 16.

111. Cunniffe, "Melfa," entry for 28 May 1944; McAvity, *Record of Achievement*, 87; author's interview with J.W. Lynch, 19 July 2001. The white crosses so carefully painted by Trooper Lynch and the graves cared for by the Scottish-Italian woman are no longer there, nor are the graves prepared by the Westminster Regiment. After the war, the fatal casualties from the battle were re-interred in the Commonwealth War Graves Commission Cemetery at Cassino where those Canadians killed in the Liri Valley on 24 and 25 May 1944 lie with 855 other Canadian soldiers among 3,411 Commonwealth soldiers in all.

Index

THE CONTRIBUTORS TO *MORE FIGHTING FOR CANADA*

Donald E. Graves, editor

The author, co-author or editor of fifteen books, including *Fighting for Canada*, the companion volume to *More Fighting for Canada*, Donald E. Graves is one of Canada's best known military historians. His study of a wartime Canadian armoured unit, *South Albertas: A Canadian Regiment at War*, is regarded as a classic and his many titles on the War of 1812 have established him as an authority on that subject. His current writing project is a history of the South Alberta Light Horse.

Donald E. Graves is the managing director of Ensign Heritage, a consulting firm with interests in historic sites, museums and heritage touring. He is in demand as a battlefield tour leader for both military units and civilian groups. He resides with his author wife, Dianne, in Wolf Grove, a small village in Upper Canada near Ottawa – but not too near.

Christopher Johnson, illustrator

The cartographer and graphics illustrator for this book and the companion volume to *More Fighting for Canada*, Christopher Johnson is a graduate in history from Queen's University in Kingston. A serving officer of the Ontario Provincial Police for 25 years, Christopher Johnson has long had a fascination with armoured fighting vehicles and military history. These interests have led him into the field of computer-generated graphic art, including maps and drawings, and he has contributed illustrations to many books including: Michael Green, *Patton and the Battle of the Bulge*; Donald E. Graves, *South Albertas: A* *Canadian Regiment at War, Field of Glory: The Battle of Crysler's Farm, 1813; Guns Across the River, The Battle of the Windmill, 1838; Quebec 1759: The Siege and the Battle* and *Incredible War of 1812*; John Marteinson, *The Royal Canadian Armoured Corps* and *Second to None: The Governor General's Horse Guards*; John Morris, *Sword of the Border: Major General Jacob Jennings Brown, 1775-1828.* He is currently engaged in creating map and graphic work for five more books.

Chris Johnson resides with his wife, Debby, and children, Amanda and Michael, in Newcastle, Ontario.

Robert H. Caldwell, author of the study on Cut Knife Hill, 1885

Robert (Bob) Caldwell is a westerner who joined the Canadian army in 1960. Commissioned into the Fort Garry Horse in 1961, he served for 35 years in command and staff appointments, mostly at the unit, base and militia district level. He spent nine years in Europe, in double tours with the Canadian NATO brigade in Germany and in Great Britain, where he attended the Staff College at Shrivenham and Camberley. He also served in two United Nations tours in the Middle East. When the Fort Garry Horse were cut from the regular army, Caldwell rebadged to the Royal Canadian Dragoons and his final postings were in the Operational Research and Analysis Establishment, and the Directorate of History and Heritage in Ottawa.

Bob Caldwell has an MA in War Studies from the Royal Military College in Kingston and his thesis topic was on the Canadian militia, Indian and Métis ways of war in the 1885 North West Rebellion. He completed much of his research on three staff postings in western Canada before moving to Kingston in 1985, and that year the late Professor John Foster at the University of Alberta had urged him to "Keep one foot in both camps - one on the St. Lawrence and one on the Saskatchewan -- that's the only way to tell the story with balance, and above all else, we need balance."

Since 1995 Bob Caldwell has been researching and writing naval and military history as part of the staff of Directorate of History and Heritage and is one of the authors of *No Higher Purpose: The Official Operational History of the Royal Canadian Navy in the Second World War, 1939-1945*.

John R. Grodzinski, author of the study on the Melfa Crossing, 1944

John R. Grodzinski is a native of Hamilton, Ontario, and a graduate in Political Science from McMaster University. After a year as a field engineer, he transferred to the Royal Canadian Armoured Corps, where he received his commission and served two tours with his regiment, Lord Strathcona's Horse (Royal Canadians), in Calgary, and later in staff positions in Winnipeg, Halifax and Kingston. Major Grodzinski spent six years as the Managing Editor of *The Army Doctrine and Training Bulletin*, a professional quarterly journal on Canadian army issues. He has also held appointments as museum officer for his regiment; director of public relations and historian at the Museum of the Regiments in Calgary; and executive secretary of the Army Museum in Halifax. He is author of *The Battle of Moreuil Wood* (1993), *The Operational Handbook on the First Canadian Army* (1996), and co-author of a study of Moreuil Wood in *Fighting for Canada: Seven Battles, 1758-1945*, and is

also a regular contributor to other journals. In 2002, Major Grodzinski completed a Masters of Arts in War Studies at the Royal Military College of Canada and his thesis on the War of 1812 on the Upper St Lawrence River was nominated for the Governor General's Gold Medal for Academic Excellence. His interests include 18th and 19th century North American warfare; formation and unit organization and tactics; and the evolution and application of tactical doctrine from 1750 to the present. Major Grodzinski has also led many military battlefield tours of battle sites both in North America and Europe.

John and his wife, Helga, enjoy music, reading, any product of the grape, hiking and spending time with their three children, Sylvia, Karl and Natasha and Chucky, their compulsive dog.

Ian M. McCulloch, author of the study on Sillery, 1760

A native of Halifax. Educated in Scotland and Switzerland, Ian McCulloch holds a degree in journalism from Carleton University in Ottawa and a Master's Degree in War Studies from the Royal Military College of Canada. He joined the Canadian army in 1977 and served in a variety of regimental and staff appointments in Canada and Germany before assuming command of The Black Watch (Royal Highland Regiment) of Canada in 1993. In 1996 he was appointed Deputy Director of History and Heritage of the Canadian Forces in Ottawa and, since 2000, he has been the Special Assistant to the Director General, Health Services, Ottawa. A military historian specializing in the Seven Years War in North America, Ian McCulloch has published numerous articles on that subject in such periodicals as the *Osprey Military Journal, Battlefield Review, Canadian Military History, The Beaver, Canadian Infantry Journal* and *The Bulletin of the Fort Ticonderoga Museum* as well as serving as an historical consultant for the Canadian Broadcasting Corporation's documentary "Canada: A People's History." A contributor to *Fighting for Canada*, Ian McCulloch's current projects include a book entitled *British Light Infantryman of the Seven Years War, 1756-1763, North America* (Osprey, Oxford, 2004), and co-editing a rare "voice-from-the-ranks" memoir (initially published in 1775) entitled *"Through So Many Dangers:" The Memoirs and Adventures of Robert Kirk; Late of the Royal Highland Regiment* to be published by Purple Mountain Press in 2004.

Ian McCulloch and his wife Susan live in Ottawa, where he is currently engaged in writing his next book, *Sons of the Mountains: A History of the Highland Regiments in North America, 1756-1767*.

Michael R. McNorgan, author of the study on Iwuy, 1918

Major (Retd.) Michael McNorgan is a native of London, Ontario, and holds a Master's Degree in History from Carleton University. A former member of the First Hussars, he has recently retired after more than 30 years of service in the Canadian Forces. A lifelong student of mounted warfare, Mike McNorgan is the author of a study in the companion volume to *More Fighting For Canada* and co-author of *The Royal Canadian Armoured Corps: An Illustrated History*.

Mike McNorgan's latest book, which will be appearing shortly, is *The Gallant Hussars: A History of the First Hussars Regiment, 1856-2004.*

Brian Reid, author of the study on Paardeberg, 1900

Lieutenant Colonel (Retd.) Brian Reid was born in Fort Erie, Ontario, and joined the regular Canadian army in 1957 as a gunner before being commissioned through the Officer Candidate Programme in 1961. During a military career that spanned nearly four decades, Brian Reid served in regimental, staff and liaison appointments in Canada, Europe and the United States. His last appointment, prior to his retirement in 1994, was in the Joint Plans and Operations Staff at National Defence Headquarters in Ottawa. Brian Reid is the author of *Our Little Army in the Field: The Canadians in South Africa*, two studies in *Fighting For Canada, Seven Battles, 1758-1945*, co-author of *RCHA – Right of the Line*, and has contributed a number of magazine articles on military history topics. He is currently working on a study of Operations TOTALIZE and TRACTABLE in Normandy in 1944, and on a history of the Royal Winnipeg Rifles.

Brian Reid resides with his wife, Patricia, near Ottawa and his interests include, besides military history, travel, cooking and big Labrador Retrievers.

ALSO PUBLISHED BY ROBIN BRASS STUDIO, THE COMPANION VOLUME TO *MORE FIGHTING FOR CANADA*

Fighting for Canada: Seven Battles, 1758–1945
Edited by Donald E. Graves

A fascinating detailed study of seven battles fought either to defend Canada or by Canadians overseas on behalf of their nation. "Military history as it should be written; sound in reasoning, precise in detail and firmly placed within the relevant political, military and social contexts. It incorporates the testimony of private and general and does not shirk, where necessary, from passing judgement or according praise." Michael Cessford, *Canadian Military Journal.* The actions described are:

- **Ticonderoga, 1758:** the bloodiest military action in North America before the American Civil War, as a French force defeats a large British and American army – *by Ian M. McCulloch;*

- **Queenston Heights, 1812:** an outnumbered but professional force defeats a major American invasion – *by Robert Malcomson;*

- **Ridgeway, 1866:** experience proves superior to numbers when Irish Fenians invade Canada and embarrass the Canadian militia – *by Brian A. Reid;*

- **Leliefontein, 1900:** a Boer War mounted rearguard action fought with great valour by both sides – *by Brian A. Reid;*

- **Moreuil Wood, 1918:** a rare First World War cavalry action that was a turning point on the Western Front – *by John R. Grodzinski & Michael R. McNorgan;*

- **Le Mesnil-Patry, 1944:** enthusiasm and courage prove unavailing against the ruthless determination of the Waffen SS in Normandy – *by Michael R. McNorgan;*

- **Kapelsche Veer, 1945:** a grim and unrelenting account of a tragic and costly battle that should never have been fought – *by Donald E. Graves.*

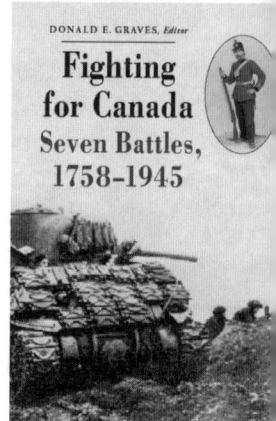

446 pages • 6.75 x 9.75 inches • about 160 pictures, maps • hardcover ISBN 1-896941-15-x, • paperback ISBN 1-896941-16-8